Eva Kuss

Hermann Czech
An Architect in Vienna

Eva Kuss

Hermann Czech
An Architect in Vienna

With an Introduction by
Liane Lefaivre
and an Essay by
Elisabeth Nemeth

Content

9 **Introduction** Liane Lefaivre

13 **Prologue**

21 **Progress and Criticism: Viennese Modernism**
   21 The Aftermath of the Enlightenment in 19th-Century Vienna | **25** In the Center of the Discourse: "Language" | **26** Otto Wagner–Vienna around 1900 | **29** Adolf Loos and Karl Kraus–Vienna before the First World War | **33** Josef Frank and the Vienna Circle–Vienna around 1930 | **40** Viennese Living Culture–Viennese Modernism

43 **"Background"–Childhood, Youth, Studies**

43 *Vienna 1936–1954*
   43 The Era of National Socialism | **47** The Topic of National Socialism in Czech's Later Life | **48** Postwar Period (1945-1954) | **49** The Political and Cultural Situation | **54** Catholicism in the Postwar Period

55 *Study at the Technical University of Vienna and with Konrad Wachsmann from 1954 to 1963*
   55 First Years of Study | **57** Karl Kraus–A New Dimension of Language | **59** Austrian Architecture in the 1950s | **61** The Viennese Art and Cultural Scene/Galerie St. Stephan | **66** Lectures at the Faculty of Philosophy | **67** arbeitsgruppe 4/Johann Georg Gsteu | **70** Konrad Wachsmann and the Salzburg Summer Academy | **74** The Influence of the "wiener gruppe" | **76** Serial Music/Journal and Ensemble *die Reihe* | **77** Metrical Film/Peter Kubelka | **79** From Contemporary Impulses to Restaurant Ballhaus

81 *Study at the Academy of Fine Arts 1963–1971*
   81 The Scene in the 1960s–*Die Furche*/Galerie nächst St. Stephan/Klubseminar | **84** Study under Ernst Anton Plischke | **89** Europa Symposium, 1963 | **91** Viennese Urban Development Discussion | **98** Retractable Roof over the Graben | **103** Christopher Alexander | **104** The Vienna Subway Discussion | **106** Travels to Italy and England | **107** City Structure and Terrace House | **112** Criticism of "Irrationalism" in Architecture | **114** trigon '69 and "Spatial City Planning" | **115** The Magazine *Bau* | **117** The Viennese Actionists | **118** Josef Frank | **122** The Loos House | **128** Kleines Café | **129** Completion of Studies | **132** Czech's Language and "Terms" | **134** No Need for Panic | **136** For a Change

143 **"Newer Objectivity"**

147 **An Essay.** On the Relationship between Architecture and Philosophy in Hermann Czech's Work **Elisabeth Nemeth**

161	**Selected Projects**	366	Furnishing of the Swiss Re Centre
		376	"Area of Tolerance"
162	Restaurant Ballhaus	380	Hadersdorf Model Housing Estate
168	Transformation Summer House Nussdorf	386	Hotel Messe Vienna
176	Kleines Café	396	"Housing for Generations" Am Mühlgrund
194	Antiquarian Bookshop Löcker	404	Rooftop Extension Günthergasse
200	Wunder-Bar	412	Exhibition *Josef Frank: Against Design*
206	Villa Pflaum	420	Sigmund Freud Museum Architecture and Exhibition Design
216	House M.		
226	Galerie Hummel		
234	House S.	430	**Appendix**
248	Salzamt Restaurant		
256	Basement Remodeling in Palais Schwarzenberg	431	Hermann Czech – Biography
		432	Buildings, Plans and Projects
268	Exhibition *Von hier aus. Zwei Monate neue deutsche Kunst* (*Up from here – Two months of new German art in Düsseldorf*)	439	Significant Assistants at Atelier Czech 1979–2020
		440	Writings by Hermann Czech
276	Stadtparksteg Pedestrian Bridge	449	Articles on and Critiques of Hermann Czech and His Work
282	Residential Block Petrusgasse	453	Sources Used
290	Exhibition *Wien 1938* (*Vienna 1938*)	463	Register
298	Exhibition Design *Wunderblock: A History of the Modern Soul*		
		469	About the Author
304	Brunner Gasse Residential Block	469	Thanks
314	Atelier Czech, Singerstraße	470	Image Credits
322	Arcadia Music Shop	471	Funders and Sponsors
328	Block Development at the U3-West Ottakring Turnaround	471	Imprint
336	MAK Café and Thonet Chair		
346	Winter Glazing of the Vienna State Opera Loggia		
352	Rosa Jochmann School		
358	Urbanization of Oranienburg		

Introduction
Liane Lefaivre

Although the architect Hermann Czech is a truly beloved cult figure in Vienna, he is not as well-known as he should be outside the German-speaking world. This monograph by the architect and architectural historian Eva Kuss has made his work available in full in English for the first time.

Czech stands out among the Viennese architects of his generation, a generation dominated by counterculture figures of the late 1950s and 1960s. Austrians were different from their equivalents elsewhere—Cedric Price and Archigram's Peter Cook in Britain, Ant Farm in the US, Archizoom and Superstudio in Italy. First of all, the Austrians were far more numerous. Vienna alone had almost ten groups of them. Hans Hollein and Coop Himmelb(l)au are just the most well-known internationally. In addition, there were Zünd-Up (Ignite), Missing Link, Salz der Erde (Salt of the Earth), not to mention the Graz School, among others. And second, these architects could be politically radical firebrands, not just madcap pranksters. There was often an unusually angry side to their performances and visual works, not to mention their many manifestos.

This aspect of the postwar Vienna architecture scene is hardly surprising. Much has been written about Austria's "memory problem" at the time, which amounted to a denial of its role during World War II. Parallel to the Viennese architectural counterculture were artistic counterculture movements—the Wiener Gruppe and the Vienna Actionists in particular—that engaged in violent, often gruesome tactics which veered towards the scatological, bloody self-lacerating. Their rage provided these cultural guerrilla warriors with a weapon for venting their often-obscene fury and breaking down the wall of silence and amnesia about the harrowing realities of Austria's Nazi involvement in the Holocaust. In one typical performance, Günter Brus, who has incidentally since gone on to be awarded the Grand Austrian State Prize, sang the national anthem while masturbating, then shitting. These artists were the extremely radical expression of what I have elsewhere called Vienna's deep-seated tradition of Modernist Rebels engaged in a *Kulturkampf* (cultural war) against the established order, beginning with Otto Wagner (once he had written his iconoclastic, anti-historicist manifesto, *Modern Architecture*), Gustav Klimt, Josef Maria Olbrich, Koloman Moser and other members of the iconoclastic Secession.

In the midst of Vienna's postwar cultural turmoil, the cerebral Hermann Czech followed his own path. He distanced himself from the confrontational, "angry young man" shock tactics of many of his contemporaries and chose instead the other extreme of the spectrum. To Hans Hollein's supremely hyperbolic declaration that "Everything is architecture," Czech countered with "Architecture is *background*, everything else is *not* architecture." To the incendiary Wolf Prix, who would proclaim that "Architecture must burn," Czech preferred the attempt of postwar, more rationally and structurally orientated architects such as Johannes Spalt, Friedrich Kurrent or Johann Georg Gsteu to study prewar Viennese modernism, in particular of Adolf Loos, in search of consistent approaches. He saw in this return a way of re-affirming what one may call the architecturalness of architecture which, in his view, would provide the foundation on which modern architecture could be built anew. Not surprisingly, Czech's projects have always tended towards litotic understatement and reserve. Far from inflammatory, his aim is and has always been to reconstruct the world, to put it back together again with fragments of memory retrieved from under a veil of amnesia.

When I first arrived in Vienna to take up my position as the Chair of Architectural History and Theory at the University of Applied Arts, the *Angewandte*, in Vienna in 2003, I would often find myself invited to one or the other of Czech's now legendary cafés and restaurants—the Kleines Café, the Salzamt, Immervoll and the MAK Café (unfortunately demolished in 2005). To an outsider Canadian like me, each appeared to be another legendary, atmospheric Viennese café. But my companions would begin to point out the meaning of the details: the mirrors, the floor tiles, the chairs, the lighting. There is no item that was not pregnant with a meaningful reference. Suddenly, almost everything required a doubletake and the place became like a riddle, or a story written in an architectural language that needed an interpreter.

Does this mean that Czech's architecture is a nostalgic Proustian attempt to dwell in a remembered past as a form of resistance to the modern world? On the contrary. As in any creative act, memory serves as a toolbox for creative rethinking. This tendency to re-use the past in a modern construction of the present is perhaps most obvious in Czech's large-scale projects. His housing project for Hadersdorf and in Mühlgrund with Krischanitz and Neuwirth, his Hotel Messe, his Blockbebauung in Ottakring in Vienna. As Elie Wiesel wrote in his *Function of Memory*: "Without memory, there is no culture. Without memory, there would be no civilization, no society, no culture."

Besides a reserve that has become legendary, another of Czech's traits is his meticulous devotion to the smallest detail—and the more imperfect the detail the better—that characterizes his exploration into what he poetically refers to as the barely perceivable "shimmering of the real." For all his reserve, Czech has been perhaps the most influential of the architects of his contemporaries on younger Austrian architects. Jabornegg and Palffy's work, for example, as well as Martin Feiersinger and ARTEC's Bettina Götz and Richard Manahl. Not surprisingly, it also has inspired Eva Kuss's own architectural design. All should be more well-known outside Austria.

With this book, entirely based on original research, Eva Kuss has become the one, single, indispensable interpreter of Czech's architectural language, grounded on an extensive oral history compiled from lengthy and detailed conversations with Hermann Czech himself. It is divided in two sections.

The first section sketches the cultural milieu from which Czech *forma mentis* emerged. Eva Kuss has an insightful and highly original way of seeing things, a good match for Czech's own modus operandi. This section deals with the historical period from Otto Wagner until the Second World War, which formed a cultural background for Czech, that is the literary and artistic movements of Vienna, before the rise of Austrofascism, Nazism and the role of Austria in World War II, marked by Otto Wagner, marked by Hugo von Hofmannsthal, Adolf Loos, Karl Kraus and Sigmund Freud.

For as long as I have known Eva (full disclosure: this book began as a doctorate with me), she has never tired of repeating that Czech's architecture has its intellectual origins in the uniquely Viennese cultural movement of *Sprachkritik*, a reflection on the inadequacies and limits of language and the attempt to formulate a new one. This tradition goes back to the late 19th- and early 20th-century philosophical writings of Fritz Mauthner and Ernst Mach. It shaped Ludwig Wittgenstein's *Tractatus*, which in turn influenced the Vienna Circle during the 1920s. One of Kuss's main contributions is to have drawn parallels between these thinkers and Czech's way of designing, which she sees as an attempt to rethink the architectural language inherited from the great Viennese past, an architectural language that has broken down. She likens Czech in this sense to the postwar Viennese filmmaker Peter Kubelka, who strove to re-invent filmic language.

Among Czech's sources of inspiration, the book singles out the architecture and writings of the Viennese architect Josef Frank. Frank is little known in the English-speaking world. He, too, was a highly respected, individualistic and unorthodox presence in the movements of the 1920s. Le Corbusier, Gropius, and Mies among many others, not to mention Adolf Loos, all condemned not only ornament but also disorder as a crime. Frank embraced both on the other hand. Opposed to what he saw as an authoritarian over-regimentation and a negation of the taste of what he called ordinary people, he incorporated not only whimsical ornamentation in his designs but also an asymmetrical, almost haphazard approach to composing façades and arranging interiors, an approach which he would eventually theorize about as "accidentism." As a Jewish émigré in New York following the Nazi takeover of Austria with the Anschluss in 1938, Frank was struggling to make a living. Still, nothing could make him conform to what he perceived as reductive architectural correctness.

The second section of Kuss's book is a catalogue raisonné of a selection of Czech's manifold works of different scales. He has designed shops, hotels, public and private housing and urban planning projects for Vienna, along with his furniture design, exhibition design and curatorship, and his cafés. Each work is accompanied by a close and meticulously revealing interpretation and rich visual documentation that unlocks the riddles of Czech's architectural language and brings to the surface the subliminal references nested deep inside his designs.

This section is most significant because it makes the implicit messages of Czech's work explicit. These are up to the reader to discover. The book makes us understand the importance and originality of Hermann Czech's architecture and design within the historical knowledge of the astonishing originality of Viennese modernity and vice versa, Vienna today by the knowledge of Hermann Czech. Eva Kuss has provided an essential introduction to both.

Prologue

The thought process of this work began with my first experiences as an architect and the concrete implementation of architectural concepts into built reality. When transforming an abstract thought into a material object, it is inevitable that the materials, building components and construction methods, their history and meanings, influence and overlay the materialization process. "But history is sedimented in the material itself […]. Only another phrase for this is that the material does not consist of abstract, atomistic urelements, which as such would be completely without intention and which could randomly usurp the artistic intentions, but that themselves already bring intentions to the work."[1]

Architects have been trying to eliminate these unwanted meanings since modernism: for example, by using new, "uncontaminated" building materials, by abstraction in the structural details or by alienation. One can also distinguish between the methods of "concretion" and "abstraction." "When concretizing, one starts with abstract, general ideas and tries to inscribe them into the world of things."[2] The attempt is made to get by with as few resources as possible and to make the material and constructive presence necessary for implementation "uninteresting."[3] "When abstracting, on the other hand, one starts from the representational and seeks to sort out certain symbolic meanings."[4] Through the way they are used, materials and constructions are detached from their traditional associative meanings and brought into connection with the design concept.[5] The method of concretion produces a form of abstractness which, at least for the uninformed user, often remains inexplicably banal and provokes "attempts at embellishment." That of abstraction, in turn, leads to an auratic charge of the architecture. In both cases, I think there is something artificial about the end product.

1 Theodor W. Adorno: "Ohne Leitbild," in: Adorno: *Ohne Leitbild. Parva Aesthetica*, 1967, 7–19: 17.
2 Hans Frei: "Neuerdings Einfachheit," in: *minimal tradition. Max Bill und die "einfache" Architektur 1942–1996*, XIX. Triennale di Milano 1996, 113–131: 126f.
3 Ibid., 127.
4 Ibid.
5 Ibid.

At this point, Hermann Czech's works became interesting for me: They do not convey any superficial meanings, are neither banal nor auratic or artificial, and instead create spaces of astonishing self-evidence and pleasant "normality." In Vienna, which has shaped Czech in his attitude and has always been the center of his work and life, there is traditionally a different approach to the concept of "meaning" in architecture. Here, with Otto Wagner, Adolf Loos, Josef Frank and others, a modernist architecture developed from the turn of the 20th century up into the interwar period, which remained connected to the tradition of consciously using the visual impact of a building and precisely generated something new from it.

Adolf Loos wrote in 1910: "Architecture arouses moods in people, so the task of the architect is to give these moods concrete expression. A room must look cozy, a house comfortable to live in. To secret vice the law courts must seem to make a threatening gesture. A bank must say, 'Here your money is safe in the hands of honest people.'" And further: "An architect can only achieve this by going back to those buildings of the past which aroused these moods in people."[6] What Loos calls "mood" means for Josef Frank understanding architecture as "symbol." Both terms see architecture as something that visually communicates meaning. For Frank, the symbolic content of architecture was an essential part of it, which he refused to abolish because he was convinced: "Humanity needs symbols today as ever before […]."[7]

With "postmodernism's"[8] international criticism of "modernism" at the end of the 1960s, a new interest in dealing with the visual impact of architecture established itself. In 1972, Venturi, Scott Brown and Izenour defined the building types they found in their study *Learning from Las Vegas*[9] as "decorated sheds" or "ducks." The "decorated sheds" need a sign to communicate their content; the "ducks"[10] convey their function through their outer appearance. As early as 1966, Robert Venturi had spoken out in favor of a "complex and contradictory" architecture in view of the increasingly banal international style and postwar functionalism.[11] Charles Jencks was the first to use the term "postmodernism" in architecture in 1977 to denote a direction that was characterized by pluralism and turned against the rigid formal rules of dogmatic modernism. He defined a postmodern building as one that, unlike modern buildings, has several levels of meaning.[12] And in 1979, Peter Eisenman described "the presence of an intentional sign" as perhaps being "the most important quality which distinguishes architecture from geometry."[13] Czech's architecture also incorporates postmodern

---

6 Adolf Loos: "Architecture" (1910), trans. Michael Mitchell, in: Adolf Loos: *On Architecture* (Studies in Austrian Literature, Culture and Thought), Riverside, CA: Ariadne Press, 2002, 73–85: 84.

7 Josef Frank: *Architektur als Symbol. Elemente deutschen neuen Bauens* (1931), edited and with an index compiled by Hermann Czech, 1981, 11, reprinted in: Frank 2012, Vol. 2, 9–191: 25. English translation by John Sands, *Architecture as Symbol*, in: Frank 2012, Vol. 2, 9–191: 26.

8 See Robert Venturi: *Complexity and Contradiction in Architecture*, 1966. The term "postmodern" has a different significance in architecture than in philosophy, where postmodernism principally marks the realization that truth can no longer be seen as absolute: see Jean-François Lyotard, *Das postmoderne Wissen* (1979), 1986.

9 See Robert Venturi, Denise Scott Brown, Steven Izenour: *Learning from Las Vegas*, 1972.

10 The "duck" as a building was a restaurant that served grilled chicken and duck, and actually had the shape of a duck on the outside.

11 See Venturi: *Complexity and Contradiction in Architecture*, op. cit.

12 See Charles Jencks: *The Language of Post-Modern Architecture*, 1977.

13 Peter Eisenman: "Aspects of Modernism: The Maison Dom-ino and the Self-Referential Sign," *Log*, No. 30, 2014, 139–151: 144, *JSTOR*, www.jstor.org/stable/43631742 (accessed November 10, 2020).

principles: He refers to historical models, uses "quotations," many of his works seem to contain ironic comments and there is a superimposition of different levels of meaning.

In 1980, Hermann Czech, Boris Podrecca, Heinz Tesar and Hans Hollein, who designed the main contribution, were the Austrian participants in the first Venice Architecture Biennale, a key event in the postmodern movement. There the "End of Prohibition" through dogmatic modernism and the "reusability" of the classical column was proclaimed.[14] One opposed a modernism experienced as purist, in which "both the trivial aesthetics of the user and the appropriation of history were frowned upon."[15] As a result, the focus of the architectural discourse shifted more and more to a discussion about the form or the formal expression of a building that does not need to derive its legitimation from the emphasis on its content and materiality, but from the "pure" form. As early as 1978, Lefaivre and Tzonis had described postmodernism as the "narcissistic" phase of architecture.[16] They related it to the decline of the American welfare state and the expectation of functionalism to be able to solve social problems technically. As a reaction to these sobering circumstances, architects would begin to refer to themselves and to gain their legitimacy exclusively from the resources of the profession. With this withdrawal, they would regain their—weakened—raison d'être and maintain a misunderstood impression of power and control, similar to the narcissist who suffers from a disturbed perception of his/her relationship with the world. Their criticism of this development was directed against the associated loss of the social agenda in architecture: "In this new phase, there is an absence of human concern, an inability to acknowledge facts incompatible with evidence; issues of form are handled with the greatest naiveté and arbitrariness."[17]

Even if the Austrian situation differed greatly from the American in terms of economic circumstances, and the welfare state in Austria reached a peak in the 1970s, there was also an increased orientation towards formal experiments in architecture.[18] Czech rejected the idea that the form need not be justified from the start. In 1963, he had already written: "Objectivity as a reflective stance does indeed constitute a level of consciousness that cannot be relinquished. Refraining from thinking results in a loss of quality"[19] In a text about Otto Wagner written in 1974, he formulated the "only real art problem" as: "[…] if I am entitled to annoy others with my individuality."[20] He did not see his concepts as a criticism of modernism and functionalism, but on the contrary as a

14 *The Presence of the Past: First International Exhibition of Architecture*, La Biennale di Venezia, 1980.
15 Czech: Text accompanying the exhibition at the Architekturmuseum Basel, 1996.
16 Liane Lefaivre and Alexander Tzonis: "The Narcissist Phase in Architecture," in: *Harvard Architectural Review* 1, 1980, 53–61: 59; see also Alexander Tzonis, Liane Lefaivre and Richard Diamond, "Introduction," in: *Architecture in North America since 1960*, London: Thames and Hudson, 1995.
17 Lefaivre and Tzonis: "The Narcissist Phase," op. cit., 59.
18 See, e.g., Hans Hollein and Walter Pichler: *Architektur*, 1963.
19 Czech: "Newer Objectivity" (1963), trans. Elise Feiersinger, in: Hermann Czech: *Essays on Architecture and City Planning*, Zurich: Park Books, 2019, 41–46: 45.
20 Czech: "Die Sprache Otto Wagners" (1974), in: Czech 1996, 73–76: 76. English translation by Michael Loudon, "The Work and Diction of Otto Wagner," in: *a+u* (Tokyo) 7/1977, 45–66: 66.

continuation of an Austrian modernism, especially in the understanding of Adolf Loos and Josef Frank, who had already anticipated the later criticism.[21] Their rejection of the more dogmatic German modernism of the Bauhaus primarily related to the breach with traditional building elements of architectural history and the establishment of rigid, almost morally understood design principles. In Loos's case, Czech recognized a way of working that reused the everyday and the proven: "Loos was, of course, a lifestyle reformer, though his aim was not to create an ideal, parallel culture for outsiders, but rather to filter out the existing culture's viable elements," wrote Czech in 1984.[22] Loos himself explained: "And I found out the most important thing, namely that the style of 1900 only differs from the style of 1800 to the same extent as the tail coat of 1900 differs from that of 1800. By not very much, that is. […] In its external appearance a building can at most have changed as much as a tail coat. By not very much, that is."[23] When designing an armchair, for example, both Loos and Frank used typical, everyday models as a starting point for their own designs. For Frank, the tubular steel armchair was an example of the misunderstood modernist view that the cubic shape is more important than the comfort of the seated person and that the shape and the material became an ideology and a moral issue. "This is a commercialized world view that is demonstrated to every visitor, just like the 'material authenticity' that, when used demonstratively, proclaims to everyone who sees it: 'I am honest,' and delivers to them a moral sermon, 'I no longer want to appear as I am and therefore I am more than you. Go forth and be likewise.' But how pleasant were the people who used imitations, of material, yes, but not of spirit; people with true humility who flaunted material but never ideals, and who showed no morality."[24] Loos and Frank shared this opinion with all modernist architects that the project of modernism should be seen in the tradition of enlightened humanism, when the focus was on the emancipation of human beings. This commitment to the Enlightenment is also, in my view, the big difference between Czech and most postmodern architects. In the aforementioned text on Maison Dom-ino, Peter Eisenman analyzed Le Corbusier's design as a system of signs that point to the architecture itself and no longer to people. For him, this "self-referential condition of sign" constitutes the true modernity of Le Corbusier's design and represents a "true and seminal break from the 400-year-old tradition of Western humanist architecture."[25] Czech was never able to understand considerations that questioned the

21 Czech: "Was bedeutet 'postmodern'?" (1985), in: Czech 1996, 110.
22 Czech: "Adolf Loos – Widersprüche und Aktualität," in: *Mitteilungsblatt der Architektenkammer der Provinz Bozen*, 1984 and in other publications, last version in: Inge Podbrecky; Rainald Franz (eds.): *Leben mit Loos*, 2008, 17–25: 22. English translation by Elise Feiersinger, "A Conceptual Matrix for the Current Interpretation of Josef Frank" (1985), in: Hermann Czech: *Essays on Architecture and City Planning*, 2019, 151–191: 159.
23 Loos: "Architecture," trans. Michael Mitchell, in: Adolf Loos: *On Architecture* (Studies in Austrian Literature, Culture and Thought), Riverside, CA: Ariadne Press, 2002, 73–85: 80–81. Loos related this statement to his House on Michaelerplatz.
24 Frank, *Architecture as Symbol* (1931), trans John Sands, in: Frank 2012, Vol. 2, 9–191: 133.
25 Eisenman: "Aspects of Modernism," 151.

Enlightenment. For him, these ideas are the leitmotif of his work as an architect. On the occasion of an exhibition on Austrian architecture at the Institute for Architecture and Urban Studies in New York, in which Hermann Czech also took part, Kenneth Frampton already wrote in 1980: "Whatever its idiosyncrasies this collection certainly serves to remind us that 'after modern architecture' need not degenerate into the deliquescence of endless pastiche or be reduced to a game in which little remains but to arbitrarily adopt one historicist mask after another."[26] Frampton ascribed this to the historical circumstances in Austria as a country that had "lost its innocence" much earlier than any other, that had become a "land without qualities" and had brought forth personalities such as Loos and Frank, Musil and Schönberg, but also Otto Mühl and Walter Pichler.[27]

Perhaps the difference between Hermann Czech and postmodern architects can be compared to the difference between humor and irony: Postmodernism uses ironic elements to demonstrate a distance from society. Architecture is no longer understood as a social project. Hermann Czech, on the other hand, uses humorous elements in his work. For him, humor is the last chance to practice architecture as an enlightening, emancipatory project in a world of consumerism.[28]

Friedrich Achleitner described "the strange phenomenon of a *backward oriented utopia*, which means that Vienna seeks to complete its past always with a delay and mostly under totally different conditions."[29] In this context, he refers to prominent examples of Viennese architectural history: from Fischer von Erlach's St. Charles Church to Otto Wagner's Church at Steinhof and Adolf Loos's House on Michaelerplatz to Hans Hollein's Haas House. In his opinion, these represent works that refer to the history of architecture and thus attempt to retrospectively make concepts that were not realized in earlier times real. Achleitner wonders whether this approach is a "psychological compulsion to make amends for a traumatized historical error."[30] In this logic, Czech's work can also be understood as an attempt to retrospectively realize the conception of Viennese modernism by Loos and Frank.

This book assesses the preoccupation with architectural history as a reference and inspiration for architectural work more positively. In my view, a critical look at the past is first possible by consciously examining the past and new things can actually arise only through this examination. "If you want to convey new thoughts, you cannot use a new language at the same time."[31]

26 Kenneth Frampton: "Preface," *A New Wave of Austrian Architecture*, 1980, 1.
27 Ibid.
28 Czech: "Can Architecture Be Conceived by Way of Consumption?" (2011), trans. Elise Feiersinger, in: Hermann Czech: *Essays on Architecture and City Planning*, 2019, 229–247. See more detailed information on this topic: "Wunder-Bar," 205.
29 Friedrich Achleitner: *Die rückwärtsgewandte Utopie: Motor des Fortschritts in der Wiener Architektur?*, 1993, 48f.
30 Ibid., 49.
31 Czech: "Adolf Loos – Widersprüche und Aktualität," in: Podbrecky; Franz (eds.): *Leben mit Loos*, op. cit., 22.

The standard method for a biographical work on a living person is "oral history," i.e., the method of the narrative interview.[32] The method is based on making a certain period of time experienceable through a person's individual perspective. In the narrative interview, the interviewer asks a general question and lets the interviewee tell his/her stories and associations on the subject as unaffectedly as possible. The interviewer mainly listens and does not try to influence the narrative by asking questions. She is aware that the story of the narrator and his/her view of the past and what has been experienced are influenced by the current present. The interviewer also knows that the narrating person structures the experience in retrospect in order to give it meaning.

Hermann Czech avoided this method from the start. He has no finished view of his own past. He does not like to think "out loud," and rarely tells personal anecdotes. Whenever possible, he looked for thoughts that had already been formulated in our conversations in the form of texts that he gave me to read. Silence was also part of our communication. His private life, friendships, and personal views of his colleagues were not topics of our conversations. Rather, it was about the environment in which he moved, which books he had read, which events he had gone to, what he had thought about. Our conversations were more like a neutral informing about places and contents than conveying personal memories of the respective time and its events. At the same time, we went through the projects and works in his archive.

Hermann Czech prefers the written word to the spoken word,[33] which is why his text archive became an important source alongside the conversations. However, he is not only a writer, but also a meticulously reading architect and his studio includes a comprehensive specialist library. Part of the work, therefore, also involved reading, at least excerpts of, the same texts and books that he had read in certain phases of his theoretical examination—for example, the writings of Adolf Loos and Josef Frank, Konrad Wachsmann or Christopher Alexander.

As an "intellectual biography," this book shows the development of an architect in dealing with the cultural context to which he belongs. It begins under the title "Progress and Criticism: Viennese Modernism" with a presentation of this cultural and historical environment, addresses the aftermath of the Enlightenment in 19th-century Vienna, as well as the consequently emerging, specifically Austrian philosophy that emphasized an empirical basic attitude, scientific theory, logic and language criticism,

---

32 Uwe Flick, *Qualitative Sozialforschung. Eine Einführung*, 2007, 227–238. The following summary of the narrative interview is based on Flick's description.

33 Interview by Shinichi Eto with Hermann Czech for the Japanese magazine *Toshi-Jutaku – Urban Housing*, 186, 1983, reprinted: "Was ist Ihre Kunst im speziellen?" (1983), in: Czech 1996, 91–94: 94.

up to its most important representatives in architecture: Otto Wagner, Adolf Loos and Josef Frank.

This introductory chapter is followed by the biographical part of the work, which encompasses Czech's childhood and adolescence, as well as the years of his studies—the most formative time for him, when he framed the questions that were to accompany him throughout his professional life. There are no breaches or phases in his conception of architecture in which he completely reoriented himself and rejected earlier ideas or models. On the contrary, his work to this day consists of continuous further development, improvement, enrichment and specification of an attitude that he developed during his studies, which began in 1954 and lasted until 1971, and was accompanied by independent design activities from an early age.

Furthermore, selected projects by Hermann Czech are presented in chronological order, placed in reference to his texts and the historical context worked out in the first part, and interpreted, as well as supplemented by a list of works and writings.

The structure of the research work in the biographical section can be understood with the help of graphical means: The texts that arose directly from interviews with Hermann Czech are set in a different font[34] than my research and conclusions. At this point, I would like to mention that text additions by Hermann Czech have also been included in the project part. In the interests of better readability, however, because these supplements are much more interlinked with my texts, they were, in consultation with Hermann Czech, not specifically highlighted.

34 These texts are set in "Bodoni," a font that Czech used in his text collection *Zur Abwechslung*, as well as in the study *Das Looshaus*, which was co-written with Wolfgang Mistelbauer, because, among other things, he valued it as a classic font that had never been "in fashion" (with reference to Karl Kraus et al.). "Bodoni" is a classicistic font (actually several fonts), which was designed around 1790 by the Italian typographer Giambattista Bodoni.

20

Progress and Criticism: Viennese Modernism

The Aftermath of the Enlightenment in 19th-Century Vienna

In the second half of the 18th century, reforms in the spirit of the Enlightenment were carried out in Austria by Emperor Joseph II (1741–1790). The reason of the individual was to take precedence over outdated traditional hierarchies, the individual was to become part of a rational structure of the state and the goal was a society of reasonable individuals, supported by common humanitarian values.[1] Between 1781 and 1789, Joseph II issued a series of so-called tolerance patents to equate all religions (especially Protestants, Greek Orthodox and Jews) with Catholicism; the focus was on the individual and his or her value for the state. The tolerance patents were particularly well-received by the Jews,[2] since they opened an individual life outside the ghetto and social advancement within the emerging civil society.

Education was a major concern of the Enlightenment, which fell on fertile ground, especially with liberal Jews, since the language and reading of the Holy Scriptures had always been of central importance in Judaism. In this sense, the Bible was exchanged for the scientific book, the study of Hebrew for intensive preoccupation with the German language.[3] Many Jewish women and men of the Habsburg Monarchy, particularly in Vienna, devoted themselves entirely to the new culture of reason and progress, and saw the Enlightenment, above all the idea of the ethically superior human being, as a kind of further development of Judaism.[4] The assimilation of the Jews can be understood as a "project" in order to define an identity between adaptation and Jewish tradition with the help of aesthetics.[5]

---

[1] The following compilation is essentially based on the studies by Steven Beller, *Vienna and the Jews, 1867–1938. A Cultural History*, 1990 (German: *Wien und die Juden. 1867–1938*, 1993), 125, and was initiated by a lecture Joseph Koerner gave in Vienna, Joseph Koerner: "The Viennese Interior," March 14, 2013, Vienna Secession.

[2] According to the lecture "Josephine Tolerance Patents for the Jewish Population of the Habsburg Monarchy" by Svjatoslav Pacholkiv on October 16, 2013 as part of the lecture series "The Austrian History of Judaism" organized by the Center for Jewish Studies, Karl-Franzens-Universität Graz.

[3] Beller: *Vienna and the Jews*, op. cit., 127.

[4] Ibid., 142f; see also Arthur Schnitzler: *Der Weg ins Freie*, quoted in Elana Shapira: "Jüdisches Mäzenatentum," in: Claudia Theune; Tina Walzer (eds.): *Jüdische Friedhöfe. Kultstätte, Erinnerungsort, Denkmal*, 2011, 182: "Do you know what the final conclusion will probably prove? That we, we Jews I mean, have been a sort of ferment of humanity."

[5] Ibid., 171.

In addition to the legal upheavals caused by the ideas of the Enlightenment, the effects of the Industrial Revolution were the second important impetus for the emergence of a liberal and enlightened bourgeoisie in the Habsburg Monarchy. As a result of the trade in industrially manufactured goods, a broad middle class achieved prosperity; merchants especially began to process the purchased raw materials themselves in factories and to resell them as end products with greater profit. This new class, which appeared as a political group under the name "The Liberals," pushed for participation in political life and public presence.

In 1867, the full legal equality of the Jewish population, accompanied by the right of assembly and association, was finally achieved and led to the establishment of the *Israelitische Kultusgemeinde* (The Jewish Community of Vienna). The freedom to convert to another religious denomination prompted many Jews to join the Catholic or Protestant faith. However, their origins as Jews remained in the social consciousness. "The emperor and the liberal system offered status to the Jews without demanding nationality; they became the supra-national people of the multi-national state, the one folk which, in effect, stepped into the shoes of the earlier aristocracy."[6]

In Vienna, as an expression of the liberal bourgeoisie, the Vienna Ringstrasse with its representative buildings and private houses was created. "The inner city was dominated architecturally by the symbols of the first and second estates: the Baroque Hofburg, residence of the emperor; the elegant palais of the aristocracy; the Gothic Cathedral of St. Stephen and a host of small churches scattered through the narrow streets. In the new Ringstrasse development, the third estate celebrated in architecture the triumph of constitutional *Recht* over imperial *Macht*, of secular culture over religious belief."[7] The representative buildings of the Ringstrasse symbolized the new values of the liberal bourgeoisie, the parliament, the democratic constitutional state, the university, the education of the elite of an early democratic society, the theaters and museums, the education of the whole society and the possibility for aspiring citizens to rise into the so-called "intellectual nobility."[8]

The Ringstrasse was built in the style of Historicism. A distinction is made between Romantic Historicism, Strict Historicism and Late Historicism.[9] Strict Historicism aimed to define a vocabulary of forms from the most

---

6   Carl E. Schorske: *Fin de Siècle Vienna: Politics and Culture*, New York: Vintage Books, 1981, 129.
7   Ibid., 31.
8   Ibid., 42.
9   Renate Wagner-Rieger: *Wiens Architektur im 19. Jahrhundert*, 1970.

"pure elements" possible, which could be applied to the most varied of contemporary building tasks.[10] The aim was to eliminate the subjective and to find a scientifically sound, objective style. In this spirit, for example, the Austrian Museum of Art and Industry[11] was founded in 1864. It was to offer contemporary artists a collection of models for their work using historical objects and also with the help of plaster replicas. In 1867, the museum was augmented by the establishment of a School of Arts and Crafts. Both institutions obtained a building designed by Heinrich Ferstel on Stubenring in 1871, which was expanded in 1877 with a school wing.[12] Ferstel took the Italian High Renaissance as a design model and reproduced ornaments from the Circle of Raphael for the façade. He used a modern, glass-steel construction for the roofing of the central hall, showing how new spatial qualities could be generated by combining classic models with modern constructions.[13] This phase of Historicism produced a kind of Austrian architectural language in which the stylistic elements became assignable codes.[14] To put it simply, the official style of the monarchy was the Neo-Baroque. The administrative buildings, as well as the theaters and museums of the court, were built in this style. Neo-Gothic, on the other hand, was received as a style in which the national or communal could be emphasized as opposed to the multi-ethnic state of the monarchy. The liberal urban bourgeoisie, who wanted to draw attention to their humanistic and cosmopolitan attitude, had their representative houses and palaces built in the Neo-Renaissance style, which then also took up the largest part of the Ringstrasse.[15]

The bourgeois houses, on the other hand, differed significantly in their structural concept from the palais of the nobility. Right from the start, they were planned with several rentable apartments and shops in the ground floor zone. The first such urban residential building was erected in 1844 by Ludwig Förster on behalf of Adolph Pereira on Rennweg.[16] Sparsely embellished with classical ornaments around the windows and a few strong fascia, the façade was rational, but the latest construction methods were used for the implementation.

With this linear but high-quality building, Pereira wanted to create a new urban style.[17] In 1861—again by the architects Förster and Hansen—the first Ringstrasse residential building belonging to Jewish owners was constructed for the bankers Eduard and Moritz Todesco—in a prominent location right next to the opera, which was then under construction. The most famous and type-forming urban, block-sized apartment building was

10 Ibid., 150.
11 Later the Vienna Museum of Applied Arts, now the MAK—the Austrian Museum of Applied Arts.
12 Today: University of Applied Arts, Stubenring; see Otto Kapfinger; Matthias Boeckl: *Abgelehnt – nicht ausgeführt: Die Bau- und Projektgeschichte der Hochschule für Angewandte Kunst in Wien 1873–1993*, 1993.
13 Wagner-Rieger: *Wiens Architektur…*, op. cit., 182ff; Ákos Moravánszky: *Die Architektur der Donaumonarchie*, 1988, 49f.
14 Moravánszky, ibid., 37ff.
15 Ibid., 44–61.
16 Fredric Bedoire: *The Jewish Contribution to Modern Architecture*, 2004, 304.
17 This representation by Fredric Bedoire contradicts common art historical interpretations that the bourgeois residential buildings were primarily false copies of the aristocratic mansions. Adolf Loos certainly made a major contribution to this in Austria with his polemic "Die potemkinsche stadt" (1898). However, since he strictly opposed new forms and advocated the continuation of the existing tradition, in my opinion, his polemic aimed at a certain development of Late Historicism and not the design of residential buildings in the Historicist style in general. In 1911, Loos wrote about "Otto Wagner" in *Die Reichspost*: "In Vienna one took the good where one found it. The Corinthian orders, profiles and ornaments from two millennia were amassed and used on a building. The master was able to build the opera and Palais Larisch according to this recipe, but the pupils failed because of the unbridled eclecticism." (Loos: *Gesammelte Schriften*, 2010, 409–414: 410).

the Heinrichhof, opposite the opera and designed by Theophil Hansen for the brick manufacturer Heinrich von Drasche, a liberal Christian.

From 1880 onwards, the classifications of Strict Historicism became blurred, the national component moved more into focus, the Neo-Baroque was used as the "Austrian style," mixed with that of the "German Renaissance," without differentiating between the function.[18] Towards the end of the 19th century, the use of foreign styles as an expression of one's own identity led to increasingly quirky results and to corresponding criticism. Nascent nationalism, in turn, tried to employ historical symbols to express the separate nation. Ödön Lechner, the architect of the Museum of Applied Arts in Budapest, used façade ornaments that were supposed to refer to the oriental origins of Hungary.[19]

The unchecked application of different styles also affected the design of interiors. Egon Friedell described the typical living culture of the liberal bourgeoisie at the turn of the century as follows: "These rooms of theirs were not living-rooms, but pawnshops and curiosity-shops. Simultaneously there is displayed a craze for satin-like surfaces […] as also for totally meaningless articles of decoration such as Rococo mirrors in several pieces, multi-coloured Venetian glass, fat-bellied Old German pots, a skin rug on the floor, complete with head and terrifying jaws, and, in the hall, a life-size wooden Negro. Everything was mixed, too, without rhyme or reason: in the boudoir a set of Buhl, in the drawing room an Empire suite, next door a Cinquecento dining-room, and next to that a Gothic bedroom. […] We note with astonishment that the best-situated, most comfortable and airy room in a house (the 'best room') was not intended to be lived in at all, but was only there to be exhibited to friends."[20]

At the end of the 19th century, criticism towards historicism became increasingly vehement. Otto Wagner's book *Moderne Architektur* appeared in 1896, the Secession was founded in 1897, and Adolf Loos wrote his polemic about Vienna's Ringstrasse, "Die potemkinsche stadt" ("Potemkin City"), in 1898.[21]

18 Wagner-Rieger: *Wiens Architektur...*, op. cit., 252ff.
19 Moravánszky: *Die Architektur der Donaumonarchie*, op. cit., 39.
20 Egon Friedell: *A Cultural History of the Modern Age. Volume III. The Crisis of the European Soul: From the Black Death to the World War*, trans. Charles Francis Atkinson, New York: Alfred A. Knopf, Inc., 1932, 299–300.
21 Loos: "Die potemkinsche stadt" (1898), in: Loos 1962, 153–156.

In the Center of the Discourse: "Language"

The contrast between the tendencies of the Enlightenment and Baroque Catholicism, which had a lasting effect, can be seen as the key to understanding Austrian culture. Both have in common the fundamental rejection of German idealism and its fundamental concept of wanting to grasp reality as an overall system.[22] In philosophy, an independent Austrian tradition developed against idealism and its metaphysics. The focus areas of this philosophy were an empirical basic attitude, scientific theory, logic and language criticism.[23]

One characteristic of Austrian philosophy is that "it never followed or understood Kant's 'Copernican turn.' Contrary to all idealistic tendencies, Austrian philosophy is determined by its realistic orientation."[24] This orientation began towards the end of the 18th century with Johann Friedrich Herbart (1776–1841) and Bernhard Bolzano (1781–1848). The most important and, in this line, actual founder of a school tradition of Austrian philosophy was Franz Brentano (1838–1917).[25] A Catholic clergyman, he left the Church when the dogma about the infallibility of the Pope was proclaimed, taught as a philosopher in Vienna from 1874 on and married a daughter from an assimilated, liberal, Jewish middle-class family. Brentano's method of practicing philosophy as a scientific discipline, understanding one's own perception as the only possibility of cognition and having clarity as the primary goal, went hand in hand with the use of linguistic-analytical and language-critical methods to expose pseudo-problems.[26] His teaching already contained a criticism of language which was consolidated in Austria at the turn of the century with the linguistic despair expressed in Hugo von Hofmannsthal's *Chandos Brief* (*The Lord Chandos Letter*), the radical language skepticism of Fritz Mauthner and the relentless language criticism of Karl Kraus.[27]

Ernst Mach—a special chair for the "History and Theory of Inductive Sciences" was set up for him at the University of Vienna in 1895[28]—opined that knowledge is only possible through sensations and thus hit the nerve of both writers and Secessionists. The focus was on one's own feelings and the exploration of the soul, as well as those of the liberals and socialists who found their philosophical basis in the resulting rejection of metaphysics. Mach saw the meaning of all science in replacing experience with knowledge and in the most economical way possible. In the historical process of the emergence of science, language and its concepts were created through abstraction. In

22 Peter Kampits: "Biedermeier und österreichische Philosophie," in: Ian F. Roe; John Warren (eds.): *The Biedermeier and Beyond*, 1999, 76; Rudolf Haller: *Neopositivismus. Eine historische Einführung in die Philosophie des Wiener Kreises*, 1993, 43.
23 See Rudolf Haller: *Studien zur österreichischen Philosophie: Variationen über ein Thema*, 1979.
24 Ibid., 8.
25 Ibid., 10.
26 Ibid., 12.
27 Kampits: "Biedermeier…," op. cit., 80.
28 Haller: *Studien zur österreichischen Philosophie…*, op. cit., 82. After Mach, Ludwig Boltzmann held this chair and was succeeded by Moritz Schlick.

this conception there is no "thing in itself" or something that stands behind things. In the end, everything can only be traced back to sensory experiences such as colors, sounds and smells.[29] The economic principle means that in science, when describing experiences and establishing laws and rules, one should limit oneself to the bare essentials. Already in Mach's thinking, all metaphysically classified terms disappear from philosophy. As early as 1883 he postulated in *Die Mechanik in ihrer Entwicklung* (*The Science of Mechanics*): "Where neither confirmation nor refutation is concerned, science is not concerned."[30] Mach's philosophy went beyond the purely philosophical discourse towards an "interdisciplinary world view with the inherent claim to the humanization and democratization of science and society."[31]

Otto Wagner–Vienna around 1900

At the height of historicism, the architect Otto Wagner (1841–1918) began his professional career.[32] He had studied in Berlin with the Schinkel pupil Carl Ferdinand Busse and in Vienna with the Ringstrasse architects August Sicard von Sicardsburg and Eduard van der Nüll. In 1862, he interned at Ludwig von Förster's studio. At the beginning of his own professional practice, he worked in the style of what he himself called "unbound" or "free" Renaissance. Looking back on his first years of practice, he formulated in 1889: "[…] and thus I finally reached the conviction that a certain free Renaissance that has been absorbed by our *genius loci* is, taking the greatest possible account of all our circumstances as well as of modern accomplishments in the use of materials and construction, for present and future architecture the only course […]."[33] With his treatise, *Moderne Architektur* (*Modern Architecture*) (1895),[34] Wagner turned away from historicism. Architecture should find an expression of its own time, which is determined by necessity. Wagner's key words were "realism" and "modern life." "The realism of our time must pervade the developing work of art. It will not harm it, nor will any decline of art ensue as a consequence of it; rather it will breathe a new and pulsating life into forms and in time conquer new fields that today are still devoid of art […]."[35] In the foreword to the first edition, Wagner wrote: "One idea inspires this book, namely *that the basis of today's predominant views on architecture must be shifted, and we must become fully aware that the sole departure point of our artistic work can only be modern life.*"[36]

---

29 Haller: *Neopositivismus*, op. cit., 34.
30 Ernst Mach: *The Science of Mechanics*, trans. Thomas J. McCormack, Chicago: The Open Court Publishing Co., 1893, 490.
31 Friedrich Stadler: "Zum Aufstieg der wissenschaftlichen Philosophie," in: idem; Rudolf Haller (eds.): *Wien – Berlin – Prag. Der Aufstieg der wissenschaftlichen Philosophie. Zentenarien Rudolf Carnap, Hans Reichenbach, Edgar Zilsel*, 1993, 11–37.
32 On Otto Wagner, see: Heinz Geretsegger; Max Peintner: *Otto Wagner 1841–1918. Unbegrenzte Großstadt. Beginn der modernen Architektur*, 1964; Otto Antonia Graf: *Otto Wagner*, 7 Volumes, 1985–2000; Ákos Moravánszky: *Die Architektur der Donaumonarchie*, 1988; August Sarnitz: *Otto Wagner 1841–1918. Wegbereiter der modernen Architektur*, 2005.
33 Otto Wagner: *Sketches, Projects, and Executed Buildings*, trans. Edward Vance Humphrey, New York: Rizzoli, 1987, 17.
34 Otto Wagner: *Die Baukunst unserer Zeit: dem Baukunstjünger ein Führer auf diesem Kunstgebiete*, 4th edition, 1914. Wagner changed the original title *Moderne Architektur* (1895, 1998, 1902) for this edition.
35 Otto Wagner: "Antrittsrede an der Akademie" (1894), quoted in August Sarnitz: "Realism versus *Verniedlichung*," in: Harry Francis Mallgrave (ed.): *Otto Wagner. Reflections on the Raiment of Modernity*, 1993, 85–112: 108. English translation by Harry Francis Mallgrave in: Otto Wagner: *Modern Architecture: A Guidebook for His Students to This Field of Art*, Los Angeles: Getty Center Publications, 1988, 160.
36 Wagner: *Modern Architecture: A Guidebook for His Students to This Field of Art*, trans. Harry Francis Mallgrave, 9.

Wagner's designs are to be understood as a confrontation with his era and his environment. Modern man, urban inhabitants, their needs and living conditions take center stage.[37] Otto Wagner wrote a groundbreaking urbanistic study in 1910 entitled *Die Großstadt* ("The Development of a Great City"),[38] in which he presented his ideas about urban development. For him it was clear that "the majority of people undoubtedly prefer living in a large city to living in a small town or in the country."[39] The "anonymity of the big city" was a positive term for him and he went even further: "To hark back to tradition, to make 'expression' or picturesqueness the controlling consideration in designing homes for the man of to-day, is absurd in the light of modern experience. The number of city dwellers who to-day prefer to vanish in the mass as mere numbers on apartment doors is considerably greater than of those who care to hear the daily, 'good morning, how are you' from their gossipy neighbors in single houses."[40] In addition to anonymity, the main advantages of the metropolis for Wagner lay in the possibility of finding work, in a far more convenient, more comfortable and, in terms of hygiene, healthier life than in the country, as well as in the possibilities of leisure activities through the cultural offerings. For these reasons he turned against any nostalgia in urban planning, against the picturesque, against the *Heimatstil* and—in clear opposition to Camillo Sitte—against the stylistic integration of new buildings into an existing cityscape; he designed the image of a straight-lined, grid-like city made up of regular blocks, interrupted by special administrative or art buildings and geometrically laid out green spaces. In this context, too, Wagner referred to "realism" and "modern life," which demanded this clarity, "the straight line." As the foundation of modern life, reality was to be the object of artistic interpretation; the supreme ethic was to make visible its inner structure, materials and processes.[41]

Wagner belonged to the bourgeois class, was "a liberal patrician,"[42] but the city administration was still in the hands of the imperial court and its aristocratic administration. Wagner's vision of the city was, therefore, also to be understood politically and was clearly directed against the prevailing image of the city, which, in his opinion, was characterized by preservation and a false appearance. Instead, his design proposals for the city were intended to enable real (democratic) urbanity.

37 See Sarnitz: "Realism versus Verniedlichung," op. cit.
38 Wagner: *Die Großstadt. Eine Studie über diese von Otto Wagner*, 1911.
39 Ibid., 10. English translation quoted in August Sarnitz: "Realism versus *Verniedlichung*," in: Harry Francis Mallgrave (ed.): *Otto Wagner. Reflections on the Raiment of Modernity*, 1993, 85–112: 90.
40 Otto Wagner: "The Development of a Great City," *The Architectural Record* 31 (May 1912): 485–500, http://urbanplanning.library.cornell.edu/DOCS/wagner.htm (accessed November 19, 2020). Another English translation (by Michael Loudon) of this quote can be found in: "The Work and Diction of Otto Wagner," in: *a+u* (Tokyo) 7/1977, 45–66: 45.
41 Sarnitz: "Realism versus *Verniedlichung*," op. cit., 97.
42 Ibid., 105.

In 1897, likewise as a reaction to the phase of Late Historicism, the Vienna Secession was founded as an association of visual artists and architects. It had set its sights on finding a new style, looking for an individual expression for the "new era." The transitions between the dissolving canon of forms in Late Historicism and the style of the Secession proceeded fluidly in reality. The new *Jugendstil* (Art Nouveau) used curvy and soft forms and corresponded in its understanding to the Neo-Baroque and its view of the building as a volume with a designed surface in contrast to the Neo-Renaissance of Strict Historicism. Both styles also share a preference for the use of domes.[43] Art Nouveau appealed to the next generation of bourgeois entrepreneurs who, in turn, came primarily from assimilated Jewish circles.[44] The already-established Ringstrasse families and the old aristocracy found the new style to be vulgar.

The best-known patrons of the Secession were the great industrialist of the new generation, Karl Wittgenstein, and the young banker, Fritz Wärndorfer. It was the "ascetic, mystical, dream-like, 'non-Christian'"[45] which did not refer to a historical tradition that appealed to the connoisseurs of Vienna. Josef Hoffmann and Joseph Maria Olbrich were the most famous architects among the Secessionists. Olbrich designed the Secession building, which the artists' association moved into in 1898.

In 1903, the Wiener Werkstätte was founded in order to implement this new style in handicraft products. It was supposed to modernize all areas of life, especially the furnishings. Josef Hoffmann, Joseph Maria Olbrich and the Wiener Werkstätte were co-signers of the charter of the Deutscher Werkbund,[46] established in 1907. The aim of the Deutscher Werkbund was to overcome the arts and crafts in the traditional understanding of historicism and to create a new quality in design through the cooperation of art, craft and industry. The step towards the design of large-scale industrial products was not taken in Austria; the Wiener Werkstätte remained focused on artisanal, exclusive wares.

Art Nouveau's forms were new, but its basic concept of subjecting the entire environment to an artistic expression (*Gesamtkunstwerk*) remained. This is where Adolf Loos began with his criticism and offered the liberal, enlightened client an alternative in the form of modern, urban, rational architecture based on classical and English models.

43 Wagner-Rieger: *Wiens Architektur...*, op. cit., 227ff.
44 Bedoire: *The Jewish Contribution...*, op. cit., 332.
45 Ibid.
46 Wilfried Posch: "Josef Frank, eine bedeutende Persönlichkeit des österreichischen Kulturliberalismus," in: *UM BAU* 10, 1986, 21–38: 23–25.

Adolf Loos and Karl Kraus—Vienna before the First World War

Adolf Loos[47] (1870–1933), having spent several years in the USA after dropping out of his studies, returned to Vienna in 1896. He joined the intellectual circle around Karl Kraus and Peter Altenberg and wrote critical comments on Viennese culture in the newspaper *Die Neue Freie Presse*. Just as Loos criticized the Secession and the Wiener Werkstätte with their new ornamentation, Kraus satirized the feuilleton with its phrases and hollow rhetoric. Both Loos and Kraus were key figures in the intellectual discourse in Vienna around 1900, in the context of which the philosophy of Ludwig Wittgenstein's criticism of language and the Vienna Circle came into being.[48]

Karl Kraus (1874–1936) was a typical representative of the Viennese middle class. He came from a wealthy Jewish family, and his father enabled him to live independently. At the age of barely 25, he founded the satirical journal *Die Fackel* (*The Torch*) after he had turned down a job at the renowned daily *Die Neue Freie Presse*. Kraus's controversial criticism in *Die Fackel* was directed against what he believed to be the immoral middle class. If read superficially, his relentless sweeping blows against a wide variety of people and topics are irritating. In the background, however, Kraus's conviction that the sincerity and truth of the individual personality are the most important aspects for a functioning society can also be seen. "Kraus diagnosed the state of a disintegrating epoch and a sick society by the state of its disintegrating, sick language."[49] He saw the expression of a person's moral character in his/her language; he turned bitterly against the use of language as phraseology he perceived as corrupting, and pleaded for authentic, true expression. Mere reason, whether it was effective or not, was morally neutral to him. Nevertheless, Kraus believed, the mind needs a moral direction, while a person's values arise in his/her feelings. Therefore, truth emerges from a unity of feeling and understanding, with feeling, expressed through imagination and creativity, having the upper hand. Without the right feeling, without a feeling for the value of things, reason becomes, according to Kraus, an instrument of the immoral.[50] From these considerations comes the idea of the unity of "ethics and aesthetics," which Wittgenstein was later to formulate in his *Logisch-philosophische Abhandlung* (*Tractatus Logico-Philosophicus*).[51]

47 The author is aware that Adolf Loos was convicted of pedophilia in a 1928 trial. The following text on Loos, however, focuses on Loos's architectural thinking, his architecture and the cultural scene around him, since these were important for Hermann Czech's later reflection on architecture.
48 See Allan Janik; Stephen Toulmin: *Wittgenstein's Vienna*, New York: Simon and Schuster, 1972, 143.
49 Ibid., 106.
50 Ibid., 74.
51 Ludwig Wittgenstein: *Tractatus Logico-Philosophicus. Logical-Philosophical Treatise*, Proposition 6.421. Czech quoted this sentence in: "Architektur, von der Produktion her gedacht," in: *Hintergrund* 41, 2009, 21–37: 26.

Kraus was not doctrinal in his thinking; ideas, for him, belonged to reason and had no moral dimension in themselves. For him, it was a question of how the individual behaved according to his/her own ideas.

Paul Engelmann, a former associate of Adolf Loos and, together with Ludwig Wittgenstein, architect of the house for Margarethe Stonborough-Wittgenstein on Kundmanngasse in Vienna-Landstrasse, sees a fundamental correspondence between the way Kraus, Loos and Wittgenstein thought.[52] All three are concerned with the distinction between the utterable and the unutterable—in each case from the vantage point of their respective specialist area.

Similar to Kraus's criticism of language, for Loos it was a matter of the appropriate expression in architecture and the self-presentation of people in their living spaces. The characteristics of the interiors of the private inner spaces were to match the life of the residents.[53]

Loos entered the Viennese stage in 1897 with a series of articles in the *Neue Freie Presse* which ran for months on the occasion of the Vienna Anniversary Exhibition of 1898.[54] The exhibition lasted from May to November and showcased Emperor Franz Joseph's achievements from Austrian industry and commerce to mark the 50th anniversary of his reign. Loos began his series with the article "Lederwaren und Gold- und Silberschmiedekunst" ("The Leather Goods and Gold- and Silversmith Trades").[55] In it, he praised the professions mentioned, as they were the only ones that made usable products in Austria and did not follow the trend of covering them with historical ornaments. He wrote that "the strong wind of America and England"[56] had changed his mind about the arts and crafts. "We were always supposed to look back; we were always supposed to take another age as our model. But all of this has now retreated from me like a bad dream"[57] His second article was devoted to "Herrenmode" ("Men's Fashion").[58] In it, he stated that one is "dressed correctly" if one stands out as little as possible "at the center of culture." He defined London as this center of Western culture and praised those Viennese tailors who worked according to the English model. In the third article, "Der neue stil und die bronze-industrie" ("The New Style and the Bronze Industry"),[59] he summarized his stance by asserting that the search for a new style was in vain. Instead, everything that is useful should be copied. Western culture, for him, was the English and American way of life, from the tuxedo to the Chippendale chair. With this attitude, Loos met with open ears among most of the Austrian liberals who, like him, were Anglophile.[60]

---

52 Ilse Somavilla (ed.): *Wittgenstein – Engelmann. Briefe, Begegnungen, Erinnerungen*, 2006, 126.
53 See Bernhard Langer: "Rhetorik, Bild, Utopie. Adolf Loos und die Wiener Sprachkritik," in: Ákos Moravánszky et al. (eds.): *Adolf Loos. Die Kultivierung der Architektur*, 2008, 117–128 and 137–146.
54 These articles were included by Loos in the anthology *Ins Leere gesprochen* (1921). See also the lecture by Christopher Long: "Adolf Loos and the Strategy of Sorting" in the scope of the exhibition *Loos zeitgenössisch* at the MAK, Vienna from 13.3.–23.6.2013.
55 Originally the text was called "Der Silberhof und seine Nachbarschaft" (*Neue Freie Presse*) – and also in the 1st edition of *Ins Leere gesprochen* (1921). In the 2nd edition (1932) Loos changed the title and details in the text. See Loos 1962, 15–18. English translation by Jane O. Newman and John H. Smith, "The Leather Goods and Gold- and Silversmith Trades," in: Adolf Loos: *Spoken into the Void: Collected Essays 1897–1900*, Cambridge, MA and London: The MIT Press, 1982, 6–9.
56 Ibid., 7.
57 Ibid., 7.
58 Adolf Loos: "Men's Fashion" (1898), trans. Jane O. Newman and John H. Smith, in: Adolf Loos: *Spoken into the Void: Collected Essays 1897–1900*, 10–14: 12.
59 Adolf Loos: "The New Style and the Bronze Industry" (1898), trans. Jane O. Newman and John H. Smith, in: Adolf Loos: *Spoken into the Void: Collected Essays 1897–1900*, 15–17.
60 See Carl E. Schorske: *Fin de Siècle Vienna: Politics and Culture*, 45.

Like Kraus, Loos used exaggeration and polemics to convey his point of view. In an article from 1900, he told the story "Von einem armen reichen manne" ("The Poor Little Rich Man"),[61] whose quality of life was robbed through the design of his entire house down to the last detail, and contrasted this picture with the memory of his childhood living room, which could take everything up in it: the family heirlooms, children's handicrafts, family pictures. "The house was never finished; it grew along with us and we grew within it. Of course it did not have any style to it. That means there was no strangeness, no age. But there was one style that our home did have—the style of its occupants, the style of our family."[62] Loos demanded: "Everyone should be his own decorator."[63] In a similar way, Jakob von Falke had already made the case in 1871 in his book *Die Kunst im Haus* (*Art in the House*)[64] for a house that would make "the changefulness and unrest of modern life" possible. It is not the furnishing that should determine the user, but the user his furnishing.

With his polarizing views, Loos wanted to particularly address the class of liberal assimilated Jews. He offered them the possibility of a new kind of self-representation that differed from the criticized Art Nouveau and the Wiener Werkstätte.[65] Loos compared the Secessionist institutions with the Jewish caftan. "Jews who have long since put aside their caftans are happy to be able to slide back into one again. For these Secessionist interiors are only caftans in disguise…," he wrote in 1900. "[…] I deplore the man who wishes to overcome his caftan […] and relapses into Olbrich again […]."[66] "In place of the pseudo-modern caftan of the Secession interior, Loos offered with his architecture an alternative form of clothing to his clients—an English raincoat"[67] or rather the English men's suit. His architecture used simple geometries and high-quality materials, perfectly crafted in detail. Loos was concerned with creating the expression for a new cultural elite.[68]

Loos was attacked in the 1920s by the Bauhaus architects, who did not see him as a consistent modernist and accused him of failing to meet his own demand for the abolition of ornament. At the latest with Loos's design for the Chicago Tribune Tower in 1922, none of the contemporary modern architects had any use for his architecture.[69] Loos himself responded to the criticism in 1924: "Twenty-six years ago I maintained that the use of ornamentation on objects of practical use would disappear with the development of mankind, a constant and consistent development, which was as natural a process as the atrophy

61 Adolf Loos: "The Poor Little Rich Man" (1900), trans. Jane O. Newman and John H. Smith, in: Adolf Loos: *Spoken into the Void: Collected Essays 1897–1900*, 124–129.
62 Adolf Loos: "The Interiors in the Rotunda" (1898), trans. Jane O. Newman and John H. Smith, in: Adolf Loos: *Spoken into the Void: Collected Essays 1897–1900*, 22–27: 24.
63 Ibid., 23.
64 Eva B. Ottillinger: *Adolf Loos. Wohnkonzepte und Möbelentwürfe*, 1994, 24.
65 Elana Shapira: "Tailored Authorship. Adolf Loos and the Ethos of Men's Fashion," in: Podbrecky; Franz (eds.): *Leben mit Loos*, op. cit., 53–72: 64.
66 Adolf Loos: "Die Emanzipation des Judentums" (Manuscript 1900), in: Loos: *Gesammelte Schriften*, 2010, 268. English translation by Roger Tanner, quoted in: Jonathan C. Kaplan: *"Kleider machen Leute": Jewish Men and Dress Politics in Vienna, 1890–1938*, University of Technology Sydney, Master's Thesis, 2019, 144.
67 Beatriz Colomina: "Sex, Lies and Decoration: Adolf Loos and Gustav Klimt," in: Yehuda E. Safran (ed.): *Adolf Loos. Our Contemporary*, 1–12: 3.
68 Bedoire: *The Jewish Contribution…*, op. cit., 335.
69 Nikolaus Pevsner described Adolf Loos as an "enigma" in 1966 in the English-language edition of Münz und Künstler's Loos monograph.

of vowels in final syllables in popular speech. By that I did not mean what some purists have maintained ad absurdum, namely that ornament should be systematically and consistently eliminated. What I did mean was that where it had disappeared as a necessary consequence of human development, it could not be restored [...]."[70]

Loos limited ornament to furnishings that would be subject to fashion, such as fabrics and wallpaper, and otherwise to the use of classic, already existing shapes: "Classical ornament brings order into the shaping of our objects of everyday use, orders us and our forms, and creates, despite ethnographic and linguistic differences, a common fund of forms and aesthetic concepts."[71]

But there were also similarities between Loos and the architects of the Bauhaus or the so-called "New Objectivity" and they related to the rejection of superfluous decor. While Loos was primarily concerned with a conceptual and not aesthetic reduction, in his opinion the architects of the Bauhaus made a new design out of simplicity and thus unconsciously introduced a new type of ornament.[72] An essential difference between Loos or Viennese modernism and Bauhaus modernism was a fundamentally different understanding of truth.[73] In Loos's case, truth is thought individually, not collectively. At the same time, however, he was also convinced that forms are collective, arise in a cultural process and cannot be created by an individual. However, the individual would have an individual responsibility as a bearer of culture and part of a tradition. According to Loos, architecture is part of the common culture, the "everyday culture," and not an artistic vision of an individual.[74]

---

70 Adolf Loos: "Ornament und erziehung" (1924), in: Loos 1962, 391–398: 395. English translation quoted in: Christopher Long: "Ornament Is Not Exactly a Crime: On the Long and Curious Afterlife of Adolf Loos's Famed Essay," in Yehuda E. Safran (ed.): *Adolf Loos. Our Contemporary*, 31–48: 38–39.

71 Adolf Loos: "Ornament and Education" (1924), trans. Michael Mitchell, in: *Ornament and Crime: Selected Essays by Adolf Loos*, Riverside, CA: Ariadne Press, 1998, 188.

72 Somavilla: *Wittgenstein – Engelmann*, op. cit., 130.

73 Christian Kühn: *Das Schöne, das Wahre und das Richtige. Adolf Loos und das Haus Müller in Prag*, 2001, 98–100.

74 Ibid., 89.

Josef Frank and the Vienna Circle—Vienna around 1930

After the collapse of the monarchy and the multi-ethnic state, the term "Jewish" took on a new linguistic connotation.[75] As one of the remaining "Austrian traditions," the Catholic Church became stronger, as did anti-Semitism. Especially in the years after the collapse, "the Jews" were blamed for the lost war and the miserable economic situation. With the end of the monarchy as the guarantor of the multi-ethnic state, a new situation arose for the Jewish population: In the process of identifying the new Republic of (German-) Austria, they were quickly misused as outsiders, if not even as negative identification figures. Anti-Semitism grew and was particularly supported by the Christian Social Party, which is why many Jews began to get involved in the Social Democratic movement. Because of their desire to be accepted as "Austrians," their ties to the country and Christian culture, artists from assimilated Jewish families made a major contribution to Austria's cultural self-image and identity. A well-known example of this is the founding of the Salzburg Festival by Hugo von Hofmannsthal and Max Reinhardt.[76]

Josef Frank (1885–1967) was a typical representative of this cultural commitment by Jewish intellectuals. His occasional colleague, Ernst Anton Plischke, describes Frank in his memoirs as a person with a strong ethical attitude, who was committed to democratic socialism, and which he also realized in his buildings.[77] Frank was actively engaged in social housing and had a decisive influence on the so-called *Wiener Wohnkultur* (the culture of modern domestic living in Vienna) that saw itself as an alternative to the German Bauhaus, which he perceived as too dogmatic and formalistic.[78] In addition to his important position in the architectural discourse in Vienna, Josef Frank also belonged to a group of intellectuals associated with the *Wiener Kreis* (Vienna Circle). His brother, the physicist Philipp Frank, was a member and Josef Frank himself was listed as a "friend."

Due to its liberal, modern and anti-metaphysical stance and the fact that eight of the fourteen members were of Jewish origin, the Vienna Circle was regarded as "Jewish."[79] The case of Moritz Schlick shows how far such an attribution could go.[80] Schlick himself was not a Jew but was considered "Jewish" in public because of his prominent standing in the Vienna Circle. In 1936, he was shot dead by his former student, Hans Nelböck, at the University of Vienna. Although Nelböck had already threatened Schlick in

75 Lisa Silverman: "Introduction," in: *Becoming Austrians. Jews and Culture between the World Wars*, 2012, 8–27.
76 Ibid., 141–171.
77 Ernst A. Plischke: *Ein Leben mit Architektur*, 1989, 95.
78 Ruth Hanisch: "Vom Wienerwald zum Central Park: Wiener Wohnen im New Yorker Exil," in: Eva B. Ottillinger (ed.): *Wohnen zwischen den Kriegen. Wiener Möbel 1914–1941*, 2009, 131–140: 133.
79 Silverman: *Becoming Austrians*, op. cit., 60.
80 Ibid., 60–65.

1931 and 1932, and had been in psychiatric treatment for some time, he was later able to assert the threat to his Christian values through Schlick's "Jewish" views in the anti-Semitic climate during his trial in 1937. He consequently received a lighter sentence and a shorter imprisonment, getting released in October 1938 in the course of the "Anschluss."[81]

The Vienna Circle was a group of philosophers, mathematicians, physicists and social scientists who met for mutual exchange.[82] They felt obligated to the tradition of the French Enlightenment and wanted to counter the backward-looking and irrational tendencies in society with the help of science.[83] In conservative-Catholic Austria at that time, the group stood for the nothing less than revolutionary stance that philosophy should be freed from all metaphysics and concentrate on the philosophy of science with the basic theme of a logical analysis of language. This standpoint led to strong resistance to the Vienna Circle, especially in the Catholic part of Austrian society, which regarded it as an attack on its own Christian (metaphysical) convictions. The Vienna Circle did not establish a self-contained, dogmatic doctrine; the individual members had different points of view and the Circle's stance developed and changed in the course of its existence. What the protagonists shared, however, were the following basic attitudes:[84] First, there is only one type of existence and reality, namely that which the individual can perceive sensually, and secondly, human reason possesses autonomy; its sensory experiences are the sole source of knowledge. From this follows the postulate of the unity of knowledge and the unity of the sciences. The consequence of these three statements is that all indescribable assertions, everything that cannot be called true or false, do not fall within the realm of science. This also affects the value judgments, which earned the Vienna Circle the greatest criticism and was translated by its opponents into the effect that its members were generally against values.

The movement saw an important impetus for social engagement in the basic idea that the discussion of values does more damage than achieving anything positive. One followed Bertrand Russell's argument: "Those who forget good and evil and seek only to know the facts are more likely to achieve good than those who view the world through the distorting medium of their own desires."[85]

---

81 Likewise involved in the case was Leo Gabriel, who, according to Nelböck, had told him that Schlick had prevented his appointment as a teacher. Gabriel had also been one of Schlick's students but distanced himself from positivism early on and became actively engaged as a conservative Catholic in the 1930s, where he also played a role in the *Vaterländische Front* (Fatherland Front) of the *Ständestaat* (Corporate State). After the end of National Socialism, he received a professorship at the Department of Philosophy at the University of Vienna. Hermann Czech attended his lectures there in the late 1950s.
82 The best-known members of the Vienna Circle were Rudolf Carnap, Philipp Frank, Hans Hahn, Otto Neurath and Moritz Schlick.
83 Rudolf Haller: *Neopositivismus. Eine historische Einführung in die Philosophie des Wiener Kreises*, 1993, 2.
84 Ibid., 11–12.
85 Quotation from Haller, ibid., 15: Bertrand Russell: *Mysticism and Logic*, 1914.

Not a closed philosophical fraternity, the Vienna Circle understood its own work politically, culturally and socially, and was closely allied with the project of social and political modernism. There was a lively interchange with parallel developments in other fields such as the "Austrian School of Economics," the "Vienna Psychoanalytic Society" around Sigmund Freud, the "Vienna School of Jurisprudence," the "Settlement Movement" and the "Society for Private Musical Performances" founded by Arnold Schönberg. Moreover, the members of the Vienna Circle were involved in worker education.[86] The "Ernst Mach Society" strove to place the discussions of the Vienna Circle on a broader public basis and to convey the concern of "promoting the scientific world conception" to a larger audience, addressed as "Friends of the Scientific World Conception."[87] The Society's initial event was a series of lectures, the first one given by Josef Frank on the subject of "The Modern World Conception and Modern Architecture."[88] Members of the Vienna Circle, particularly Otto Neurath, saw the advancement in philosophy and science in connection with the advancement of society and the social reforms.[89]

One can assume that Josef Frank knew Neurath through Frank's brother, Philipp, who had already been on friendly terms with him since 1907 in the first "Vienna Circle."[90] Frank's approach "to seeing things not in absolute terms, but in relative terms, can certainly be traced back to the influences of the Vienna Circle and his brother Philipp."[91] Starting in 1920, Neurath got involved in the Viennese Settlement Movement, where he worked with Josef Frank.[92] Both were convinced that education and thus the strengthening of personal responsibility could enable people to have a better life and that architecture was an effective instrument in the development towards a social and democratic society.[93] Frank and Neurath also maintained correspondence during the years of their exile.[94]

In the first few years after World War I, a food and housing shortage prevailed in Vienna. The new republic only managed to cope with the situation from 1923 onwards. As a result, many middle- and working-class people moved to the periphery of the city, either in allotments or by occupying open land. They built their own homes there and provided themselves with food from their gardens. The so-called "Viennese Settlement Movement" arose.[95] Many architects like Adolf Loos, Margarete Lihotzky and Josef Frank got involved to support the settlers. From 1920 to 1924, Adolf Loos was chief architect of the City of Vienna Settlement Office and during this

86 Haller, ibid., 13f.
87 This is the name given on the first poster announcing lectures by the society in 1929.
88 See the corresponding passages in Christopher Long: *Josef Frank. Life and Work*, 2002; Maria Welzig: *Josef Frank 1885–1967*, 1998; Peter Galison: "Aufbau/Bauhaus," in: *Critical Inquiry* 4/1990; German: in: *ARCH+* 156/2001.
89 Haller: *Neopositivism*, op. cit., 32.
90 Ibid., 45.
91 Posch: "Josef Frank...," op. cit., 33.
92 See Nader Vossoughian: *Otto Neurath. The Language of the Global Polis*, 2011.
93 Eve Blau: "Isotype and Architecture in Red Vienna: The Modern Projects of Otto Neurath and Josef Frank," in: Judith Beniston; Robert Vilain (eds.): *Austrian Studies. Volume 14. Culture and Politics in Red Vienna*, 2006, 227–259: 233.
94 Nader Vossoughian: "Die Architektur der wissenschaftlichen Weltauffassung," in: Iris Meder (ed.): *Josef Frank 1885–1967. Eine Moderne der Unordnung*, 2008, 59–65: 64.
95 On the Viennese Settlement Movement see: Klaus Novy; Wolfgang Förster; Ernst Koch (eds.): *Einfach bauen: genossenschaftliche Selbsthilfe nach der Jahrhundertwende. Zur Rekonstruktion der Wiener Siedlerbewegung*, 1991.

time he campaigned strongly for the garden city (as a continuation of the settlement idea of self-sufficiency through one's own garden). He planned several terraced houses himself and looked for the "cheapest construction method."[96]

Otto Neurath was secretary of the "Austrian Settlement and Allotment Garden Association" and initiated a series of learning programs to facilitate the self-organization of the settlers. Together with the Vienna *Volkshochschule* (Adult Education Center), he organized the Settlement School, in which Loos and Frank also taught.[97] In 1923, Neurath founded the "Settlement Museum," from which the "Social and Economic Museum of Vienna" emerged in 1925. Neurath's concern was to depict social relationships in simple pictorial symbols so that even people without education could understand them. In this way, he wanted to strengthen the self-confidence of the working class and society's sense of belonging in general. Designed according to the "scientific world conception" of the Vienna Circle, these illustrations showed statistics on social issues such as production, immigration, mortality, unemployment, alcoholism, health, sports, etc. ("Vienna Method of Picture Statistics"), in a graphically understandable form. In doing so, Neurath also complied with the Vienna Circle's demand to combine science with everyday life.[98] In 1927, the museum moved to the Vienna City Hall and was able to use the so-called *Volkshalle* (People's Hall), a large, elongated room in Neo-Gothic style. Josef Frank designed the exhibition furnishings for this hall: wooden panels that could be changed with simple means and formed separate spaces of various sizes. Lamps were attached to the top of these panels, the light of which directed the visitor's gaze to the pictorial statistics and pushed the space into the background. These panels could easily be dismantled and put back up. In the concept, they were intended to be endlessly expandable and could therefore be used in the appropriate number depending on the type of exhibition and room size. In this manner, Neurath and Frank conceived a completely new type of museum that neither referred to authentic exhibition objects nor to a privileged place.[99] Neurath described the exhibition design in a letter with the words: "The museum is bursting with Old Objectivity."[100]

As the sole representative of Austria, Josef Frank took part in the 1927 International Building Exhibition initiated by Ludwig Mies van der Rohe in Stuttgart-Weissenhof. For the avant-garde of modern architects associated with the German Bauhaus, Adolf Loos was merely considered a

---

96 See, inter alia, Ludwig Münz; Gustav Künstler: *Der Architekt Adolf Loos*, 1964, and Burkhardt Rukschcio; Roland Schachel: *Adolf Loos. Leben und Werk*, 1982. During this time Loos built, among other things, the Heuberg Model Estate and patented the "House with One Wall."
97 Vossoughian: *Otto Neurath*, op. cit., 31–32.
98 Ibid., 55–57.
99 Ibid., 72–79.
100 Otto Neurath: *Gesammelte Schriften 1*, 307, cited above by Vossoughian, ibid.

forerunner of true modernism. The *Bauhäusler* advocated for completely abstracted houses and apartments; people were supposed to leave all the ballast of the past behind and live only in sober surroundings liberated from all sentimentality. But this was too dogmatic for Josef Frank; again, like the Viennese Secessionists, architecture was understood as a total work of art and design became a dictate. His contribution to the Weissenhof Estate looked different: Frank did without any "machine aesthetics" in the interior and instead used Persian carpets and colorfully patterned fabrics for curtains, cushions and lamps with fabric covers. When the criticism of his draft began, he replied: "[...]; every human being has a certain measure of sentimentality, which he has to satisfy."[101]

In another essay, also from this period, he wrote: "Modern man, whose work is becoming increasingly strenuous and stressful, needs a home that is a great deal more cozy and comfortable than those of former times, so that he can find focused peace as quickly as possible. The home, thus, is the absolute opposite of the workplace. […] The home is not a work of art; it does not have to be stirring, which would be the opposite of its true purpose. Uniformity and plainness foster restlessness, ornament and variety promote a sense of calm and alleviate the pathos of pure functional form. Because our era is incapable of creating decoration and ornamentation, modern man reuses old materials and patterns."[102]

From the very beginning of his professional practice, Josef Frank spoke out against architecture that understood living as a total work of art. Together with a group of younger Viennese architects (including Oskar Strnad, Oskar Wlach, Viktor Lurje and Hugo Gorge), he continued to work on Adolf Loos's concept of the apartment as something that develops over time and through its users.[103] Even more radically than Loos, he detached the furniture from the wall and placed it completely open in the room. He thus dispensed with the built-in cabinets propagated by Loos and preferred light, free-standing, individually designed ones. The walls were hardly covered or decorated in any way, but the rooms were for the most part painted white. The individual spaces were regarded as more or less neutral containers for the furnishings. Frank used historical models much more freely than Loos and took them as the starting point for his own new designs.

Josef Frank was the only Austrian representative to take part in the founding meeting of the Congrès Internationaux d'Architecture Moderne (CIAM) in La Sarraz, Switzerland in 1928. However, he already withdrew

101 Josef Frank: "Frippery for the Soul and Frippery as a Problem" (1927), trans. Christopher Long, in: Frank 2012, Vol. 1, 288–298: 289.
102 Josef Frank: "Modern Furnishings in the Home" (1927), trans. Kimi Lum, in: Frank 2012, Vol. 1, 340–343: 341.
103 See Christopher Long: "Wiener Wohnkultur: Interior Design in Vienna, 1910–1938," in: *Studies in the Decorative Arts*, 1997–1998, 29–51.

his membership after the second congress in Frankfurt in 1929, as the differences of opinion on what constituted modern architecture turned out to be too great.[104] Frank's views on modern architecture, as championed primarily by the German architects around Walter Gropius and the Swiss Sigfried Giedion, were too doctrinal and too strongly determined by aesthetic rather than conceptual considerations. He saw therein a new "pathos" and a return to outdated metaphysical, irrational thinking, something that, in his opinion, had to be overcome in the sense of the "scientific world conception."

Josef Frank had been associated with the Deutscher Werkbund since its founding, had attended its first annual meeting in 1908 and was a member from 1910 to 1912.[105] A serious crisis in the Austrian Werkbund flared up in 1920 about the preference for individually, artistically designed single-unit production (Josef Hoffmann and the Wiener Werkstätte) over artisanal or industrially manufactured products for broader sections of the population (Josef Frank, Oskar Strnad and other younger architects). This pinnacled in Josef Hoffmann's resignation, along with the entire board, and the establishment of a separate Viennese Werkbund.[106]

In 1925, Frank founded the company *Haus & Garten* together with Oskar Wlach, where he countered the theoretical discussions about applied arts, handcraft and industrial production with a practice-oriented position.[107] In the exhibition space on Bösendorferstrasse, in which furniture and fittings were shown, individual furnishings could be purchased or a complete interior design commissioned. Due to his disenchantment with CIAM and the Bauhaus, Frank campaigned in the late 1920s to reunite the Austrian Werkbund.[108] By 1928 the time had come: Hermann Neubacher, the general director of GESIBA (Gemeinnützige Siedlungs- und Bau AG), became the new president; Josef Frank and Josef Hoffmann were appointed as vice-presidents. Along with Frank, Otto Neurath and the younger generation of architects—Max Fellerer, Oswald Haerdtl, Walter Sobotka and Oskar Strnad—joined the board and committee of the Werkbund. Frank saw in his work in the Austrian Werkbund an opportunity to disseminate his alternative view of modern architecture, which differed from Bauhaus and CIAM.[109] In 1929, he started with lectures on "New Building" throughout Austria; in 1930, an exhibition of the Werkbund was shown at the Austrian Museum of Art and Industry; in 1932, the Werkbundsiedlung, which had been planned for 1930, was finally built. In summary, Frank published his

---

104 See Long: *Josef Frank*, op. cit., 110–113; Welzig: *Josef Frank*, op. cit., 136–141.
105 Posch: "Josef Frank…," op. cit., 23.
106 Ibid., 27f.
107 Ibid., 29f.
108 Ibid., 31.
109 Long: *Josef Frank*, op. cit., 119.

own conception of modern architecture in 1931 in *Architektur als Symbol* (*Architecture as Symbol*), a collection of sixty articles. With this book, he also addressed his engagement with the Bauhaus and the representatives of "New Objectivity." The work begins with three quotes from members of the Bauhaus, and with the subtitle "Elements of the German New Building," Frank explicitly takes a position against this "German new" type of construction.

The essential difference between Frank and the Bauhaus representatives lay in a fundamental disagreement over the interpretation of the term *Sachlichkeit* (objectivity).[110] Josef Frank followed the Viennese context of Otto Wagner and Adolf Loos, which regarded objectivity as the examination of the existing, also cultural conditions (reality, real life) and the search for the right expression for this life, which could also include criticism and change in the existing conditions. In the Bauhaus view, the changes brought about by industrial mass production, the mechanization of work and the industrialization of building methods stood in the foreground. They wanted to express these changes in a new style (machine aesthetics).[111] Josef Frank found this approach unethical because it prescribed the worker an aesthetic from above that was in complete contrast to his needs. Such a demand can only be made by someone who has never worked in a factory himself and therefore has a different idea of rest.[112] In *Architecture as Symbol*, under the heading "What Is Modern?," he ultimately argued against purely functional architecture: "*Modern German architecture* may be objective, practical, correct in principle, and sometimes even appealing, but it remains *lifeless*."[113] Instead, he called for an undogmatic and empathic modern architecture, an architecture that includes the diversity of the world, the feelings of the people, the real modern life. "Modern is the house that can assimilate all the vitality of our time and still be an *organically* developed entity."[114] Frank made a distinction between a vapid and a lively banality of everyday life. He distanced himself from the former and tried to integrate the latter into his architecture.[115]

In 1932, the Werkbundsiedlung was the high point of Frank's commitment to realizing the Viennese understanding of modernism. The interior furnishings, in particular, were intended to offer an alternative to the uniform, austere, minimalist designs in the Weissenhof Estate.[116] The objective was to create living spaces that were modern, yet comfortable and pleasant, and related to the past.[117]

110 Blau: "Isotype and Architecture in Red Vienna...," op. cit., 235.
111 Ibid., 239.
112 Frank: "Frippery...," op. cit., 293.
113 Frank: *Architecture as Symbol* (1931), trans. John Sands, in: Frank 2012, Vol. 2, 9–191: 135.
114 Ibid.
115 Plischke mentioned this in his biography: *Ein Leben mit Architektur*, op. cit., 95.
116 Long: "Wiener Wohnkultur...," op. cit., 44.
117 Ibid., 45.

Just as he rejected the modernity of the Bauhaus because it was not oriented towards human needs, Frank also increasingly criticized Austrian arts and crafts, which, in his opinion, were outdated in their individual artistic form.[118] From 1931 to 1932, he designed an exhibition at the Werkbund entitled *Der gute, billige Gegenstand* (*The Good, Inexpensive Object*). In 1933, Clemens Holzmeister used this dispute in the intensifying anti-Semitic and conservative political climate to found a "New Austrian Werkbund" together with Josef Hoffmann and Peter Behrens against the ideas of Josef Frank and his group. At the end of the same year, in view of Hitler's takeover in Germany and the emergence of Austrofascism, Josef Frank and his wife Anna decided to move to Sweden, where Frank played a decisive role in shaping the so-called Scandinavian style of living—a style that ultimately became a commercial success story thanks to the furniture store IKEA. In a 1958 article, he summarized his view of modernism under the term "Accidentism." He argued, "Every human being needs a certain degree of sentimentality to feel free. That will be taken from him if he is forced to make moral demands of every object, including aesthetic ones."[119]

Viennese Living Culture–Viennese Modernism

The described cultural milieu in Vienna produced its own architectural expression that clearly differed from the modernism of the German Bauhaus and the later International Style, namely an "other" or a "differentiated" modernism, which is also referred to as *Wiener Wohnkultur* ("Viennese Living Culture").

In Viennese modernism, "objectivity" was understood conceptually and grounded on a discourse about the relationship between design and society as a whole. "Modern life" in all its facets, of which new building methods were only a small part, was to find its expression in the design. The concept of type was also understood in this discursive context. Gottfried Semper's theory of dressing already distinguished between structure and dressing. Together they form the architectural type that is in constant evolutionary development. Structure and dressing are subject to constant changes in the available techniques depending on the time and place. In this sense, the façade was understood as covering which has a communication function (language) that expresses itself between the content of the building and its relationship to the city. Otto Wagner's work, as well as

118 Posch: "Josef Frank…," op. cit., 33–35.
119 Frank: "Accidentism" (1958), trans. Christopher Long, in: *Frank 2012*, Vol. 2, 372–387: 385.

that of Loos, stands on this idea of modernism as a dialectic between type and individuality, tradition and new, and the search for its expression (its language). Frank further developed this conception away from the cultural discussion about the architectural expression of the middle class towards a completely changed world of social, economic and political upheavals to which Austria was exposed after the fall of the monarchy. He saw the task of architecture in saying something about people's living conditions and their experiences with modern life.[120] This understanding of ("old") objectivity takes the existing cultural conditions as the starting point for a critical analysis and for a design process that ends with the new form. The aspect of criticism[121] (self-criticism, cultural criticism, language criticism) is of essential importance and distinguishes it from conventional, historicizing approaches. This modern architecture is formed by individual solutions, not by a prescribed canon of forms. It cannot break with the past because, in its logic, the encountered traditions and their critical consideration are the springboard for new, innovative solutions. The focus is on people as individuals with their needs, especially for physical and psychological comfort. In this view, cultural progress arises evolutionarily (from below), not revolutionarily through individuals (from above).

[120] Blau: "Isotype and Architecture…," op. cit., 248f.
[121] Stanford Anderson: "Sachlichkeit and Modernity, or Realist Architecture," in: Mallgrave (ed.): *Otto Wagner*, op. cit., 323–360: 341f.

"Background"–Childhood, Youth, Studies

Vienna 1936–1954

The Era of National Socialism

Hermann Czech was born in Vienna in 1936. The family lived in a two-room apartment on the mezzanine at Halbgasse 8 in Vienna-Neubau. His father, Josef Czech (born in 1913), originally came from Leobersdorf. His mother, Anna, called Jane (German pronunciation), hailed from Brno and had immigrated to Laa an der Thaya with her family as a child. Both worked in the restaurant trade, the father as a waiter, the mother as a cashier. They met in the "O.K." (Otto Kaserer), a "restaurant for everyone" near the State Opera House that was very popular up into the postwar period. Hermann Czech has only vague memories of his childhood, most of which he reconstructed from the stories of others. According to his own estimation, he appears "always grumpy" in the photographs of this time. His first conscious perceptions are from the time of the Second World War and National Socialism.

His mother had originally sympathized with the National Socialists, which his father forbade her to do. He did not think much of the new regime and believed that "it couldn't go well." One of the few memories Hermann Czech can classify politically is that of a warehouse from which one could take office supplies—as he suspects, "Aryanized" goods. His parents were there, too, but his mother conveyed to him that it was something wrong.

Czech has no recollections from this period of the persecution of Jews or of Jews in general. But he has the image in his head of SA men marching on the street, confronting passers-by who did not raise their arms in the Hitler salute. His parents kept political topics and especially "hostile" radio broadcasts secret from him. Not wanting to go to war, his

Hermann Czech with his mother   Hermann Czech (front right) with his father (bottom center) in the air raid shelter

father faked an accident when he was called up for the first time so that he could go back to Vienna. He had even volunteered for military service so that the accident seemed more believable. In order to avoid later drafts, he continued to pretend to be suffering and lastly even injured himself. Czech's parents were probably very afraid that some of this might leak out through their son, but Czech does not remember it himself and was only told this story much later.

Hermann Czech grew up very sheltered in his parents' apartment. The family spent the weekends and summer in various rented gardens on Satzberg Hill behind Steinhof or on the Danube towards Klosterneuburg. He remembers the Schmelz, where the Stadthalle event center is now located, the villa in Döbling, where his paternal grandmother served as the caretaker, and the rectory in Laa an der Thaya, where his maternal grandparents lived.

From 1942 to 1945, Hermann Czech attended elementary school in the immediate vicinity of his parents' apartment. He was allowed to walk to school alone, as well as to the Non-Stop-Kino on Mariahilfer

Strasse, where the newsreels and short films were shown. On the way there he took notice of a high portal made of dark stone, which flowed into his imagination of the rainy city in the evening. Much later, in 1970, Friedrich Kurrent identified the Zentralsparkasse portal as a work by Adolf Loos.

At the elementary school there was a teacher who was enthusiastic about literature. He once asked the class if someone had a library at home because he wanted to read Ibsen.[1] Czech's mother owned the complete edition and loaned it to the teacher, a fact that Czech was proud of.

As a cohort of the so-called "white year of birth," Hermann Czech was too young for the Hitler Youth and too old for the military (of the Second Republic). At the end of 1944 and the beginning of 1945, no school classes took place for months because Vienna was already a war zone. In the house on Halbgasse there was an air raid shelter in which the family and the other residents of the house spent a whole week in 1945, as the front stretched from the Gürtel belt road to the 7th district (Vienna-Neubau). For a while, no one knew who was in control of the area. His father repeatedly attached a white flag to the façade and then removed it again. "I didn't notice anything; I sat protected in the shelter." In retrospect, however, Hermann Czech cannot name a place in his childhood where he would have really felt comfortable.

The awareness of those born between 1927 and 1947 as children traumatized by the war began relatively late in the German-speaking world, namely in the context of research on "children of war." Czech first found out about this topic from his partner, the psychoanalyst Sabine Götz, in the late 1990s. He had never considered himself a "war child."

Today, research on the Second World War in Germany and Austria pursues an interdisciplinary approach that includes the historical environment of a person and that of the previous generation (generation approach[2]) in individual treatment and, conversely, individual socialization in general historical research.[3] Current historical scholarship thus sees the causes of the Second World War in connection with the First World War and its psychosocial effects on a generation. In this approach, the cohorts 1905 to 1920 in Germany and Austria are the first war-affected generation, the cohorts 1927 to 1947 are the second, and their children are the third (indirectly) war-affected generation.[4]

[1] Henrik Ibsen's dramas were used by the National Socialists to support their ideology, but not in Ibsen's Enlightenment spirit, but rather abridged and partially rewritten in the German translation. On the subject see: Uwe Englert: *Magus und Rechenmeister. Henrik Ibsens Werk auf den Bühnen des Dritten Reiches* (Beiträge zur nordischen Philologie; 30), 2001.

[2] Hartmut Radebold; Werner Bohleber; Jürgen Zinnecker (eds.): *Transgenerationale Weitergabe kriegsbelasteter Kindheiten. Interdisziplinäre Studien zur Nachhaltigkeit historischer Erfahrungen über vier Generationen*, 2008.

[3] See Jürgen Reulecke: "Die 'Junge Generation' von 1930 wird alt," in: Hartmut Radebold (ed.): *Kindheiten im II. Weltkrieg und ihre Folgen*, 2004.

[4] The author only became aware of her own connection with the story while dealing with the subject, namely that of belonging to the third generation affected by the war. The perspective of an outsider in relation to European history (Liane Lefaivre) first made this perspective visible. Interview with Dr. Brigitte Lueger-Schuster, University of Vienna, Institute of Clinical, Biological and Differential Psychology, research project on war children in Vienna on November 3, 2010.

There are further subdivisions within the second generation, which is decisive for this research. Depending on the year of birth and family background, the children were exposed to very different burdens. The National Socialist regime intervened massively in everyday life from early childhood on. Right from the outset, child-rearing was to follow the aim of turning girls into "mothers" and boys into "soldiers." Mothers were offered training courses in which parents were encouraged not to "pamper" children, but rather to impose strict rules on them. Physical contact was to be kept to a minimum, the child was to sleep separately from the mother if possible, and cleanliness was the top priority.[5] The schools were also reshaped according to the National Socialist ideology; "*Volk, Wehr, Rasse and Führertum* ['the people, defense, race and leadership'] took center stage."[6] School subjects were reassessed, with local history, German and sports given priority, "so military training already began with the six-year-olds."[7] From the age of ten, the children had to join the youth organizations of the NSDAP: boys to the *Hitlerjugend* (Hitler Youth) and girls to the *Bund Deutscher Mädel* (League of German Girls). Using experiential educational approaches with excursions and tent camps, they were trained in a paramilitary manner. During the war, the 10- to 14-year-olds were separated from their parents as part of the *Kinderlandverschickungsprogramm* (an evacuation program which moved children to areas less exposed to the war). Towards the end of the war, the over-14-year-olds were first called in for military assistance operations such as clean-up work after bombing raids or as flak helpers. From 1944 on, they were integrated into the so-called Volkssturm as "soldiers."

Besides the influence of the regime on the everyday life of the children at school and in their free time, their lives were also particularly marked by the absence of their fathers. From a psychological point of view, one can also assume that the mothers were often emotionally unable to offer their children a stable relationship due to their own traumas and overburdening.[8]

When looking at Czech's biography, it is noticeable that—in relation to his generation—it takes up a special position to some extent. From a historical-sociological perspective, those born between 1933 and 1938 are fortunate in relation to those immediately before and after,[9] because they were too young to be with the Hitler Youth and lived through a few years without war and dictatorship in their early childhood. In contrast

---

5   This ideology was widely disseminated based on the guidelines of Johanna Haarer's educational guide *Die deutsche Mutter und ihr erstes Kind*. Documented and analyzed in its scope in 1997 by Sigrid Chamberlain: *Adolf Hitler, die deutsche Mutter und ihr erstes Kind*.
6   Wilfried Breyvogel: "Erziehung im Nationalsozialismus," in: Radebold et al. (eds.): *Transgenerationale Weitergabe…*, op. cit., 35.
7   As in footnote 4.
8   Radebold: "Kriegsbedingte Kindheiten und Jugendzeit. Teil 1: Zeitgeschichtliche Erfahrungen, Folgen und transgenerationale Auswirkungen," in: idem et al. (eds.): *Transgenerationale Weitergabe*, op. cit., 49.
9   Interview with Mag. Harald Knoll from the Ludwig Boltzmann Institute for Research on the Consequences of War in Graz on January 24, 2012.

to many of his peers, Czech neither had to cope with displacement nor a long absence from his father, and the family was not bombed out. Since the family was politically inconspicuous, they were not subjected to any direct persecution. However, they were probably strongly influenced by Josef Czech's decision to evade military service, as conscientious objection was socially outlawed and punishable by the death penalty. Therefore, the parents led a very isolated life and made sure that their child had as little contact as possible with the outside world. This isolation was probably frightening, but it made the child much less exposed to National Socialist propaganda than his peers. The first two weeks of April 1945 must have been particularly dramatic, when Vienna was a battle zone and the family had to hide in the cellar; at that time Hermann Czech was eight-and-a-half years old. His family was happy about the end of the war and the collapse of the National Socialist regime—in contrast to many others.

The Topic of National Socialism in Czech's Later Life

During his student years from the mid-1950s to the early 1960s, Czech dealt with the Nazi era: He read Alexander Mitscherlich's reports on the Nuremberg Trials[10] and studied the titles of the Fischer paperback series on National Socialism. At that time, he could not imagine—or he did not notice at all—that there were still people with a Nazi mindset. Czech remembers a conversation with Konrad Bayer in 1963,[11] in which he conjured the "Nazis" as a danger, while he himself assessed that "naively as a purely theoretical problem." It was on the occasion of the student protests against Taras Borodajkewycz when rallies for this highly controversial university teacher took place that he first understood what Bayer had meant.[12] The events surrounding Borodajkewycz are one of the few political events that Czech mentioned in our conversations.

In his professional life, Hermann Czech occupied himself intensively with the Nazi era on two occasions: from 1986 to 1988 in the design of the *Vienna 1938* exhibition and from 1992 to 1993 in the competition for the Oranienburg urban planning expertise (*Wettbewerb zum städtebaulichen Gutachten Oranienburg*).

10 Alexander Mitscherlich; Fred Mielke: *Das Diktat der Menschenverachtung. Der Nürnberger Ärzteprozeß und seine Quellen*, 1947; idem: *Wissenschaft ohne Menschlichkeit: Medizinische und eugenische Irrwege unter Diktatur, Bürokratie und Krieg*, 1949.

11 In an interview on June 12, 2009 while going through the notebooks from this time.

12 Taras Borodajkewycz was a professor at the University of World Trade in Vienna and was known for making Nazi and anti-Semitic statements in his lectures. In 1965, there were demonstrations against and for him, in which the former resistance fighter Ernst Kirchweger was fatally injured.

Postwar Period (1945–1954)

Czech did not experience the postwar period negatively. He completed the last year of elementary school at a new school and then attended grammar school at a boarding school. Since his father was good at organizing and improvising, there was always enough food and heating material. Czech remembers, for example, that his father tapped electricity for a heating coil and hid it so well in the wood-burning stove that it looked like a piece of wood was glowing in it, or that he organized poppy seeds and pasta on the black market, which he hid behind a wall panel in the apartment. "The gray of the postwar period didn't affect me; Vienna had always been a gray city. Only later, in the '80s, did they begin to paint the houses in hideous colors."[13]

After the war, the Czech family's economic and social situation improved. Starting in 1946, his parents jointly operated the police canteen on Schauflergasse in the 1st district. In 1945, his father accidentally discovered a fire in the police barracks on the Rossauer Lände and immediately called together volunteers, with whom he organized a fire chain from the nearby Danube Canal. As a thank you for this effort, he received an offer to run the police canteen. It was a simple inn featuring a set meal for lunch and the police had to bring their own cutlery. Later, Josef Czech expanded it into a restaurant, the so-called "Hofburg Restaurant," which was open to everyone and where Hermann Czech often helped out as a teenager.

From 1946, he attended the Catholic boarding school St. Josef, a grammar school in Strebersdorf, in the 21st district (Vienna-Floridsdorf). He spent the week at boarding school and every second or third weekend at home. Back then it was quite common to send children to Catholic schools, as the church with its traditional values was viewed positively. Czech cites his parents' practical considerations as the main reasons for the boarding school: Both worked all day and it was important to them that he received a profound education. Both parents only had compulsory schooling themselves, but his mother was very interested in culture, read a lot and went to the opera, and it was her wish that her son should go to a higher school and study later. The Catholic faith played no role in Czech's parents' home—for him as a schoolboy it acquired a certain significance for some time. There was a Neo-Gothic church in St. Josef with blue vaulted ceilings and gold stars that he remembers well. He continued to

13 Quote from Hermann Czech in an interview on November 3, 2010.

Reading of the school leaving examination results, St. Josef

School trip, Hermann Czech in front right

associate architecture with Gothic in general for a long time, and Gothic elements appear in an ironically alienated form in his work, for example, in the Wunder-Bar. For Czech, Catholicism is part of the personal cultural background and has nothing disconcerting about it. After leaving school, he also became a member of a Catholic student association of the *Österreichischer Kartellverband* for a few years. Moreover, he began to deal with Marxism and came to the conclusion that Marxism also had the features of a religion.

The Political and Cultural Situation

During her stay in Vienna in February 1946, the writer and journalist Hilde Spiel, who had come from exile in London, attended the editorial conference of the literary and art magazine *Plan* published by Otto Basil. She noted the following observation in her diary: "[…] a strange sense of déjà vu […] took hold of me as soon as I entered the room. When, finally, a young artist opens his portfolio to leaf through a series of abstract drawings, over which all heads are bowed, it becomes clear to me that this scene is a mere repetition. All this had already taken place in Vienna before the First World War [...]. At that time it was my parents who spent long evenings discussing modern art, in whose apartment young Cubists and Expressionists would appear, opening their portfolios with awkward eagerness. [...] So far, not a single original thought, no new aspect of art or literature has come to light at this table. The abstract drawings look forced, like copies or imitations. What we are offered here is a brew of old ingredients. [...] The modernism of these young people is for the time being no more than the negation of Nazi banality. Thirteen years of provincial mentality have torn a hole in their development, and they are just beginning to find their way back to where it began."[14]

Peter Weibel described the situation in the following words: "After the gigantic rupture (World War II), Europe could have, to paraphrase two film titles of Roberto Rossellini, *Germania anno zero* (1947) and *Europa '51* (1952), redefined its concept of culture in the zero hour. But only a few people have tried; the majority has opted for continuity rather than breach. The continuity of Fascism persisted, as did the continuity of modernism. The Neo-Modernism of the '50s naively continued the prewar modernism, partly with the same people who had adapted opportunistically or voluntaristically to the totalitarian systems in the previous decades as if there had been no interruption. The totalitarian systems of Fascism, National Socialism, and Communism have undermined and broken modernism in several ways. First, through the partial collaboration of modernists like Marinetti, Wyndham Lewis, Ezra Pound, G. Benn, L. Fontana, etc., with Fascism and National Socialism. Second, through the violent, historical termination of the modernist project. Thirdly, modernism continued to be suppressed even after 1945 through the interruption of the breach. The National Socialists stayed for the most part in their offices and institutions and continued to fight modernism. Only the vocabulary changed. Instead of 'degenerate art' (1937), the 'lost center' (Hans Sedlmayr, 1948) was being spoken of. Likewise, the displaced remained banned in exile."[15]

With the establishment of the Second Republic in 1945, official policy pursued the goal of "extraterritorializing" National Socialism.[16] The strategy of the first postwar government was to convince the Allies that Austria had been occupied by Germany and that it had not voluntarily become part of the German Reich. Austria was presented as an independent nation, clearly separated from Germany. With this reasoning, the country's

14 Hilde Spiel: *Return to Vienna; A Journal*, trans. Christine Shuttleworth, Riverside, CA: Ariadne Press, 2011, 70–71.
15 Christa Steinle; Peter Weibel: *Identität: Differenz: Tribüne Trigon 1949–1990. Eine Topografie der Moderne*, 1992, 3.
16 Erika Thurner: *Nationale Identität und Geschlecht in Österreich nach 1945*, 2000.

"Background"–Childhood, Youth, Studies

independence was to be achieved. It was about manifesting the Austrian culture, the Austrian language, even the Austrian people. Mozart was performed in the opera houses and Grillparzer in the theaters. The school did not teach "German," but the "Austrian language of instruction." This line was supported by all four occupying powers, who, as an antithesis to the Greater German Reich, likewise pushed an Austrian identity set apart from Germany. Political Austria still suffered from the extreme diminishment of its territory due to the collapse of the Danube Monarchy after the First World War. The shibboleth of the First Republic that this country was not viable and that an annexation to the German Reich was therefore necessary was finally disqualified by the experienced history of the renewed war. The longed-for "greatness" was henceforth constituted in a spiritual realm, in the cultural heyday of the past. These efforts culminated in a sentence by the historian Heinrich Benedikt in 1954: "Austria's future lies in the past."[17]

A regional and cultural studies handbook published in 1955 defines the "cultural nation of Austria" through Haydn, Mozart, Beethoven, Schubert, Burgtheater, Staatsoper, Philharmoniker, Vienna Boys' Choir and the Salzburg Festival.[18] The glorified gaze was thus directed towards a very special, politically unencumbered past, namely that of the Danube Monarchy and its Catholic-Baroque background. The Imperial and Royal Monarchy was stylized into the myth of a peaceful country with harmless, musically gifted people. This image of Austria was particularly pursued by the conservative People's Party and deliberately blanked out Viennese modernism in the interwar period.[19] During the First Republic, the Social Democratic Workers' Party had strongly urged for an annexation to Germany in order to strengthen the break with the monarchy. After the collapse of the Third Reich, the newly founded Socialist Party of Austria (SPÖ) still had not resolved the national question internally and generally distanced itself from the concept of the nation.[20] The party stayed out of the cultural-political debate until 1970 or followed the opinion of the bourgeois coalition partner ÖVP (Austrian People's Party).[21]

Modernism—at least in Vienna—was often ascribed to the Communist Party and discredited because of its proximity to the Soviet occupying power and the Cold War that was already beginning.[22] Therefore, the Neues Theater in der Scala, which opened in 1948 and did not limit itself to Austrian classics, but also staged contemporary, critical plays related to Austria such as *Der Bockerer*, was politically attributed to the Communists and thus artistically disqualified. After the Soviet occupying troops had withdrawn,

17 Heinrich Benedikt (ed.): *Geschichte der Republik Österreich*, 1954. English quotation in: Architekturzentrum Wien (ed.): *The Austrian Phenomenon 1: Architektur Avantgarde Österreich 1956–1973*, Basel: Birkhäuser, 2009, 110.
18 Oliver Rathkolb: *Die paradoxe Republik. Österreich 1945–2005*, 2005, 328.
19 Siegfried Mattl: "Autoritäre Modernisten und skeptische Avantgarde. Österreich um 1959," in: *Die Wiener Gruppe*, 1998, 14–19.
20 Rudolf Haller (ed.): *Identität und Nationalstolz der Österreicher*, 1996, 283.
21 Rathkolb: *Die paradoxe Republik…*, op. cit., 308.
22 Especially in the form of the Communist Party of Austria (KPÖ) City Councilor for Culture Viktor Matejka.

the theater, which was located in the Soviet zone and had received funding from this side, was stripped of public subsidies and had to close again in 1956. The defamation went so far that the actors had problems getting new engagements.

The conservative forces were the only ones who filled the idea of the nation of Austria with content and concepts. One of their theoretical minds was the art historian Hans Sedlmayr, who, in 1948, published a polemic against modernism called *Der Verlust der Mitte* (*The Lost Center*).[23] In the book Sedlmayr attempted a "diagnosis of the suffering of the time" by interpreting the "pathological symptoms" by which he understands the productions of modern art. According to Sedlmayr, the "loss of center" is the loss of God and His replacement through secular terms such as nature, reason, art, machine or chaos. Sedlmayr closes the book with the hope of a "recovery" of time and a return to a Catholic order. This recourse to the conservative Catholic cultural policy of the Habsburg Monarchy and its cultural achievements met with broad approval among the population. "Instead of participating in—and probably also taking responsibility for—the less glorious history of the 'Thousand-Year Greater German Empire,' the 'true Austrians' could refer back to their own thousand-year past."[24] In order to make the population aware of this myth, the first government celebrated the high-publicity event "950th Anniversary of Ostarrichi" in 1946. The images established at the time related to a "small and beautiful country of musicians with magnificent Baroque buildings, embedded in an enchanting landscape."[25] The majority of the population gladly took up the orientation to a glorified past; just think of the popularity of the film productions of this time, from *Hofrat Geiger* (1947) to the *Sissi* trilogy (1955–1957).

Hermann Czech remembers the discussion about the distinction between Austrian and German, but did not understand at the time why this was being questioned. It was clear to him that there are differences. He has always resisted the concept of the nation, since it is not a frame of reference for him. If there is to be a sense of connectedness, then a regional one.

The dissociation of Austria from Germany, however, has a longer and more intellectual tradition than what politics at the time conveyed in a populist way. The discourse about an "Austrian man" began with the fall of the monarchy and was also carried out in literature.[26] A well-known example

23 Hans Sedlmayr: *Der Verlust der Mitte. Die bildende Kunst des neunzehnten und zwanzigsten Jahrhunderts als Symptom und Symbol der Zeit*, 1948. According to Sedlmayr's own statements in the afterword, the content of the book arose in lectures that he had given between 1941 and 1944 at the University of Vienna. The book achieved great popularity in German-speaking countries.
24 Thurner: *Nationale Identität…*, op. cit., 2000, 41.
25 Ibid., 42.

of this is Robert Musil's "man of possibility" in the novel *Der Mann ohne Eigenschaften* (*The Man without Qualities*).

Ingeborg Bachmann differentiated in an interview between the "House of Austria" and the "Country of Austria":[27] In her opinion, the "Country of Austria," which was only "agreed upon in some kind of treaties," did not exist. By "House of Austria" she meant the cultural heritage, which encompassed much more than the new state. It included the background of the multi-ethnic state, but also that of the interwar period, the many languages and cultures, and the numerous Jewish intellectuals. Peter Weibel stated that Austria's art and the Austrian state are not identical: "Because Austria's art of standing builds on the culture of Vienna around 1900. Austria's neo-modern, postwar art stems from international influences [...] and from the art of the artists exiled, driven out and killed by the First Republic."[28] The Austrian state in those days, however, could not identify with this culture because it then would have acknowledged the victims and would have to remove itself from the victim role.[29]

Domestically, the postwar years up to Austria's sovereignty in 1955 were characterized by the unconditional striving for consensus and reconciliation; everything else was ignored. The Second Republic was founded in part by the same people who had held central positions in the First Republic. New was the basic agreement on a policy of compromise, power sharing and proportional representation.[30]

In 1946, the exhibition *Niemals vergessen!* (*Never Forget!*) opened at the Künstlerhaus in Vienna. Initiated by the Communists, it was supposed to be a show against Fascism in Austria. Long quarrels and political tactics preceded its implementation, "because the spirit that supported the new state could only flourish if the recent past was viewed selectively and skillfully instrumentalized."[31] The exhibition ultimately pursued several goals: One wanted to demonstrate to the Allies the renunciation of Fascism and at the same time show the followers and supporters of National Socialism a way out of guilt by abstracting Fascism and portraying the individual as the victim of a grand "seduction machinery." In the first government declaration, Leopold Figl spoke of the "Hitler regime" instead of Germany or German-Austria and communicated with it: "One person is to blame, but the people are exempted."[32] The exhibition turned out to be a spectacular public success. In the media, the population was portrayed as diligent and working without exception on the reconstruction. The Allied

26 See William M. Johnston: *Der Österreichische Mensch. Kulturgeschichte der Eigenart Österreichs*, 2010.
27 Ingeborg Bachmann in a conversation with Veit Mölter, "23. März 1971," in: Christine Koschel; Inge Weidenbaum (eds.): *Ingeborg Bachmann: Wir müssen wahre Sätze finden*, 1983, 79.
28 Weibel: "Probleme der Neomoderne," in: Steinle; Weibel (eds.): *Identität: Differenz…*, op. cit., 1992, 3–21: 18.
29 Ibid.
30 Anton Pelinka: "Zur Gründung der Zweiten Republik," in: *Wien 1945 davor/danach*, 1985, 21–22: 21.
31 Wolfgang Kos: *Eigenheim Österreich. Zu Politik, Kultur und Alltag nach 1945*, 1994, 9.
32 Ruth Wodak: "Herrschaft durch Sprache? Sprachwandel als Symbol und Ausdruck des gesellschaftlichen Wandels," in: *Wien 1945 davor/danach*, 1985, 75–89: 82.

occupation became increasingly incomprehensible in this conception of history and from the end of the 1940s the call for withdrawal became more and more urgent. When the Austrian State Treaty was signed in 1955 and the country regained its independence, the actual reasons for the occupation were no longer a topic of public discourse.

Catholicism in the Postwar Period

The church experienced a new blossoming in postwar Austria; politicians and the populace gladly tied in with the long and culturally anchored tradition of Catholicism. The suppression of the faith by the National Socialist ideology had been problematic for the majority of Austrians and had led to resistance against the regime. Especially in rural areas, for example, the Austrian greeting *Grüß Gott* could never be completely supplanted by the *Heil Hitler* ordered by the Nazis.

During these years, the church not only acted as a preserving force, but also became involved, even if only through a controversial minority within the institution, in the field of contemporary art and architecture. The individual parishes were organized autonomously and open-minded pastors were the first publicly effective clients, even before the state. In Innsbruck, for example, the painter Max Weiler was commissioned in 1945 with the execution of the frescoes for the Theresienkirche in Innsbruck's Hungerburg Fortress.[33] From 1954 onwards, the Galerie St. Stephan, run by the Diocese of Vienna, established itself as a meeting place for the art scene. In 1958, the *Internationales Kunstgespräch*, a discussion forum for young artists, took place at the Seckau Abbey in Styria.[34]

---

33 The frescoes sparked heated public controversy. In 1947, Weiler was forced to give the face of God "more majestic features." Those frescoes that had not yet been executed had to be submitted to the client in sketch form for approval and from 1950 to 1958, three of the frescoes remained covered after an intervention by the Vatican.

34 Robert Fleck: *Avantgarde in Wien. Die Geschichte der Galerie nächst St. Stephan 1954–1982. Kunst und Kunstbetrieb in Österreich. Band 1. Die Chronik*, 1982, 171.

Study at the Technical University of Vienna and with Konrad Wachsmann from 1954 to 1963

First Years of Study

Czech's mother died in 1954, and his father married twice afterwards. Hermann Czech will realize his first projects for him: Restaurant Ballhaus (1962) and a summer house in Nussdorf (1968). In 1977, he dedicated the book *Zur Abwechslung* (*For a Change*) to his father.[35]

In 1954, Hermann Czech began to study film at the University of Music and Performing Arts and architecture at the Technical University. He found both studies to be not in-depth enough, experienced them as selective and arbitrary, and began searching early on for theoretical backgrounds and critical discourses. During this time he read a lot, attended lectures, exhibitions—especially those at the Galerie St. Stephan—and philosophy lectures at the University of Vienna. In 1958 and 1959, he attended the architecture class of the Summer Academy in Salzburg held by Konrad Wachsmann. In 1963, he moved from the Technical University to the Academy of Fine Arts and into the master school of Ernst Anton Plischke, who had returned from emigration in New Zealand, and completed his studies in 1971 under Plischke's tutelage. He experienced his student years as a time of great self-doubt, which he also sees as a hindrance in retrospect. Czech justifies his final turn to architecture with the realization that it suits his temperament, since in architecture, in contrast to film, which requires quick decisions during filming, it is possible to think about the respective topic for a long time and also "repair weaknesses and enhance quality" afterwards.[36]

Hermann Czech's general picture of this time paints an intellectual narrowness that is difficult to imagine today. There was absolutely no interest in contemporary art among the general public. There were

35 Czech: *Zur Abwechslung. Ausgewählte Schriften zur Architektur Wien*, 1977.
36 Czech: "Was ist Ihre Kunst im speziellen?" (1983), in: Czech, 1996, 94.

hardly any personalities who could communicate something. He found the training at the film school to be uninspiring, as he got an idea of the craft, but no impulses for artistic issues. In connection with his film studies, he had delved into acting theory and discovered a parallel to architecture in acting, since the actor and the architect would have to create an effect artificially. And he read Brecht's theories on acting, Denis Diderot's *Paradox of the Actor* and Konstantin Stanislavski's work on method acting. The latter two play a role for him as comparative approaches to architecture.[37]

However, Czech was also disappointed with his studies at the Technical University, since in his opinion the theoretical subjects were taught at a low level, there were no discussion partners, there were hardly any practical applications in the design exercises and the designs were again discussed without a theoretical background.[38] One had only limited opportunities to acquire knowledge. International architecture magazines were hardly available and lectures on architectural history ended in the Rococo. Because of this, he spent a lot of time at the National Library. The writings of Karl Kraus became particularly important to him. Kraus's texts, especially the issues of *Die Fackel*,[39] opened the art and culture scene in Vienna at the turn of the century and the interwar period up to Czech. As a result, he understood, among other things, Adolf Loos and his dispute with the Vienna Secession and his peer Josef Hoffmann.

When Hermann Czech began studying in the mid-1950s, there was still no relevant scholarly reception of the period since the turn of the century. The continuity of professors at the universities, for whom dealing with the cultural heyday before the Corporate State and National Socialism would have threatened their own existence, was too big. The loss of the Austrian "intelligentsia," especially the assimilated Jews, the liberal Christians and the Social Democrats as exponents of the Enlightenment, liberalism and language criticism, was not offset after the end of the war. On the contrary: The basic anti-liberal and anti-intellectual tendency was transferred almost seamlessly into the resurrected republic; hardly any attempts were made to bring emigrants back to Austria and preferably people with a connection to the Corporate State and Catholic conservatism were appointed to positions at the universities. The first reception of the intellectual discourse of modernism in Austria after the war was partly

37 Czech: "A Conceptual Matrix for the Current Interpretation of Josef Frank" (1985), trans. Elise Feiersinger, in: Hermann Czech: *Essays on Architecture and City Planning*, 2019, 151–181.
38 Czech: "Zum Jubiläum" (1965), in: ibid., 49.
39 Karl Kraus: *Die Fackel*, 1899–1936.

negative, partly characterized by individual approaches or still hesitant and cursory.[40] A culturally broader scholarly discussion began much later with the burgeoning interest of the Anglo-Saxon region and the Italian architectural theorists in Vienna at the turn of the century up to Red Vienna.[41] Czech's imprint through the intellectual world around Adolf Loos and Josef Frank took place through contact with a group of young architects called "arbeitsgruppe 4" and its circle, through the intensive self-study of original texts, as well as through reading *Die Fackel* or Dadaist writings, e.g., by Hugo Ball.

Karl Kraus—A New Dimension of Language

Czech did not regard Karl Kraus's writings as literature in the narrower sense, but as a source that informed him about the cultural discourse of the years after the turn of the century. In addition to the issues of *Die Fackel*, he was particularly impressed by the montage drama *Die letzten Tage der Menschheit* (*The Last Days of Mankind*), from which he can quote entire passages and which he named as one of his favorite books for the exhibition *ex libris*.[42] Czech particularly values the text as a testimony to its era and because of the biting irony. What has made a lasting impression on him about Kraus is his attitude as a moralist, for whom morality does not follow an abstract, general ethic, but an examination of the specific case. In his criticisms, Kraus traced every doctrine back to the problem of artistic and human truthfulness: behind the "ideas" it was the people who turned out to be moral or immoral.[43] For Czech, it was important at this time to find a methodical approach that was to deliver "more than an abstract ideology; it has to be useful all the way down to the concrete design decisions, down to a floor plan, down to the solution of a corner, that of a railing, the choice of a color, in the arrangement of a mirror. […] His [Kraus's] writings, as well as the writings and works of Adolf Loos, had become for me—around the same time as Wachsmann—models of such precision in concrete terms."[44]

Karl Kraus[45] (1874–1936) was a writer and critic who worked primarily with the linguistic means of satire and polemics. He made a name for himself as a relentless fighter against corruption, as a revelator of double

40 E.g., Ottokar Uhl: *Moderne Architektur in Wien von Otto Wagner bis heute*, 1966.

41 See Manfredo Tafuri: *Vienna Rossa: la politica residenziale nella Vienna socialista, 1919–1933*, Milan: Electa, 1970; Allan Janik; Stephen Toulmin: *Wittgenstein's Vienna*, New York: Touchstone, 1972. From the mid-1970s onwards there are a large number of analytical and compiling works, both nationally and internationally. For example, Carl E. Schorske: *Fin de Siècle Vienna – Politics and Culture*, New York 1981; in 1985, the exhibition *Traum und Wirklichkeit* (*Dream and Reality*), curated and designed by Hans Hollein, took place in Vienna.

42 *ex libris*, book exhibition February 22–April 5, 2002, curated by Arno Ritter at the Architekturforum Tirol, Innsbruck.

43 Janik; Toulmin: *Wittgenstein's Vienna*, 1972, 88.

44 *ex libris*, see footnote 42, exhibition text.

45 The paragraph about Kraus is essentially based on the analysis by Janik and Toulmin in *Wittgenstein's Vienna*, op. cit., 67–91.

standards and as a critic of the "linguistic and cultural decay." His special concern was language and its use. Kraus criticized the superficiality of ordinary language and relentlessly exposed phrases and clichés. In his opinion, language was to be used carefully and with great responsibility. He was the founder and editor of *Die Fackel*, a kind of "anti-newspaper" that served as a mouthpiece for his position. From 1899 to 1936, 922 self-published issues appeared with attacks on the police and the judiciary, with criticism of bourgeois sexual morality, with satires about fellow artists such as Hofmannsthal and Lehár, and polemical ridicule of articles in the *Neue Freie Presse*, the most important bourgeois daily newspaper at the time. Kraus founded *Die Fackel* because he had a particular aversion towards the daily press, which, in his opinion, mixed up fact and opinion in a shifty language and thus committed fraud against the public. "If human beings had no clichés, they wouldn't need any weapons,"[46] was his conviction. In the first edition of *Die Fackel*, he wrote that he wanted to "speak from an independent platform to a forum where, thanks to the market shouting of public opinion, which is falsified twice a day, the honest man cannot hear his own word."[47] Kraus's central thought in relation to language was the strict separation between factual reports and texts with artistic expression. He equated the aesthetic value of an autonomous, truthful and authentic artistic expression with its moral content.[48] There are parallels here to the mode of thought of Adolf Loos, who limited art in architecture to the design of "monuments,"[49] and to Ludwig Wittgenstein, who wrote in the *Tractatus*, "… (Ethics and aesthetics are one.)."[50]

Kraus's most famous work, *The Last Days of Mankind*, is a satirical drama he wrote between 1915 and 1922 in response to the First World War. It is a montage of a wide variety of texts, for which Kraus used original quotations from newspapers, court decisions and other official reports, and which he condensed into over 200 scenes depicting various everyday situations during the war. "The most implausible conversations in this play were spoken verbatim; the shrillest inventions are quotations."[51]

Controversial during his lifetime, Kraus "only had fanatic admirers and fanatic opponents […]. Most of the fanatic enemies had started out as fanatic admirers."[52] Hans Weigel writes about these years: "Looking backwards, you can see the Karl Kraus picture in a new way. The onslaught of his no was always defensiveness. He insulted the Burgtheater to defend Shakespeare and Nestroy, he attacked the powerful for the sake of oppression, the

---

46 Quotation from Wodak: "Herrschaft durch Sprache?" op. cit., 75. English translation of quote in: Marjorie Perloff: "Avant-Garde in a Different Key: Karl Kraus's *The Last Days of Mankind*," *Critical Inquiry*, Volume 40, Number 2, 2014, https://criticalinquiry.uchicago.edu/Avant_Garde_in_a_Different_Key (accessed December 12, 2020).

47 Kraus: *Die Fackel*, No. 1, Vienna, beginning of April 1899, 4.

48 Janik; Toulmin: *Wittgenstein's Vienna*, op. cit., 89.

49 Adolf Loos: "Architecture" (1909), trans. Michael Mitchell, in: Adolf Loos: *On Architecture* (Studies in Austrian Literature, Culture and Thought), Riverside, CA: Ariadne Press, 2002, 73–85: 83.

50 Ludwig Wittgenstein: *Tractatus logico-philosophicus*, Proposition 6.421, trans. C. K. Ogden, New York and London: Kegan Paul and Harcourt Brace and Company, 1922: 88.

51 Kraus: "Vorwort," in: *Die letzten Tage der Menschheit. Tragödie in fünf Akten mit Vorspiel und Epilog* (1926), 5. English translation by Michael Russell in Kraus: "Preface," in: *The Last Days of Mankind*, https://thelastdaysofmankind.org/preface (accessed December 10, 2020), n.p.

52 Kurt Wolff on Karl Kraus in: Daniel Keel (ed.): *Denken mit Karl Kraus*, 2007, 9. English translation by Deborah Lucas Schneider in: Michael Ermarth (ed.): *Kurt Wolff: A Portrait in Essays and Letters*, Chicago: University of Chicago Press, 1991: 83.

generals for the sake of the common soldiers, the judiciary for the sake of the victims, the late Gerhart Hauptmann for the sake of *Die Weber* (*The Weavers*) and *Hanneles Himmelfahrt* (*The Assumption of Hannele*), Austria for Austria's sake."[53] In *Karl Kraus: Schule des Widerstands* (*Karl Kraus: The School of Resistance*), the writer Elias Canetti described what he had learned from him.[54] This included the "feeling of absolute responsibility" and a "new dimension of language"—both of which are also very important in the work and attitude of Hermann Czech.

Austrian Architecture in the 1950s

"The situation around 1945 seemed hopeless: not only the economic one which, by its very nature, strongly determines building, but also the political and cultural one […]. Not only had most of the architects of the thirties emigrated or died, but Vienna in 1945 no longer knew what to do with the survivors from that time," wrote Friedrich Achleitner, who was six years older than Czech, in 1965.[55]

The architecture of the first postwar years was marked by the need for "pure rebuilding," on the one hand, and the "reconstruction" of some of the architectural monuments that are important for the cultural identity, such as the Vienna State Opera or St. Stephan's Cathedral, on the other.[56] "In the postwar period, architecture as 'art' was to above all represent and not question the social position of the client."[57]

Public attitude towards architecture in Austria was shaped by the conservative heritage, especially by the cultural policy of Austrofascism with its rejection of modern tendencies and the turn to a kind of traditionalist, glorified *Heimatstil* (Domestic Revival style). Commissions were awarded according to political convictions; the surviving prominent architects only got marginally involved in the construction process.[58] The few exceptions orientated themselves towards developments in Austria during the interwar period.[59]

Only a small number of the architects who followed the modernist tradition, such as Oswald Haerdtl, Max Fellerer and Eugen Wörle, received significant public commissions. Wilhelm Schütte returned to Vienna in 1947, but, as a self-confessed Communist, was not employed by the public sector. Josef Hoffmann was already 75 years old and no longer

53 Hans Weigel on Karl Kraus, in: ibid., 151.
54 Friedrich Achleitner: "Aufforderung zum Vertrauen" (1967), in: idem: *Aufforderung zum Vertrauen*, 1997, 48–76: 49.
55 Achleitner: "Entwicklung und Situation der österreichischen Architektur seit 1945," in: *Bauen + Wohnen* 9/1965 ("Österreich baut"), 339.
56 See Achleitner: "Besser als ihr Ruf. Zur Architektur der fünfziger Jahre" (1982), in: idem: *Wiener Architektur*, 1996, 111–117: 112.
57 Matthias Boeckl: "Zeichen und Wunder. Die magische Form als Erfolgsmotor einiger zeitgenössischer Architekturwegbereiter aus Österreich," in: *Parnass* 18/2001, 106.
58 Achleitner—in: *Aufforderung zum Vertrauen*, op. cit.—lists the following architects: Josef Hoffmann, Clemens Holzmeister, Lois Welzenbacher, Max Fellerer, Oswald Haerdtl and Franz Schuster. Oswald Haerdtl was entrusted with the refurbishment of the Federal Chancellery and Max Fellerer and Eugen Wörle with the reconstruction of the Parliament and several residential buildings.
59 Achleitner: *Aufforderung zum Vertrauen*, op. cit., 49.

active professionally. Clemens Holzmeister and Lois Welzenbacher were appointed professors at the Academy of Fine Arts Vienna. Holzmeister remained firmly anchored as an architect in Turkey and was only able to realize his first major project after the war with the Large Festival Hall in Salzburg in 1956.[60] In spite of this, he "resumed the role of the state-supporting artist, which he had already played before the war in the era of the Austro-Fascist Corporate State."[61] Welzenbacher, who tried to tie in with Classical Modernism (e.g., with the Danube Canal control structure project), remained isolated.[62] Holzmeister had been a member of the State Council in the authoritarian Catholic Corporate State from 1934 to 1938.[63] At this time he was already a professor at the Academy of Fine Arts in Vienna, at times also its rector, and was on the board of the most important professional associations, such as the *Zentralvereinigung der Architekten* (Central Association of Architects) and the *Neuer Werkbund*. Not least, he had led the split in the Werkbund in 1933. Holzmeister had taken on the leading role in architecture during these years. "His handwritten, monumentalism-prone, strongly emotional architecture displaces the intellectual, sensitive, skeptical and contemplative building ethos."[64] Architects who thought differently were denounced by him as "cultural Bolsheviks" and he succeeded in preventing them from receiving any public contracts.[65] At the invitation of Kemal Pasha Atatürk and Ernst Egli, Clemens Holzmeister had already planned and built the new capital of Ankara starting in 1926. From 1938 on, he took over, among other things, the execution of the new parliament building. As a high-ranking member of the Corporate State, he would have been considered a political enemy under the National Socialists in the Third Reich, which is why he had to spend the years of Nazi rule in Turkish exile, but was able to take on a certain role as a mentor and protector of Austrian emigrants and resistance fighters.[66] When Josef Frank was repeatedly invited to Austria in 1947 and 1948 to give lectures, he supposedly rebuffed the audience at the only lecture in Vienna: "I see sitting in the *front row* the same *gentlemen*, who in the old days, with flags flying and their tails between their legs, went running from the old Werkbund to the new one."[67]

At the Academy of Applied Arts, Oswald Haerdtl and Franz Schuster, who had been appointed before 1938, kept their professorships. Max Fellerer was brought back from the forced retirement effected in 1938. Haerdtl was regarded as liberal, Schuster as social—the latter had a particular impact

60 Wilfried Posch: *Clemens Holzmeister. Architekt zwischen Kunst und Politik*, 2010, 283ff.
61 Christian Kühn: "Entweder, oder. Oder dazwischen." in: *Parnass* 18/2001, 96–105: 97.
62 Ibid.
63 Posch: *Clemens Holzmeister*, op. cit., 201f, 230.
64 Achleitner: "Aufforderung zum Vertrauen," op. cit., 50.
65 As reported by Ernst Plischke, for example, in his biographical texts—Plischke: *Ein Leben mit Architektur*, 1989, 181.
66 The Graz architect Herbert Eichholzer spent two years in exile in Turkey and worked for Holzmeister. From there he tried to build up a resistance group against Nazi rule, which Margarete Schütte-Lihotzky also belonged to. During a stay in Austria, Eichholzer was betrayed and executed. Schütte-Lihotzky was also arrested with others and was the only one of the group to survive. See Heimo Halbrainer: "Ein Leben für soziale Architektur und Freiheit," in: Heimo Halbrainer; Antje Senarclens de Grancy: *Totes Leben gibt es nicht. Herbert Eichholzer*, 2004, 23–74: 58; Margarete Schütte-Lihotzky: *Erinnerungen aus dem Widerstand 1938–1945*, 1985.
67 Quote passed down by Herbert Thurner according to Friedrich Kurrent: "Frank und frei," in: *UM BAU* 10/1986, 85–93, 88; English translation by Christopher Long in: *Josef Frank. Life and Work*, 2002, 238.

on postwar residential housing construction.[68] Oswald Haerdtl pursued a modernist architecture, regardless of the respective regime, which then became generally accepted in the late 1950s.[69] After 1945, he re-founded the Austrian CIAM group and tried to bring emigrated colleagues back to Austria. For example, Josef Frank's aforementioned lecture was held in Vienna at the invitation of Haerdtl, and Frank was also able to make suggestions for the redesign of St. Stephan's Square during this visit.[70]

In the 1950s, Roland Rainer and Karl Schwanzer, two other architects who shaped the Austrian postwar period, appeared on the scene. Rainer took over the architecture school from Lois Welzenbacher in 1955 and became head of the Vienna City Planning Office in 1958 after building the Wiener Stadthalle between 1953 and 1958. Schwanzer planned the Austrian Pavilion for the World's Fair in Brussels in 1958, which was the first international symbol of a modernized, new Austria. Both advocated an uncompromisingly modern design language, but without the intellectual depth of the discussion between Frank and Loos.[71] This functionalist view of modernism has greater parallels to the functionalism of the Nazi planning offices than to the modernism of the interwar period.[72] Rainer's theoretical focus was on urban planning. Published in 1947 together with Johannes Göderitz and Hubert Hoffmann, *Die gegliederte und aufgelockerte Stadt* (*The Structured and Dispersed City*) traces back to studies on the "expansion, re-establishment and reconstruction of cities" from 1944.[73] Rainer's vision of the city was based on the idea of the garden city and densified low-rise construction with an access to a private garden for everyone.

arbeitsgruppe 4 also became active in the mid-1950s, first with success in competitions and a new school building concept, and ultimately with the realization of the church *Zum kostbaren Blut* (Precious Blood Church) in Salzburg-Parsch (1953–1956), taking up theoretical approaches in their work and building upon the modernist tradition in Austria before 1938.[74]

The Viennese Art and Cultural Scene/Galerie St. Stephan

Beyond official university instruction, young artists began to occupy themselves with the tradition and developments since the turn of the century. The group of painters at the Galerie St. Stephan discovered Surrealism for themselves.[75] Ingeborg Bachmann wrote her dissertation

68 Matthias Boeckl: "Kulturnation Österreich," in: Patrick Werkner (ed.): *Kunst in Österreich 1945–95. Symposium der Hochschule für angewandte Kunst in Wien*, 1996.
69 Ibid., 33
70 See Maria Welzig: *Josef Frank 1885–1967. Das architektonische Werk*, 1998, 229; Long: *Josef Frank*, op. cit., 238. Friedrich Kurrent; Johannes Spalt: "Josef Frank" (1965), in: Kurrent: *Texte zur Architektur*, 2006, 122–127: 122.
71 See Kühn: "Entweder oder…," op. cit.
72 See ibid.
73 Ibid., 98.
74 See the *arbeitsgruppe 4* exhibition catalog edited by Architekturzentrum Wien, 2010.
75 Fleck: *Avantgarde in Wien*, op. cit.

at the University of Vienna under the supervision of the philosopher and last representative of the Vienna Circle, Viktor Kraft. The *wiener gruppe*, an interdisciplinary group of artists (Friedrich Achleitner, H. C. Artmann, Konrad Bayer, Gerhard Rühm and Oswald Wiener), devoted themselves to Dadaism and the tradition of language criticism; one read Karl Kraus and took an interest in the Vienna Circle.[76] Oswald Wiener, in particular, began to deal with Ludwig Wittgenstein and Fritz Mauthner[77] and used sentences from the *Tractatus* for a speaking performance with the title *Mens sana in corpore sano* at the first "literary cabaret" in December 1958.[78] "We were all Neopositivists," said Friedrich Achleitner during a lecture on the 1950s at the Architekturzentrum Wien. And in the context of the exhibition he curated about the wiener gruppe at the Venice Art Biennale in 1997, Peter Weibel called it a "moment of modernity" in Austria.[79] According to Weibel's analysis, there is a tradition against modernism in Austrian art, a tradition of the exclusion of reason. Art should be expressive, emotional and irrational. The wiener gruppe drew upon the ostracized rational aesthetics of Viennese modernism, from the New Vienna School of Music to the Vienna Circle. "as regards their production, the interest in instruction manuals, in the principle of construction and in the system is also greater than the interest in the product. they are not interested in how work sounds rather in how it is made."[80]

While attending film school, Czech met the Hungarian-born painter Jakob Laub, who was part of the Galerie St. Stephan in the early days.[81] He was introduced personally and intellectually to the art scene through Laub; in the friendship of the following years, the information about and the productive understanding of art laid the foundation for what Czech later referred to as "thinking towards design."[82] The Catholic background of Galerie St. Stephan was familiar to him from his school days at the St. Josef boarding school. From Czech's point of view, Monsignor Mauer, who ran the Galerie, formulated art theologically, because it corresponded to his conceptuality. However, it was more important for Czech that he experienced this gallery as a place where rationality was not ostracized. A method was sought to go beyond rationality, "but at least according to a method!" He perceived the group around the Galerie St. Stephan as a small, open-minded minority within the church, and particularly appreciated the breadth of its content.

76 Friedrich Achleitner in a conversation on June 13, 2013.
77 See Peter Weibel (ed.): *die wiener gruppe. a moment of modernity 1954–1960. visual works and actions*, 1997, 653.
78 Czech interview.
79 See Weibel (ed.): *die wiener gruppe*, op. cit. (subtitle).
80 Peter Weibel: "the vienna group in the international context," trans. Tom Eppleton, in: ibid., 778.
81 One of the first exhibitions at Galerie St. Stephan was dedicated to Jakob Laub (born in 1930) in 1955. Fleck: *Avantgarde in Wien*, op. cit., 63. Fleck writes a text accompanying the one from Laub, initialed with "J. L.," which was mistakenly ascribed to the art critic Jörg Lampe.
82 Czech: untitled, in: *Hintergrund* 46–47 (Friedrich Achleitner 80), 2010, 38–39.

Hermann Czech and Jakob Laub, 1959

Fresco painting of the Schwanberg Josefikirche by Jakob Laub, 1957-1960/1993

Along with the Galerie Würthle, the Galerie St. Stephan,[83] opened by Otto Mauer in 1954, was an important meeting place for young artists and those interested in contemporary art. The director Otto Mauer was a priest and cathedral preacher at St. Stephan's Cathedral. For him, art was a tool of faith and included humanitarian commitment and a clear metaphysical orientation. He opposed the then-customary attitude of accusing modern art of having turned away from God and wanted it to be interpreted as an expression of faith. Like Willi Baumeister, he opined that art is the attempt to "make the unknown, that is, God, visible."[84] He did not see the Galerie as a sales gallery, but as a religion-related educational institute.[85]

Works by Herbert Boeckl were shown at the first exhibition. In his opening address, Otto Mauer announced "a series of encounters with contemporary, religious art."[86] Otto Mauer was not a gallery owner, but an art lover, a "speaker, collector, organizer, friend of artists […], valued as an art-philosophical interlocutor."[87] The artists themselves were also able to influence and set programmatic priorities. In the first four years of its

83 The paragraph about the Galerie St. Stephan mainly draws upon Fleck: *Avantgarde in Wien*, op. cit.
84 Ibid., 402.
85 Ibid., 43.
86 According to Alfred Schmeller in: *Neuer Kurier*, 9 Nov. 1954; quoted by ibid., 54.
87 Ibid., 62.

existence, the Galerie transformed from a theologically-oriented collection of graphics into a meeting place for the young Viennese art scene. Otto Mauer's achievement was to have created an inspiring intellectual climate through his personality: "When Mauer was in top form during an opening speech, the Galerie actually became a different world, an intellectual laboratory."[88]

In those years, the art scene was quite small; people knew each other and felt like a loose grouping of outsiders. As such, they did not have a common approach, but consisted of artists from various movements and directions. People met at Galerie St. Stephan, at Galerie Würthle or at coffee houses such as Café Hawelka. "In the coffee houses they sat side by side in groups. Each group occupied a table. There were hardly any border crossings. Everyone referred to himself as an artist, but denied the others this honorary title."[89] Because everyone knew everyone, everyone was in competition with everyone else and endeavored to differentiate their own work from that of the other. "Our thoughts are there to free ourselves and others from the thoughts of others. Since the thoughts of others are meters thick everywhere," said Konrad Bayer and Oswald Wiener.[90]

What the individual persons had in common was that they stood outside the "official" position, which was very narrow at the time. "Since the end of the war brought little liberation in the cultural field, the 'no longer fine arts' were not considered worthy to live by either the population or the political parties."[91] Gerhard Rühm described the situation in the 1950s as follows: "it very soon became obvious that the majority, although opposed to the nazi wartime policy, basically had little reservation about a 'healthy' cultural policy. now that the so-called 'decadent' art could be encountered again freely, it stirred up emotions, occasionally not even stopping short of violence. anyone who showed an interest was declared insane, perverted, and even more so its representatives."[92]

Modernist movements had been completely eliminated in Austria by the Corporate State and National Socialism. This loss was further decisive in the 1950s, despite the reintroduction of the republic.[93] There was no breach in the understanding of art and culture as a result of the end of National Socialism. Reconstruction was determined by the pragmatism of necessity, in which cultural issues were considered a luxury.[94]

In the late 1950s, when Czech also regularly visited the Galerie, representatives of the St. Stephan painters' group (Arnulf Rainer, Markus Prachensky, Josef Mikl and Wolfgang Hollegha), the wiener gruppe

---

88 Ibid., 63.
89 Ibid., 171.
90 Quoted according to ibid., 173.
91 Ibid., 19f.
92 Gerhard Rühm: "the phenomenon of the 'wiener gruppe' in the vienna of the fifties and sixties," trans. Tom Eppleton, in: Weibel (ed.): *die wiener gruppe*, op. cit., 16–28: 16.
93 Kos: *Eigenheim Österreich*, op. cit., 160ff.
94 Friedrich Achleitner: "Rund um die arbeitsgruppe 4," in: *arbeitsgruppe 4*, op. cit., 7.

Vienna ca. 1960

(Gerhard Rühm, Oswald Wiener, H. C. Artmann, Friedrich Achleitner and Konrad Bayer), arbeitsgruppe 4 (Friedrich Kurrent, Wilhelm Holzbauer and Johannes Spalt), the composers of the "reihe" and filmmakers such as Peter Kubelka, Ferry Radax, Kurt Kren and Marc Adrian were present.[95]

Oswald Wiener, born in 1935, said of this time: "[…] in the vienna of my adolescence there was no choice of contacts […]. it was impossible to take note of another person simply because he bore premises and themes with him which ran counter to one's own. pressure from the compact society kept all divergence from outsiders together, one had to deal with them in detail and was forced to think along lines which one had not selected of one's own free will. some of my friends backed me in attempts not to be what one thinks but to see one's own thinking as foreign."[96]

[95] Fleck: *Avantgarde in Wien*, op. cit., 173.
[96] Oswald Wiener: "some remarks on konrad bayer," trans. Tom Eppleton, in: Weibel (ed.): *die wiener gruppe*, op. cit., 42–48: 42.

Lectures at the Faculty of Philosophy

From 1957 to 1974, Hermann Czech kept notebooks (at the same time, later exclusively, dated notepads). They contain very diverse entries: names, book titles, art theoretical and philosophical quotations, shorthand transcripts of lectures and talks, transcriptions and excerpts from publications, as well as his own thoughts, in key words and in full sentences. Among others, he quotes Frank Lloyd Wright, Karl Kraus, Jean-Paul Sartre, Bertolt Brecht, Hugo Ball, Le Corbusier, Friedrich Heer and Martin Heidegger. Many entries deal with the subject of "form and content." In search of theoretical approaches, Czech attended philosophy lectures at the University of Vienna held by Erich Heintel and Leo Gabriel for several years, between 1957 and 1959. Heintel, whose lectures on Hegel and aesthetics Czech remembers in particular, was more important to him, as Heintel's lectures inspired him to "conceive architecture by way of production."[97]

At the Philosophical Faculty, two philosophers who would later be described as "two pioneers of backward-looking philosophy,"[98] Erich Heintel and Leo Gabriel, set the tone. They decidedly polemicized against any progressive philosophizing based on the empirical sciences. They consciously followed the metaphysical tradition and tried, with the help of the history of philosophy, to make the arguments of the modern philosophy of science (on which—along with other international movements—the Vienna Circle had worked) downright ridiculous. In the 1950s, Viktor Kraft was the sole representative of the Vienna Circle at the Institute for Philosophy, albeit in the position of an outsider.

This politically conservative attitude was commonplace at the time. A critical reception of the position of Heintel and Gabriel first began in the late 1960s with the student movement. For Czech, the philosophy lectures with them were the only opportunity in Vienna at the end of the 1950s to deal with theoretical approaches. Heintel and Gabriel dominated philosophy at the University of Vienna until the 1970s. Internally, at the Department of Philosophy, the two were bitter opponents and rivals: Gabriel as a representative of a Christian existential philosophy, Heintel as an exponent of a direction based on the transcendental philosophy of German Idealism in which Hegel played a central role.

---

97 Presented in greater detail in the essay by Elisabeth Nemeth in this volume.

98 Haller: *Fragen zu Wittgenstein und Aufsätze zur Österreichischen Philosophie*, 1986, 228. For the historical background see: Hans-Joachim Dahms; Friedrich Stadler: "Die Philosophie an der Universität Wien von 1848 bis zur Gegenwart," in: Katharina Kniefacz et al. (eds.): *Universität – Forschung – Lehre. Themen und Perspektiven im langen 20. Jahrhundert*, 2015, 115–127. On the problem of postwar philosophy at the University of Vienna and the influence on Hermann Czech's thinking, see Elisabeth Nemeth's essay.

arbeitsgruppe 4/Johann Georg Gsteu

Hermann Czech knew the architects of arbeitsgruppe 4 from the Galerie St. Stephan. He was impressed by their method of operation, always leading a theoretical discourse, finding arguments for certain architectural decisions and justifying the design in this way. Czech names arbeitsgruppe 4 and Johann Georg Gsteu—along with Konrad Wachsmann—as crucial for the realization that designing is a conceptual process.[99] It was just as important for him that these architects committed themselves to rediscovering the Austrian tradition of modernism—Wagner, Loos, Hoffmann, Plečnik, Frank—and to make it known and to protect its buildings. Important projects of arbeitsgruppe 4 for Czech at that time were the *Wohnraumschule* (Living Space School), the Precious Blood Church in Salzburg-Parsch, the Steyr-Ennsleite Pastoral Care Center, the Kolleg St. Josef in Salzburg-Aigen and the Music Store ¾ in Vienna.

Founded in 1950, arbeitsgruppe 4[100] was a working group of Wilhelm Holzbauer, Friedrich Kurrent, Otto Leitner and Johannes Spalt, who had studied together under Clemens Holzmeister and who, in addition to their work as architects, were also involved in the field of the architectural history of Viennese modernism. The architects of arbeitsgruppe 4 were among the first to build upon the tradition of modernist architecture at the turn of the century and the interwar period, particularly upon Otto Wagner, Josef Hoffmann, Adolf Loos and Josef Frank.

Johann Georg Gsteu was not a member of arbeitsgruppe 4, but maintained a friendly and professional relationship with them. Holzmeister was able to convince his students with a charismatic demeanor and authority, but less with theoretical depth. An independent culture of discussion developed among the students, in which Johannes Spalt, who was ten years older, assumed a substitute teacher position.[101] Due to the shortages of the postwar years, this generation hardly had any access to international architectural publications and the Austrian ones were still conservative or even a continuation of National Socialist ideology.

As already mentioned, Hans Sedlmayr's book *Verlust der Mitte* (*Lost Center*) was published in 1948, in which, to put it simply, modernism was presented as "the derailment of art."[102] In postwar architecture, as in the planning of the National Socialists, modernism was only accepted

arbeitsgruppe 4 with J. G. Gsteu: Pastoral Care Center Steyr-Ennsleite, 1961

99 Untitled (Czech on Gsteu) in: Claudia Enengl: *Johann Georg Gsteu. Architektur sichtbar und spürbar machen*, 2010, 128.
100 See *arbeitsgruppe 4*, 2010.
101 Maria Welzig; Gerhard Steixner: *Die Architektur und ich. Eine Bilanz der österreichischen Architektur seit 1945 vermittelt durch ihre Protagonisten*, 2003: 9.
102 Sedlmayr: *Verlust der Mitte*, op. cit., dust cover blurb, 1998.

in terms of its functionalistic aspect.[103] Owing to the lack of available literature, Sedlmayr's book functioned primarily as a source in which modern architecture was at least depicted. To this end, the students began to occupy themselves with international, as well as Viennese architecture and art.

"So the young generation of architects had little to learn from their fathers. It was left up to their own initiative to re-establish contact with international architecture and their own tradition," wrote Friedrich Achleitner in 1967 in a first look back at this time.[104] Johannes Spalt and Friedrich Kurrent, in particular, continued to promote a lively discourse after their studies: They initiated exhibitions and lectures, worked to bring emigrated architects back to Vienna (E. A. Plischke, Josef Frank) and, as assistants to Konrad Wachsmann, organized his summer class for architecture at the "International Summer Academy for Fine Arts" in Salzburg in 1957.[105] Their aim was to rediscover the forgotten and ostracized Austrian modernism and to make international modernist trends known in Vienna. In this context, Johann Georg Gsteu designed the first postwar exhibition on Adolf Loos in Vienna in 1961.[106]

In general, an attempt was made to use exhibitions and texts to bring a scholarly systemization into the development of prewar and interwar architecture. Besides the exhibitions on modernism (*Adolf Loos; Vienna um 1900; Josef Frank*), there were also a number of typological exhibitions, e.g., on church, theater and school construction. The most productive time of arbeitsgruppe 4 in relation to exhibitions (*Kirchen unserer Zeit* [Churches of Our Time], 1956; *Internationale Kirchenbau-Ausstellung*, [International Church Building Exhibition] 1966), coincides with Czech's student days. His friend and fellow student from the Technical University, Wolfgang Mistelbauer, worked for arbeitsgruppe 4 during this time, so Hermann Czech was often in the office to visit. Friedrich Kurrent writes in his biography: "The Fuhrmanngasse studio became a 'secret school.' 'Tutoring lessons' on architecture were given, even though we were not teachers. Did we have pupils? Wolfgang Mistelbauer worked in the studio. Often the studio door opened and Hermann Czech visited us."[107] This was also the time when Hermann Czech and Wolfgang Mistelbauer developed their analysis of Adolf Loos's House on Michaelerplatz.[108]

---

103 Kühn: "Entweder, oder…," op. cit., 97.
104 Achleitner: "Aufforderung zum Vertrauen," op. cit., 50f.
105 Friedrich Kurrent: *Einige Häuser, Kirchen und Dergleichen*, 2001, 36.
106 Enengl: *Johann Georg Gsteu*, op. cit., 17; *Adolf Loos 1870–1933: Ausstellung veranstaltet von der Galerie Würthle, Wien, unter dem Protektorat der Zentralvereinigung der Architekten Österreichs, 7. April–6. Mai 1962*, exhibition catalog compiled by Maria Münz.
107 Kurrent: *Einige Häuser*, op. cit., 72.
108 A later result of this examination was the book: Hermann Czech; Wolfgang Mistelbauer: *Das Looshaus*, Vienna 1977 and 1984.

Besides their commitment to architectural discourse, the members of arbeitsgruppe 4 also took part in competitions during their own studies. Dissatisfied with the conservative and pragmatic architecture of the reconstruction, they wanted to show how projects could be solved in a contemporary way.[109] arbeitsgruppe 4's discourse was not limited to functional and constructive decisions, but aimed at working out the "typical."[110] In this way, buildings with a pronounced physiognomy emerged and the preoccupation with architectural history flowed directly into them as a reference which one drew upon and as a tradition in which one saw one's own work.[111] "One design seems to arise from the other logically and in small steps, integrated into a comprehensive architectural concept that again shows continuity, the diverse interweaving with Austrian modernism and antennae for the movements of the present,"[112] is how Friedrich Achleitner describes the projects of arbeitsgruppe 4. And he describes their way of working as a "kind of systematic exploration of the possibilities, a constant weighing and selection in relation to the characteristics and particularities of the task, so that the solution almost inevitably results from the sum of these individual decisions."[113] arbeitsgruppe 4 received its first commissions from the Catholic Church, which had a lot of catching up to do in church construction in the postwar period. The church in Salzburg-Parsch was completed in 1956, followed in 1961 by the Steyr-Ennsleite Pastoral Care Center together with Johann Georg Gsteu, and in 1964 by the Kolleg St. Josef (a Catholic seminar house) in Salzburg-Aigen.

Wolfgang Mistelbauer, 1961

The theoretical considerations of arbeitsgruppe 4 concerned the constructive, geometric and modular aspects of architecture. Hermann Czech himself soon began to include other topics such as effects and content as design-determining parameters, like Restaurant Ballhaus, which he planned for his father together with Wolfgang Mistelbauer and Reinald Nohàl in 1962. He formulated the further development of these approaches in 1973 in the essay "Zur Abwechslung," ("For a Change"). Here he complements the attitude of a logic of all decisions, from which a solution inevitably results, with the recognition that in the end there is a solution that can be understood but is not logically clear, similar to the chaos theory, which says that one can explain complex conditions, but cannot predict them: "[…] we can attain diversity if we allow all of our motivations to flow into every design and follow up on all the ramifications

109 Achleitner: "Rund um die arbeitsgruppe 4," op. cit., 6–9.
110 Achleitner: "Die Entwurfsmethode der 'arbeitsgruppe 4,'" in: Johannes Spalt: *Johannes Spalt*, 1993, 23.
111 Gabriele Kaiser: "Bilanzen mit Ausblick. Die Ausstellungen der arbeitsgruppe 4," in: *arbeitsgruppe 4*, op. cit., 142–159: 144.
112 Achleitner: untitled, in: *Johannes Spalt*, op. cit., 7.
113 Achleitner: "Die Entwurfsmethode der 'arbeitsgruppe 4,'" in: ibid., 23.

and thought processes instead of sticking to some hare-brained recipe or hanging on to a shallow discipline. The aim is a congruence of all considerations in a result that is definite but transparent and allows the multi-layered network of relationships to carry on."[114]

Konrad Wachsmann and the Salzburg Summer Academy

Hermann Czech calls Konrad Wachsmann's Summer Academy, in which he participated in 1958 and 1959, immensely important for his training. He found out about Wachsmann through an exhibition at Galerie Würthle in early 1958. Here the insight was to be gained "that planning decisions could not be based on 'ideas,' but had to be worked out in a strict, methodical way," if only because they would be "infinitely reproducible on the scale of industrial production." For Czech, the essential insight in the seminars was the analytical approach to the design, which did not begin with an idea or formal deliberations.[115] At last, someone taught an actual method of creating shapes. Basics and prerequisites were defined, which, when analyzed individually, made the design process a sequence of logical decisions. "Wachsmann's teaching was carried by the belief in the technology of prefabrication; but behind it stood the intellectual dimension of the responsibility for planning and the architectural quality. Based on the modular problems of prefabrication, Wachsmann was also able to open one's eyes to the structure of a Gothic hall or the corner solution of a Renaissance palace."[116] For him it was a matter of introducing the scientific knowledge of modernism, scientific thinking in general, into architecture, and not just about a formally new expression in architecture.[117] "There will probably be less to see; however, the little there is will be all the more significant."[118]

Wachsmann brought the international discourse on industrialized construction methods and modular construction to Austria and also invited guest speakers such as Frei Otto to the seminar. Besides the ostensible economic benefits of industrial production, Czech recognized an attitude in this approach that saw architecture as the responsibility of the planner with regard to architectural quality,[119] because every decision also had to be lasting in terms of duplication.

Hermann Czech at the blackboard, Salzburg Summer Academy with Konrad Wachsmann, 1959

114 Czech: "For a Change" (1973), trans. Elise Feiersinger, in: Czech 2019, 109–115: 115.
115 Czech: "Was ist Ihre Kunst im speziellen?" (1983), in: Czech 1996, 91–94: 94.
116 Ibid., also the following quotations.
117 The Grünings call him an "early building scientist," see Christa and Michael Grüning: "Konrad Wachsmann – Architekt Albert Einsteins und Pionier des Industriellen Bauens," in: Konrad Wachsmann: *Holzhausbau. Technik und Gestaltung*, 1995, 5–17.
118 Konrad Wachsmann: *The Turning Point of Building: Structure and Design*, trans. Thomas E. Burton, New York: Reinhold Publishing Corporation, 1961, 231.
119 Ibid.

Seminar project (information hall made of wooden elements), 1958

Wachsmann also communicated a differentiated conception of space, as the modular design requires that the individual components in the space fit together ("thinking around the corner"). Years later, Czech described him in a lecture: "He was able to combine a spiritual dimension of architecture with the ostensibly technological approach. That was the real, almost moral experience one could have with him."[120]

Still completely under the impression of Wachsmann, Hermann Czech submitted a design to the Technical University in 1960 in two construction variants—namely as a solid and a steel frame construction with correspondingly different characteristics—with the comment that he could not find any decisive reason for one or the other building material. The first theoretical texts and lists of design parameters to

[120] Hermann Czech lecture as part of the series "Monday Evening Conversations. Cue Giver Hermann Czech," Theory of Architecture, RWTH Aachen University, on December 3, 2012.

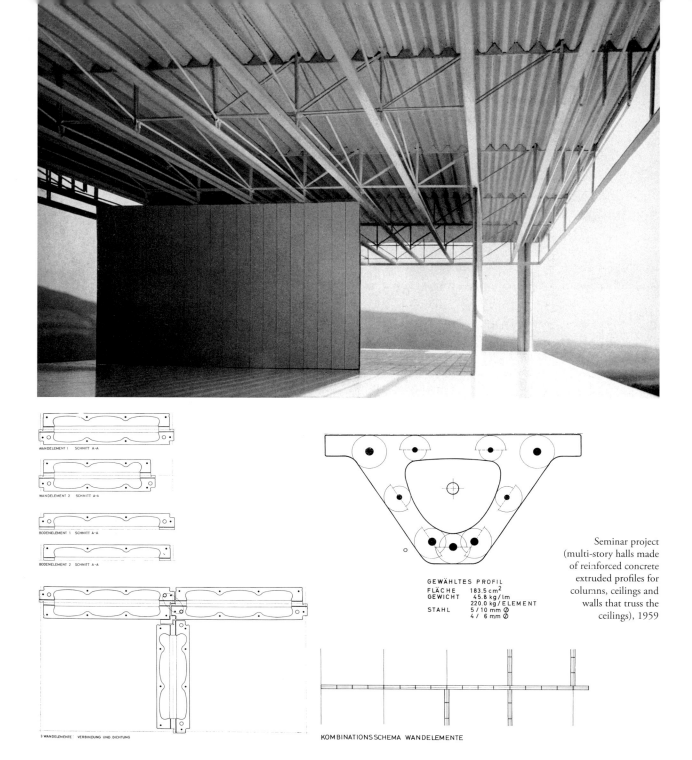

Seminar project (multi-story halls made of reinforced concrete extruded profiles for columns, ceilings and walls that truss the ceilings), 1959

which, in addition to Wachsmann's constructive aspects, he added further ones such as light and acoustics, likewise come from this period. In a text from 1959 he wrote: "The external appearance of a building is not the result of aesthetic considerations, neither is it an expression of functional planning, but rather one of many possibilities of an abstract order."[121]

Konrad Wachsmann headed the architecture class of the "International Summer Academy of Fine Arts Salzburg" from 1956 to 1960. Founded in 1953 by Oskar Kokoschka and Friedrich Welz, the Academy offered courses in various artistic fields that were open (and still are open today) to all interested parties, even without previous (academic) training. For the young generation of architects after the war, the Wachsmann class at the Summer Academy was a rare opportunity to get to know an international point of view.[122] In 1958 and 1959, when Czech attended Wachsmann's courses, the latter dealt intensively with industrial prefabrication and lightweight construction, and also incorporated this into the courses. Wachsmann saw the new technologies as a prerequisite for any future architecture and building production. He approached the design scientifically and analytically and in teamwork, a method that was impressive for many students and often stands in the foreground in the stories about the courses: structural aspects were worked on in teams of three, then discussed by everyone and passed on to the next group for continuation.[123] In this process, the form was first the result and not the impetus for the design process,[124] a well-thought-out, reasoned and anonymous solution.[125]

Like Josef Frank, Konrad Wachsmann came from an assimilated Jewish family. His father was a pharmacist and the family lived without religious affiliation.[126] When asked what the atmosphere was like in his parents' house, Wachsmann replied in an interview: "Artistically inclined and liberal Prussian, enlightened, educated and self-confident bourgeoisie. We were brought up to be free thinkers."[127] Wachsmann's first commission as a freelance architect in 1929 was a summer home for Albert Einstein. During the course of the assignment, he got to know Einstein and his wife well and also spent a lot of time with them privately. Einstein made it possible for him to leave France for the USA in 1941. Josef Frank's brother Philipp, as a physicist and member of the Vienna Circle, was also closely connected to Einstein both professionally and privately. On Einstein's

121 Czech: "Allgemeine Gesichtspunkte zum vorliegenden Entwurf" (explanation of a residential building design by Wolfgang Mistelbauer), unpublished, November 1959.
122 Welzig; Steixner: *Die Architektur und ich*, op. cit., 10.
123 Bernhard Steger: *Vom Bauen. Zu Leben und Werk von Ottokar Uhl*, 2007, 28f.
124 Czech: "Was ist Ihre Kunst im speziellen?" (1983), op. cit., 94.
125 Kurrent: *Einige Häuser, Kirchen und dergleichen*, op. cit., 36.
126 Michael Grüning: *Der Architekt Konrad Wachsmann. Erinnerungen und Selbstauskünfte*, 1986, 102. Grüning: "Konrad Wachsmann…," op. cit., 6.
127 Ibid., 99.

recommendation, he took over his chair in Prague in 1912. He later met Einstein again in the USA, where he also wrote a biography about him.[128] Einstein's way of thinking had a lasting influence on Philipp Frank and, through him, the theories of the Vienna Circle and Konrad Wachsmann. Frank dedicated separate chapters in the book to the subjects of "Einstein's Theories as Political Weapons and Targets" and "Einstein's Theories as Arguments for Religion."

The Influence of the "wiener gruppe"

An important impulse for Hermann Czech was the work of the wiener gruppe,[129] especially the "literary cabarets" of 1958 and 1959, which he both attended. On a photograph in the Biennale catalog about the wiener gruppe, Hermann Czech and Wolfgang Mistelbauer can be seen laughing in the audience.[130]

The wiener gruppe was a circle of artist friends who dealt intensively with language and came from different artistic directions: Gerhard Rühm and Oswald Wiener from music, H. C. Artmann and Konrad Bayer from literature and Friedrich Achleitner from architecture. However, this group of people did not see themselves as a uniform formation and the name wiener gruppe[131] also led to internal differences. Moreover, there was no defined beginning or a specific end of the wiener gruppe; they simply had similar views and goals and saw each other as discussion partners. The first joint appearances of H. C. Artmann and Gerhard Rühm took place in 1950, Friedrich Achleitner first joined them in 1955 and H. C. Artmann left the group in 1958. They studied the modern cultural movements before Fascism in Austria and Europe and read, among others, Wittgenstein, took a lively interest in Surrealism, Expressionism, Bauhaus, serial music and in the different manifestations of language, such as vernacular, dialect, idioms, the language in dictionaries or technical instructions, the sound of language, as well as the aesthetic qualities of the written word. Language was understood as material and the possibility of a methodical production of literature was intensely discussed and tried out. Old encyclopedias, textbooks or newspapers were used as the starting material for literary montages that were mutually produced and in which parts of the text were rearranged. "'*die montage über die montage*' (a montage created by

---

128 Philipp Frank: *Einstein. Sein Leben und seine Zeit*, 1949 (English original edition *Einstein: His Life and Times*, New York: Alfred A. Knopf, 1947).

129 The wiener gruppe was a collaboration between the writers H. C. Artmann, Friedrich Achleitner, Konrad Bayer, Gerhard Rühm and Oswald Wiener, who wrote joint texts from 1954 to 1963 and organized events with experimental performances.

130 Weibel (ed.): *die wiener gruppe*, op. cit., 351.

131 The name "wiener gruppe" comes from the journalist and writer Dora Zeemann, who, after a reading, wrote a review entitled "Die neue Wiener Dichtergruppe. Untersuchungen an der Sprache. Vorlesung in der Galerie St. Stephan" in *Der Kurier* on June 23, 1958. Friedrich Achleitner recalled in an interview that they had a guest appearance in Switzerland and were introduced there as a "Viennese group."

juxtaposing sections from a reference book on the installation of machines. this text is intended for reading out on the factory floor of a large firm. we will all wear overalls)."[132]

The Situationists in France, the Independent Group in England and representatives of Concept Art in the USA worked similarly to the wiener gruppe. They all dealt with language, which was recognized as a medium that constructs reality. "Doubt and criticism of language are therefore preconditions for a criticism of reality"[133] and, as a result, of the state, which helps to construct social reality and thus society with the help of language.

The "literary cabarets"[134] in 1958 and 1959 were geared to present the many expressive possibilities and peculiarities of language. Gerhard Rühm saw them as an opportunity to "try out aspects of a 'holistic theater'" all the way up to a "theatre unleashed."[135] In the "cabarets," the group attempted to deconstruct and reveal the relationship between language and society by "controlling concrete situations through the use of language." Konrad Bayer wrote the following about the "cabarets": "we voice criticism by depicting realities. (real radio broadcast – a critical contribution: on a small wireless on stage we hear a genuine, random, but above all awful programme). we sing, act, dance and amaze."[136] Oswald Wiener, on the other hand, said, "one of the basic ideas of the event we were planning was to exhibit 'reality' and thus, consequently, to abandon it. another idea was to consider the audience as a group of actors and ourselves as spectators, and yet another to offer the spectators, viz. ourselves, something really worth seeing [...]. the audience as an object, in every sense of the word."[137]

The evenings consisted of a sequence of the most diverse performance formats, from the classical chanson, the telling of jokes (which were not all actually jokes), the first "Franz" text (later known in "Humanic" ad spots), actions that are atypical on the stage (the audience could not distinguish whether something belonged to the performance or just happened by chance), all the way to performative formats that were later described under the term "happening." Oswald Wiener named the following contribution as typical: "in 'friedrich achleitner as beer-drinker', he [Achleitner] was sitting by himself at a table, with a bottle of beer and a glass before him, while bayer read the text behind the stage. the scene developed in the form of prophecy, statement and recollection. achleitner reacted only to sentences in present tense, doing exactly what the respective sentence

Gerhard Rühm, on the occasion of a recording by Czech for a publication of DU-Plastik, 1963

132 Konrad Bayer: "hans carl artmann and the viennese poets," trans. Tom Eppleton, in: Weibel (ed.): *die wiener gruppe*, op. cit., 32–39: 36 and 39.

133 Peter Weibel: "Laudatio für Oswald Wiener, manuskripte-Preisträger 2006," in: *manuskripte* 174, 2006 [see manuskripte.at/texte/peter%20 weibel174.pdf].

134 Oswald Wiener: "the 'literary cabaret' of the vienna group," trans. Tom Eppleton, in: Weibel (ed.): *die wiener gruppe*, op. cit., 308–321.

135 Gerhard Rühm: "the phenomenon of the 'wiener gruppe' in the vienna of the fifties and sixties," trans. Tom Eppleton, in: Weibel (ed.): *die wiener gruppe*, op. cit., 16–28: 26.

136 Bayer: "hans carl artmann…," op. cit., 38.

137 Wiener: "the 'literary cabaret' of the vienna group," trans. Tom Eppleton, op. cit. 308–321: 308 and 310.

pretended to describe. he poured himself a glass of beer ('gray beer'), then raised and drank it. this number expressed vividly what our cabaret was intended to be. it developed at an embarrassing rhythm, conspicuously showing the ridiculous character of any description in view of the actual event, and – with the exception of a little joke at the end – caught the silent attention of the audience."[138]

Serial Music/Journal and Ensemble "*die Reihe*"

Czech was made aware of the music journal *die Reihe* by Gerhard Rühm and subscribed to it. At this time, he also attended concerts by the "Ensemble for New Music." Theoretical considerations about serial and electronic music brought him to the question of the quantifiability of spatial properties and their limits, i.e., the relationship between quantity and quality; using the example of a mirror, for instance: At one point the quantitative increase in the degree of gloss of a surface changes into a new quality, in this case that of the mirror, "an additional element of the concept."[139]

From 1955 to 1962, Herbert Eimert and Karlheinz Stockhausen published the journal *die Reihe. Information über serielle Musik* in which they theoretically analyzed this genre and discussed it with other disciplines. A total of eight issues were published, including one entitled *Form – Raum* (Universal Edition, 1960). Due to new technical developments, sounds could be produced electronically for the first time without any restriction in pitch or duration, and "premiered" on tapes in the concert hall. The composer was no longer only the producer of a piece of music theoretically, but also practically. *die Reihe* discussed these developments and their significance for music, although there is an interesting linguistic proximity to architecture: the contributions speak of music as "material," of "electronic sound material" or of "structures of the new building material." Serial music sees itself as a further development of twelve-note music, in which "rational control" is applied to all musical elements such as pitch, duration or intensity.[140] The music should be completely free of any emotion and based only on mathematical rules such as series of proportions.[141] In issue Number 1 of *die Reihe*, the composer Paul Gredinger described the new way of composing on the basis of the

138 Ibid., 312.
139 Unpublished entry in a notebook in 1960. See "Zur Abwechslung" (1973), in: Czech 1996, 76–79: 77.
140 Herbert Eimert: "Vorwort," in: *die Reihe, Band 1: elektronische Musik*, Vienna, 1955, 7.
141 Markus Bandur: *Aesthetics of Total Serialism. Contemporary Research from Music to Architecture*, Basel 2001, 11.

technical possibilities of electronic music: "The first stages of creation are inherent in the proportioning of the material and must mean a breathing of life into the dead numbers, an 'awakening' of proportions into live forms. They become music when they sound—previously I said that they were part of mathematics. Once more I repeat that the ultimate aim is the creation of quality out of quantity."[142] In Czech's notebooks from the late 1950s, there are several entries on Karlheinz Stockhausen, including one on *Gesang der Jünglinge* (*Song of the Youths*), a central early work by the composer and of electronic music in general. Stockhausen succeeded in letting natural music (singing) and electronic music become one. He used different types of language in this work: the language of music, the sung language and the spoken word. As a composer, Gerhard Rühm himself dealt with serial music and later tried to apply these strict rules to literature in his work in the wiener gruppe.[143]

Friedrich Cerha and Kurt Schwertsik founded the "Ensemble for New Music" in Vienna in 1958, also under the name "die reihe." In its early years it was mainly devoted to the works of the "Second Viennese School" around Arnold Schönberg, Alban Berg and Anton Webern, as well to contemporary music from 1945 onwards—in the late 1950s it was mainly serial music.

Metrical Film/Peter Kubelka

After film school, Czech continued to study architecture, but remained interested in both métiers. He valued the filmmaker Peter Kubelka, whose film *Arnulf Rainer* left a lasting impression on Czech at the premiere in 1960.

Peter Kubelka, born in 1934, came onto the Viennese art scene with the premiere of his film *Mosaik im Vertrauen* (*Mosaic in Trust*) in 1955 and has been an integral part of it ever since. *Arnulf Rainer* arose from the painter's commission to make a film about him and his work. The film was shot quickly, but when Kubelka looked at the material, he began to think about painting and art in general: "I wanted to be not less than Michelangelo; […] I wanted to put cinema where it can stand with every musician and every painter."[144] He analyzed what constitutes the traditional arts and came across harmony: "The incredible thing is that our music and architecture operate out of the same principles of harmony […]. When

142 Paul Gredlinger: "Serial Technique," in *die Reihe*, Bryn Mawr, PA: Theodore Presser Company/Universal Edition, 1958, 38–44: 43. English translation uncredited (the English-language translations of the texts were prepared by Hans O. Holms, Leo Black, Eric Smith, Cornelius Cardew, Ruth Koenig and Margaret Shenfield).
143 Sabine Hahlweg: *Das Verhältnis von Kunst und Politik in Österreich am Beispiel der Wiener Gruppe*, 2009, 62.
144 Peter Kubelka: "The Theory of Metrical Film," in: P. Adams Sitney (ed.): *The Avant-Garde Film: A Reader of Theory and Criticism*, New York: Film Culture/New York University Press, 1978, 139–159: 155.

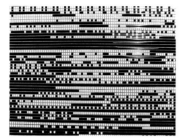

Peter Kubelka: The Film *Arnulf Rainer*

you take the string and hang it between two points, you get one sound. When you divide this string in half—what do you get? You get a sound that is exactly one octave higher than the first note. This is the point where architecture, painting, geometry, and music come together." For Peter Kubelka, film consists in its essence of light, sound and time. Just like in the other arts, the temporal factor makes it possible to introduce harmonious series of numbers: "I can give you a visual signal which lasts half time, double time, fourth, third, as I choose."[145] Kubelka recognized as one of the possibilities of cinema: "Well, what I can do in the cinema is to make a rhythmic building between light and sound which is complex, exact, fast and has a certain strength. Also, it must have exact measure, harmony and beat."[146] For *Arnulf Rainer*, Kubelka made use of the four no longer reducible basic forms of film: a completely transparent blank film, a completely exposed black film, a tape without any acoustic signal and a tape with continuous "white sound." This includes all sound frequencies, just as white light includes all visible wavelengths. From these four strips he made the film "like the tailor."[147] It was produced without a film camera: "[…] No camera, no editing tables, just right into a core."[148] The film consists of nothing other than transparent and black or opaque frames, as well as silence and white noise. Silence is the negation of all tones, just as black is the negation of all colors. The sequence of the individual film strips (black, transparent, with sound, without sound) was carried out according to harmonious mathematical series. Peter Kubelka said the following about his film: "My *Arnulf Rainer* film is a documentary; it is an objective film; it is a world where there is lightning and thunder twenty-four times a second, let's say."[149]

Similar to Czech, Kubelka dealt extremely intensively and persistently with a given topic. Ultimately, he worked on *Arnulf Rainer* for two years—the film lasts six minutes.

---

145 Ibid., 156.
146 Ibid., 157.
147 Ibid., 159.
148 Ibid.
149 Ibid., 144.

Hermann Czech in front of the Hoffmann wallpaper in Restaurant Ballhaus, 1962

From Contemporary Impulses to Restaurant Ballhaus

When comparing the contemporary influences on Hermann Czech at the end of the 1950s—the wiener gruppe, Peter Kubelka, the arbeitsgruppe 4 and the journal *die Reihe*—one recognizes an intensive and sustained preoccupation with the essential fundamentals of the respective direction, with its material and language. The works resulting from this preoccupation appear rudimentary, they "stammer" like someone learning a new language. The work of the wiener gruppe revolves around spoken language, sometimes actually stammering, as in the joint work of Konrad Bayer and Gerhard Rühm, *bissen brot*;[150] mostly surreal, collage-like words and sentences that linger without a clear statement, end unexpectedly or could go on forever. Kubelka's metrical film reduces the film to light and darkness; what remains from the possible richness of the images and movements of a film is a rhythmic flickering. The buildings of arbeitsgruppe 4 also reduce the

150 Gerhard Rühm (ed.): *Die Wiener Gruppe. Achleitner, Artmann, Bayer, Rühm, Wiener*, 1967, expanded new edition 1985, 297.

space to its essential properties; raw materials form simple geometries. All of these works deliberately set themselves apart from the romanticizing, "sentimental" world of 1950s popular culture; they were supposed to be explained solely on the basis of their rationality.

Hermann Czech's first realized project, the furnishing of Restaurant Ballhaus (together with Wolfgang Mistelbauer and Reinald Nohàl), arose from this attitude, but also speaks the language of fin-de-siècle architecture in its refined, Viennese depth, with ambiguities, abysses and hints, interspersed wit and historical references, but without sentimentality and with a clear reference to the current reality. In addition to methodical approaches that Czech had become familiar with through Konrad Wachsmann, aspects and elements with which the architect is still concerned flowed into the design. These were the use of existing (as-found) products (armchairs, wallpapers and fabrics based on designs by Josef Hoffmann), the engagement with colors, light and illusionistic components (also as a result of the engagement with cinema and music) and the strategy of montage to create new references and perspectives (which was also used by Karl Kraus and the wiener gruppe). On a more abstract level, those terms that still play a central role in Czech's work came into use in Restaurant Ballhaus: transformation, the existing fabric, multi-layeredness and irony.[151]

---

151 A detailed project description can be found on pages 162–167.

Study at the Academy of Fine Arts 1963–1971

The Scene in the 1960s—*Die Furche*/ Galerie nächst St. Stephan/Klubseminar

In May 1963, Czech began publishing articles on current architectural themes in *Die Furche*. The arts editors were Ladislaus Rosdy, later Anton Pelinka, Trautl Brandstaller and Horst Friedrich Mayer. Czech's first piece, entitled "Die Stadtbahn wird unterschätzt" ("Otto Wagner's Vienna Metropolitan Railway"), campaigned for the preservation of Otto Wagner's metropolitan railway facilities. Yet he was not only interested in the historical value of the Wagner buildings, but also made a case for the metropolis, as it was laid out during the Gründerzeit.

The editorial line, which had been liberal until then under the editor-in-chief Kurt Skalnik, was stopped at the end of 1967 and the main staff left the editorial office. Czech also discontinued his contributions.

Likewise in 1963, with the exhibition *Architektur* (*Architecture*) by Hollein and Pichler at the Galerie St. Stephan, a development that was incomprehensible for Hermann Czech began. At first, he thought he could "just dive through" it, but in the years that followed it attracted the public's whole attention.[152] Since thought precedes form for Czech, and every form is considered meaningless to him without a thought, he could not get anything out of the new scene and its work seemed completely insignificant to him.[153]

Starting that same year, Günther Feuerstein, at that time Karl Schwanzer's assistant at the Technical University, organized the so-called *Klubseminar* for architecture students and published periodic documentation of the content in the magazine *Klub*. Czech rarely

[152] Peter Cook gave the scene the name "The Austrian Phenomenon" in 1970. The catalog for the eponymous exhibition at the Architekturzentrum Wien offers detailed documentation: Johannes Porsch; Architekturzentrum Wien (eds.): *The Austrian Phenomenon (Conceptions, Experiments, Vienna Graz 1956–1973)*, 2009.

[153] Czech: "Zukunft und Architektur," in: *Die Furche* 9/1967, 9.

attended the *Klubseminar* and found the discussions to be characterized by simplifications. However, he has kept all issues of *Klub*, some featuring a personal dedication by Günther Feuerstein, in his library.

In the 1960s, the Viennese art and architecture scene expanded and radicalized. The events cannot be represented linearly, as the years were marked by several parallel, mutually influencing occurrences. Roland Rainer became the Director of Planning for the City of Vienna in 1958; his plans sparked a discussion about future urban development, in which the young architecture scene also actively participated. From May 1963 on, Czech worked as a freelancer in the architecture and urban planning editorial department of the weekly newspaper *Die Furche* and, up to 1967, regularly penned articles related to the topical discourse in Vienna. Hans Hollein entered the scene in 1962 with the lecture "Zurück zur Architektur" ("Back to Architecture)." In May 1963, he and Walter Pichler presented the highly acclaimed *Architektur* (*Architecture*) exhibition. Two years later, Hollein became editor-in-chief of the architecture magazine *(Der) Bau* and thus initiated a new movement that pursued irrational, anti-functionalist, utopian ideas. In 1963, Czech decided to continue his studies in the master school at the Academy of Fine Arts, which was newly headed by Ernst Anton Plischke. In the same winter semester, Günther Feuerstein started the aforementioned *Klubseminar* for architecture students at the Technical University, which he understood as a platform for broader discussions and more visionary work on architecture than was usual at the university back then. The art scene associated with the Galerie (nächst) St. Stephan split into new groups and became radicalized. Several artists had started to go public with sensational campaigns, which were to reach one of their climaxes in 1968 in the "Kunst und Revolution" ("Art and Revolution") event in Lecture Hall 1 of the New Institute Building of the University of Vienna.

Die Furche was founded in 1945 as a "cultural-political weekly journal" and as a discussion forum on the future of Austria by Friedrich Funder, former editor-in-chief of the Christian-Social *Reichspost*, a daily newspaper that had greatly contributed to the worsening of the political climate during the time of the Corporate State. Clearly oriented towards Catholicism, *Die Furche* arose from the firm desire to avoid the mistakes of the First Republic and to support the establishment of a Second Republic.[154]

154 Trautl Brandstaller: "Friedrich Heer und 'Die Furche' (1946–60)," in: Richard Faber et al. (eds.): *Offener Humanismus zwischen den Fronten des Kalten Krieges. Über den Universalhistoriker, politischen Publizisten und religiösen Essayisten Friedrich Heer*, 2005, 37.

In the 1960s, when Czech wrote for *Die Furche*, it was led by a liberal editorial team. These were the years of the Second Vatican Council, when an epochal spirit of optimism characterized the Catholic Church.

The Galerie St. Stephan underwent a phase of change in the early 1960s. It came under greater pressure from the "official" Catholic Church, which at the end of 1963 insisted on renaming it to Galerie nächst St. Stephan (the Gallery "next to" St. Stephan), in order to no longer be compromised by the exhibitions that the public perceived as too provocative.[155]

The second change came from within; the artist collectives that had previously worked together dissolved. For instance, the wiener gruppe, whose work interested Czech the most, fell apart: H. C. Artmann had already left it in 1958; Friedrich Achleitner began to devote himself to the history and criticism of architecture, wrote articles for *Die Presse* as of 1962, and started working on his documentation of 20th-century Austrian architecture; Oswald Wiener joined the more radical Actionists and Konrad Bayer's suicide in 1964 ultimately marked the definitive end of the wiener gruppe.[156]

In 1962, Hans Hollein returned from his stay in the USA and that same year gave the lecture "Back to Architecture" at Galerie St. Stephan. He had studied architecture under Holzmeister (after Kurrent and Spalt) and then continued his training in Chicago and Berkeley with the help of a scholarship. In his lecture, Hollein took a stand against "a philosophy that sees architecture as the shaping of a material function instead of the transformation of an idea through building."[157] His criticism was of postwar functionalism, perceived as dry and dreary. This criticism was shared by the architecture scene, but what made Hollein's position new was the general departure from rationally-based architecture. At the *Architektur* exhibition, architectural models were displayed for the first time without any statement about function or use. Hollein and Pichler exhibited sculptural architectural objects as pure form and for form's sake, anti-rationally, emotionally and without scale. "The shape of a building does not develop from the material conditions of a purpose. A building should not show its type of use, is not an expression of structure and construction, is not a covering or shelter. It is a building itself. Architecture is pointless."[158] Hollein and Pichler demonstrated that architectural forms can also exist regardless of any preconditions, and they sparked

155 Fleck: *Avantgarde in Wien*, op. cit., 456.
156 In one of Czech's notebooks from 1964 there is an uncommented entry, "1964 Suicide Konrad Bayer," although the notebooks otherwise have no diary-like character.
157 Hans Hollein, "Zurück zur Architektur (1962)," https://www.hollein.com/ger/Schriften/Texte/Zurueck-zur-Architektur.
158 Fleck: *Avantgarde in Wien*, op. cit., 573.

enthusiasm in the next generation of architects, while the scene associated with arbeitsgruppe 4, which Czech felt close to, reacted with rejection.[159]

As of 1963, the Feuersteinian *Klubseminars* took place in the evenings in the rooms of the Galerie (nächst) St. Stephan.[160] Architects were invited to a discussion, where they introduced current articles from international architecture magazines to each other or they jointly visited exhibitions. The topics were influenced by Feuerstein's stance, which he had published in 1958 in the *Thesen zu einer inzidenten Architektur* (*Theses on Incidental Architecture*).[161] In this work, he called for an emotional, changeable, random architecture, one opposed to technical perfection and classic aesthetics: "Incidental architecture does not judge according to beautiful and ugly, but according to good and bad, wrong and right. Architecture is a moral category."

Study under Ernst Anton Plischke

In 1963, the Viennese architect of interwar modernism, Ernst Anton Plischke, returning from exile in New Zealand, was appointed to the master school for architecture at the Academy of Fine Arts as the successor to Clemens Holzmeister. Unsatisfied with his education at the Technical University, Czech switched to Plischke's class. Roland Rainer, the director of the second architecture school at the Academy, was out of the question for him as a teacher due to his linear approach to design. In reference to Rainer's dogma of the compact low-rise building, Czech later hung a poster in the Plischke class stating: "Architecture is at least two-storied." Plischke attracted his interest because he had been part of the architecture scene of Viennese modernism in the interwar period[162]– someone who had known Adolf Loos personally, worked for Josef Frank and planned a house for the Vienna Werkbundsiedlung. Czech valued his clear, humanistic, cosmopolitan and democratic approach. From his lectures, Czech particularly remembered Plischke's criticism of symmetry "as a habit to be overcome." In a presentation in the context of the weekly lecture, Czech tried to argue that symmetry is a permissible possibility in certain cases, using examples of Le Corbusier, whose symmetry he described as "disturbed." Plischke replied: "So, then make a disturbed symmetry."[163]

159 Czech's stenographic notes on and in the exhibition catalog. On a picture page with rockets, bulldozers, oil rigs, etc., he wrote: "What is fascinating about these things is what they can do." Regarding the sketch of a "building that radiates power": "Refusing a telephone connection, switching off escalators is a stronger exercise of power," "Light, air conditioning, communication more important than formed material." These were lines of thought that also played a role for Hollein a few years later.

160 See Feuerstein: *Visionäre Architektur in Wien 1958–1988*, Berlin 1988. Beatriz Colomina; Craig Buckley (eds.): *Clip, Stamp, Fold. The Radical Architecture of Little Magazines. 196X to 197X*, 2014, 91.

161 Günther Feuerstein: "Thesen zu einer inzidenten Architektur," in: *Klub*, Heft 24, publications of the Klubseminar, Vienna 1965; reprinted in Feuerstein: *Visionäre Architektur Wien 1958/1988*, 1988, 51–54.

162 According to Friedrich Kurrent: "This brought probably the best of the young Austrian architects of the interwar period back from emigration," Kurrent: "Schule machen. Die zweite Wiener Zeit," in: *E.A.P. Ernst Anton Plischke. Architekt und Lehrer*, 2003, 168–181: 168.

163 Czech: "Das Arbeitsamt Liesing und seine Wiederherstellung 1996–97" in: *E.A.P.*, op. cit., 40–47: 47, as well as Czech: "Der Hoffmann-Pavillon," in: Diener & Diener: *Common Pavilions*, installation at the 13th Architecture Biennale in Venice 2012.

Plischke's instruction began with the design of a single-family house. Czech analyzed several modern single-family houses, such as Mies van der Rohe's Farnsworth House and those of Loos and Frank, and found Loos to be the most productive. He worked on the design with a ribbed concrete ceiling with a prefabricated formwork system that was common at the time. Derived in a purely technical logic, the rounded ribs left room for the specially shaped skylights. This detail gave the house an unexpected Moorish expression and Czech recognized that architecture also contains associative effects. Further projects from the initial period under Plischke included an exhibition space, a diving platform, a commercial building on Stephansplatz and the urban redevelopment of Schottenfeld as part of a conceptual renewal of the Gründerzeit city.

Plischke took his teaching activities very seriously. Every morning from 9 a.m. to 1 p.m. the design projects were corrected. There were no grades, all parts of the draft had to meet his requirements and was only considered finished when Plischke placed his signature below it. Architectural differentiation was crucial for him and he demanded detailed drawings on a 1:5 scale for all projects to clarify the visual appearance. His pencil-marked points in the drawings were feared—they had to be worked out in detail.[164] For Plischke, it was not about the students following his building aesthetics, but rather that they produced projects with an inner logic and coherence. It was important to him that the designs were geared towards the users and their specific needs.[165]

Ernst A. Plischke: Frey House, 1972

Every Tuesday morning in the lecture, Plischke conveyed his own understanding of architecture using examples with which he passed on his view of the architecture of the interwar period and of architects he had known personally (including Behrens, Frank, Strnad, Wright and Le Corbusier). Plischke's lectures "were conversations about problems that [in his opinion] move planning architects and are essential for them."[166] He had a completely different view of Viennese modernism than the young Viennese architecture scene around arbeitsgruppe 4. He named Otto Wagner in connection with purely decorative strivings in architecture. He saw no continuity in the development of architecture from Adolf Loos to Josef Frank, but rather both as dissimilar, individual personalities who, on closer inspection, had little in common. Plischke's judgment of Loos was not very flattering; he compared the House on Michaelerplatz with the

164 Kurrent: "Schule machen," op. cit., 170.
165 Georg Friedler: "Ernst Anton Plischke – ein politischer Mensch?" in: *E.A.P.*, op. cit., 70–73: 73.
166 Alessandro Alvera: "Vermittlung," in: ibid., 98–99.

Study at the Academy of Fine Arts 1963–1971

Single-family house, 1963

167 Plischke: *Ein Leben mit Architektur*, op. cit., 95.
168 "Gehört und geschrieben, Auszüge aus den Dienstag-Vorlesungen von E.A.P. Eine exemplarische Auswahl von Alessandro Alvera und Hermann Czech," in: *E.A.P.*, op. cit., 100–109: 101.
169 Ibid., 109.
170 Martin Spühler: "Reflexionen eines Schülers aus der Schweiz," in: ibid., 130–133: 133.

façade of the Federal Reserve Bank in Chicago and said that Loos had only been able to impress the ignorant Viennese with this design. In Frank, however, he recognized an ethical attitude committed to a democratic socialism that he saw realized in his buildings.[167] "What one […] builds or does not build, design, etc., is not essential—it is a by-product of the mind. The adeptness of the t-square is not important; developing the mind and character are important for us […]."[168] Plischke was convinced of the reality and meaning of the metaphysical and quoted Meister Eckhart, Plato and Lao Tze. It was about having a "building attitude" that was "a matter of knowledge, restraint, tact."[169] Plischke opposed fads and formalisms: "You have to enjoy visiting your buildings even after twenty years," he pointed out to his students.[170]

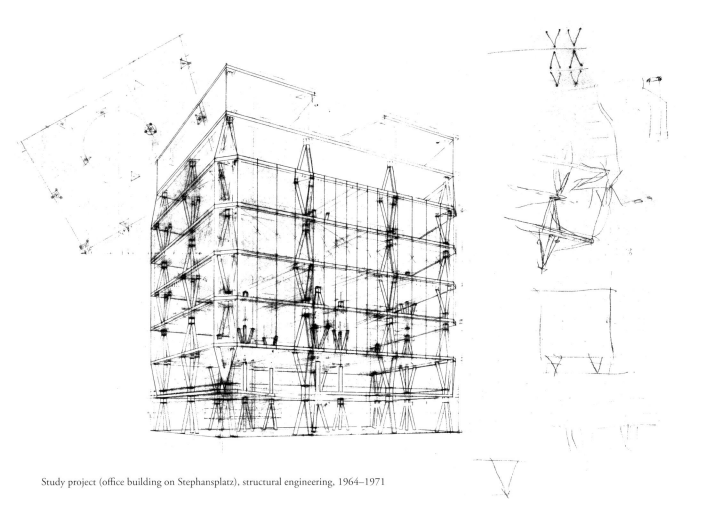

Study project (office building on Stephansplatz), structural engineering, 1964–1971

Because of the inhuman scale and the demonstration of power inherent in the symmetry, he detested both monumentalism and symmetry. Moreover, he was an enemy of classicism, symbolism and all decoration; only the modern architectural style came into question; nevertheless, he protested vehemently against a pure utilitarianism. For him, modernism was not over yet, but still needed time to develop fully.[171] Function and form were to be enriched by a differentiated structural elaboration of the construction and a specific spatial concept that includes path and time.

171 A position very close to that of Team X members. During his emigration, however, Plischke had lost contact with the international scene and dismissed the young scene as a "clique" that talks too much; see "Gehört und Geschrieben," in: ibid., 102.

Perspective of an elementary school, 1964–1970

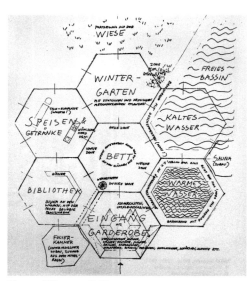

House of Pleasure, 1963

Diving tower, 1965
(class exercise)

Europa Symposium, 1963

During this time, Czech likewise grappled with a criticism of functionalism, albeit without questioning it as a legitimate stage in an intellectual development. Rather, it had more to do with how to get beyond functionalism without falling behind it. He gave a first answer in the article "Neuere Sachlichkeit" ("Newer Objectivity") in *Die Furche* in June 1963 to mark the Europa Symposium on the topic of "Die europäische Großstadt – Licht und Irrlicht" ("The European Big City – Vision and Mirage"), the lectures and discussions of which he followed as a reporter. His article was preceded by a quote from Theodor W. Adorno's lecture, which the latter had given in the scope of the event: "It is only possible to go beyond objectivity by being *even more objective*." In this piece, Czech attempted to conceptualize the word "functionalism." He traced the term back to the word "purpose" and to Kant's definition of the art of building, "that makes things pleasant that have 'their determining basis' in an 'arbitrary purpose,'" as well as to the popular notion that a consequent functionalist is "someone who has his buildings find their determining basis in an arbitrary purpose and refrains from making them pleasant." Another popular conclusion in this logic would be to see artistic freedom in architecture only in areas free of purpose, to perceive the purpose as "contamination" and therefore to strive for functionless architecture. Czech suggests replacing the concept of functionalism with Adorno's concept of "objectivity" and seeing objectivity as the material of architecture: "What the above-mentioned attempts to define functionalism have in common is that they identify, as Kant does, the determining basis in purposes that lie outside architecture. One could go so far as to hand over the decisions to the user or client—the consumer—who must, after all, know best what he needs. 'Objectivity,' on the other hand, tends in the exact opposite direction. In the face of 'what the thing itself demands,'" the consumer loses his rights. Those demands present themselves to the artist in the material that he processes."[172]

In addition to Adorno, Czech refers to Golo Mann at the beginning of his article by stating that the metropolis does not really pose a problem, and with the attitude that a city is fundamentally unplannable, it cannot be something that has a form, and that urban planning can only supply the "'grain' that permits change," he refers to Lucius Burckhardt

172 Quoted from Czech: "Newer Objectivity" (1963), trans. Elise Feiersinger, in: Czech 2019, 42f.

as well. Associated with the piece is an interview with Richard Neutra and a photo of his Lovell Health House from 1927. Czech interprets Neutra's approach as "absolute functionalism," as he advocates aligning architecture with scientific knowledge about the nature of man and what he needs for his health. In the way he conducts the interview, Czech draws closer to this approach critically by opposing it with the thinking consciousness of a human being who eludes a linear conditioning and patronization through architecture.

As of 1958, on the initiative of Vienna Mayor Franz Jonas, the Europa Symposium took place at the end of the Wiener Festwochen as a freely accessible event with international thinkers on current issues. In June 1963, the architects Richard Neutra, Victor Gruen, Lucius Burckhardt and Jacob Bakema, the philosopher Theodor W. Adorno and the historian Golo Mann were invited.[173] The speakers largely agreed that the historically grown, European city still offers the highest urban quality that new residential areas could not match. As problems of the big city, they identified the increasing private car traffic, the phenomenon of the mass society in which the individual grows emotionally and mentally lonely, as well as the preference of technology over humans. The solution approaches were different. Neutra and Gruen were committed to paying more attention in planning to people as individuals. Adorno believed on a theoretical level that the critical mind should be strengthened and saw the only hope for change in the autonomous mind of man. Bakema identified potential in the design of the infrastructure with which the individual could identify in his social consciousness. Burckhardt saw the role of urban planning the most optimistically: He considered the city as being in constant development, supported by urban planners who would accompany the participatory processes and the balancing of interests. What is special about every city is its "grain," not its shape, that is, the relationship between built and non-built space. Burckhardt also recognized the possibility of regionalism in this grain, regardless of the style and architecture of the individual buildings.

173 *Europa-Gespräch 1963*, 1964.

Viennese Urban Development Discussion

One of the urban planning discussions that Hermann Czech followed with interest in the late 1950s and early 1960s was the question of how to deal with the flak towers in Vienna. In the first years of the postwar period, a number of speculative building projects for the pair of flak towers in Augarten were proposed. All of the discussed projects envisaged a complete conversion and new uses (hotel, office, etc.) while simultaneously allowing their visual identity to disappear. Friedrich Kurrent began to devote himself to the flak towers in 1958 and was the first to plead for their unchanged preservation. Czech took up these considerations in 1964 after an exhibition by arbeitsgruppe 4 and carried out his own research. The importance of their urban location was first recognized by Rudolf Oertel in 1947 in the publication *Die schönste Stadt der Welt – ein utopisches Buch (The Most Beautiful City in the World – A Utopian Book)*[174]: The idea of the Kaiserforum by Semper and Hasenauer is incorporated into it and called the "Vienna Forum" and further thought out with the flak tower of the Stiftskaserne as a conclusion. Czech suspected that the flak towers, which had been erected as of the winter of 1943/44 and, in addition to the installation of anti-aircraft guns on their roof platforms, also served as air raid shelters for the population and as protective structures for works of art, could have been consciously placed as a part of urban planning. In 1965, he established contact with Friedrich Tamms, the architect of the flak towers. There is an exchange of letters between the two of them in which Tamms confirms the deliberate urban planning position of the three pairs of towers in a triangle bordering the city center. Czech found the consideration of arbeitsgruppe 4 to use the militarily determined position of the flak towers for a new development impressive and made a comparison with the Ringstrasse, which had also been created by the reinterpretation of a formerly militarily determined geometry.[175] In 1960, Hans Hollein sketched a project in which the flak towers were sculpturally built over, and presented it at the *Architektur* exhibition held in 1963.[176] This purely formally conceived approach was less interesting for Czech. arbeitsgruppe 4, on the other hand, suggested using the flak towers as a base for glass skyscrapers and thus making use of their urban planning position.

174 Rudolf Oertel: *Die schönste Stadt der Welt: ein utopisches Buch*, published by Wiener Verlag, Vienna.
175 Interview with Hermann Czech on April 12, 2012. arbeitsgruppe 4 referred to Czech's argument of the reinterpretation in: Friedrich Kurrent; Johannes Spalt: "Gebrauchsanweisung für Flaktürme," in: *Forum* 138–139, 325–328: 328. Further articles by Kurrent and Spalt on the topics of their exhibition *Wien der Zukunft* in: *Forum* 136, April 1965, and 144, December 1965.
176 *architektur aktuell* 3/1968, 30.

arbeitsgruppe 4: 2nd flak tower project, 1963

In 1964, at the *Wien der Zukunft* (*Vienna of the Future*) exhibition[177] in the showrooms of the Olivetti Gallery, arbeitsgruppe 4 presented their project for the re-use of the flak towers, which could not be blasted away due to their inner-city location and which the Austrian government had urged the occupying powers early on to preserve and convert. Friedrich Kurrent had been dealing with these war relics for a long time and visualized them in their position around the inner city. In his sketch from 1958, he positioned a helicopter landing pad on the flak tower of the Stiftskaserne exactly in the axis of the Heldenplatz monument and the two court museums. In 1963, arbeitsgruppe 4 came up with the idea of erecting a superstructure over the flak towers consisting of transparent, high-rise buildings in skeleton construction.[178] In the accompanying project text, they analyzed the effective urban planning location of the flak towers that they wanted to use for high-rise buildings with diverse urban functions (apartments, offices, hotels, restaurants, etc.). The goal was to add a new order to the historic city silhouette with the church towers protruding from the landscape of houses. arbeitsgruppe 4 saw their proposal as a realistic project, not a utopian one; for them it was a matter of dealing with the historical architectural heritage and its potential for a possible reinterpretation.[179]

Roland Rainer became the Director of Planning for the City of Vienna in 1958 and in this role was supposed to create a "basic urban planning concept" for the future development of the city. This was decided upon in 1961 and published in 1963 under the aforementioned title *Planungskonzept Wien* (*Planning Concept for Vienna*). Rainer's analyses concluded that Vienna was

177 See the eponymous exhibition catalog: *Wien der Zukunft*, arbeitsgruppe 4, Vienna 1964.
178 Ute Waditschatka: "Im Vordergrund das Bauen," in: *arbeitsgruppe 4*, op. cit., 20–77: 72.
179 Ibid. 73. In her essay: "Zurück in die Zukunft," in: *arbeitsgruppe 4*, op. cit., 160–175: 174, Karin Wilhelm sees the flak tower project as part of a "work of mourning [...] whose own history remains visible as one of the entanglements in the contrast between war and peace architecture." The flak towers would be respected as part of history and at the same time their effect would be deconstructed by the light superstructures.

a city with a shrinking population in the 1960s. He found the historic city quarters to be too densely built up and compared them with a "sick and overburdened organism": "We have to distinguish between that culturally valuable Vienna up to 1850, which is absolutely worthy of protection, and the later tenement blocks of the Gründerzeit, which are completely insignificant and unhealthy as buildings."[180] According to his ideas, the Vienna of the Baroque and Biedermeier periods, when the gardens and parks had a high cultural value, was the one that should be drawn upon, and he described the city around 1850 as a garden city that had already been realized. In the *Planungskonzept Wien*, he therefore proposed breaking up the historical zones and expanding the city with residential buildings, differentiated according to specific requirements (for old people, families, singles, students, etc.) to accommodate the inner-city residents. For the 1st district he defined a precise plan of the monuments and street lines to be preserved. The urban functions (living, working, leisure) were to be separated, based on his ideas of a "structured and dispersed city."[181] Rainer made a case for a sensible unmixing of functions. Disturbing commercial operations were to be separated from the residential areas, whereas non-disturbing ones were to be "interspersed" to keep the transport routes short. According to Rainer, the expansion was to go south like a linear city, since the greatest number of inbound and outbound commuters had already been heading in this direction. For the area north of the Danube, he suggested revitalizing the three existing centers (Stadlau, Kagran, Floridsdorf), as well as loosely built-up residential areas, mixed with commercial spaces. This proposal defined, for the first time, a still-to-be-created "Danube Island" as a green space and recreational area. Rainer vehemently opposed high-rise buildings and any kind of monumentality in urban development, rather preferring dense, low-rise residential areas. He did not go into the topic of the flak towers in his study.

An ideological discourse had arisen around urban development; the conception of the city included the notion of a "proper way of living." arbeitsgruppe 4 responded to Roland Rainer's *Planungskonzept Wien*[182] with *Wien der Zukunft*.

In their exhibition, arbeitsgruppe 4 contrasted the triangle of high-rise buildings on the flak towers around the city center with a concentric, dense urban expansion beyond the Danube, with a center as a generously curved, longitudinal structure that surrounds the Alte Donau (Old

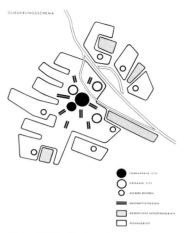

Roland Rainer's urban development concept, 1963

180 Rainer: *Planungskonzept Wien*, op. cit., 8.
181 Johannes Göderitz; Roland Rainer; Hubert Hoffmann: *Die gegliederte und aufgelockerte Stadt*, 1957. For decades, this book shaped the teaching of urban planning at Austrian universities. Only recently has it been regarded more critically. It goes back to work that Rainer did in Berlin during the Nazi era and that was also created under the aspect of planning a city that is more difficult to destroy in an air war. See, e.g., Kühn: "Entweder, oder…," op. cit., 98.
182 Roland Rainer: *Planungskonzept Wien*, 1963.

Study at the Academy of Fine Arts 1963–1971

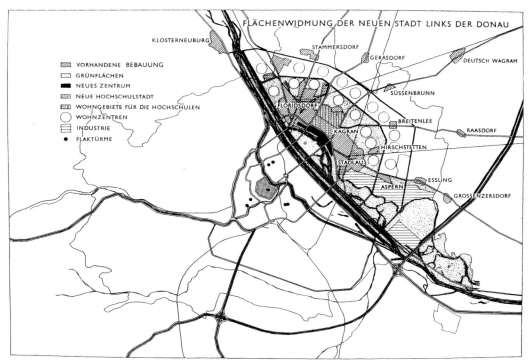

arbeitsgruppe 4: "City expansion proposal," 1964

Danube), a university district and a wreath of "housing mountains" which, however, contained mixed use. The proposal was a counter-model to Roland Rainer's *Planungskonzept Wien*[183] published in 1963 and resumed Otto Wagner's concentric continuation of the urban structure north of the Danube. It also featured a principal concept for public and private transport.

Ernst Plischke and his students examined the area north of the Danube on the basis of Rainer's suggestions.[184] The "Old Danube" project foresaw a center with public spaces and dense buildings for commercial, cultural and administrative purposes on the banks of the Danube, based on the modernist model, as well as a traffic-calmed residential area with one-way streets and dead ends, arranged radially around it. There was to be a continuous green zone between the residential areas with a variety of community facilities for recreational activities. Like Rainer, Plischke stood against any monumentality in urban planning, but he made an argument

183 Kaiser: "Bilanzen mit Ausblick…," in: *arbeitsgruppe 4*, op. cit., 154.
184 See Plischke: *Ein Leben mit Architektur*, op. cit., 451ff.

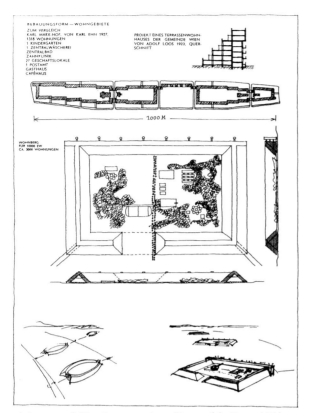
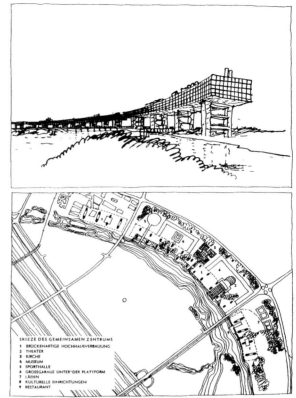

arbeitsgruppe 4: Housing mountains – *Vienna of the Future*, 1964

for a differentiation in height development and planned high-rise buildings both in the city center and in the residential areas. As a student of Plischke's Master School, Czech consciously did not participate in this project. His interest lay in the existing city and its possible further development. Czech's articles in *Die Furche* corresponded to the latter positions. In order to underpin the prevailing vision of the city, all discussants cited historical references as the respectively valid tradition.

At the same time, Max Peintner and Heinz Geretsegger's Otto Wagner monograph, designed by Walter Pichler, appeared in Residenz Verlag.[185] All three belonged to the circle of artists and architects associated with the Galerie nächst St. Stephan. One of the main focuses of the book is the chapter entitled "Die unbegrenzte Großstadt" ("The Unlimited Metropolis"). In it, the authors describe Otto Wagner's idea of thinking

185 Geretsegger; Peintner: *Otto Wagner 1841–1918*, 1964.

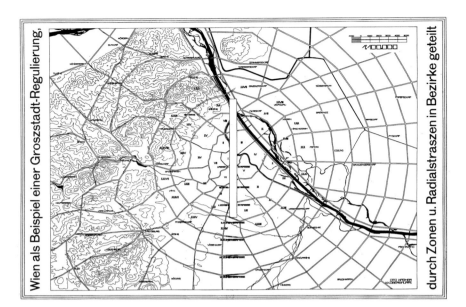

Otto Wagner: The Unlimited Metropolis, 1911

of Vienna as a metropolis that could theoretically expand radially without limits. In Wagner's proposal, district after district, each one autonomous, concentrically surrounded the existing city. The individual districts consisted of residential buildings in perimeter block development, loosened up by green areas or separately highlighted structures with special functions such as churches or administrative buildings. The authors used Wagner's urban planning concepts to argue the case for the dense metropolis and thus took a critical stance on Rainer's planning concept for Vienna as a loosened garden city, too. They quoted Otto Wagner: "In the light of our present experience the expansion of a city must be unlimited,"[186] and said the "longing for a simple life" (Rainer's Garden City) could not be fulfilled because, in their opinion, it was no longer possible to return to a "simple life."

Czech's texts regularly made reference to Vienna's urban development. A recurring term was the "metropolis," by which Czech means the existing urban structure. In 1965, he explicitly stated his position on Roland Rainer's urban planning ideas: "What is appalling about Rainer's ideal city design is not the brutality, but the methodical frumpiness."[187] In 1966, he wrote the text "Für eine neue Großstadt" ("Towards a New

186 Otto Wagner: "The Development of a Great City," *The Architectural Record* 31 (May 1912): 485–500, 500ff.

187 Czech: "Umweltgestaltung," in: Czech 1996, 46–47. Czech wrote this article on the occasion of a Roland Rainer exhibition at the Academy of Fine Arts, but did not publish it at the time. It first appeared in the original edition of Czech's *Zur Abwechslung*, in 1976.

Metropolis"),[188] in which he again called for the mixing of functions and proposed the terrace house as a new urban building type. In the discussion contribution to the *Neue städtische Wohnformen* (*New Forms of Urban Housing*) exhibition in 1967, Czech asked the question "Was geschieht mit der bestehenden Stadt?" ("What Will Happen to the Existing City?") and said, "It is pointless to want to produce a metropolis. The metropolis already exists. Urban planning does not involve creating something new, but setting up new relationships in the existing."[189] He advocated for the creation of new levels of traffic and proposed laying public mass transit and highways underground (in exceptional cases: elevated), local traffic on ground level, and pedestrians on ground level or one level above. He spoke out in favor of a mixing of functions in the city, as well as neutral forms of development that made their respective use possible through individual design, and formulated the following: "[…] instead of the separation of functions: the building should accommodate a variety of functions. Instead of 'reducing density': a higher floor-space ratio (not population density) […]."[190]

Another urban development controversy of the 1960s revolved around the discussion about the demolition and rebuilding of St. Florian Church on Wiedner Hauptstrasse. This place of worship held a singular position in terms of urban development in that it stood in the middle of the street, surrounded by traffic. The City of Vienna argued in favor of the demolition primarily with a planned tunneling under the road, as well as with the attainment of higher traffic safety and the supposedly merely average quality of the existing structure. The church leadership agreed to a new building on the left, eastern, side of the street. When this was finished, the city's plans had changed. Nevertheless, they insisted on tearing down the old church, since it no longer had any function. Although architects and neighbors mounted a protest movement, the church was knocked down in 1966. Czech wrote two articles on this subject in *Die Furche*, in which he, on the one hand, emphasized the lost urban development value of the position of the church, regardless of its architectural or functional importance, and, on the other hand, polemicized against the project, which now completely sanctioned this act of vandalism by erecting a bell tower as a "landmark."[191]

188 Ibid., 41.
189 Czech: "What Will Happen to the Existing City?" (1967), trans. Elise Feiersinger, in: Czech 2019, 63–70: 67.
190 Ibid., 69.
191 Czech: "Die Chance (Der falsche Weg)," in: *Die Furche* 31/1966 (an interview with Fritz Wotruba, juror in the bell tower competition), and "Stadtbild und Moral," in: *Die Furche* 39/1966, both reprinted in: Czech 1996, 34–37.

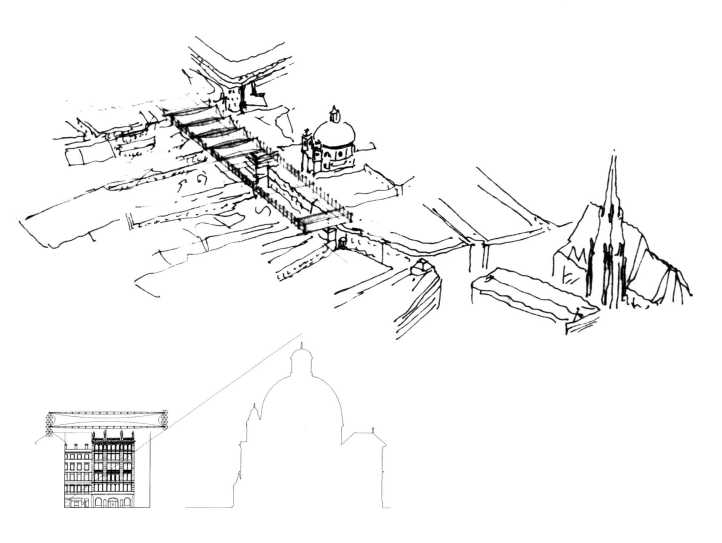

Retractable Roof over the Graben

From 1965 onwards, as part of his studies, Czech also dealt with the self-raised issue of constructing a retractable roof over the Graben, one of the most famous street plazas in the center of Vienna. He proposed a flexible construction consisting of pull cables, compression struts and a membrane, which was to be placed on the ridge walls of the houses bordering the street, thus tying into the concepts of Frei Otto.[192] Czech considered the experience of high-ceilinged space to be essential.

192 Frei Otto was also a guest at the Wachsmann Seminar and Czech had followed his publications since then.

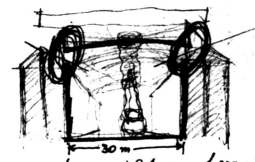

Sept. 66

windschiefe Linie!
keine ebene Membran

Heizung entlang des unteren Seils. Ent-
wärmungsrinne eben-
falls aus Membran?
Könnte mitfahren!

Druchglieder mit betreffenden Seil beweglich.
obere Seilspannung bleibt durch Eigengewicht,
unteres Seil wird schlaff

Peterskirche!

"Portal" über dem
Förster-Haus?

"Portal" zum
Stock im Eisen-Platz

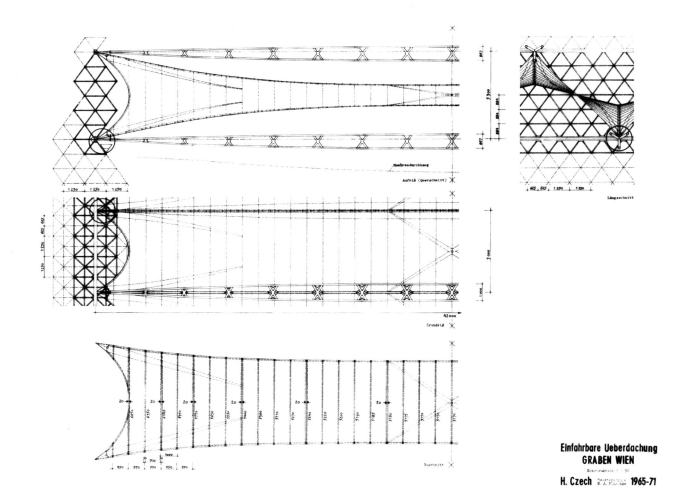

**Einfahrbare Ueberdachung
GRABEN WIEN**

H. Czech 1965-71

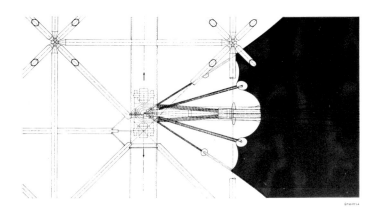

Christopher Alexander

In search of well-founded theoretical approaches, Hermann Czech had subscribed to the *Journal of the American Institute of Planners* and had become aware of articles by Christopher Alexander. He remembers "The Pattern of Streets" (1966)[193] and "Thick Walls" (1968) as early publications. Czech applied the scheme from "The Pattern of Streets" to Vienna's radial-concentric street grid in his Schottenfeld urban redevelopment project.

Christopher Alexander is a British-American architect, likewise born in Vienna in 1936. Similar to Czech, he was interested in architecture in its essence from an early age. Dissatisfied with his education at Trinity College in Cambridge, where he studied architecture and mathematics, he went to Harvard University and began his dissertation on "what people do in buildings, what human needs are developed in buildings, and how one deals with them."[194] His dissertation, *Notes on the Synthesis of Form*,[195] was published in 1964. In it, Alexander argues that in most design tasks there is the problem of too many variables. He tries to minimize these according to mathematical models by organizing them in sub-sets. The designer can first find a solution for each subgroup separately and then combine them into a common solution. In 1965, he published the text "A City is Not a Tree,"[196] with which he also became known in Europe. This essay criticizes the tree-like organization of new urban structures which, due to their linearity, rigidity and separation of functions, are unable to create true living spaces. Like Czech, he also recognizes the qualities of the historic city. Alexander analyzes this quality using the mathematical term "semilattice," which describes a complex structure of overlaps. "The city is a receptacle for life,"[197] and this should not be cut up by the linearity of a hierarchical "tree structure."

In the text "The Pattern of Streets," Alexander develops a new form of street organization in a neighborhood. All streets are parallel, with superordinate cross streets every three to five kilometers. The parallel streets are designed as one-way streets with alternating directions. In this way, detours have to be taken, but the flow of traffic is not disturbed by left turns. The shorter the journeys, the longer the detours, which again means that one does not drive the car for short distances. Alexander calls this structure a "pattern." A few years later he and his team put together a whole book of

193 *Journal of the American Institute of Planners*, Vol. 32, No. 5, 1966, 273–278.
194 Christopher Alexander in an interview with Georg Schrom, *architektur aktuell* 181/182, 92–101: 93.
195 Alexander: *Notes on the Synthesis of Form*, 1964.
196 Alexander: "A City is Not a Tree," in German: "Die Stadt ist kein Baum," in: *Bauen+Wohnen* 7/1967, 283–290.
197 Ibid., 290.

such patterns: *A Pattern Language*,[198] as the basis of every design—from urban planning to interior design, from the "independent region" to "half-inch trim."

The theoretical examination of Christopher Alexander's ideas was to occupy Czech for a long time in his later professional life, which led to the editorship of the German edition of *A Pattern Language* under the title *Eine Muster-Sprache* (1995).

The Vienna Subway Discussion

"The renouncement of a subway corresponded to Rainer's urban planning ideas, which did not go far from the natural ground, either upwards or downwards," wrote Hermann Czech in a 1966 article in *Die Furche*,[199] further criticizing that the official planning of the subway network was seen as a purely technical problem and not as an essential creative contribution to everyday life and understanding of the city. That same year, Czech collaborated with Friedrich Kurrent, Hugo Potyka, Johannes Spalt and Otto Steinmann on a basic proposal for a subway network. This alternative plan essentially proposed two points that differed from the official planning: the inner city was to not only be accessed via a single point (Stephansplatz), but via a triangle of points that are close together (Stephansplatz, Freyung and Albertinaplatz), and Mariahilfer Strasse was to be connected as an important shopping street to the subway network. There was no official reaction from the Planning Department of the City of Vienna to these suggestions, but years later Mariahilfer Strasse was actually included in the subsequently implemented network.

The Vienna underground discussion at the beginning of the 1960s was strongly influenced by politics, after the ÖVP (Austrian People's Party) had spoken out in favor of the subway in several election campaigns and the SPÖ (Socialist Party of Austria) argued that public housing should be put first. Roland Rainer's *Planungskonzept* spoke out against building a subway. Instead, the existing tram lines and the rapid transit system should continue to be used and expanded and only be laid underground where it was absolutely necessary (as a so-called "Ustraba" ["Unterpflasterstrassenbahn"]—an underground tramway). In 1964,

198 Christopher Alexander; Sara Ishikawa; Murray Silverstein: *A Pattern Language. Towns. Buildings. Construction*, 1977.
199 Czech: "Zwei entscheidende Fehler," in: *Die Furche* 43/1966.

Together with Kurrent, Potyka, Spalt and Steinmann: Alternative network design, 1967

this approach was used to lower the tram on the so-called Lastenstrasse parallel to the Ring and on the southern Gürtel belt road as far as Wiedner Hauptstrasse. In 1968, the city government decided to build a regular subway in Vienna and began to upgrade the existing urban railway lines for the subway. In 1978, the first newly constructed section from Karlsplatz to Reumannplatz went into operation.

Travels to Italy and England

Hermann Czech journeyed to Italy several times during his study years. He travelled to Rome for the first time in 1950 on the occasion of the "Holy Year" with his middle school class; visits to Venice and Northern Italy followed later. He remembers that, even as a grammar school student, he noticed that the campanile in Venice with its uniform brick structure looks dead and artificial. Later, as an architecture student, he learned that the campanile had been rebuilt after its collapse in 1902.

In 1964, he undertook a study trip to Milan, which he wrote an article about in *Die Furche*. Influenced by the discussion on the expansion of Vienna and the Hollein-Pichler exhibition, he analyzed individual examples of Milanese architecture, including the Torre Velasca and the Galleria Vittorio Emanuele II. He judged the buildings to be fashionable in style and adapted to their time, but convincing in their concept: "Their greatness lies in the concept. Where no one is repelled by unfamiliar shapes, the thought can be understood all the better. The banality of the individual recedes behind the intelligence of the arrangement. Great architecture is individual. What defines a city is the architectural way of life—spaciousness and intelligence. Not grand architecture, but rather metropolitan."[200] In addition to Milan, he visited Venice again on this trip; a note about the larger and the smaller square near San Marco can be found in a 1964 notebook, stating that a large square facing the sea would be "ineffective and infantile" compared to the effect of the shorter, deeper insight while driving past. This realization led 30 years later in his consultant project for the Donau City to perpendicular structures not parallel to the river which, however, did not prevail in the lead project.

In 1973, at the time of the design for the Kleines Café extension, Czech participated in an excursion to Andrea Palladio's buildings, which was organized by the Austrian Society for Architecture (ÖGfA).

During his school days (1953), Czech's first trip to England, not yet marked by a conscious architectural interest, took place. In February 1965, he then visited England as part of an excursion by the Academy of Fine Arts, which he extended out of personal interest, spending several weeks in London, Bath and Brighton, among other places. The memories of these two trips are blurred. What is clearly remembered, however, besides the preoccupation with "English classicism, that is, with Nash or the much more brittle Soane [...] before I really knew contemporaneous

200 Czech: "Großstädtische Architektur," in: *Die Furche* 47/1964; also in: Czech 1996, 13–14: 14.
201 Czech 1996, 93.

Viennese classicism"[201] is the observation that the ceilings of many English pubs are painted with glossy oil paint and that this creates a reflection that is effective in terms of space, despite the unevenness.

As he was used to from Vienna, Czech also spent some time in libraries in London. A notebook contains quotes from the article "Words on Theory" in the February 1965 issue of the *Architectural Review* and from the book *Modern Architecture* by Vincent Scully. He visited Regent's Park, the John Soane Museum, the Crescents in Bath and the Royal Pavilion in Brighton. A rejection of classicism because of its misuse by National Socialism was never an issue for Czech. In his opinion, Speer, for example, used the formal language of classicism "in a simplifying and uncritical manner."

City Structure and Terrace House

From 1966 onwards, under Plischke's supervision, Czech worked on the self-chosen design task of the "Schottenfeld Urban Redevelopment Project," where he picked up on the terrace house type for inner-city densification. The lower, deep floors would accommodate parking spaces and commercial functions, the upper floors would take in apartments. Depending on the cardinal direction and the type of existing building, the terrace house could be steeper, flatter or higher in the existing fabric. The result would be different spatial configurations of streets and courtyards, open, closed or covered by a superstructure. The terrace house and its models from the interwar period (such as Henri Sauvage, Adolf Loos) entered into international discussion and also played a role in the designs of arbeitsgruppe 4. The terrace house was the logical further development of the garden city idea in a densified, metropolitan form; at the same time, it favored a mixture of functions: the buildings, becoming increasingly wider at the bottom, would lead away from the pure residential building and the doctrine of the spatial separation of urban functions—and lead back to the historic "metropolitan house with multiple purposes." Czech also addressed the subject in *Die Furche*: "The practical difficulties of new building forms do not lie in the technical or financial realm, but—since residential construction is largely fed by public funds—in the hesitant insight of the responsible politicians and officials."[202]

202 Czech: "Terrassenhäuser," in: *Die Furche* 25/1966.

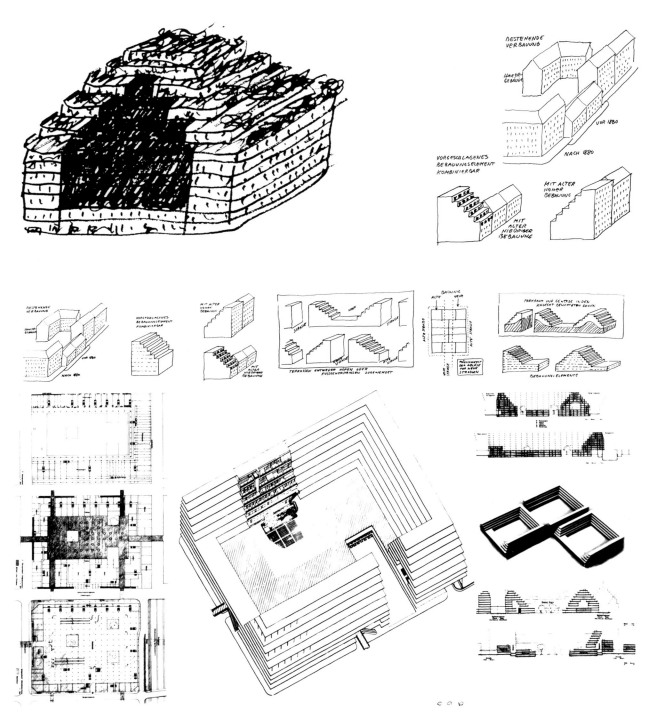

Terrace house project, 1966–1969

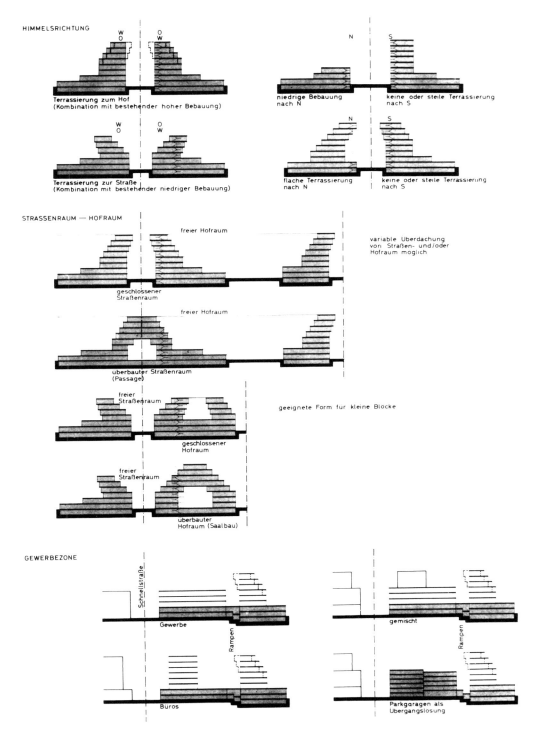

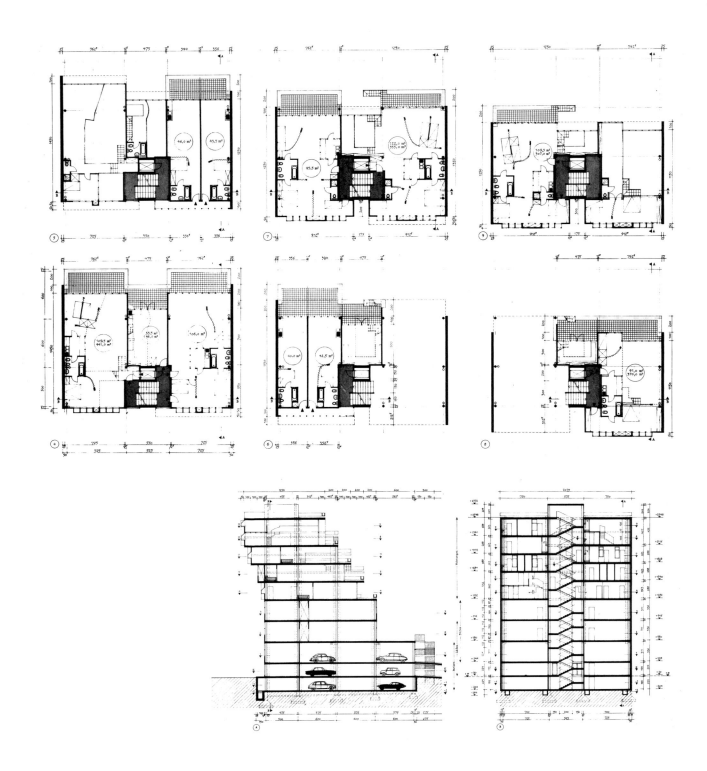

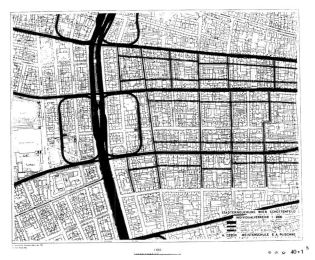 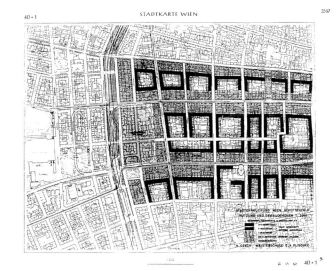

Schottenfeld urban redevelopment project, 1966–1969

In Czech's study project, the individual house object respectively fulfills the reinterpretation of the Gründerzeit urban structure—based on a superordinate regulation. However, as in the historic city, this principally requires parcel-wise realization. Nevertheless, the individual project increasingly does not follow a development plan in the planning reality, but the plan rather follows a respective larger-scale project. Not only in new development areas, but also in the Gründerzeit city, the new building structure "comes about gradually, on the basis of different proposals, competition results, in short, on the basis of successive paradigms of planning and architecture [...]."[203] Decades later, Czech therefore contrasts the regularity of planning with "chaos," the term "emptiness, [...] the space in between [...] the area one has no use for—or not yet [...] the [also inner] 'periphery'—the blank space in the system," its "future aspect" contains "utopian potential" not only in the new development area, but also in the historical city.[204]

The terrace house was first introduced into the discussion in Vienna in 1922 by Adolf Loos in search of a form of living that combines the advantages of the garden city with the density of the big city,[205] and was taken up again in the 1960s by arbeitsgruppe 4 as a "housing mountain." A cross-section of the

203 Czech: "Elements of Urban Conception" (1990), trans. Elise Feiersinger, in: Czech 2019, 195–209: 204.
204 Ibid., 202–205.
205 See Münz; Künstler: *Der Architekt Adolf Loos*, 1964, op. cit., 111–120, 150–153; Rukschcio; Schachel: *Adolf Loos*, op. cit., 285–286.

models discussed at the time was shown at the *Neue städtische Wohnformen* exhibition[206] organized in 1967 by the ÖGfA. The catalog was edited by Czech, whereby in the introductory sequence he takes a look back at international and Viennese architectural examples from the turn of the century to the present, including the various terrace house plans from Loos to Strnad, Le Corbusier and Henri Sauvage, to Walter Jonas's Funnel House and highlights Atelier 5's Halen Housing Development. The presented, meanwhile established Austrian groups of architects of the late 1950s were represented with various autonomous, to some extent utopian living models and terrace house plans for new settlement areas.[207] Hermann Czech's personal contribution was the only one to deal with the existing city and attempted to argue using the terrace house type to densify and modernize the existing urban structures. What ensued was a literal terrace house boom in the Austrian architectural scene, ranging from Hans Puchhammer and Gunther Wawrik's terrace house estate "Goldtruhe" in Brunn am Gebirge to the residential towers of Alt-Erlaa by Harry Glück with Kurt Hlaweniczka and Requat & Reinthaller & Partner in Vienna, and the Graz terraced housing estate of the Werkgruppe Graz.

Criticism of "Irrationalism" in Architecture

In 1965, Hans Hollein realized his first project in Vienna with the Retti candle shop in the 1st district. Czech wrote a favorable article in *Die Furche*.[208] He analyzed the design as starting from the form and called this an "uncertain path," but in this case it was to be regarded as "convincing," "because it succeeded in actually giving these forms an architectural sense."

The following year, the *Klubseminar*, a students' studio organized by Günther Feuerstein at the Technical University of Vienna, showed an exhibition of utopian city models at the Galerie nächst St. Stephan under the title *urban fiction*, which had been conceived by the students of the *Klubseminar* and a number of invited architects of the younger Austrian scene. The exhibition design and contributions took up Archigram's pop aesthetic and revolved around technoid, monumental structures. Architects such as Laurids Ortner and Wolf Prix presented their work for the first time. A new, younger, more rambunctious, less reflective scene with an "emotional, irrationalistic conception of architecture"[209] turned up.[210] In the 1967 article "Zukunft und Architektur" ("The

---

206 *Neue städtische Wohnformen* (*New Forms of Urban Living*), exhibition compiled by Viktor Hufnagl, Wolfgang and Traude Windbrechtinger, ÖGfA, 1967.
207 In this exhibition, respectively, in the catalog, apart from a sketch by Hollein, there were no references to the utopian models of the younger architects associated with the Klubseminar or—except for the Werkgruppe Graz—from the Graz scene.
208 Czech: "Ein Geschäft am Kohlmarkt," in: *Die Furche* 50/1965.
209 Achleitner: *Aufforderung zum Vertrauen*, op. cit., 74.
210 These works later became known under the title "The Austrian Phenomenon" (based on a formulation by Peter Cook), to which the Az W devoted a comprehensive exhibition and exhibition catalog in 2004 under the eponymous title.

Future and Architecture"),²¹¹ Hermann Czech publicly replied to the suggestions for utopian city models it contained. He asked whether "one can seriously be interested in what something might look like if one simultaneously knows exactly that the prediction is methodologically impossible?" Czech does not see a quality criterion in the newness of a structure in itself. He tried to approach the debate methodically and argued: "Every architectural design relates to the future, insofar as it lacks the execution into reality." Accordingly, it is banal to use the term "future" in architecture: "In architecture, 'future' has no place at all. Architecture is either contemporary design or nothing at all."²¹² In 2004, in an interview on the occasion of *The Austrian Phenomenon* exhibition at the Architekturzentrum Wien, Czech recapitulated his attitude about this phase: "I was less bothered by the utopian approach than by the formalism that these 'concepts' and 'experiments' implied. I only saw the decorative in this 'awakening.'"²¹³

In the summer of 1967, Richard Buckminster Fuller gave a lecture in Vienna at the invitation of the *ZV der Architekten* (Central Association of Austrian Architects). On this occasion, Czech published the lecture "Das Jahr 2000" ("The Year 2000") in *Die Furche*²¹⁴ with a comment pointing out that he sees this publication in connection with the article "Zukunft und Architektur" because it "documents the vision of a designer who, for decades, has been ahead of those who use the 'future' as wallpaper today." In this lecture, Fuller analyzed the most essential changes of the future, which would not lie in technology, but in a new, peaceful, positive interpersonal relationship that would be made possible by it.

In November of the same year, Czech wrote a review of Walter Pichler's *Prototypen* (*Prototypes*) exhibition at the Galerie nächst St. Stephan entitled "Mißverständnisse" ("Misunderstandings").²¹⁵ At this exhibition, Pichler displayed sculptures that looked like machine parts. Czech attributed a high degree of formal intelligence, taste and sensitivity, a sense of material and craftsmanship to the work, but he could not do anything with it conceptually. In it he saw "the emperor's new clothes" as a fascination without conceptuality. After an initial, superficial respect for the aesthetics, what will linger one day is a "musty aroma."²¹⁶ He can only explain his success with the "desire for the strong hand that overcomes the audience from time to time." Later he also attempted to name these tendencies with the help of the term "irrationalism."

Hans Hollein: Retti candle shop, 1965

211 Czech: "Zukunft und Architektur," in: *Die Furche* 9/1967.
212 Ibid.
213 "Die Ausstellung tappt in eine Falle," interview by Matthias Dusini with Czech, in: *Falter* 16/2004, 22 and 55: 22.
214 Czech: "Das Jahr 2000," in: *Die Furche* 28/1967.
215 Czech: "Mißverständnisse," in: *Die Furche* 46/1967; also in: Czech 1996, 61.
216 Later, Czech revised his prophecy in view of Pichler's "Prototypes," which were restored in 1998 and "did not leave a musty aroma," as he wrote in a 2009 catalog article for a Pichler retrospective in the USA that ultimately did not take place.

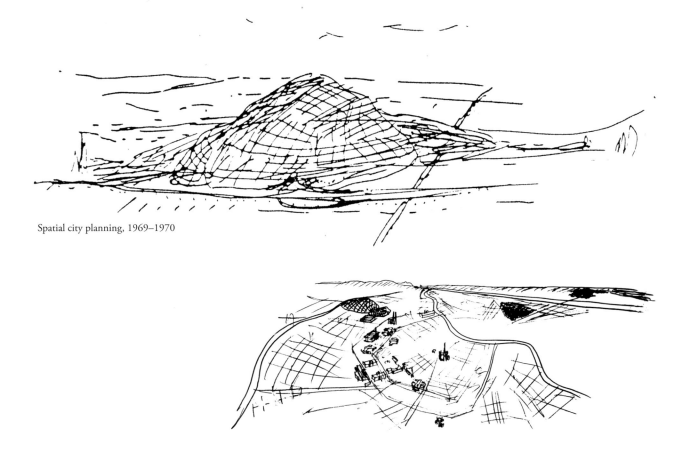

Spatial city planning, 1969–1970

trigon '69 and "Spatial City Planning"

Starting in 1963, the *Dreiländerbiennale Trigon* took place annually in Graz.[217] Contemporary trends in the visual arts from Austria, Italy and Yugoslavia were highlighted. trigon '69 devoted its focus for the first time on architecture and announced an open ideas competition under the title *Architektur und Freiheit (Architecture and Freedom)*. For this competition and on the occasion of the 1970 Austrian Architecture Congress in Payerbach, Czech brought the concept of "Spatial City Planning"[218] into the discussion. He developed a conceptual model that tries to spatially conceive the structure of the existing city, in which every point in space is only accessible from ground level: "Grand

217 *trigon '69. Architektur und Freiheit*, Graz 1969.
218 Czech: "Spatial City Planning" (1969), trans. Elise Feiersinger, in: Czech 2019, 99–101.

volumes are generated; not merely larger versions of slabs, towers, or other building types, but *rampant, amoeba-like growing and roaming entities*—yet clearly distinguishable individualities." Instead of a "plug-in" structure that would only allow the pluggable and unpluggable capsules to be replaced and merely function as a kind of "minimal apartment," this structure, due to its static overdimensioning, was to allow the replacement of a wide variety of elements, depending on the type and size of rooms required. Instead of a large climatic envelope over a conventionally conceived development, the large envelope and building structure were to be identical. In his piece for the Austrian Architecture Congress, Czech wrote: "The large structure resembles an anthill in four ways: The volume is completely built up. Constructive changes are possible during operation. Climatic effects such as condensation and heat radiation are used for the indoor air conditioning. The external shape is, in detail, coincidental." For Czech himself, the most interesting aspect of his concept was the theoretical approach of a "shapeless shape."

Out of the 70 works received, 27 were selected for trigon '69, but Hermann Czech's "Spatial Urban Planning" was not among them and there were no other reactions from the ranks of architects. The majority of the shown contributions dealt with utopian, sometimes ironic city models. Well-known works from the exhibition are the grid-like superstructures covering city and country by Superstudio, "Soul Flipper" by Coop Himmelb(l)au and the "Architecture Pill" by Hans Hollein.

The Magazine *Bau*

In 1965, Hans Hollein, Sokratis Dimitriou, Günther Feuerstein and Gustav Peichl, as well as Walter Pichler, who made drawings for the graphic design and later contributed to the content, took over the editing of the architecture magazine *Der Bau*, which then dropped the article and called itself *Bau. Schrift für Architektur und Städtebau*. It introduced a completely new aesthetic to Austrian architectural mediation: colorful, with large-format pictures spread across double pages and with references to Pop Art and advertising graphics. The first issue already featured a graphic by Roy Lichtenstein on its cover: *Whaam!* Dimitriou and Feuerstein left the editorial team after a year, while Feuerstein remained connected to the medium as a freelancer. Hollein brought Oswald Oberhuber on board, who also took over the graphic design after Pichler had left. Following Oberhuber's departure, the design of the magazine largely ended up in Hollein's hands. The Loos issue, designed by Czech as a guest editor (to which Hollein added a short Hoffmann section),[219] is the last issue of this era. In 1970, the specialist magazine publisher separated from the *Zentralvereinigung der Architekten* (ZV) and the previous editorial team, and appointed Rudolf Kohoutek as the new editor-in-chief. In 1971, the medium was finally discontinued.

The new line stood in stark contrast to the modular, strict, black-and-white graphics of the exhibitions and articles by arbeitsgruppe 4.[220] In the years that followed, the magazine became an important mouthpiece for Hans Hollein's architecture scene. In 1968, he proclaimed "Alles ist Architektur" ("Everything Is Architecture") as the title of an issue.[221] Below the headline one can see the skyline of Vienna on the cover, complemented by a slice of Emmentaler cheese. Hollein's programmatic text is followed by a heterogeneous selection of images—each with the heading "Alles ist Architektur"—from lipstick and a faux Ford advertisement to Arnulf Rainer's overpainting of the Votive Church and the "Ballon für Zwei" ("Balloon for Two") by Haus-Rucker-Co. Hollein saw building as the "artificial transformation and determination of man's world." He opined that, in the past, the environment could only be changed through building, but today through a multitude of media, all of which belonged to the expanded concept of architecture. Architects should stop thinking only in terms of buildings; architecture would be determined more by its effect than by its symbolism and could become completely immaterial in the media space.

However, *Bau* also partially represented the rest of the spectrum of the architectural scene at the time and monopolized it to a certain extent. There were articles about forgotten Austrian modernism, about Austrians in exile such as Rudolph Schindler and Frederick Kiesler, an issue about the Stonborough House by Ludwig Wittgenstein, one about arbeitsgruppe 4 and one entitled "Wiener Architekturstandpunkte 1969" ("Viennese Architectural Standpoints 1969"). Articles by Hermann Czech appeared three times in *Bau*: a piece about competitions in the first issue, the text "Mehr Licht" ("More Light") in the Vienna issue of 1969, and in 1970, when he served as chief editor for the Loos issue.

219 *Bau* 1/1970. Czech's guest editorship is mentioned in Hollein's editorial preface, but not in all mutations of the imprint.
220 Kaiser: "Bilanzen mit Ausblick…," op. cit. 144.
221 *Bau* 1-2/1968 (*Alles ist Architektur*). Colomina; Buckley (eds.): *Clip, Stamp, Fold*…, op. cit., 105.

The Viennese Actionists

Czech knew the scene associated with the Viennese Actionists through Oswald Wiener, but had not followed their activities closely. He liked the association "Zeugen e.V.," which defined passive participation in events as an artistic action.[222] **During an occupation of the Burgtheater (which was not carried out because of a police operation), in which Oswald Wiener invited him to participate, he wore a suit and tie and had an entrance ticket as a precaution. He was a spectator in the "Kunst und Revolution" ("Art and Revolution") action. Kurt Kalb had taken** *Express* **reporter Michael Jeanée to the event, whose article subsequently triggered the media turmoil.**

At the beginning of the 1960s, the first actions aimed against the established art business took place in Vienna. Günter Brus, Otto Mühl, Hermann Nitsch and Rudolf Schwarzkogler belonged to the circle of friends who called themselves the *Wiener Aktionsgruppe* (Vienna Action Group). Together they wanted to go beyond painting and language as a means of expression and tried to find artistic expression in direct, elementary body experiences.[223] In the middle of the decade, the actionists and the avant-garde writers began to appear together, pursuing a cultural revolutionary claim. Over time, the scene radicalized and the artists undertook actions in public space. Well-known examples of this are Günter Brus's *Wiener Stadtspaziergang* (*Vienna Walk*) as a walking painting (1965), and the action in which VALIE EXPORT led Peter Weibel on a dog leash and on all fours through Kärntnerstrasse (1968). The actions subsequently became even more radical and destructive, and at the same time experienced their climax and end with the "Art and Revolution" action in 1968 in Lecture Hall 1 of the New Institute Building of the University of Vienna, organized by Günter Brus, Otto Mühl, Peter Weibel, Franz Kaltenbäck and Oswald Wiener. The latter wrote a leaflet about the action, which ended with the appeal: "Abolish the madness of everyday life! Away with the labor camp of the State!! Redeploy the billions spent on the army for the construction of lust machines! Psychotherapy for all artists! Liberation of all slaves of marriage! End reality!"[224] In order to change the repressive and philistine Austrian postwar society, the artists broke numerous prevailing taboos in the scope of the action. They performed naked, relieved themselves in public, masturbated, vomited

222   The association was founded in 1965 by Oswald Wiener, Ingrid Schuppan, Kurt Kalb and Dominik Steiger according to Fleck: *Avantgarde in Wien*, op. cit., 590.

223   Peter Gorsen: "Der Wiener Aktionismus: Begriff und Theorie," in: Werkner (ed.): *Kunst in Österreich 1945–1995*, op. cit., 141.

224   VALIE EXPORT; Peter Weibel: *Wien: Bildkompendium Wiener Aktionismus und Film*, 1970. See Fleck: *Avantgarde in Wien*, op. cit., 595–596. English translation in: Günter Berghaus: "Happenings in Europe," in: Mariellen R. Sanford (ed.): *Happenings and Other Acts*, London and New York: Routledge, 2005, 373.

and whipped one another, sang the national anthem and also included the Austrian flag in their activities.

The *Neue Kronen Zeitung*, in particular, reported luridly about the incidents under the title "Uni-Ferkelei" ("University Obscenity") and the waves of indignation over such "fecal art" swelled in the population. The action had legal consequences, with Brus, Mühl and Wiener being sentenced to imprisonment for "degrading the symbols of the Austrian state."

Josef Frank

In addition to the work of Adolf Loos, that of Josef Frank became one of the most important sources of intensive architectural and theoretical discussion for Hermann Czech. Both of these were originally inspired by research by arbeitsgruppe 4, who saw Frank as a direct successor to Adolf Loos and Josef Hoffmann, even as their synthesis.[225] **In an obituary entitled "Josef Frank—Intellekt, Liebenswürdigkeit, Ironie" ("Josef Frank—Intellect, Amiability, Irony")**[226] **Czech emphasized that Frank was never doctrinal, but that "his creative engine" consisted "rather in seeing through doctrines."**

In 1968, Hermann Czech applied for the first Josef Frank Scholarship awarded by the ÖGfA, which financed a stay in Sweden. He stated that the purpose of the study trip was to examine Josef Frank's estate in order to prepare a publication on his work. However, Roland Hagmüller was awarded the scholarship, prompting Czech to leave the ÖGfA. He reapplied in 1969, saying that the application from 1968 was still valid. When asked to submit a project for application, Czech sent a critical article "Über die Vergabe des Frank-Stipendiums" ("About the Awarding of the Frank Scholarship") as a "theoretical work" in which he justified his displeasure with the first awarding. He received the scholarship, traveled to Sweden in 1969, and first visited Frank's houses in Falsterbo. In Stockholm he lived with Dagmar Grill,[227] **who managed Frank's estate and had partly deposited it in the Architecture Museum in Stockholm.**[228] **Here, Czech sifted through and arranged Frank's imaginary designs for residential buildings, many of which were initially sketches from letters to Dagmar Grill.**

225 Kurrent; Spalt: "Josef Frank," in: Kurrent: *Texte zur Architektur*, op. cit., 122–127: 126.
226 Czech: "Josef Frank—Intellekt, Liebenswürdigkeit, Ironie," in: *Die Furche* 3/1967.
227 Dagmar Grill was a cousin of Frank's wife. She worked in Frank's *Haus & Garten* shop and was his conversation partner in discussions about architecture. After the death of his wife, Frank lived with Dagmar Grill in the last years of his life.
228 With the exception of the part relating to Stockholm, she later transferred the archive to the Albertina in Vienna.

In 1965, on the initiative of Friedrich Kurrent and others, the Austrian Society for Architecture (ÖGfA) was founded with the aim of giving architecture a higher profile in public perception and counteracting the ignorance of politics.[229] Back then, Otto Wagner's metropolitan railway stations had begun to be demolished, despite protests from the architects. As part of the 1964 Wiener Festwochen, arbeitsgruppe 4 had already realized the *Architektur in Wien um 1900* (*Architecture in Vienna around 1900*) exhibition on the initiative of the Österreichisches Bauzentrum,[230] in which the work of Otto Wagner, Josef Hoffmann, Adolf Loos, Joseph Maria Olbrich, Josef Plečnik and other representatives of the Wagner School, as well as early works by Josef Frank, Oskar Strnad and Oskar Wlach were shown. The works were arranged according to typologies and compared to international examples. Contrasts in terms of content were also included and presented—such as Camillo Sitte's urban planning considerations, together with those of Otto Wagner.[231]

With the establishment of the ÖGfA, however, the intention was not only to make a connection to the Viennese tradition of modernism from the years 1900 to 1934, but also to provide an alternative platform to the presence of Hans Hollein and Günther Feuerstein at the Galerie nächst St. Stephan, as well as to *Bau* magazine and its anti-rational architectural concept.

ÖGfA's first public event was the *Josef Frank* exhibition,[232] designed by Friedrich Kurrent and Johannes Spalt, which was supposed to be understood programmatically. The architects of arbeitsgruppe 4 had already discovered Frank during their student years through their involvement with the Vienna Werkbundsiedlung, of which Frank had been the initiator and artistic director. In a talk in 1985, Kurrent described the visit to the Werkbundsiedlung as a realization "that we should start here." They researched and visited Frank's Viennese buildings and discovered his book *Architektur als Symbol*[233] for themselves. They used Frank's 80th birthday as an opportunity to bring him back into the public eye and initiated the awarding of the "Grand Austrian State Prize for Architecture" in 1965. Due to illness, Frank was unable to attend the award ceremony and died in Stockholm in 1967 without ever returning to Vienna.

Also on the occasion of Frank's 80th birthday in July 1965, Kurrent and Spalt wrote the article "Ein Architekt aus Wien" ("An Architect from Vienna") for *Die Furche*.[234] Frank is described as a role model, in the direct genealogy of Loos and Hoffmann, who continued and developed the great

229 Kurrent: "Zur Gründungsgeschichte der Österreichischen Gesellschaft für Architektur" (1997), in: Kurrent: *Texte zur Architektur*, op. cit., 203–206.
230 *Architektur in Wien um 1900* exhibition by arbeitsgruppe 4, held from May 20 to August 23, 1964.
231 Kaiser: "Bilanzen mit Ausblick…," op. cit., 150.
232 December 18, 1965 to January 29, 1966 at the clubhouse of the ÖGfA.
233 Josef Frank: *Architektur als Symbol. Elemente neuen deutschen Bauens*, 1931.
234 Kurrent; Spalt: "Josef Frank," in: Kurrent: *Texte zur Architektur*, op. cit., 122ff.

tradition of modern Viennese living culture, but was also internationally recognized for his participation in the Werkbundsiedlung in Stuttgart. The article mentioned Frank's residential houses in Vienna and his commitment to social housing, as well as to interior design and furniture designs—first in Vienna with the *Haus & Garten* furniture store he and Wlach founded, and later in emigration in Sweden at the Svenskt Tenn interior design company. Kurrent and Spalt also addressed Frank as a skeptic of modernism who affiliated himself with the Austrian building tradition. They quoted from *Architecture as Symbol* in which Frank warned against "functionalism, constructivism, elementarism," the "religion of norms," the "New Design" and the "international style," and saw his stance ending in an avowal of antiquity and the forms of East Asia: "These forms, granted us by fate, are as distinct and at the same time as diverse as the human form and could express every character and every feeling; a quest for new ones is hopeless."[235] Kurrent and Spalt repeated in the last paragraph of their article that Frank should be seen as the successor to Loos and Hoffmann, and that his "third path" produced a synthesis between the paths of Adolf Loos and Josef Hoffmann, which in their time seemed incompatible. "[…] We owe Frank the continuation of the Austrian architectural tradition and the deepening of Viennese living culture. His criteria, which are still valid for us today, were above all individuality, transparency, lightness, flexibility and the rejection of everything monumental and heavy."[236] They closed the article by emphasizing the anti-formal tradition of modernism and quoted Frank again as saying: "They created works that led in straight succession to the architecture of the present day. Vienna need only to uphold this tradition—in contrast to other countries, which must abandon theirs."[237] Friedrich Achleitner shared this opinion about Josef Frank. In 1967, he wrote: "Since the death of Adolf Loos (1933) and the emigration of Josef Frank (1934), Austrian architects have lacked a clear intellectual orientation."[238] Plischke, who had worked in Frank's office from 1927 to 1929, also mentioned him very positively in his lectures, in contrast to Loos. He regarded Frank's attitude of "looseness" as essential in his personal lifestyle, as well as in his architecture.[239] Frank opposed all forms of doctrines and force. At the same time, however, he also attached importance to an "intellectually developed order." According to Plischke, his designs were never monumental, but nevertheless very precisely worked through; Plischke saw Frank as the antipole to Hoffmann and the Wiener Werkstätte, who pursued the notion of the *Gesamtkunstwerk* in architecture.

235 Frank: *Architecture as Symbol* (1931), trans. John Sands, in: Frank 2012, Vol. 2, 9–191: 125.
236 Kurrent; Spalt: "Josef Frank," op. cit., 126.
237 Ibid. This quote is also used repeatedly by Hermann Czech. English translation by Elise Feiersinger, "Vienna's Modern Architecture to 1914" (1926), in: Frank 2012, Vol. 1, 277.
238 Achleitner: "Aufforderung zum Vertrauen," op. cit., 50.
239 Plischke: "Josef Frank, wie ich ihn kannte," in: Johannes Spalt; Hermann Czech (eds.): *Josef Frank 1885–1967*, 1981, 8–9.

In 1966, Czech published excerpts from Frank's text "Akzidentismus" ("Accidentism")[240] in *Die Furche*. "Accidentism" is considered as Frank's last attempt to get to the heart of his attitude towards architecture and his criticism of functionalist modernism. He argued that modern architecture was developing into a style that determined in a totalitarian way what was allowed and what was not, from which monotonous and uniform cities would emerge. Modernism regards architecture as art, but a work of art places aesthetic demands on its surroundings, which makes people unfree, and he argued with the already quoted sentence: "Every human being needs a certain degree of sentimentality to feel free. This will be taken from him if he is forced to make moral demands of every object, including aesthetic ones."[241] Frank anticipated—as already in 1931, for example, in *Architecture as Symbol*—a criticism of modernism that was to be widely adopted in 1966 by Robert Venturi in *Complexity and Contradiction in Architecture*.[242] In the catalog for the *Österreichische Architektur 1960–1970* (*Austrian Architecture 1960–1970*) exhibition, which was shown by the ÖGfA and curated and designed by Viktor Hufnagl, Friedrich Achleitner spans an arc from the time before the Second World War into the past: "Austria was never a country of architectural inventions. The geographical area lacked security and stability, the political and cultural continuity of development for that. The different parts of the country lay and lie in different ethnic, economic and intellectual spheres of influence, and when Vienna received the function of an imperial metropolis, its task was to unite the heterogeneous elements at least symbolically. Therefore, Austrian architecture has always had a pluralism that is charged with internal tensions and forced early on to accept the coexistence of views. […] His [Fischer von Erlach's] *Entwurff Einer Historischen Architectur* (*Outline of a Historical Architecture*) has remained the unspoken basis of architectural thought to this day. 'Our time is the entirety of history as we know it' writes Josef Frank around 1930, thus polemicizing from Vienna not only against a narrow-minded belief in progress in architecture, but also acknowledging a scale of values that is independent of the time, indeed, of inherent laws and the individuality of things."[243]

240 Frank: "Akzidentismus," first publication in Swedish, "Accidentism," in: *Form*, Vol. 54, Stockholm 1958; the first German-language publication in: *Baukunst und Werkform* 4/1961, excerpts published in: *Die Furche* 3/1966, reprinted in: Spalt; Czech: Josef Frank, op. cit., 236–242.
241 Frank: "Accidentism" (1958), trans. Christopher Long, in: Frank 2012, Vol. 2, 372–387: 385.
242 Long: *Josef Frank*, op. cit., 255; Denise Scott Brown: "Reclaiming Frank's Seat at the Table," in: Frank 2012, Vol. 1, 20–45.
243 Achleitner: "Bemerkungen zum Thema 'österreichische Architektur,'" in: Viktor Hufnagl (ed.): *Österreichische Architektur 1960–1970*, 1969, n.p.

The Loos House

Restaurant Ballhaus, the first work by Czech, Mistelbauer and Nohàl, received little enthusiasm in the architectural scene. At the same time, Czech and Mistelbauer began to devote themselves to the Loos House on Michaelerplatz as part of a study project by Walter Frodl at the Technical University. The investigation soon went beyond the scope of a student thesis and was self-published in 1968 as a research work.[244]

Czech also had a personal and practical connection to Michaelerplatz: Restaurant Ballhaus was right around the corner on Schauflergasse and the Loos House had been a familiar sight to him for a long time. Czech's initial interest in Adolf Loos arose—in addition to the stimulus from arbeitsgruppe 4—when reading issues of Karl Kraus's *Die Fackel* in the mid-1950s. Kraus and Loos had been close friends and Kraus sided with Loos in *Die Fackel*, offering him a platform for his articles. In a conversation, Czech cited the article "Heine und die Folgen" ("Heine and the Consequences")[245] by Karl Kraus as particularly important for his own understanding of architecture.

In this essay, Kraus makes Heinrich Heine responsible for the pleasing confusion of the form and content of language. He sees two fundamental strains of "intellectual vulgarity": "The one experiences only the material side of art. [...] The other experiences even the rawest of materials artistically."[246] Heine has obscured language in the latter sense. The result is the feuilleton Kraus fought against, one in which the journalist feels like an artist instead of communicating facts. A comparable insight opens up the role of ornament. Kraus: "Paralleling the kitschification of practical life via ornament, as traced by the good American Adolf Loos, is an interlarding of journalism with intellectual elements, but here the resulting confusion is even more catastrophic."[247] But also "the literary ornament doesn't get demolished, it gets modernized in the Wiener Werkstätten of the mind."[248] "The phrase is the ornament of the mind," Kraus states more precisely in an earlier version of this argument.[249]

Czech and Mistelbauer's publication, *Das Looshaus*, the first monograph on a single work of modernist architecture altogether, is divided into five chapters: a historical and urban planning analysis of Michaelerplatz, the building history of the Loos House, the description of its architectural and

244 Hermann Czech; Wolfgang Mistelbauer: *Das Looshaus*, manuscript copied for study purposes, self-published by Hermann Czech, Vienna 1968, Verlag Löcker & Wögenstein, Vienna 1976, 2nd revised edition, Löcker & Wögenstein, Vienna 1977, 3rd supplemented edition, Löcker, Vienna 1984.
245 Karl Kraus: "Heine und die Folgen," in: idem (ed.): *Die Fackel*, XIII., 329–330, August 31, 1911, 1–33.
246 Karl Kraus: "Heine and the Consequences," trans. Jonathan Franzen, in: Franzen: *The Kraus Project: Essays by Karl Kraus*, New York: Farrar, Straus & Giroux, 2013, 3–114: 7.
247 Ibid., 35.
248 Ibid.
249 *Die Fackel*, XI., 279–280, May 13, 1909, 8.

constructional details, a collection of personal testimonies and reviews with a reconstruction of the then-unpublished Loos lecture in the Sophiensaal[250] and, finally, Czech and Mistelbauer's own analysis of the work. Its central statement is that Loos's architecture is not a rudimentary forerunner, but a profound path to modernism and, due to its complexity and intellectual depth, even more sustainable than the path of the International Style or the New Objectivity.[251] Loos did not destroy Michaelerplatz, as many contemporaries accused him of, but first completed it.[252]

Czech and Mistelbauer's analysis[253] deals with the role of the house in the perception of Michaelerplatz, as well as extensively with all functional, architectural, structural, spatial and stylistic aspects of the building. As a metropolitan, multi-purpose commercial structure, it differs from the monofunctional type of department store; the publicly accessible lower part is different from the privately accessible upper part; the ferro-concrete (as it was called that back then) enables the diverse dissolution of the outer wall into glass surfaces; Loos's main design motivation is not shaped by the constructive structure, but rather by a more artisanal world of ideas, which is shown in typical details. "This is how material and thought become form; but form and material remain a thought: no material becomes independent in the sense of a rustic romanticism; every invention of form solves a certain problem. The 'ornament' condemned by Loos can be defined as form that is not thought."[254]

Besides the "spatial plan"[255] already used at the Loos House, the analysis discusses the relationship between the undecorated plastered façade not only to the later "objectivity," but also to the contemporary debate about the Art Nouveau style as its continuation; with the column as a signal for "representation," the world of forms from antiquity is finally adopted, but not used canonically, but rethought and thus—as in America—subject to commercial representation. In addition to many other contradictions, one that is obvious and had been already criticized by his contemporaries manifests itself here in the "inconsistency of the axes between the upper and lower part," in which "two principles: the additive of the apartment building and the holistic of a column position" confront each other.[256] Czech and Mistelbauer conclude: "This work is to be understood less from the context of function and construction than from an intellectual will. That's the only reason it struck the chord of a city and its culture."[257]

250 Czech; Mistelbauer: *Das Looshaus*, 1976, 64–71.
251 Among others, Vincent Scully: *Modern Architecture. The Architecture of Democracy*, 1961, revised edition 1974, 24. Czech read the book when he was in England in 1965. Scully describes the beginnings of modernism as a revolt against the Art Nouveau style and names Otto Wagner and Adolf Loos as the first to "strip" the façade of decoration. He quotes Adolf Loos without further explanation and concludes that this ornament has been equated with crime and has suspected anyone who uses it of sexual perversion. According to Scully, Peter Behrens, Walter Gropius and Mies van der Rohe were the first who consequently realized and consolidated modernism.
252 Czech; Mistelbauer: *Das Looshaus*, 1976, 91.
253 Ibid., 90–115.
254 Ibid., 102.
255 Heinrich Kulka's name for Loos's design thinking with different room heights. Kulka: *Adolf Loos*, op. cit., 13–14.
256 Czech; Mistelbauer: *Das Looshaus*, 1976, 113.
257 Ibid., 115.

When Czech and Mistelbauer were working on their study of the Loos House, the broad, contemporary opinion, both internationally and in Vienna, considered Loos to be a forerunner of actual modernism, who one assigned, for instance, to the Bauhaus, and criticized for not having fulfilled his demand for the abolition of ornament in his own projects.[258] In November 1959, however, the Loos issue of the magazine *Casabella continuità*, introduced by Ernesto N. Rogers and Aldo Rossi, was published.[259] In 1961, the first Loos exhibition of the postwar period, curated by Johann Georg Gsteu, took place at Galerie Würthle in Vienna with previously unknown plans and drawings from Ludwig Münz's private Loos archive.[260] In 1962, on the occasion of the opening of the Center Culture Autrichien, arbeitsgruppe 4 designed an exhibition about Adolf Loos in Paris, which was shown two years later in Vienna. According to Friedrich Kurrent, this was to provide for the first time a complete overview of Loos's work and make people aware of the exemplary nature of his oeuvre.[261] At the exhibition in Vienna, Czech and Mistelbauer presented panels for the Loos House. Using the preparatory work by Ludwig Münz, Gustav Künstler's Loos monograph appeared in 1964.[262] Czech discussed the book in an article in *Die Furche*. It begins with the words: "The work of Adolf Loos has again been unpublished."[263] The book was a disappointment for Czech, as, once more, not all available documents had been published. In view of the later research by Rukschcio and Schachel, it was probably asking too much. In terms of older literature, there was the book by Heinrich Kulka from 1931[264] and a text by Karl Kraus on the House on Michaelerplatz.[265] The latter is primarily a polemic against the Viennese understanding of art and its representatives and was—among other things through the sentence: "There he has built you a thought"— an important impulse for Czech and Mistelbauer to consider the priority of the thought over the form in Loos's work as pivotal.

Heinrich Kulka writes about Loos's understanding of ornament: "If an object of daily use is created primarily from an aesthetic point of view, it is an ornament, however smooth it may be," and quotes Loos with the words: "The new form? How uninteresting is that for the creative person. It all depends on the new spirit. It turns the old forms into what we new people necessarily need."[266]

Czech and Mistelbauer described Loos's architecture as "complex and contadictory"[267] and recognized it as a design strategy and not a design weakness. At the same time, Robert Venturi described the

---

258 Like Günther Feuerstein in the Klubseminar, for example.
259 *Casabella continuità* 233, 1–53.
260 *Adolf Loos 1870–1933*, 1961; Ludwig Münz was an art historian in Vienna who still knew Loos personally and had already started to set up a private archive of Loos's works during his lifetime. He planned to publish a biography about Loos, but died in 1957 without having realized this project.
261 Architekturzentrum Wien (ed.): *arbeitsgruppe 4. Wilhelm Holzbauer, Friedrich Kurrent, Johannes Spalt 1950–1970*, Salzburg: Müry Salzmann, 2010.
262 Münz; Künstler: *Der Architekt Adolf Loos*, op. cit.
263 Czech: "Das Loos-Buch," in: *Die Furche* 24/1965; also in: Czech 1996, 59–60: 59.
264 Kulka: *Adolf Loos*, op. cit. Heinrich Kulka had been a long-time employee and office partner of Adolf Loos. Because of his Jewish origins, he emigrated to New Zealand in 1940.
265 Kraus: "Das Haus auf dem Michaelerplatz," in: Kraus: *Die Fackel*, XII., 313–314, December 31, 1910, 4–6.
265 Kulka: *Adolf Loos*, op. cit., 15–16.
266 Czech; Mistelbauer: *Das Looshaus*, op. cit., 113.

buildings of Le Corbusier and Alvar Aalto in the USA under the aspect of complexity and contradiction in architecture.[268] In contrast to Czech's analysis, Venturi's is a general critique of modernism and seeks answers in mannerist art epochs such as the Baroque or Hellenism and, based on the example of Pop Art, in the trivialities of everyday American life—"Is not Main Street almost all right?" Czech did not question modernism in itself, which would have been a historical step backwards for him and just as impossible as a return to a premodern lifestyle, but saw in Loos's architecture a neglected parallel development that had the potential to advance modernism.

In 1970, at the invitation of Hans Hollein, Hermann Czech designed an edition of *Bau* magazine as a guest editor on the occasion of Loos's 100th birthday.[269] Originally intended solely as a magazine about Loos, Hollein decided at short notice to also address Josef Hoffmann, Loos's counterpart, who would have turned 100 that same year, and put a few pages on a hitherto unknown Hoffmann project—the Wiener House in the US—together.

Cover of *Bau* 1/1970, Czech and Hollein. Hollein added a Hoffmann project to the Loos issue edited by Czech.

Czech wrote the article "Der Loos Gedanke" ("The Loos Thought") for this issue and for the first time affords Josef Frank a broad place as an architect who is on a par with Loos. With a collection of quotations from Adolf Loos and Josef Frank, Czech worked out the "Viennese standpoint" of the discussion on modernism. He analyzed it as anti-doctrinal, reflective and able to individualize, to think concretely and not abstractly. "Every building is a thought" and further: "Loos's formal elements are consistently—although repeatedly—solutions to certain structural and spatial problems."[270]

For other articles, Czech chose his own photos as well as historical ones of the sugar factory and villa by Adolf Loos in Hrušovany (Rohrbach) near Brno, part of his and Wolfgang Mistelbauer's text on the Loos House, an excerpt of pictures from the Loos exhibition compiled by Kurrent and Spalt, and a contribution by artist Heinz Frank, a fellow student and friend of Czech from the Plischke Master School. Heinz Frank titled his article: "Adolf Loos. Eine Bewältigung" ("Coming to Terms with Adolf Loos")[271] and combined Loos quotes on proper dress with photos of himself in different clothing in front of Loos's business portals.

268 Robert Venturi: *Complexity and Contradiction in Architecture*, 1966; 18.
269 *Bau* 1/1970, foreword by Hans Hollein.
270 Czech: "Der Loos-Gedanke," in: *Bau* 1/1970, 2–4; also in: Czech 1996, 69–72: 71, 72.
271 Heinz Frank: "Adolf Loos. Eine Bewältigung," in: *Bau* 1/1970, 16–19.

In 1970 as well, Hermann Czech made a 19-minute documentary about Adolf Loos on behalf of the Federal Ministry of Education and Art.[272] *Ins Leere gesprochen* (*Spoken into the Void*) begins with the white title on a black background and a spoken quote from Loos's "Ornament and Crime": "The child is amoral..." The film shows the House on Michaelerplatz, home furnishings and conversions, housing developments, terraced houses, urban development projects for Vienna, the design for the Chicago Tribune, Landhaus Khuner, Villa Müller in Prague, the men's fashion store Kniže and the American Bar, but Czech also developed intellectual arguments: Loos's polemic against Art Nouveau, the concept of the spatial plan, the model of America (the contrast between comfort and representation), the use of traditional forms, Loos's complex attitude to ornament, etc. The medium of film itself is also reflected upon: the incompatibility of art and consumer goods prohibits anything like accompanying music. Historical photographs and new film footage of Loos's buildings (mostly shot with a moving camera while walking) are combined. There are three different levels of speakers: one recites quotes from Loos's texts, one articulates the explanations of the author and the interviewed people speak as well. The latter were filmed in their personal environment and are Loos experts in their own way: architects, art historians (Spalt, Kurrent, Glück, Kulka) and residents of Loos's houses. The film ends with the following words about the architecture of Loos, which also summarize and define Czech's own attitude towards architecture: "Architecture that is not based on ornamentation, but on spatial effects, does not become obsolete. It remains an expression and background for the contradicting tendencies of modern man: convenience, representation, irony."

In his book about Adolf Loos, Heinrich Kulka wrote: "Tradition means a tremendous reservoir of strength for countless generations. Those connected to it have energies that an individual, no matter how ingenious, can never attain. In the case of Adolf Loos, even the new that he brought to architecture is a child of the old, whose features it bears. There are family stories and a resemblance to ancestors. One can enumerate father and grandfather. From Kornhäusel to Fischer von Erlach to antiquity."[273] This can be applied to arbeitsgruppe 4, who themselves draw upon Wagner, Loos and Frank, and subsequently to Hermann Czech, who in turn comes from the generation of arbeitsgruppe 4 and the work that they have created.[274] Friedrich Achleitner implies

272 Czech: *Ins Leere gesprochen. Der Architekt Adolf Loos*, documentary film, "cultural film" for cinemas and television, ORF Archive, Vienna 1970.
273 Kulka: *Adolf Loos*, op. cit., 16.
274 Architects with an attitude comparable to that of arbeitsgruppe 4, according to Czech, are Johann Georg Gsteu, Ottokar Uhl, Hans Puchhammer, Gunther Wawrik and Anton Schweighofer. In addition to Wolfgang Mistelbauer, Czech counts the IGIRIEN group (Elsa Prochazka, Franz E. Kneissl and Werner Appelt), Luigi Blau and Adolf Krischanitz among those of his generation. See also footnote 289.

a barrier, a "glass wall," which, in the processing of the models by the first—his—generation, "let through the historical not as a concrete form, but at most as a system, type or principle."[275] Czech was more carefree in adopting concrete elements, even as quotations: "We (for instance, Wolfgang Mistelbauer and others of a later Wachsmann year) expanded the reflection on geometry, construction, modularity [...] into a reflection on effects and content, which Gsteu and his generation did not accept until much later,"[276] because—according to Kurrent when referring to Restaurant Ballhaus—"we [arbeitsgruppe 4] could never have done that ourselves, nor did we."[277]

The central design theme, how form can be justified in architecture, continued to occupy Czech's reflections in the 1960s: In addition to the criticism—externally—of irrationalism, there was an internal clarification of the design rationality, the basis of which could not be a functionalism however formulated. In Czech's notes dating from 1969, there are conclusive considerations on this: There can be no compelling causal connection between form and function. Even the function cannot only be justified objectively: "The function is conveyed," is therefore a work of the design, already in its compilation prior to that. The form is concrete: "Something is existent. Material, shape," while the function is abstract: "Something should be made possible. Process, change." Both are reflected, "meaning free, and not causally determined."

[275] Achleitner: "Franks Weiterwirken in der neueren Wiener Architektur," in: *UM BAU* 10, op. cit., 123.
[276] Czech's commentary in: Enengl: *Johann Georg Gsteu*, op. cit., 128.
[277] Letter from Friedrich Kurrent to Hermann Czech on the occasion of his 70th birthday, Kurrent: *Einige Projekte, Architekturtexte und dergleichen*, 2016, 43–44: 44.

Kleines Café

Parallel to his preoccupation with Loos, Hermann Czech realized his third work after Restaurant Ballhaus and the summer house in Nussdorf with the Kleines Café on Franziskanerplatz. Again, there were two successive "conversions," namely the adaptation of a merely 25 m²-large space that had previously accommodated a café with the same name, and the extension of similarly-sized space around the corner in the back with a portal at the other house front. Here, Czech not only realized his formula "Architecture is *background*," but also the later remark: "That doesn't mean it has to be inconspicuous, it can be precise or distinctive. Background also means that you can lean on it—and that it holds."[278] Every change entailed a deepening and supplementation of the overall concept and its spatial ideas, but at the same time created a further usability, "as if it had always been that way." The venue still exists as an equally light-footed and complex manifestation of the diverse Czechian levels of meaning.[279]

278 Interview "Architektur ist nicht das Leben," in: *a3 BAU*, Mödling, 11/2008, 24–26: 24.
279 See the detailed project description in this book.

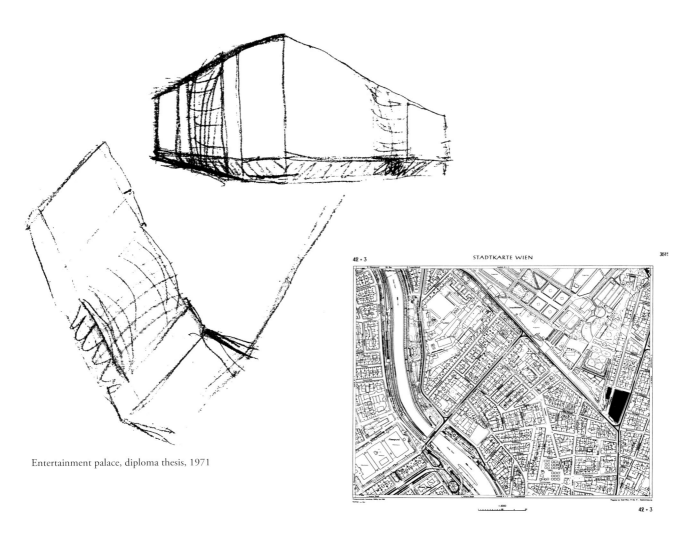

Entertainment palace, diploma thesis, 1971

Completion of Studies

In 1971, Czech completed his studies with Plischke with the design of an "entertainment palace" as a diploma thesis. Situated in the inner courtyard of an existing block building, this structure contained a wide variety of functions such as sports facilities, a department store, a hotel, offices and entertainment options that are interleaved in and above one another. Cedric Price's "Fun Palace" was a reference, but Czech's "entertainment palace" differed from it in the complexity of more concrete uses and its positioning on a real site.

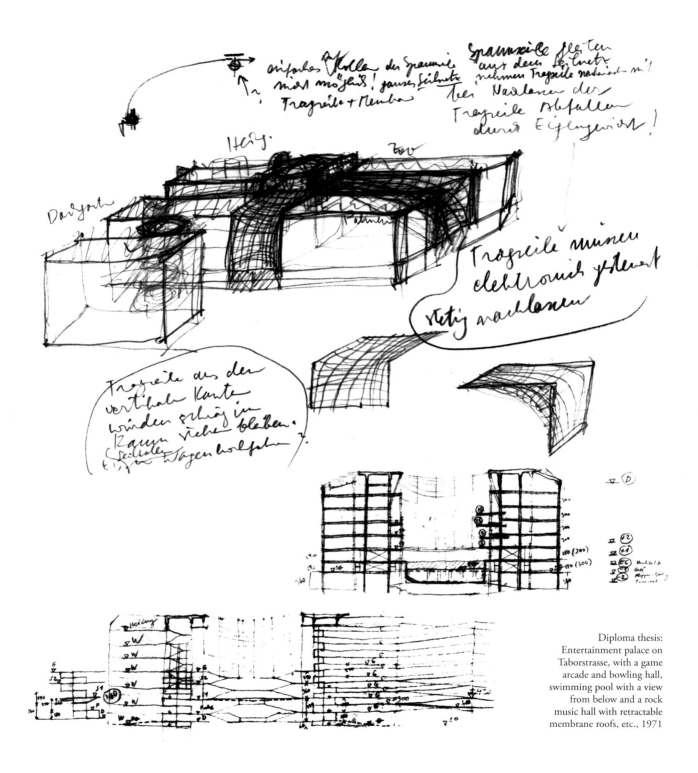

Diploma thesis: Entertainment palace on Taborstrasse, with a game arcade and bowling hall, swimming pool with a view from below and a rock music hall with retractable membrane roofs, etc., 1971

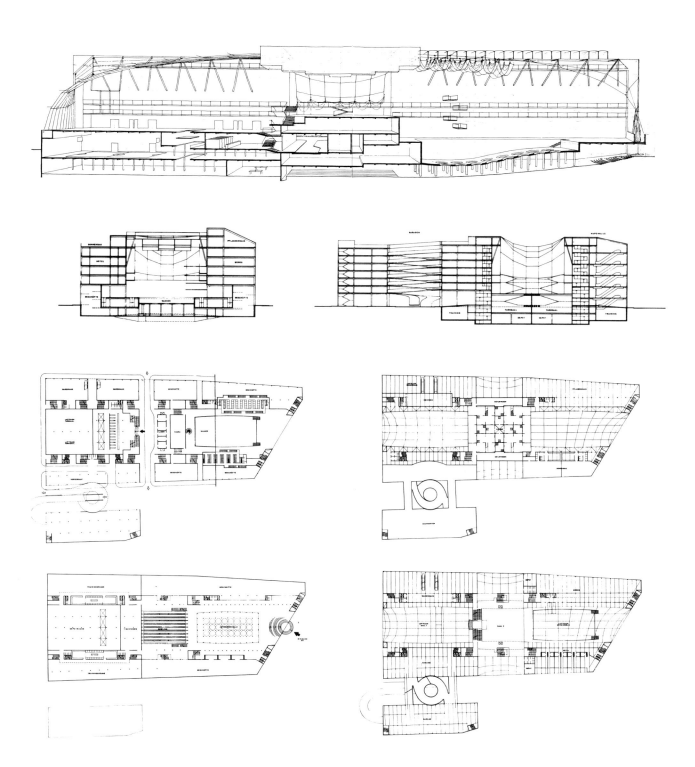

Study at the Academy of Fine Arts 1963–1971

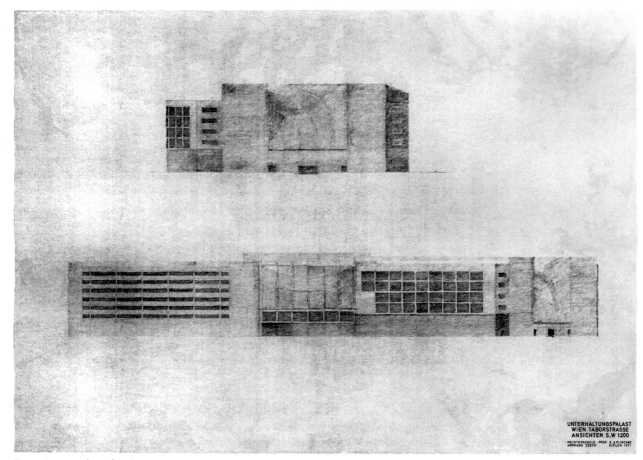

Entertainment palace, elevations

Czech's Language and "Terms"

As already mentioned several times, Viennese modernism was rediscovered in the 1950s and 1960s by the young generation of architects associated with Spalt, Kurrent, Achleitner, J. G. Gsteu and Uhl, and in their successors Hollein, Geretsegger, Peintner and Czech, and later Otto Kapfinger, Adolf Krischanitz and others. The first public reception of this engagement took place in the early 1960s in the local Viennese daily press. In addition to Czech's articles for *Die Furche*, Achleitner wrote a large number of articles, particularly for the *Abend-Zeitung* and *Die Presse*, dealing with the architecture of Viennese modernism, Art Nouveau and the Gründerzeit era.[280] The main reason for this first public presentation was the disdain for these buildings in the public perception and, as a result, their threat of being demolished. Most of the articles are stormy calls to protect this architecture and to finally recognize it for what it embodied in the eyes of the young generation of architects, namely a grand cultural heritage.

Achleitner, for instance, began a piece with the "sad result: of the around 15 Adolf Loos buildings in Vienna, eight have been converted or even destroyed!"[281] The Steiner House served as an example of the ignorant handling of the building fabric by its new owner and the authorities. In the article "Jenseits von Kitsch und Mode" ("Beyond Kitsch and Fashion")[282] Achleitner focused on the "legendary Viennese living culture." He analyzed this as spacious, open living in the hall and living space for residents and visitors, in contrast to the petty bourgeois *Gutstube* (parlor), which was only used for visitors for representation and was "too good" for one's own living. As a "little-known" example, Achleitner presented Frank's Beer House (*Hietzinger Wohnhaus*) with illustrations and floor plans in the article. Achleitner summed up: "It [Viennese living culture] was essentially the achievement of a few architects and clients. It would be an interesting historical task for sociology, which is concerned with building, to examine the elite circle of clients who had an effect here. Perhaps it would turn out that this so-called Viennese living culture was sustained by a society that had very little attachment to the city. In other words, those aristocrats, Jews and artists whose absence makes Vienna a provincial city today."[283]

The linguistic reflection accompanies Czech's designs throughout. In this linguistic debate, he developed a number of terms in the course of his practice, which he uses to convey his understanding of architecture. Entirely in keeping with the logic of the described individual and undogmatic quality of Viennese modernism, he considers architectural theory as "thinking towards design."[284] "The city itself is the existent. It is stronger than anything one can invent in its place. […]," Czech writes in 1973.[285] What he does not explicitly mention, but does address in his architecture, is that the preoccupation with the existing city, Vienna at the turn of the 20th century and the Second Republic, is a preoccupation with its own contemporary

280 Achleitner began in the Abend-Zeitung in 1961 with the article series "Bausünden" ("Architectural Eyesores"), Czech in 1963 with articles for *Die Furche*. See both collections of articles: Achleitner: *Nieder mit Fischer von Erlach*, 1986, and Czech: *Zur Abwechslung*, 1977 and 1996.
281 Achleitner: "Loos-Haus Steiner," in: *Abend-Zeitung*, April 11, 1961.
282 Achleitner: "Jenseits von Kitsch und Mode," *Die Presse* April 18–19, 1964, also in ibid.: Nieder mit…, op. cit., 100–107.
283 Ibid., 105.
284 Among others Czech: "Cleaning the Tools for Design," in: Tom Fecht; Dietmar Kamper (ed.): *Umzug ins Offene*, 2000, 286–287: 286.
285 Czech: "For a Change" (1973), trans. Elise Feiersinger, in: Czech 2019, 113.

history and most recent past, an undertaking that the majority of Austrians did not want to face at the time. What is existent not only consists of noble motives, but also of the abysses of cultural history.

The most important terms used by Czech and developed over a long period of time are the following:[286]

> *Background method*
> *Irony*
> *the existent*
> *architectural multi-layeredness and overlap (vibration)*
> *the normal and trivial*
> *Individualization*
> *Eclecticism as a path to associations that cannot be reached otherwise (Abbreviation, 'Short-Cut')*
> *Mannerism as the only credible basis for participation*
> *Form destruction (deformation) not through the use of 'destroyed forms'*
> *Transformation as a central concept of architectural theory*
> *Comfort as an object of architectural theory*

No Need for Panic

In 1971, Czech published an article entitled "Nur keine Panik" ("No Need for Panic") and a picture of the interior of the Kleines Café I from 1970.[287] In this text, Czech argues polemically for a return to what architecture can do and actually is. In his opinion, architecture is both over- and underestimated. He contrasts "the arrogance to believe that architecture can save the world," and "the modesty to believe that this can be achieved by rounding off all its corners," describes "project architecture" as *Schmunzelkunst* (art that makes people chuckle) and suggests that "all attempts to extort another role for architecture apart from standing there and keeping quiet" is suspicious. The essay ends with the sentences "Architecture is not life. Architecture is *background*. Everything else is *not* architecture." The conclusion can also be read as a response to Hollein's 1968 manifesto "Alles ist Architektur" ("Everything Is Architecture").

---

286 Notepad, Czech Archives.
287 Czech: "Nur keine Panik," in: *Protokolle* 71/2, 142; also in: Czech 1996, 63. English translation by Elise Feiersinger, "No Need for Panic" (1971), in: Czech 2019, 105–107. Robert Fleck says in his work on the Viennese avant-garde that around 1968 there were "three aesthetics […] in competition with one another (and within one another)": " – cultural revolutionary actionism – impressionist technologism, a new form of Art Nouveau [and] – an aesthetic of truthfulness and self-conquest." For the first position he gives an example of the "Art and Revolution" event of the Viennese Actionists, for the second, the *Superdesign* exhibition with a text by Hollein (and a reply by Otto Mauer) and for the third, Czech's essay "Nur keine Panik," see: Fleck: *Avantgarde in Wien*, op. cit., 595–599.

Hermann Czech

NO NEED FOR PANIC (1971)

Architecture is overestimated. Fifty years ago people were convinced that modern architecture could cure tuberculosis. Now that tuberculosis really has vanished, architects feel called upon to solve problems of greater scope. They flock to the mass media to inform us about population explosion, space flight, pollution, and—above all—the importance of mass media, telling us what they have learned from mass media.
That's public relations; it demands a certain journalistic attitude; that flickering between two states of consciousness that complement and necessitate one another: first, one is confronted with people dumber than oneself who need a schoolmaster, and second, one must play the fool in order to be understood. There is already evidence of a division—as in the music business—between popular architecture and serious architecture, referring of course to individual approach, not to its pretensions: architects mimic scientific teams or act like geniuses. In between are the sort of teams who rise as one to the rank of genius, which eliminates individual inhibitions and is therefore definitely the most economical of methods. For what counts is: although we are continually being assured that personality is out, anyone who wants to rate on the market has to become important straight away.
Architecture is in fact *under*estimated. Although the seizers of power want to design life in its name, they think the intention to be progressive will suffice. In the word "environment" this continuously overturning nonsense has crystallized: the arrogance to believe that architecture can save the world, and the modesty to believe that this can be achieved by rounding off all corners.
But it's all vain. No architectural product, however flexible or inflated, can play as important a role as the dome or the rib vault once played. The promises of a subjugated nature find fulfilment elsewhere. They don't want to accept this reality—and so they produce architectural imitations, similar to Pacific Islanders who create replicas of aircraft on stopover and worship them.
To calm everything down I propose to view all public relations with suspicion: all publicity that is not theory or design, all "social engagement" that is not political action, all "project architecture" and related *Schmunzelkunst*,* all obscenity that is not produced for its own sake—in short, all attempts to extort another role for architecture apart from standing there and keeping quiet. Architecture is not life. Architecture is *background*. Everything else is *not* architecture.

The original German version, entitled "Nur keine Panik," was first published in: *Protokolle* 2 (1971).
Schmunzelkunst: art that makes people chuckle.—Trans.

For a Change

In 1973, Hermann Czech published the text "Zur Abwechslung" ("For a Change"), in which he formulated his now consolidated architectural stance[288]—his "personal path and that of a certain scene."[289] In it he defines four terms: "methods," "irony," "the existent" and "multi-layeredness." Using these four terms, Czech draws a summary of the development of his architectural concept.

He begins with the term "methods," the late 1950s and Wachsmann: "Those lacking experience must begin with methodology. [...] We start from square one—of course there is historical architecture, but the previous generation lives in musty ignorance."[290] The method Wachsmann conveyed is to create a "retraceable series of thoughts" from the analysis of all framework conditions, making decisions possible. That alone is no longer functionalism—the "purposes" are just decision-making materials, and not the only ones. From the exact method in the end—not at all understood as a program—"mustn't something original and irreverent evolve from this approach?"

This is followed by the term "irony," referring to the early 1960s and the first years in the Plischke Master School: "The self-contained image is fiction, because, when given thorough consideration, each detail breaks out of its framework." One cannot miss the subjectivity of the decisions in the design process. "…the motivation must come from individuality. It reacts with irony; possibly out of uncertainty because its motives are not definite enough."

Already in the second half of the 1960s (the "Schottenfeld" study project, 1966), when American postmodernism discovered irony for itself, Czech went beyond this and identified "the existent" as a criterion for decisions. "It is remarkable how little of reality architects perceive." And he continues with the sentence already quoted above: "The city itself is the existent. It is stronger than anything one can invent in its place. It is not a matter of erecting a world on the basis of a plan: we have at hand a powerful built mass to which we can only make minor additions—to change, estrange, reinterpret, and perhaps regulate it."

Czech ends his programmatic essay with the term "multi-layeredness." At that time, he had already dealt intensively with Adolf Loos, had been to Sweden to research Josef Frank and had completed the design of the first (lower) part of the Kleines Café. Working with the existent led him to

288 First published in: *architektur aktuell* 34, 1973.
289 Czech: "Architektur, von der Produktion her gedacht," in: *Hintergrund*, 41, 2009, 20–37: 21. This publication contains the first printing of the article "Zur Abwechslung"—with the correction of the Czech layout that was not exactly followed in 1973—with a reproduction and commentary. The "specific scene" means above all Wolfgang Mistelbauer, but also other Wachsmann seminar participants involved in the discourse such as Klaus Bolterauer, Roland Ertl, Herbert Reinagl, Wilfried Richter or Peter Schmid, and ultimately the painter and director Jakob Laub.
290 Czech: "For a Change" (1973), trans. Elise Feiersinger, in: Czech: 2019, 109–115: 110f. With regard to the following approaches, which respectively "rescind" the previous ones, the first is already formulated ironically.

the concept of "conversion," while his preoccupation with Frank made him think about "chance" as a design method. Czech recognized that what was available did not come about through "chance" or a puzzling process, "but as a result of innumerable, intelligible motivations of earlier individuals. Correspondingly, we can attain diversity if we allow all of our motivations to flow into every design and follow up on all the ramifications and thought processes instead of sticking to some hare-brained recipe or hanging on to a shallow discipline. The aim is a congruence of all considerations in a result that is definite but transparent and allows the multi-layered network of relationships to carry on."[291]

"For a change, architectural theory should concern itself with architecture again so that one might understand the where and the how," was the first sentence of the preliminary remark. Josef Frank's criticism of functionalism summarized in the text "Accidentism" closes with the demand: "What we need is variety and not stereotyped monumentality. [...] and by that I mean that we should design our surroundings as if they originated by chance."[292] Even if Frank uses the term "variety" in a different context than Czech, the congruence is interesting. For him, Josef Frank is the last Austrian architect who dealt extensively with architecture in his writings on architecture (architectural theory) and tried to express his understanding of architecture in language.[293] Frank's demand for a design "as if it originated by chance" has accompanied Czech's thinking throughout his life.

Czech dedicated the publication, also titled *Zur Abwechslung* (*For a Change*), which appeared in Löcker Verlag in 1977, to his father. Here he collected 40—or, in the 1996 extended new edition, 55—reviews and essays since 1963, in which his attitude, still valid today, is documented in a precise language and well-thought-out terminology that he had learned during his studies. Because: "Mere thinking has to be reintroduced into architecture first."[294]

291 All quotations from Czech: "For a Change" (1973), trans. Elise Feiersinger, in: Czech 2019, 109–115.
292 Frank: "Accidentismus" (1958), trans. Christopher Long, in: Frank 2012, Vol. 2, 372–387: 385. In German, "Abwechslung" fits to both meanings, "change" and "variety."
293 Especially in Frank: *Architektur als Symbol*, 1931.
294 Czech: "Vorwort zur Neuausgabe," in: Czech 1996, 8.

FOR A CHANGE (1973)
Architectural theory should concern itself with architecture again so that one might understand the where and the how.

Dynamism is popular and there's no harm in calling a building—along with digestion and other production—a process. That shouldn't, at any rate, distract us from the fact that thinking is a process. Theory is practicing theory. The course of events has biographical and historical aspects. It's called contemporary history when the two cannot yet be separated. I start in the late nineteen-fifties.

METHODS
Those lacking experience must begin with methodology. What is architecture? We have space; the human inhabits it, has needs. How do we get a handle on that? The three dimensions, light (and color), climatology, and sound are quantifiable.
Everything else is only partially so. We try to set exact objectives on the basis of the function, the structure, and the determinate economy; ordering principles will emerge out of this material that, in a retraceable series of thoughts, lead to the necessary decisions. We start from square one— of course there is historical architecture, but the previous generation lives in musty ignorance. Everything flows; therefore the building must be variable. It must allow for all possibilities. It must be a world that is bounded and completely mastered within a continuity of

Einkaufszentrum (Entwurf), 1960

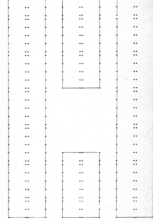

Notizen zu einem Nachtlokal, 1961/62

Hermann Czech:
ZUR ABWECHSLUNG
könnte sich Architekturtheorie einmal wieder mit Architektur befassen: damit man doch sieht, wo und wie.

Dynamik ist beliebt; und es verschlägt ja nichts, neben Verdauung und anderer Produktion auch das Bauen als Prozeß zu bezeichnen. Man sollte aber nicht davon ablenken, daß jedenfalls Denken ein Prozeß ist. Theorie ist Vollzug von Theorie. Der Ablauf hat eine biographische und eine historische Seite. Zeitgeschichte ist, wenn beide noch nicht zu trennen sind. Ich beginne Ende der fünfziger Jahre.

METHODE
Wer keine Erfahrung hat, muß bei der Methodik anfangen. Was ist Architektur? Da haben wir den Raum; der Mensch hält sich darin auf; er hat Zwecke. Wie bekommen wir das in den Griff? Quantifizierbar sind Raumdimensionen, Licht (und Farbe), Klima, Schall; anderes nur teilweise. Wir versuchen aus den Zwecken, aus der Konstruktion, aus der vermittelnden Ökonomie begrenzte, exakte Problemansätze zu machen; aus diesem Material werden sich Ordnungsprinzipien

Schule (Entwurf), 1964/70

"Background"–Childhood, Youth, Studies

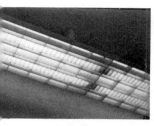

Restaurant unter Verwendung von Tapeten-, Stoff- und Sesselentwürfen von Josef Hoffmann (mit Wolfgang Mistelbauer und Reinald Nohàl), 1962

ergeben, die in einer nachvollziehbaren Gedankenreihe zu den nötigen Entscheidungen führen. Wir fangen ganz von vorne an — sicher gibt es historische Architektur, aber die vorige Generation lebt in dumpfem Unwissen. Alles fließt, deshalb muß der Bau variabel sein (Feuerstein ist damals dagegen); er muß alle Möglichkeiten bieten, eine begrenzte, in einem Kontinuum aller Parameter völlig beherrschbare Welt. Ein aus den Voraussetzungen entwickelter Typus — jedoch nicht als Ergebnis vorgestellt, weil nur der Weg exakt sein kann; und vor allem unter Ausschluß von Subjektivität. Aber — da noch niemand so gedacht hat' — muß hier nicht überraschend das Originale und Originelle entstehen?

Manchen genügt heute noch Modularkoordination.

IRONIE

Das geschlossene Bild ist eine Fiktion, denn jede Einzelheit sprengt, durchdacht, den Rahmen. Man kann an der Lichtfarbe drehen, aber wenn die Fleischfarbe nicht mehr normal erscheint, wird es plötzlich interessanter. Eine Oberfläche kann alle möglichen Reflexionseigenschaften haben, aber die Bedeutung eines Spiegels kann man so nicht erklären. Man kann mit Raumeigenschaften bis an Schmerzgrenzen gehen und darüber — aber nun wird klar, daß ich das wollen muß. Ich kann eine Wand nicht nur beleuchten, sondern auch darauf projizieren; aber was? Begriffe und ihre Dialektik werden wichtiger als Parameter; die Individualität kann sich den Entscheidungen nicht entziehen. Auch nicht durch Variabilität; das Wesen des Entwurfs

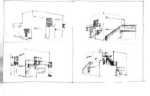

Gasthaus (Entwurf), 1963

Villa (Entwurf), 1963—65

all parameters. A standard type developed in answer to prerequisites—though not seen as a result, because only the path can be exact—and, above all, to the exclusion of subjectivity. Even so—considering that no one has ever had such thoughts before—mustn't something original and irreverent evolve from this approach?
Some still make do with modular coordination.

IRONY

The self-contained image is fiction because, when given thorough consideration, each detail breaks out of its framework. The color of light can be regulated, but when the flesh tones no longer appear normal, things suddenly become more interesting. A surface can have all sorts of reflection characteristics, but that doesn't tell us anything about the significance of a mirror. I can go to the threshold of pain and beyond with spatial characteristics—but now it becomes evident that this must be a conscious decision. I can not only illuminate a wall, but also project something onto it—but what? Concepts and their dialectic become more important than parameters; individuality cannot steer clear of decisions. Not even through variability; underlying it is the essence of the design, which will no more be affected by making use of the preplanned variability than by the opening and closing of a shutter. The essence appears as a form of expression; to just accept this result is not satisfying in the long run. It too

Study at the Academy of Fine Arts 1963–1971

becomes a means: the forms of all epochs are available to us. Decisions cannot be derived from the material—the motivation must come from individuality. It reacts with irony; possibly out of uncertainty because its motives are not definite enough. The quote is the medium of historical irony. Architecture can even become thematic; compared to the conceptual impact, the actual realization can indeed be boring.

Some still make do with conceptual art.

THE EXISTENT

The theory expands and is filled with information; one notices that hardly anything is new, neither the problems nor the solutions. Only a well-developed theory can bring the existent into play. It is remarkable how little of reality architects perceive. The city itself is the existent. It is stronger than anything one can invent in its place. It is not a matter of erecting a world on the basis of a plan: we have at hand a powerful built mass to which we can only make minor additions—to change, estrange, reinterpret, and perhaps regulate it. But like nature this mass is much more an object of cognition than of change. Change also demands that we hoist ourselves into the saddle of the colossus—and the personal question arises whether the company we find there is to our liking.

One can also settle for the pleasures of the existent, as for those of nature.

Some have given up architecture.

Einfahrbare Überdachung des westlichen Grabens in Wien (Entwurf), 1965/71

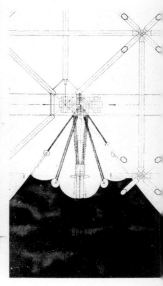

liegt dahinter und ist durch Konsum einer eingeplanten Variabilität nicht mehr betroffen als durch Öffnen und Schließen eines Fensterladens. Das Wesen erscheint als Ausdruckswert; diesen als Ergebnis hinzunehmen, befriedigt nicht auf die Dauer; er wird ebenfalls zum Mittel, die Formen aller Zeiten stehen als Verfügung. Aus dem Material ist die angestrebte Verbindlichkeit nicht zu gewinnen — die Begründung muß aus der Individualität kommen. Diese reagiert mit Ironie; vielleicht aus einer Unsicherheit, gerade weil ihre Motive nicht bestimmt genug sind. Das Mittel der historischen Ironie ist das Zitat. Überhaupt kann Architektur geradezu thematisch werden; neben der begrifflichen Wirkung kann sogar die tatsächliche Ausführung langweilen.

Manchen genügt heute noch concept art.

DAS VORHANDENE

Die Theorie gedeiht und füllt sich mit Information; man bemerkt, daß kaum etwas neu ist, Probleme so wenig wie Lösungen. Erst einer entwickelten Theorie erschließt sich das Vorhandene. Es ist verblüffend, wie wenig Architekten von der Realität wahrnehmen. Das Vorhandene ist die Stadt. Sie ist stärker als alles, was einer statt ihrer erfinden kann. Statt eine planmäßige Welt zu errichten, finden wir eine gewaltige Masse vor, die wir nur durch Hinzufügen von Kleinigkeiten verändern können, verfremden, umdeuten, vielleicht steuern. Aber wie die Natur ist diese Masse viel mehr ein Gegenstand der Erkenntnis als der Veränderung. Auch erfordert Veränderung, daß wir in den Sattel des Kolosses gelangen; und es erhebt sich die persönliche Frage, ob uns die Gesellschaft dort gefällt. Man

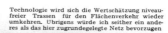

Knoten Schwarzenbergplatz (Entwurf), 1967. Es wäre natürlich bequem, eine solche Arbeit im Augenblick nicht zu zeigen. Aber mit der

Technologie wird sich die Wertschätzung niveaufreier Trassen für den Flächenverkehr wieder umkehren. Übrigens würde ich seither ein anderes als das hier zugrundegelegte Netz bevorzugen

Schemaskizzen zur Stadterneuerung, 1966

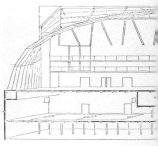

Kleines Café, Wien, 1970

kann sich auch mit dem Genuß des Vorhandenen — wie der Natur — begnügen.

Manche haben die Architektur aufgegeben.

MEHRSCHICHTIGKEIT

In der Theorie der Gartenkunst gibt es eine Dialektik verschiedener Haltungen: Gestaltung „gegen" die Natur, Bewunderung, und schließlich die Nachahmung und das Gleichnis, die Gestaltung „parallel zur Natur". Ähnlich verhalten wir uns zum Vorhandenen. Je mehr wir davon begreifen, desto weniger müssen wir uns in Gegensatz dazu bringen, desto leichter können wir unsere Entscheidungen als Fortsetzung eines Kontinuums verstehen. Ein Umbau ist interessanter als ein Neubau — weil im Grunde alles Umbau ist. Wer sich auf einem schiefwinkligen Grundstück nur mit einem rechtwinkligen Raster zu helfen weiß, ist ein Klachel. Wir wollen noch immer den zwingenden Typus, sehen aber, daß er ebensoviel Nachahmung wie Erfindung verlangt. Nach Josef Frank sollen wir „unsere Umgebung so gestalten, als wäre sie durch Zufall entstanden". In diesem „Als ob" könnte man eine Unsauberkeit, ein Verschmieren von Differenzen vermuten. Aber das Vorbild, das Vorhandene, ist ja nicht durch „Zufall" oder durch einen dunklen Wachstumsprozeß entstanden, sondern aus den zahllosen — im einzelnen nachvollziehbaren — Motivationen früherer Geister. Analog können wir Vielfalt erreichen, wenn wir alle unsere Motivationen in den Entwurf einfließen lassen, allen Verästelungen der Gedankenreihe nachgehen, statt jeweils einer Schnapsidee von einem Rezept nachzuhängen, eine flache Disziplin durchzuhalten. Das Ziel ist eine Deckung aller Überlegungen zu einem Ergebnis, das definiert, aber durchsichtig ist und das mehrschichtige Netzwerk der Beziehungen bestehen läßt.

Unterhaltungspalast in Wien II (Entwurf), 1971

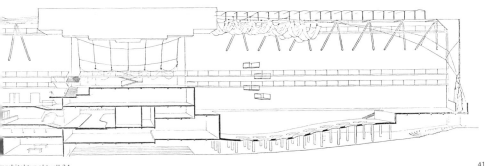

MULTI-LAYEREDNESS

In the theory of landscaping there is a dialectic of different standpoints: designing "against" nature, veneration of nature, and, finally, imitation and allegory, or, in other words, designing "parallel to nature." We approach the existent in a similar manner. The more we comprehend it, the less we must stand in opposition to it, and the easier it will be to understand our decisions as a continuation of a whole. Transforming an existing building is more interesting than building a new one—because, in essence, everything is transformation. Anyone who only comes up with a rectangular grid for an oblique-angled site is an oaf. We still want the one and only valid solution, but we see that it requires as much imitation as invention. According to Josef Frank, we should "design our surroundings as if they had originated by chance." In this "as if" one could suspect a note of uncleanliness and a blurring of differences. But our model, the existent, did not originate "by chance" or by some dark process of growth, but as the result of innumerable, intelligible motivations of earlier individuals. Correspondingly, we can attain diversity if we allow all our motivations to flow into every design and follow up on all the ramifications and thought processes instead of sticking to some harebrained recipe or hanging on to a shallow discipline. The aim is a congruence of all considerations in a result that is definite but transparent and allows the multi-layered network of relationships to carry on.

Study at the Academy of Fine Arts 1963–1971

"Newer Objectivity"

When Hermann Czech began to study in the mid-1950s, a certain canon of forms had already been established in architecture under the name *Neue Sachlichkeit* (New Objectivity) respectively, "Functionalism," which, however, increasingly faced criticism because of its empty content.[1] In 1963, Theodor W. Adorno gave a lecture in Vienna as part of the "Europa Symposium" program, which had such a criticism of functionalism as its theme and prompted Czech to write the article "Neuere Sachlichkeit" ("Newer Objectivity").[2]

In this piece he differentiates between the purposes, the "function," conceived as an external specification, and "what the thing itself demands" (which, of course, also includes the "function") that presents itself to the artist in the material he processes. This means "that function is not a compulsory specification, but the actual artistic material—, that it is not brought to the attention of the architecture, but is created by it."[3] "The 'function' does not precede the design, but is always only mediated in the design. Prior to that, it does not exist—on par with space and structure," and later he concretized: "In the same way as music must be perceivable by the ears, architecture in its essence is usable."[4] In his article about Newer Objectivity, Czech already embraced Adorno's thoughts on overcoming functionalism: "It's only possible to go beyond objectivity by being even *more objective*."[5]

Objectivity can be understood in two ways: "[…] that each thing must unfold in its own right—or that nothing is permitted except for the canon once recognized. The flatter version achieved a broader effect."[6] Now "architecture […] has to do with very many things; objectivity means treating each thing according to its requirements. Since only a few

---

1 See, e.g., Team X, 1953.
2 Czech: "Newer Objectivity" (1963), trans. Elise Feiersinger, in: Czech 2019, 41–47.
3 Czech: "Komfort und Modernität," in: Deutsches Architektur-Museum Frankfurt (ed.): *Architektur Jahrbuch* 1997, 1997, 31–34: 32.
4 Czech: "Das Lokal" (2007, unpublished); English translation by Wendy van Os-Thompson, "Cafés," in: Christoph Grafe; Franziska Bollerey (eds.): *Cafés and Bars. The Architecture of Public Display*, 2007, 113–114: 114. The reference to music is already found in the text "Newer Objectivity" from 1963.
5 Czech: "Newer Objectivity" (1963), trans. Elise Feiersinger, in: Czech 2019, 41–47: 42.
6 Czech: "Der Loos-Gedanke," in: Czech 1996, 69–72: 70.

of these things are alike, the basis of objectivity and ultimately its result is not uniformity, but heterogeneity."[7]

For him, the "very many things" of architecture are: materials, structures and technical building equipment—and the products that can be selected for them, official regulations on safety and environmental protection, the program and wishes of clients and users, aspects of comfort, the context (the "existent") and the reference to solutions (own, already tried or historical ones). The "form" or its absence ultimately results—on each of these levels—from the claim to a perceptible meaningfulness.

In the modernist discourse of the 1920s and 1930s, Adolf Loos and Josef Frank also took a critical stance towards purely aesthetic objectivity. Instead, they understood objectivity as an expression of an impartial, but differentiated examination of the existing conditions. Otto Neurath described Josef Frank's style of design as "Old Objectivity," in contrast to the "New Objectivity" currently in discourse at the time.[8]

In addition to these considerations, Josef Frank's "Accidentism," which has already been explained in detail here, with the demand for a design as if it "originated by chance,"[9] is also a central thought in Czech's work. "In this [Frank's] 'as if' one could suspect a note of uncleanliness and a blurring of differences. But our model, the existent, did not originate 'by chance' or by some dark process of growth, but as the result of innumerable, intelligible motivations of earlier individuals. Correspondingly, we can attain diversity if we allow all our motivations to flow into every design and follow up on all the ramifications and thought processes [...]."[10] In this sense, according to Czech, "chance" cannot arise from subjective, irrational or arbitrary design decisions, but must be constructed through conceptual considerations. The inclusion of several separate series of thoughts in the design process is followed by the inclusion of associations that only appear later in the design process, as well as realities and claims other than one's own.[11]

Czech's reality, the "reality" in Vienna in the postwar period and in the second half of the 20th century until today, is different from what Otto Wagner spoke of in view of the desired democratic, comfortable life in the modern metropolis. It is a less optimistic, more diverse and more contradicting reality. But through the consistent inclusion of multi-layered, also uncomfortable, irrational or absurd realities, works

---

7   Czech: "Architektur, von der Produktion her gedacht," in: *Hintergrund* 41, 2009, 20–37: 26.
8   Otto Neurath: *Gesammelte Schriften* 1, 307, quoted by Nader Vossoughian (ed.): *Otto Neurath. The Language of the Global Polis*, 2011, 79.
9   "…to design our surroundings as if they originated by chance…," Frank: "Accidentism" (1958), trans. Christopher Long, in: Frank 2012, Vol. 2, 372–387: 385.
10 Czech: "For a Change" (1973), trans. Elise Feiersinger, in: Czech 2019, 109–115: 115.
11 Czech: "Mannerism and Participation" (1977), trans. Elise Feiersinger, in: Czech 2019, 119–124.

emerged and emerge that look "superficially simple," but upon closer inspection reveal their multi-layeredness, "their complexity, through a vibration."[12]

And this includes another aspect in Hermann Czech's work, namely the "homey" character of his work. Regardless of the task at hand, this can be determined in projects as diverse as a pedestrian bridge, an elementary school or a shop furnishing—they all contain aspects of homeyness, which Czech subsumes under the term "comfort." The behavior of people is his starting point, even "the very artistic material"[13] of the architecture and not something that is added later. The notion that architecture could be "contaminated" through usage or the necessary functions is, in principle, far removed from Czech. Discomfort could also be legitimate as an artistic intention, but it would immediately make a moral demand and move to a higher level in relation to the user, which would also be diametrically opposed to Czech's position. His work is shaped by humanism, by respect for each person as an individual, even if his/her behavior may contradict the architect's idea. Nevertheless, Czech insists on an enlightening claim of architecture and tries to understand the discrepancy between this and the (often unreflecting) "wishes" of the users under the term "mannerism" and to solve it conceptually: "Mannerism is the conceptual approach of an acceptance of reality at its momentarily appropriate level; it grants the frankness and imagination that set even alien processes in motion and tolerate them, without giving voice to the disingenuous fiction that architecture has given up its claim to produce a vision: to be open yet defined, meager yet comfortable."[14] Czech has, to this day, never given up his social concern of designing a better environment for people and seeing the users "as addressees of a truthfulness."[15] "As an architect, I also speak explicitly about the freedom of the user. I aim at his active engagement with the architectural object—but in no way do I want to pre-define his mood."[16]

In 1978, Lefaivre and Tzonis called the emerging postmodernism in architecture the "narcissistic phase" and wrote: "The shortcomings of the narcissistic phase are apparent. But the forced fun in the rhetoric, the tortured rotations, mirrorings, repetitions and projections, the broken tempo of building compositions, the adolescent disco manner of current projects, conceal a bitter critique of the pitiful decay of the institution of architecture and, with it, the sunken hopes for a human

12 Czech: "Einige weitere Entwurfsgedanken," in: Czech 1996, 81.
13 Czech: "Comfort – a matter for architectural theory?", in: *wbw* 90/2003, 10–15: 15.
14 Czech: "Mannerism and Participation" (1977), trans. Elise Feiersinger, in: Czech 2019, 119–124: 123–124.
15 Czech: "Architektur, von der Produktion her gedacht," op. cit., 37.
16 "'Von Dingen, die nach nichts ausschauen.' Ein Gespräch mit Hermann Czech, Wien," in: Tom Schoper: *Ein Haus. Werk – Ding – Zeug?*, 2016, 47–73: 62.

environment physically and socially well-tempered."[17] It seems as if the digital development and the fascination it triggered kept the architectural profession in its narcissistic phase. The finding from 1978 reads surprisingly up to date at a time when architecture is perceived in the media almost exclusively as a spectacular gesture by star architects and international architecture competitions degenerate into "prize fights" for the most spectacular renderings. In their essay, Lefaivre and Tzonis suggested, as a way out of the narcissistic phase, that architects should again deal with architectural history as a scholarly discipline and not as a self-service shop for quotations or for justifying their own work. This preoccupation would focus on the investigation of the relationships between architecture as a built form and the social, societal transformations.[18]—A practice that Czech has cultivated from the beginning as "thinking towards design."[19] Seen in this way, architecture, in the understanding of the "old" Viennese objectivity, means critically examining the cultural realities of one's own time and viewing them as an expression of this reflection. When Alejandro Aravena, the commissioner of the Architecture Biennale in 2016, writes: "We believe that the advancement of architecture is not a goal in itself but a way to improve people's quality of life," this could be understood as a turning point in the broad architectural scene, as a "humanistic turn," and precisely Hermann Czech's work and theoretical considerations could serve as a model and starting point.

---

17 Lefaivre; Tzonis: "The Narcissist Phase in Architecture," in: *Harvard Architectural Review* 1, 1978, 52–61. Quoted in: Lefaivre; Tzonis: "The Narcissist Phase in Architecture," in: *Times of Creative Destruction: Shaping Buildings and Cities in the Late C20th*, London: Routledge, 2017, 109–122: 116.
18 Ibid.
19 Czech: "Vorwort zur ersten Auflage," in: Czech 1996, 7.

An Essay
On the Relationship between Architecture and Philosophy in Hermann Czech's Work

Elisabeth Nemeth

I was initially surprised that Hermann Czech had attended the philosophy lectures of Erich Heintel and Leo Gabriel in the 1950s. From today's perspective, the 1950s are by no means the University of Vienna's halcyon days. This also applies to philosophy. The two full professors Heintel and Gabriel stood for the underlying continuity of the political and intellectual milieus from the 1930s through to the years after 1945. Gabriel was close to Austrofascism, Heintel to National Socialism—at least close enough to be a member of the Nazi Party. It was not until the 1960s that the student movement made the political biographies of the two professors a topic of discussion. Admittedly, this did not detract from their determining effect on the development of philosophy in Vienna up until the 1980s. During my own philosophy studies in the 1970s, I experienced the two of them as quarreling, fiercely competing *gran profesores* who gathered their—almost all male—disciples around them. They saw themselves as representatives of opposing philosophical camps: Hegelianism with proximity to Protestantism in Heintel, French existentialism with proximity to Catholicism in Gabriel. Both sides quickly made it clear to the students in the 1970s that they had nothing in common—if we disregard two enemies fought by both in almost ritual repetition: the Marxists and the positivists. A few years ago, the philosopher Kurt Flasch, who had been invited by Heintel to give lectures on Aristotle in Vienna in the 1960s, told me that Heintel had said to him that he saw it as his greatest merit that nothing of the philosophy of the Vienna Circle remained at the University of Vienna. After that, according to Kurt Flasch, he never accepted Heintel's invitation again. — So how does the philosophy at the University of Vienna in the 1950s fit in with the architect Hermann Czech, whose work in so many ways proves its closeness to the very modernism that the philosophy of the Vienna Circle stood for? — At first glance it doesn't fit at all.

It is all the more remarkable that Hermann Czech insists he has learned something from those philosophy lectures, especially from Erich Heintel, that is of lasting value for his self-conception as an architect. First of all, I see in it a kind of intellectual honesty that refuses to resolve the dissonance existing between what we know today about the 1950s and what young people experienced in Vienna at the time. Apart from that, however, Czech's interest in philosophy has shaped his self-image as an architect more deeply than would appear at first glance. This becomes visible in the texts in which he describes what it means for him to "conceive architecture from the standpoint of production."[1]

In the following, I will first consider several ideas that are effective in Czech's reflection on what he does as an architect.[2] I will thereby sketch out connecting lines to basic philosophical attitudes, which are probably also more or less clearly echoed in the philosophy lectures Czech heard.

An architect who does not think of his work "in terms of consumption" does not aim to arouse certain moods in the consumer when designing. Czech quotes Jean-Paul Sartre, who refused to arouse predictable impulses (fear, desire or anger) in the reader and who called on literature to "turn to the freedom of the reader." Czech's architecture also addresses the freedom of the recipient. According to Czech, architecture should not aim to create atmospheres in order to "move" the recipient. Referring to the criticism of Adorno and Horkheimer, Czech maintains that the "culture industry" does that to get his money. The culture industry betrays the consumer by arousing his "emotions" that are foreseeable and manageable. In contrast, architecture, as Czech demands it, respects the freedom of the consumer. It offers him the opportunity to have his own experience, an experience not intended by the architect, not prescribed by him for consumption, as it were.

Conceiving architecture "from the standpoint of production" means, according to Czech, understanding the design as an "autonomous series of decisions," "even as it responds to external conditions or seeks to meet the most banal requirements." The notion of autonomy expressed in this understanding of architecture is very complex. Some of its facets will be discussed below. First of all, it stands in sharp contrast to the notion that the architectural design arises from a more or less ingenious

---

[1] This formulation comes from a sentence that Czech remembers as a Hegel quotation he heard from Heintel: "Art can only be conceived in terms of production, not consumption." Neither Hermann Czech nor I could verify this sentence as a quote. Czech's assumption that it could be an interpretation by Heintel is plausible. In any case, the formulation reflects a central feature of Hegel's entire philosophy, which the reader encounters at every turn in the introduction to his lectures on aesthetics—for example, in the following passages: According to Hegel, the art product is "only there in so far as it has taken its passage through the spirit and has arisen from spiritual productive activity." The same is true of scientific thinking. While scientific "production […] is active entirely in the element of pure thinking. In artistic production the spiritual and the sensuous aspects must be as one." (Georg Friedrich Wilhelm Hegel: *Vorlesungen über Ästhetik*. First Volume. Anniversary Edition, edited by Hermann Glockner, Vol. 12, 68 and 69). English translation by Bernard Bosanquet & W.M. Bryant in: Bosanquet; Bryant (eds): *Selections from Hegel's Lectures on Aesthetics*, The Journal of Speculative Philosophy, 1886; https://www.marxists.org/reference/archive/hegel/works/ae/introduction.htm (accessed January 31, 2021).

idea of the architect, which he sustains and carries through in the name of the autonomy of artistic creativity against the adversities of external conditions. For Czech, the idea on which the design is based is precisely not an idea that the architect had from the beginning and which he tries to translate into reality as directly as possible. According to Czech—as with Hegel—the thought is only really there at the end of a process, at the end of a series of decisions. At the beginning of the design process, the architect does not yet know everything about the thought he is about to realize. Rather, this is only really defined when a wide variety of questions that arise in the course of the design process have been answered.

We cannot imagine this series of decisions to be linear. It affects very different levels of the design process. Several levels are mentioned here as examples, firstly, the level of statics. When Gaudí was studying the dissipation of forces in vaults using hanging models, he was looking to answer fundamental questions about the statics of a building in new ways. His spectacular vaults are not only based on ingenious creativity, but on Gaudí's will to explore a central architectural problem with new methods. Karl Kraus described the Loos House on Michaelerplatz as a "thought." Czech takes this as a point of departure to show that not only Loos's spatial plan, but also his examination of historical architectural forms are essential components of the thought process with which this design thinks through architectural problems in a new way. A fine example from Czech's own work are the candelabra in the restaurant in the Schwarzenberg Palace, the design of which Czech impressively explains in the texts to which my considerations relate: namely as an attempt to rethink the lighting problem by dealing with the solutions that existed in the Baroque and were found in classicism and giving them a twist that meets the requirements of the specific building project in the 20th century.

In the production process of a design, quite different things are involved: dealing with static dependencies, with the formal language of historical architecture and its accomplishments in solving specific design problems, with the urban planning context and much more, but also motivations that the architect allows to flow into the design, discovering and working out their connections in the course of production. Hermann Czech: "Multi-layeredness: The planning approach cannot be one-dimensional—we can attain diversity 'if we allow all our motivations to flow into every design and follow up on all the ramifications and thought processes

2   My considerations are closely related to two texts by Hermann Czech: "Architektur, von der Produktion her gedacht," in: *Hintergrund* 41, Vienna 2009, 21–37, as well as "Architecture, Art of Consumption," trans. Kristina Galvez, quoted here according to Yehuda E. Safran (ed.): *Adolf Loos: Our Contemporary*, New York–Vienna 2012, 13–20. In order not to burden my preliminary and schematic considerations with an overly academic apparatus of references, I have only cited individual passages of these texts; I have summarized other motifs from them.

instead of sticking to some hare-brained recipe or hanging on to a shallow discipline'—or adopting a style."³ The "external conditions" and "banal requirements" such as the client's ideas, the building code requirements, the limits of the available budget… become part of the conceptual context in which the design ultimately consists. Beyond that, it will always contain elements the architect was not aware of during the design process and that will not be discovered by him afterwards, but by others. Because in a certain way the conceptual context is not finished with the completion of the built project: it can be spun on through the experiences that the "consumers" have with the building. Visitors to the Kleines Café, for example, can discover associative connections in the stone floor that arise from their own world of experience (animal skin, vagina…).

But in view of the interweaving of the design process with the most diverse motivations of the architect, as well as with external conditions and banal requirements, can one speak of an autonomy of the architect's decisions? And with what justification can these decisions be described as *rational*? Isn't this an overstretching of the term "rational"?

At first glance, Czech seems to use the term "rational" in a rather vague, relaxed way. At second glance, however, it becomes clear that his thinking about what he does as an architect is driven by an idea that has been decisive for European philosophy and its conception of the rational since ancient times. The philosopher Ernst Tugendhat calls this idea "radical accountability."⁴ Czech sees architecture as an "art of justification." It is not a question of a mere equality of words between the thinking of the philosopher and that of the architect. When asked, "Why did you do it like this, Mr. Architect? What were you thinking?," the architect states his reasons, thus making the thought that determined his decisions explicit.

For the language game of substantiated thought there are rules that have principally been valid in European philosophy since antiquity. We see two central points being consistently observed in Czech's considerations. The first rule of the game excludes justifications that are fundamentally withdrawn from intersubjective questioning. This rule, applied to architecture, has already been mentioned. It prohibits the architect from justifying the design by invoking the artist's creative power or the originality of his idea. Justifications of this kind ultimately amount to refusing the intersubjective justification of the design altogether. Of course, this refusal occurs today, as Czech observes, not only in this

3 Czech: "Architektur, von der Produktion her gedacht," op. cit., 23f. The main part of the quotation is from the essay "For a Change" (1973), trans. Elise Feiersinger, in: Czech 2019, 109–115: 115.
4 Ernst Tugendhat: "Antike und moderne Ethik (an Gadamers 80. Geburtstag)" (1980), in: idem: *Probleme der Ethik*, Stuttgart: Reclam, 1984, 41.

indirect form, i.e., in the form of referring to a source accessible only to the individual artist, but increasingly more directly and openly: In a time when star architecture reigns, the question about the justification of design decisions fits less and less in the concept: "[…] the response to the question 'Why?' is increasingly 'Why not?'"[5] The second rule in the game of rational justification consistently present in Czech's deliberations forbids the architect to rely on predetermined (philosophically speaking: determined by the will of others) purposes when justifying a design decision. Of course, that does not mean external purposes defined by others should not play a role in the design process; that would be absurd. Rather, it means that external purposes must not inadvertently come to the fore, but must be questioned about their justification. In the philosophical game of reasoning, only those purposes that we ourselves have acknowledged as well-founded are recognized as constitutive.

What I somewhat flippantly call a language game of substantiated thought here belongs to the basic structure of what was understood by rationality in European philosophy from Plato to Hegel. In order to be able to meet the demand for radical justification—of our theoretical convictions as well as our practical goals—Plato ultimately made recourse to transcendent, supra-historical ideas. By contrast, Hegel saw the justification in the development of thought itself. The thought is the result of a process in which the mind goes through a series of phases of overcoming external control towards self-determination and finally recognizes itself as this process—and thus pushes the claim of the substantiated reason of autonomy to extremes. The Hegelian interpretation of the radical (self-) justification of reason was decisive for Heintel's philosophy, and it seems to me that Hegel's philosophy—perhaps through Heintel's philosophy lectures, perhaps also through Sartre and Adorno—left its mark on Czech's thinking. If Czech describes the architectural idea as autonomous or, with reference to Stanford Anderson (and to Peter Eisenman, whom he cited) also as "self-referential," then this "self-reference" can be understood as a complex process of self-determination. As with Hegel, this self-determination is no different than going through the diverse external demands that an architectural design has to face. While the self-determination process takes place discursively in philosophy, in architecture it is a process of architectural form-finding. As in Hegel's philosophy, everything that the architect encounters and that is brought to his attention can and should

5 Czech: "Can Architecture Be Conceived by Way of Consumption?" (2011), trans. Elise Feiersinger, in: Czech 2019, 229–247: 231.

be included in this process—provided that he transforms it into an architectural form whose justification lies in the architectural thought that he develops for the respective concrete project.

Despite this proximity to Hegel's philosophy, Hermann Czech's conception of the autonomy of the design differs in essential points from the philosophy of the Hegelian Erich Heintel. While for Heintel Hegel's philosophy primarily led to the demand for an ultimately justified system of reason, the philosophical demand for autonomy takes on a different form in Czech's deliberations. By this I do not only mean that—as I said before—the philosophical-discursive process becomes a process of architectural design. I also think that Czech's demand for autonomous justification of architectural design is closer to modern philosophical approaches to radical accountability than Heintel's systematic thinking. The philosophical work of the aforementioned Ernst Tugendhat springs to mind here as an example.

Tugendhat's concept of "radical accountability" recognizes that we cannot always conclusively justify our concrete, situational judgments. From the point of view advocated by Tugendhat, what was said above also applies: that in the philosophical game of reasoning only those purposes are recognized as being substantiated which we ourselves have seen as well-founded. However, this demand does not contradict the concession "of a decisionist component" in our concrete judgments. For the "radicalized claim to justification" of modern philosophy (paradigmatically formulated by Kant) "merely demands that the status of the justification not be left indefinite. The conception that a judgment is not at all or only partially justifiable is a legitimate borderline case. Decisionism rests just as much on the foundation of autonomy as does rationalism."[6] Tugendhat has thought through the "radicalized claim to justification" for moral philosophy in ever new attempts. Proceeding from this, in his later writings on philosophical anthropology he introduced a concept of rationality that affects our theoretical judgments as well as our practical ones.

For Hermann Czech's notion of architecture as an "art of justification," Tugendhat's philosophical approach seems to me to be of interest because the architectural design concept also goes into elements that the architect cannot claim to be well-founded in themselves. As mentioned above, the architectural design also contains elements (e.g., of a psychological nature) of which the architect is not even aware. But more importantly: the design can also contain elements that the architect consciously and

6   Tugendhat: "Ancient and Modern Ethics," trans. Martin Livingston, in: Darrel E. Christensen (ed.) *Contemporary German Philosophy* Volume 4, University Park, PA: Pennsylvania State University Press, 1984, 39.

expressly considers to be ill-founded. He may, for instance, deem certain building code requirements to be incorrect and still have to observe them. In the conception of the modern (= radicalized) justification claim, as Tugendhat understands it, it is crucial "that the status of the justification" of our judgments "not be left indefinite" (and not to be a matter of looking for a final justification of the entire chain of reasoning). I think that here lies a surprising philosophical key to something that is characteristic of Hermann Czech's architecture and thinking: humor. There are always features in Czech's architecture that make me smile or laugh when I notice them or when my attention is drawn to them (which is much more often the case). I do not know how far the following consideration will go, but perhaps it would be worth trying to pursue it somewhat. Perhaps it is precisely those design decisions that make us laugh which express a tension in the design thought, consisting in the fact that (1) the elements going into the architectural thought have a different "status of justification" and that (2) the design unites conclusive, that is, well-founded thoughts. The "artistic feat" that translates this suspense into an architectural form and thus expresses it is often funny. (I do not know whether my associations fit here: I am thinking of the colored fragments of vaulted ribs in the "Wunder-Bar," the threshold of Galerie Hummel, the arrangement of the floor tiles in the Antiquariat Löcker, the winter glazing of the State Opera loggia or also because the chandeliers in the Schwarzenberg Restaurant became candelabras.)

The explanations that Czech gives to one of his housing projects fit well with what I mean: "This project of mine, dating back fifteen years, is located in a conservative community that seeks to mandate aesthetics through local building codes. But since my design does not believe in these rules, it interprets them both in a rational and efficient fashion. Users could not only request changes to the floor plans, but also to the façades: they could choose the size and position of each window within a larger structural opening — creating in this way a casual appearance through rational decisions. The design submits to the aesthetic local codes but sidesteps them at the same time, so that they fail in comparison to the reason-based advantages. I would like to call this 'critical kitsch.'"[7]

The question of how rational decisions can lead to an informal appearance was an issue for Czech early on.[8] And it runs as a central theme through his work. Here the most important architectural-historical reference point is probably Josef Frank, whose architectural

[7] Czech: "Can Architecture Be Conceived by Way of Consumption?" (2011), trans. Elise Feiersinger, in: Czech 2019, 229–247: 240.

[8] The question was already a topic for him at the Salzburg Summer Academy with Konrad Wachsmann, in which Czech participated in the late 1950s. See: "Architektur, von der Produktion her gedacht," op. cit., 25.

concept stands against the perseverance of abstract programmatic rules and for a modernism that wants to allow ambiguity and unpredictability. Josef Frank, who incidentally was the brother of the physicist and co-founder of the Vienna Circle, Philipp Frank, called his conception of modern architecture—"for the time being," as he said—"Accidentism." He wanted "to say that we should design our surroundings as if it they originated by chance."[9] One should probably take Josef Frank seriously and regard this term as a placeholder—not until a better one is found (Josef Frank was suspicious of the fashion of programmatic naming in any case), but until it is further considered how architecture that looks as if it had come about by chance can be designed. Hermann Czech's reflection on how an informal architectural appearance can arise on the basis of rational decisions seems to me to be going in precisely this direction. If I have understood correctly, one possible strategy for achieving this goal is that several levels, built according to certain systematic, rational principles, are placed in a non-systematic relationship with one another. This creates effects between the levels that are experienced as coincidental because they could not be planned as such by the architect (see, e.g., Czech's comments on Restaurant Ballhaus[10]). A kind of limbo arises, the creation of which depends on the fact that the interacting levels are precisely defined in themselves, as on the fact that their interaction is not subject to a uniform design principle.[11] Let us remember, the modernist notion of radical accountability in the Tugendhat sense does not demand that every decision be justified as part of an ultimately justified system. Rather, it requires that the justification status of the individual decisions is not left in the indefinite. It seems to me that precisely this condition is being fulfilled here. The tension between the rational definition and the unplannable effect (in which every building project is de facto inscribed) is consciously included in the architectural thought and made an issue.

Is there rationality in limbo? In fact, a large part of modern philosophical thought aimed at developing an idea of rationality that dispenses with ultimate justification—be it ontological or systematic thought. Even more sharply: It aimed to think of rationality as part of the *conditio humana*. And as such it can only be had in a state of limbo. This also applies to modern science. Otto Neurath, a prominent member of the Vienna Circle, compared science with sailors who can never bring their boat ashore to

9   Josef Frank: "Accidentism" (1958), trans. Christopher Long, in: Frank 2012, Vol. 2, 382–387.
10 As footnote 8, 24f.
11 An interview by Axel Simon about the 2015 Josef Frank exhibition shows that different levels of language can also be made to interact in the manner described. When asked: Why the title 'Against Design?', Czech replied: "'Against Design' can actually only be a German title (almost like a sentence containing 'Handy' [mobile phone] or 'Beamer' [projector]—words that do not exist in this context in English). Design has a much broader meaning in English than in German; in English one simply cannot be 'against design,' that would mean being against any goal or intention. The German meaning of 'design,' on the other hand, is abridged from the English *industrial* (or *product, fashion,* etc.) design. And that should be made suspicious as a culturally detached métier. — And, finally, the title has something of Paul Feyerabend's 'Against Method': to think concretely in the situation and not abstractly in terms of rules." "Frank war lässiger," in: *Hochparterre* 29/2016, Issue 3, 12–15.

fundamentally repair it.[12] They have to constantly rebuild it on the open sea and cannot be too choosy about the overhaul: material washed up by chance has to serve, as well as parts that have already been discarded. What a conception of rationality that expressly accepts the unsecured aspect of the *conditio humana* as the ultimate basis means for moral philosophy is Tugendhat's main theme. While explicitly renouncing any absolute justification of moral demands (including Kant's categorical imperative), he differentiates between a narrower and a broader area of practical questions. In the narrower field, the binding nature of moral judgments can be inferred from the fact that they are justified by demands that we all mutually juxtapose ("symmetrical contractualism"). In the broader area of the practically good, on the other hand, it is only about "good reasons, how to live well or better."[13] But even in the narrower field of morality, which is about getting to the nitty-gritty of ethics (such as justice, including human rights), the binding nature of the reasons is hypothetical and not categorical. Because we cannot demand of others to justify their moral judgments in the sense of "symmetrical contractualism." This is based on the conviction that traditional (mostly religious) or metaphysical (that is, referring back to a given order of being) reasons for our actions since the Enlightenment are no longer sustainable and, therefore, moral judgments are ultimately justifiable solely on the relationship between people—i.e., autonomously. But precisely this conviction cannot be demanded. Tugendhat: "To see oneself as a member of that moral community that is neither traditionally nor metaphysically justified, but in the manner of a symmetrical contractualism, is, for its part, only one possibility for which there are good reasons."[14]

The decisions made during the production of an architectural design belong neither to science nor to moral philosophy. But the architect can claim rational justification for them. Why should he do that? What are the advantages? In fact, at the end of his essay "Kann Architektur von der Konsumtion her gedacht werden?" ("Can Architecture Be Conceived by Way of Consumption?"), Hermann Czech gives his considerations a twist that could be understood as an attempt to provide good reasons why the architect should see the design as "the outcome […] achieved through conclusive deliberation," as "the productive series of design decisions" that are justified within the architecture and can thus be deemed autonomous.

12 Neurath's "parable of the sailors" was an important point of reference for Paul Feyerabend (see the previous footnote).
13 Tugendhat: "Anthropologie als 'erste Philosophie,'" in: idem: *Anthropologie statt Metaphysik*, Munich 2007, 50.
14 Ibid.

First, Czech takes a step back, as it were, to engage in a game of thought that reverses his previous considerations a little bit: Wouldn't it be possible to think of architecture from the perspective of "consumption"? In other words: Wouldn't it be possible to think of the architect's activity—following Gernot Böhme—as surrendering to an atmosphere, a perception of the "consumer"? Of course: even if the architect behaves passively towards his task, insofar as he undertakes it from the outside (e.g., to create a certain "atmospheric impression" that can be sold well at the given time), he cannot, according to Czech, avoid the practical production question: "'*How can I achieve the intended effect?*' Or even more to the point: '*Which means and which of their effects are at my disposal?*'"[15] At the latest at the point where practical questions about the production of the design come up, rationality catches up with the architect: He cannot help but ask himself why the desired atmosphere can be achieved with these architectural means rather than those. The architect cannot evade his autonomous responsibility at all. Or is there another approach?

"Even if the most delicate architectural effects are contingent upon self-referential decisions, the most rarefied design motivation is derived from production unless we were to decide to adopt a different approach. How could that be articulated in architectural terms? Only by renouncing any form of genuine communication. Viewing consumers as a means to an end involves placing them on the lowest level. A semi-consciousness that distances itself from its own production is thereby created which is only intended to be bought and sold, but is in principle superior to it and thus does not feel responsible for it."[16]

So, an alternative approach to the conscious "art of justification" of autonomous architectural decisions is actually conceivable. According to Czech, this would, of course, consist in renouncing "any form of genuine communication." How is that to be understood? — Here, too, the demand not to regard the consumer as a means to an end (a core demand of Kant's ethics of Enlightenment) plays an important role. We have already encountered it in a modified form in the places where Czech referred to Sartre, Adorno and Horkheimer. There it concerned the architect not being allowed to "move" the consumer in a calculating way and thus make him unfree. In the passage just cited, however, it becomes clear that the moral-philosophical requirement that the consumer should not be viewed as a means to an end stands for respect for the freedom of the consumer as well

---

15 Czech: "Architecture, Art of Consumption," trans. Kristina Galvez, in: Yehuda E. Safran (ed.): *Adolf Loos: Our Contemporary*, New York–Vienna 2012, 13–20: 19.
16 Ibid., 19f.

as for the architect's design activity. An architect who puts the consumer on a lower level is not so much making a moral mistake as he is damaging his relationship with his own work; because he misses the chance to gain as full an awareness of his design as possible. The contempt for the consumer is reflected in the above-quoted "semi-consciousness that distances itself from its own production […] but is in principle superior to it and thus does not feel responsible for it."

Proceeding from here, some "good reasons" that speak for the architect placing his design activity under the requirement of autonomous intellectual justification can—allusively and tentatively—crystallize. As Czech has already said: The architect can never completely escape the demand for a rational justification of the design anyway, because he always has to make decisions about the means that should lead to the goal he has in mind. Hard to imagine that an architect would deny this. It is very conceivable, however, that an architect perceives these types of practical decisions to be located on a subordinate level (he could borrow the term "merely instrumental rationality" from philosophy), while he sees the architectural idea he wants to realize with these means on a fundamentally different, higher level. Interpreted in this way, the design idea would basically be defined in advance and independently of the specific production decisions: be it through the genius of the architect, or through the interests of a client who thinks he can sell well in a certain atmosphere. In both cases, the rational justification would be limited to the realm of the instrumental. "Genuine communication" would not take place since the means for realizing the design idea would be subject to the process of rational justification, but not the architectural conception, which the architect is concerned with. — But let's return to the question: What speaks in favor of the conception itself being subjected to the claim of "radical accountability?" Or, to put it more pointedly: How does the architect benefit from placing his designing activity under this requirement? Or, to put it the other way round: What does he forego if he does not do this?

Against the background of what has been said so far, we can see a bit better what the renunciation of "any form of genuine communication" would imply. It is important to note that what Czech understands by this does not only take place where the architect explains to the client, the consumer or the audience of an exhibition opening, how his design decisions are justified. In a certain way, "genuine communication" takes place during the entire design process, namely whenever the architect asks himself in which architectural-conceptual mold he has to pour the "external conditions and banal requirements" that approach him so that he can assume architectural and intellectual responsibility for them. Refraining from this communication would deprive him of the most important instrument to pursue his "most rarefied design motivation." But if he engages in genuine communication, he embarks on a journey that allows him to further discover his design and at the same time his own motivation. If, for example, he takes his client so seriously that he implements his change requests in a form that incorporates these requests into the coherent architectural thought process, he will discover possibilities in his design that he was previously unaware of. (Perhaps one example of this is the design of the plinth façade of the Messehotel.) Ultimately, each of the diverse and complex requirements (of the technical, urban planning, social, economic… type) that every specific design task entails confronts the architect with a chance for "genuine communication" and the discoveries enabled through it.

    We can also see this journey as a research trip, and it is—we already know—not limited to the present. It also opens up the inexhaustible wealth of historical architecture to the architect, in which every design is inscribed. However, it does not reveal this wealth as a collection of arbitrary motifs that are available free of charge, so to speak, but as examples of how very specific architectural problems have been solved under specific historical conditions. The historical problem situations must first be reconstructed; attempts to solve them, as well as successful and unsuccessful answers, must be thought through so that the wealth these examples contain can be exploited in general. In this way, historical architecture can—more precisely: genuine communication with historical architecture can—lead the architect beyond individually and contemporary available "creativity." It can extend the scope of the architecturally possible beyond the imaginable of his own time. And it can sharpen the architect's view of the demands placed on him by his own era—to the point at which his most fundamental motivations are pushed to their limits: "This is the question that I submit: Equipped with the theoretical trappings of a discursive Modernism, can critical design potential also be achieved with the strategies referred to as 'branding,' 'theming' or 'imagineering?' Is it even possible in such contexts to cast consumers not as merely a means to an end, but as recipients of something genuine, even if it is cynical in nature?"[17]

17 Ibid., 19.

Postscript:

I thank Eva Kuss for inviting me to contribute an essay to her book. It enabled me to take a few steps myself on a journey of discovery through the relationships between philosophy and architecture in the work of Hermann Czech. I would like to thank Hermann Czech for information and additions that have significantly enriched this text. I would like to thank Volker Thurm-Nemeth for familiarizing me with the architecture of our time over many years. His high appreciation for the work of Hermann Czech has accompanied me for a long time and has influenced all my thoughts on it. I thank Herbert Hrachovec for very helpful comments on an earlier version of this essay.

Selected Projects

Restaurant Ballhaus
with Wolfgang Mistelbauer and Reinald Nohàl

Period of origin: 1961–1962
Address: Schauflergasse 5, 1010 Vienna
Client: Josef Czech
(demolished)

Josef Hoffmann: Wallpaper design "Leipzig," 1913

1 Czech: "Restaurant Ballhaus. Einrichtung eines Lokals in der Amalienburg, Wien 1962" (March 1963), unpublished, Czech Archive. Quote published in: Ulrike Jehle-Schulte-Strathaus: "'In welchem Style sollen wir bauen?' Gedanken zur Stil-losigkeit von Hermann Czech," *wbw* 6/1996: 21, as well as in: Achleitner: "Franks Weiterwirken in der neueren Wiener Architektur," in: UM BAU 10, 1986, 121–131: 125. English translation in: Jehle-Schulte-Strathaus: "'In welchem Style sollen wir bauen?'...," *wbw* 6/1996: 21.

When designing Restaurant Ballhaus, Czech, Mistelbauer and Nohàl applied the Konrad Wachsmann method of working with a list of parameters. But while Wachsmann mainly put together organizational and structural points (such as "construction," etc.) for the individual groups of participants in the seminars at the Summer Academy in Salzburg, the Czechian list also included categories such as light, sound, climate, but also: perception, attention, associations.

The architects used templates (chairs, wallpaper, fabric covers) from Josef Hoffmann for the furnishings. "The intention was not so much to furnish the restaurant as Josef Hoffmann would have done it at any specific time, but rather to provide the restaurant with strong characteristics by demarcable means."[1]

Czech's notebook from 1962 contains reflections on the analogy of music and architecture: Just as music reverses the time series in the repetition, the spatial effect of architecture in gravitation is just as "reversible." With regard to Restaurant Ballhaus, this consideration found expression in the addition and the illusion of continuation of the oval of the vaulted ceiling: the spaces of the restaurant became a continuous cylinder through wallpapered surfaces, which obscured the flow of gravity defined from top to bottom.

During this time, Czech was also dealing with color theory and color systems. In Restaurant Ballhaus only black, white, gray and the six colors of the traditional color wheel were used. The chosen wallpapers had a two-tone floral pattern kept in black and white (like the original) and in several combinations of primary colors (red on yellow, blue on yellow).

Based on a design by Josef Hoffmann, the chairs were unusual pieces of furniture with a hole in the middle of the seat that produced a different seating experience with the slightest movement and were chosen "because of [their] decorative and downright comical effect".[2] The chairs for Restaurant Ballhaus were reconstructed and modified in color based on historical photos.[3] The fabric covers—likewise based on Josef Hoffmann—were executed again in black and white and in two different color combinations, namely in the mixed primary colors green-orange and green-violet.

Depending on the type of wall papering, its coloring and the color of the chair covers, each room received its own atmosphere as a variant of the continuous character, with the wallpaper pattern being strongest in the rearmost room and the seat cover colored.

Since his training at the Film Academy, Hermann Czech had been interested in light, its effects and precise use. In the text "Mehr Licht" ("More Light"), he thought about an architecture "whose effect is not based on its building design, but on its lighting conditions," and which would be able "to change

2 Czech: ibid.
3 Designs by Josef Hoffmann used: wallpaper design "Leipzig" 1913 (reprinted with the original model in three shades), fabric design 1907 (rewoven in four shades), chair from Lengyel Bratislava 1930 (reconstructed from photos), stool from the business furniture shop Beyer Vienna 1940 (reconstructed inaccurately from photos), book decorations from *Ver Sacrum* 1898.

Candles also glare when they are the only sources of light. In this candleholder, the light from the candle flame, which wanders down when it burns, is solely reflected onto the table.

its effects without having to move the material."[4] For the lighting, Czech, Mistelbauer and Nohàl projected office grid lights that evenly illuminated the space and immersed it in a glare-free, shadowless light. In order to achieve freedom from glare, the lamps were shielded at an angle of 60 degrees instead of the 30 to 45 degrees that are normally used for the uniform illumination of offices.[5] Candles in a glare-free candleholder designed by Czech were also planned for evening use.

Hermann Czech mentions French director François Truffaut's black-and-white film *Jules et Jim*, which was produced using high-key technology, as a reference for the lighting mood.[6] The film tells of a friendship between two men who fall in love with the same woman, with the story ending in a strangely emotionless catastrophe. Partly shadowless, partly executed with extreme shadows, the slight overexposure gives the entire film a surreal and melancholy atmosphere that does not allow any sentimentality to arise. Only brief cuts from "reality"—scenes from the First World War or a book burning in already Nazi Germany—deviate from this basic mood.

A comparable lighting atmosphere is atypical for a restaurant; everything is far too bright, nothing is concealed. Instead of sentimental "Viennese coziness," a piece of Viennese cultural history was emotionlessly bathed in a bright light. According to Czech, the restaurant was "not a hit"[7] and too bright by Viennese standards. The reactions of colleagues like

4 Czech: "Mehr Licht" (1964), in: Czech 1996, 19–21: 19.
5 The lamp was designed together with Rudolf Gschnitzer, an employee of the Bartenbach company in Innsbruck.
6 High-key describes a type of lighting in photography in which soft light, bright colors and low contrasts predominate. The images are slightly overexposed.
7 Interview of June 12, 2009, when going through his notebooks from 1962/63.

Reconstruction of a chair from 1929, cover with a modified, rewoven fabric design from 1907 (reprinted wallpaper from 1913 in the room)—all designs by Josef Hoffmann, which he would never have combined.

After a change of ownership, the holes were papered over with reserve fabric, a copy was given to the MAK as a Hoffmann original after years and even shown—with the papered hole—in a Hoffmann exhibition worldwide in the 1980s.

Friedrich Achleitner, Friedrich Kurrent,[8] Johannes Spalt and Ottokar Uhl were reserved and ranged from "you can't do that" to "It is not Hoffmann, but also not something different." However, other people from the art scene such as Peter Kubelka, Kurt Moldovan, Konrad Bayer and Raimund Abraham appreciated Restaurant Ballhaus.

The approach of Czech, Mistelbauer and Nohàl shows parallels to the work of the English architect couple Peter and Alison Smithson (who Czech first got to know in the mid-1960s). The Smithsons coined the term *as found* in the 1950s: "In architecture, the 'as found' aesthetic was something we thought we named in the early 1950s when we first knew Nigel Henderson and saw in his photographs a perceptive recognition of the actuality around his house in Bethnal Green: children's pavement play-graphics; repetitions of 'kind' in doors used as site hoardings; the items in the detritus on bombed sites, such as the old boot, heaps of nails, fragments of sack or mesh and so on. Setting ourselves the task of rethinking architecture in the early 1950s, we meant by the 'as found' not only adjacent buildings but all those marks that constitute remembrancers [sic] in a place and that are there to be read through finding

8 In a letter to Hermann Czech from 2006, Friedrich Kurrent once again commented on the design of Restaurant Ballhaus, citing it as the first example of "Viennese mannerism" in architecture after the Second World War. He remembers that he and Spalt would have very well dealt with the "buried Austrian modernism," but never had the idea of using or recreating "parts of the past, of the treasured." That is why the design of this restaurant in 1961 marked "a new, previously unknown step." 45 years later, Kurrent cannot resist adding the word "back?" in brackets and closing the letter with his own quotation "Every mannerism is weaker than the real thing." Letter from Kurrent to Czech, 2006, Czech Archive.

out how the existing built fabric of the place had come to be as it was. […] As soon as architecture begins to be thought about its ideogram should be so touched by the 'as found' as to make it specific-to-place. […] All of this was an intellectual activity, extending to a care for 'literacy' in the language of architecture. We worked with a belief in the gradual revealing by a building-in-formation of its own rules for its required form."[9]

Czech, Mistelbauer and Nohàl also worked with *as found* elements at Restaurant Ballhaus, but did not use everyday things, but products from Viennese architectural history. They did not choose these to furnish a restaurant in the spirit of Josef Hoffmann, but to achieve a certain effect.

Analogies to approaches Czech knew and valued exist here, for example, that of Adolf Loos, who set up the coffeehouses he designed with modifications of the bentwood chairs that were quite common at the time. And just as Karl Kraus processed original quotes from various origins in *Die letzten Tage der Menschheit*, the wiener gruppe experimented in its poems and performances, namely the "literary cabarets" with found elements such as passages from grammar books. In continuation of this "tradition," Peter Weibel and his Hotel Morphila Orchestra "performed" the dubious contact ads of the tabloids in a rap song in the 1970s.

9 Alison and Peter Smithson: "The 'As Found' and the 'Found,'" in: Claude Lichtenstein; Thomas Schregenberger (eds.): *As Found. The Discovery of the Ordinary. British Architecture and Art of the 1950s*, 2001, 40–41.

The architects of Restaurant Ballhaus treated the selected designs blithely and put them in a completely new context. This technique is similar to that of montage, in which various parts in a changed context result in a new, different, but again coherent image. As with the Smithsons, the objective here was to make elements no longer consciously remembered or perceived visible in new contexts, whereby the historical context in London was completely different from that in Vienna, where its own tradition of modernism remained unappreciated and still largely forgotten at the beginning of the 1960s.

Modifying a quote from Adolf Krischanitz that Czech's work looked "like having come home from a war,"[10] one could say that Restaurant Ballhaus transported a certain language without any nostalgia, a piece of fin de siècle culture, which, although with a few wounds, would have nonetheless survived two wars after all. It is possible that this painful look at what is there, and, at the same time, at what is missing, is the reason why this first work was not well received by Czech's colleagues. For him, however, this view of "the existent" becomes a focus of his designs and texts, leading him to formulate in 1973: "Transforming an existing building is more interesting than building a new one—because, in essence, everything is transformation."[11]

10 Krischanitz describes the intensive, self-critical examination of Czech's way of working in contrast to other architects, whose examination he compares with an "adventure holiday."

11 Czech: "For a Change" (1973), trans. Elise Feiersinger, in: Czech 2019, 109–115: 114.

Transformation Summer House Nussdorf

Period of origin: 1968–1969
Address: Hackhofergasse 39, 1190 Vienna
Client: Josef Czech

The Summer House in Nussdorf is the conversion of an existing four-by-four-meter house in a garden that Czech's father had rented. Czech places the two levels in open connection with one another via a curved staircase. The ground floor serves as a kitchen-living room, the top floor as a bedroom with a bathroom. A stainless-steel bathtub, inset between the ceiling beams, is visible downward, while a tub-shaped, transparent acrylic glass dome protrudes from the steep gable roof above the bathtub. On the living floor, Czech enlarged the existing openings to create a band of foldable window elements. The floor in the sleeping area is completely covered with mattresses. From there one steps onto a balcony, a kind of gangplank, offering a spectacular view over the Danube. The construction is chosen so that both the ceiling beams and the side rail of the railing are independent, freely cantilevered supports. The wooden elements inside (beams, stairs, windowsills) are painted red—according to Loos, the strongest of the "absolute, unbroken" colors. arbeitsgruppe 4 also used this color in the Kolleg St. Josef.

The upper part of the terrain on which the house stands is extremely steep; the new access is from the lower property boundary via a straight concrete staircase with the unusual rise-to-run ratio of 20 to 30 centimeters. The width of the steps makes it easier to walk in winter without having to shovel all the snow away. To the side of the house, Czech erected a round, brick-built basement room above which a terrace area with a shower is arranged on the ground floor.

This small first conversion contains elements Hermann Czech will use again and again in residential construction: the stairs[1] wound around a support, the window set at a right angle around the corner, the round (later also oval) window (in this case "only" a mirror which is very present in the section) and accentuated colors.

---

1 The author uses the German word "Stiege" here, pointing out that "Stiege" is the Austrian word for "Treppe" in High German. "Stiege" in Austrian German means a short, steep "staircase" or open staircase in representative buildings. In High German it is the other way round.

Children's room, Klemmer Apartment, 1972–1973

2 Czech; Mistelbauer: *Das Looshaus*, self-published as a reproduction in 1968.

While working on the Summer House, Czech and Mistelbauer were just finishing their study of the House on Michaelerplatz by Adolf Loos,[2] who, like Josef Frank, had used staircases around vertical pillars. The staircase in combination with pillars is the further development of a classic element that Loos and Frank, for their part, had already further developed. Thus, the older Fischer von Erlach used a combination of supports and stairs in representative staircases: In a conversation, Czech mentioned the main staircase in Prince Eugene's Winter Palace, where the corner (turning) points are formed by Atlas figures, i.e., anthropomorphic supports.

A combination of pointed and parallel steps, the staircase in the Summer House Nussdorf turns around a square "support," the cavity of which is used as a chute for dirty laundry.

Czech also worked on this type of staircase for the Klemmer children's room (1972–1973), and House M. was even developed entirely around such a staircase that varied on each floor.

The window placed at a right angle can be found in Josef Hoffmann's structures and in Viennese municipal housing; it increasingly became a modernist attribute (which is quoted again in House M. itself). In

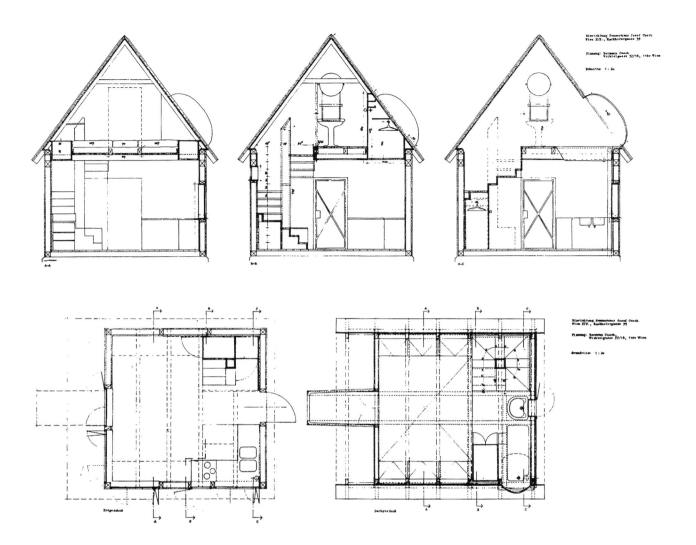

the Summer House, Czech exposed the wooden structure and made the structural logic of the house visible. A serious reference for this is Ernst A. Plischke's house on Lake Attersee, featuring, in the sense of classical modernism, a ribbon of windows leading around the corner of the building.

Oval or round windows are found in buildings of many protagonists of Viennese modernism: Adolf Loos (Villa Karma, House Nothartgasse),

On the new stairway, the shower and terrace stand above the ceiling of a storage room.

Josef Frank (Villa Beer, drafts of fantasy houses) and Josef Hoffmann (Ast Country House, Klosehof residential complex, house in the Werkbundsiedlung). Le Corbusier also used oval windows for Villa Schwob (1912) in La Chaux-de-Fonds.

In contrast to (later) international modernist projects, however, it cannot be seen as a reference of the Viennese architects to ship architecture, but rather goes back to older models such as the oval windows in many Viennese houses from the Baroque era. They can be found in Fischer von Erlach's St. Charles Church, the Court Library, the Schönborn-Batthyány Palace or the Bohemian Court Chancellery.

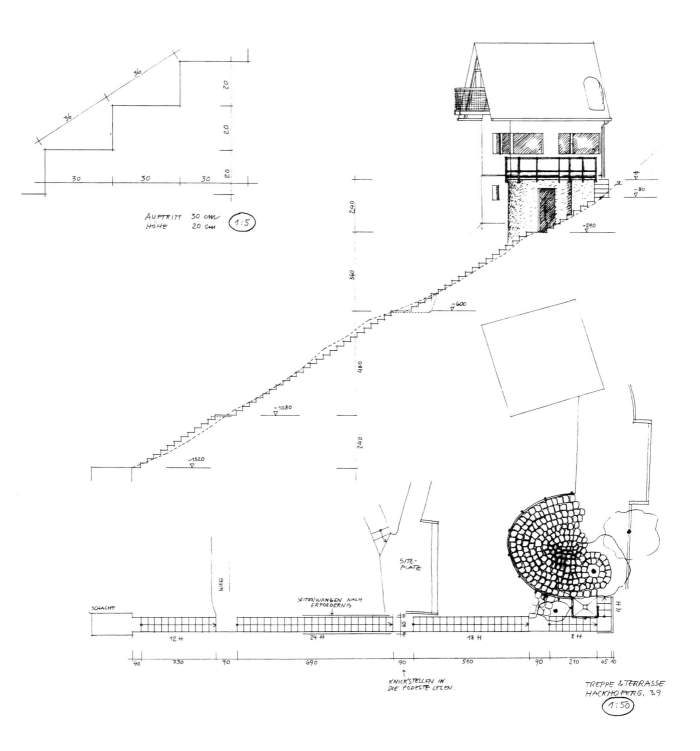

Wall covering not original

Hermann Czech later set oval or circular windows in nearly all private residential buildings (additions to Villa Pflaum, House M., House S., the Oetker or Günthergasse lofts). In the Summer House there is a rectangular window on the rear gable wall directly above the washbasin and above it a large round mirror as the first, still abstracted variant of this element.

In the text "Das prinzip der bekleidung" ("The Principle of Cladding"), Loos formulated the "law" on the use of materials: "we must work in such a way that a confusion of the material clad with its cladding is impossible. That means, for example, that wood may be painted any color except one—the color of wood."[3] Loos particularly criticized the practice at the time of making cheaper wood look "like mahogany" and praised the tram cars bought from England as a positive counter-example in which the wood appeared in its pure color. He went on to say: "Wood staining is, of course, an invention of our century. The Middle Ages painted wood bright red for the most part, the Renaissance blue; the Baroque and Rococo painted interiors white, exteriors green."[4]

In Czech's Summer House, individual components are highlighted in different colors depending on the material. Windows and doors made of iron are painted in pale ocher, windowsills, the staircase and beams made of wood in a very strong red. There are also elements in their own materiality: the stainless-steel bathtub, the handrail grips on the stairs, the transparent plastic bubble above the bathtub. The flooring on the first floor is laid out with light gray carpeting.

3   Loos: "The Principle of Cladding" (1898), in: Loos: *Spoken into the Void: Collected Essays 1897–1900*, trans. Jane O. Newman and John H. Smith, 66–69: 67.
4   Ibid., 68.

Selected Projects

In summary, two essential concepts typical of Czech can be found during his first conversion: a structural level, which is about a logical, rational type of construction and the use of materials (window, balcony, bathtub), and a historical one through which the Viennese architectural tradition is continued and further processed via references (staircase, use of color). Frank follows this logic, saying: "Our time is all of history, as it is known to us. This notion alone can be the basis of modern architecture."[5]

With regard to the history of architecture in Vienna, Czech followed Frank, who named Gottfried Semper, Theophil Hansen, Eduard van der Nüll, Otto Wagner, Josef Olbrich, Josef Hoffmann and Adolf Loos as the "Viennese development" and stated: "They created works that led in straight succession to the architecture of the present day. Vienna need only to uphold this tradition—in contrast to other countries, which must abandon theirs."[6]

Shortly before the Summer House existed as a specific conversion project, Czech had sketched a house for his father in 1968. This house as a minimal apartment in conventional, solid construction, combined with a large, open, variable space, was to consist of a pneumatic, tensile structure. "Depending on their value, the small spaces of the conventional construction open up into the large ones, which represent their expansion, supplementation (possibly covering the entire property)."[7]

---

[5] Frank: *Architecture as Symbol* (1931), trans. John Sands, in: Frank 2012, Vol. 2, 9–191: 161. Czech used this quote in "A Conceptual Matrix for the Current Interpretation of Josef Frank" (1985), trans. Elise Feiersinger, in: Czech 2019, 151–182: 160.

[6] Frank: "Vienna's Modern Architecture to 1914" (1926), trans. Elise Feiersinger, in: Frank 2012, Vol. 1, 268–276: 277. Czech used this quote in: "A Conceptual Matrix…," op. cit., 152.

[7] House for J. C. (March 1968), unpublished. Sketch with text, Czech Archive.

Kleines Café

Period of origin: 1970/1973 – 1974/1977/1985
Address: Franziskanerplatz 3, 1010 Vienna
Client: Hans Neuffer (1970), later Hanno Pöschl

Kleines Café I, 1970

Czech's redesign of the original Kleines Café, a space of around 27 m² previously used as a tavern, essentially consisted of two interventions: the introduction of a classic cornice profile and the use of a double mirror effect in the seating area.

The approach of creating a characteristic with already existing form elements can also be found in Czech's second venue design, but more differentiated than in the first, Restaurant Ballhaus. In the decade in between lay the change from the Technical University to the Plischke Master School at the Academy of Fine Arts, as well as the occupation with constructive (e.g., retractable roof over the Graben, retractable roof over a courtyard in Mödling), urban-structural (e.g., urban renewal, subway network design), historical (e.g., Adolf Loos, Josef Frank) and theoretical (e.g., functionalism and current critique of utopianism) aspects of architecture. With this design, he once again opposed all existing camps, however contradictory they appeared: The discerning architectural scene in Vienna in 1970 agreed that no classic cornice should be used.

In 20th-century Vienna, the use of classic building forms always remained present as a possibility. Besides Adolf Loos, who also often used them as "complex and contradictory"[1]—this is analyzed in detail in Czech and Mistelbauer's monograph *Das Looshaus*—Josef Frank thematized them in *Architecture as Symbol* as the only ones that are accessible to everyone.[2] In his dissertation on the churches of Alberti, he declared that Alberti was a founder of the modern style through his way of using Roman motifs.[3]

1 Czech; Mistelbauer: *Das Looshaus*, 1976, 113.
2 Frank: *Architecture as Symbol* (1931), trans. John Sands, in: Frank 2012, Vol. 2, 9–191: 23.
3 Josef Frank's dissertation: *On the Original Form of the Religious Buildings of Leone Battista Alberti* (1910), trans. Mark Gilbert, in: Frank 2012, Vol. 1, 47–119, as well as 318.

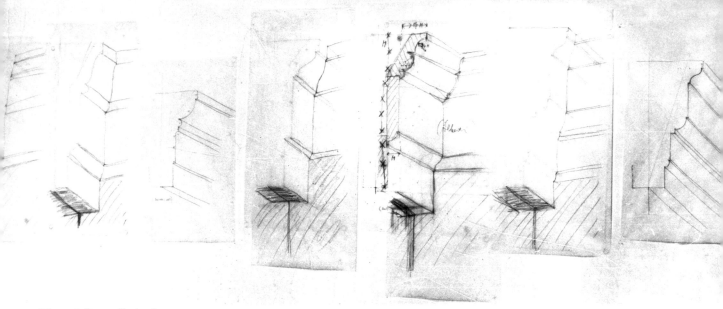

Kleines Café I, profile sketches

When deciding on the cornice profile in Kleines Café I, the choice likewise goes to Alberti: "To imitate a stone cornice profile in wood already creates a kind of ironical distance, so the (originally intended) use of this Palladio profile—which already shows mannered distortions—would have had an effect similar to a stage-set type profile."[4]

The ceiling of the space consists of two unequal cross vaults, divided by a transverse arch on pillars (the ground floor dates from the 16th century). The inserted cornice profile is bent at the height of the vault around these wall corners—this is the height at which one can still comfortably place a glass while standing—an informal comfort for those guests not standing directly at the bar, but do not consider their location as a regular standing place and therefore pay attention to people passing by them.

For the Kleines Café, Czech adopted motifs that had proven themselves in everyday life in a Viennese restaurant. Wood-paneled walls up to door height, sometimes pictures above, round or rectangular stone plates with cast-iron feet as tables, light wooden chairs with and without armrests, at times also stools, benches on walls or in niches, covered with striped or otherwise patterned plush, and globe lamps as lighting fixtures are typical Viennese coffee house features. The glossy oil paint on the

4 Czech: "Kleines Café (I)," Vienna 1970, unpublished, Czech Archive. English translation in: Ulrike Jehle-Schulte-Strathaus: "'In welchem Style sollen wir bauen?' Gedanken zur Stillosigkeit von Hermann Czech," *wbw* 6/1996, 19.

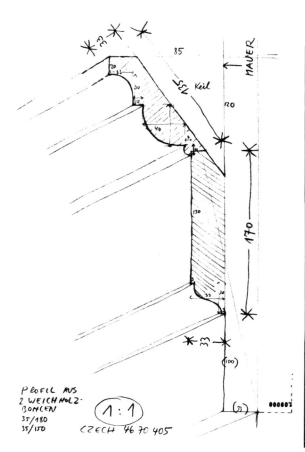

ceilings and walls above the paneling is a motif that Czech had come across in English pubs. He also left existing elements such as the double-winged, inner-glazed entrance door at Kleines Café I.

Wood, also painted glossy, served as the main material. The different colors in Kleines Café I—some of which were already used in the existing building—were to become typical for Czech: light red-orange, a pink tending towards beige, but above all a dark wine-red and a turquoise-gray. While the pure primary colors of the color wheel were strictly chosen for Restaurant Ballhaus, those of the Kleines Café are quite intense, but difficult to name and clearly attribute; they stand back as a matter of course. The "turquoise-gray" of the cornice is perceived as green by some visitors and blue by others.

Exit to the hallway toilet with swing doors and the shape of the steps responding to it (state 1977–1985)

In addition to the role colors play in the color wheel or color space, their positional relationship and combination effect, Czech speaks in an interview in 2006 of another role of color in architecture: "A color can simply vanish into the object. This is easiest to imagine with a material color but, through associations or habits, it can occur that a color paint is no longer seen as such because one is so accustomed to its use in a certain context. This is what interests me: where the color does not stand out but the object or material simply is this color. That colors exist while at the same time they are destroyed is something that is possible in architecture—it's interesting that you don't remember colors in the Kleines Café, etc. If, for example, a glazing bar has a familiar color, I don't see the color at all, but the color merges into the glazing bar, on account of habit."[5]

5 Czech: "Nein, um Gottes Willen, keinen Bezug zum Wein." Interview by Christoph Mayr Fingerle, in: wein.kaltern Gen.m.b.H. (ed.): *PUNKT*, 2006, self-published. English translation in: "Wine House PUNKT," in: *Architecture and Urbanism* 16:11,118.

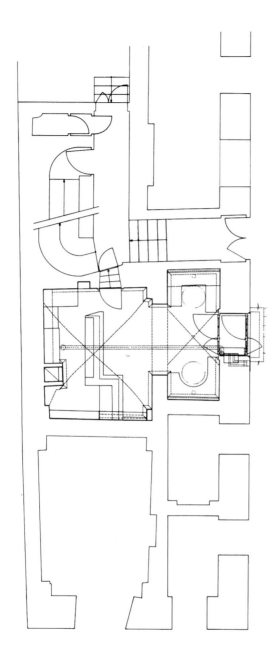

Kleines Café I, 1970. Each of the ground floor venues of the 16th century usually has a single opening—a door and a window at the same time.

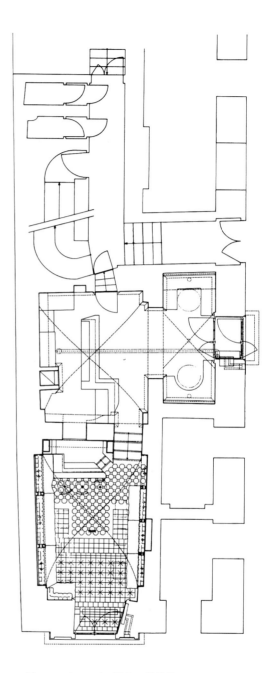

The extension to the Kleines Café II connects the two largest venues, 1973–1974.

Selected Projects

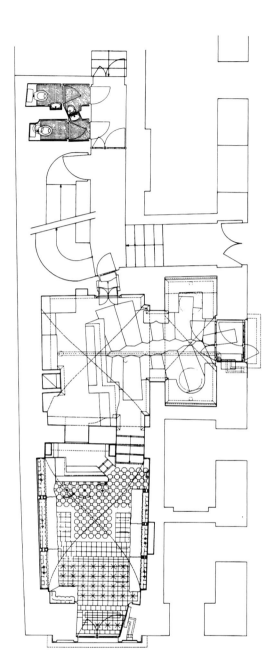

Floor in the first space, 1977

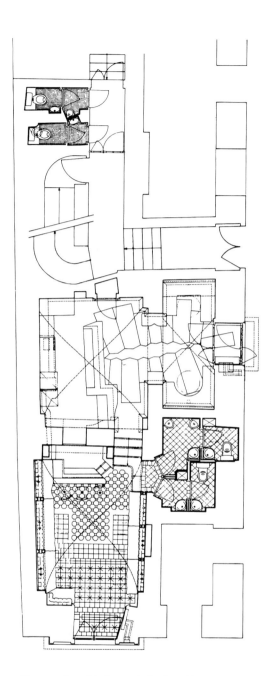

The extension with the attached toilet adds one of the small venues, but eliminates an alley portal, 1985.

Kleines Café II, Extension 1973–1974

In 1973, the Kleines Café was expanded to include a former butcher's shop with an entrance from Franziskanerplatz. The floor of the gained space is, like the square, around 60 centimeters higher than the floor of the existing café, but the vault—both vertex and transom height—continues in the same position, resulting in a more "squeezed" space. This gave rise to the basic concept of adding a "sit-down café" to the "stand-up café." "Almost all visual information is concentrated in a zone below eye level to induce people to sit down. The standing barkeeper also remains at the eye level of those seated as a result of the difference of floor levels."[6] The few years also resulted in an "age shift: those who stood in the past now sometimes want to sit down after all."[7]

The new space is almost rectangular (the side walls are not really parallel) and is spanned by a groin vault, which rests on pillars in all corners, so that the walls in between are set back under the vault and each form a flat niche. The benches are placed along the side walls in the depth of the niche; mirrors are mounted above the backrests, but above the heads of the seated people the niches are closed by what appears to be a solid wall unit that serves as storage space.

Floor plan with the reflection of the pillars and lamps

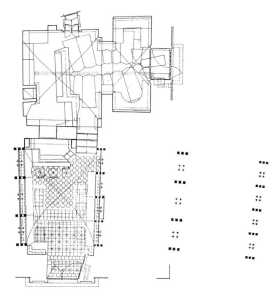

6   Czech: "Wien 1 Franziskanerplatz," in: *Bauwelt* 43/1975, 1206. English translation in: "Kleines Café," in: *Architecture and Urbanism* 16:11, 114–117: 114.
7   Ibid. (German text)

Through the mirroring above the benches, each side wall appears to be broken through in the doubled depth of the niche. This "breakthrough" in each side wall is divided into longitudinal fields by supporting pillars. The pillars are arranged in pairs, one behind the other: one at the front, free-standing with a square cross-section, and one just behind on the mirrored wall with a half cross-section. Together with the mirror image, there are three free-standing, square pillars, one behind the other, on which the wall appears to rest, with open fields between the groups of pillars in which the benches stand. "The complete system of columns and cables is created by reflection."[8] On the eastern side there are four smaller, equal fields (it is the side constricted by the position of the entrances), on the western side there are three larger, unequal ones, in "classic" division: a large field in the middle and two smaller fields on the side. The benches in the smallest fields, namely those on the "regular" side, offer space for two people each, the larger ones on the "classic" side hold three people, the largest in between four, creating a quieter seating

8 Czech: "Kleines Café," in: *Architecture and Urbanism* 16:11, 114–117: 114.

Kleines Café

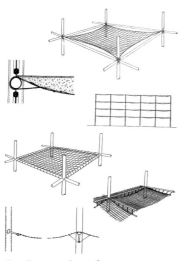

Frei Otto: tensile reinforcements in concrete ceilings

9 Czech: "Über die räumliche Wirkung von Spiegeln," in: *wbw* 6/1984, 20–25: 20.
10 A Swiss doctor and scientist, Étienne Grandjean was one of the first to study ergonomics. In 1973, he published his research in the book *Wohnphysiologie*.

area. Together with the possible chair positions, table groups of different sizes come about, although the tables are quite small, at approx. 35/50 centimeters. Since the benches protrude over the front pillars, they are not a mandatory lateral delimitation for those sitting and, depending on the situation, one can sit down on the bench or respect an occupied table. The supporting pillars are square, made of mitered stone slabs that come from demolitions. The stone grain running over the edges gives them the appearance of solid stone. The cabinet installation above the bench fields does not form a straight lintel, but is designed as a flat parabola between the pillar groups, so that the impression of a sagging cable construction emerges. This is reinforced by turned decorative molding under the lintel. Here, Czech tied in with the logic of cable constructions according to Frei Otto, with which he had already dealt intensively during several design projects (retractable roof over the Graben, over the courtyard of the Mödling shopping center). Due to the slightly different depths of the niches, the "perforated" wall appears thicker on the "classic" side; the pillar cross-sections are larger (12/12 centimeters) than on the regular side (10/10 centimeters) and even those "cables" represented by decorative strips have various diameters.

With the means of mirroring and the placement of pillars, the spatial demarcation is obscured, and an infinite sequence of rooms simulated, which is only limited by the curve of the mirror images resulting from the slight angular position of the side walls. The lighting is provided by two 15 W incandescent lamps per field, which appear to be standing under the sagging lintel in a square with their reflections. People sitting on the benches are strongly illuminated from behind and weakly illuminated from the front by the lamps opposite, which corresponds to the classic portrait light in film and photography from the interwar period and illuminates the face particularly advantageously.

The mirrors are made of crystal glass (still available until around 1975), which, thanks to its completely flat surface, provides the perfect illusion that the space behind it actually goes further. The result is the ambivalent but repeatable perception of a wall opening. In general, "mirrors in a small room [...] have an actual physical effect: the eye adjusts to the reflected distance. Therefore, fatigue and constriction appear only after a long time. Since the emmetropic eye is set to infinity in the relaxed state, every short viewing distance means an effort."[9]

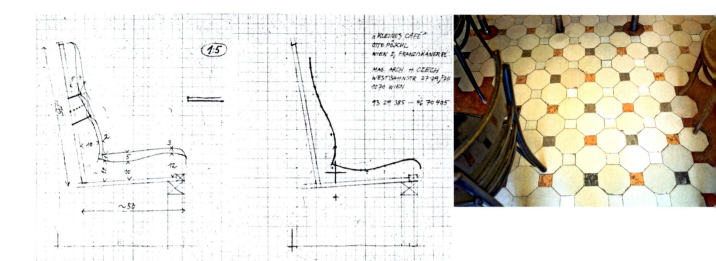

The backrests of the bench seats correspond to the optimal seating curve found by Étienne Grandjean.[10] The concave sections of the seating curve are formed in the leather covering by the buttons. Czech found this element of comfort in the upholstered seats of 19th-century carriages in the Carriage Museum (*Wagenburg*) in Schönbrunn.

The floor in the front part of the room was existing building stock, that in the rear part was supplemented with octagonal floor tiles from a demolition. The small square plates in between were added from the stone of the pillar plates. A regular row of red and black stones alternates with a row of gray stones into which a bright white stone is occasionally set. The laying direction follows the direction of the room with a circumferential frieze that compensates for the irregularities of the space. The laying pattern corresponds to that of the State Hall of the Austrian National Library.

In this expansion of the Kleines Café, Czech used the typical furnishings of the classic Viennese café again, this time more precisely and in a slightly higher quality: tables with marble tops, bentwood chairs, niches with upholstered benches, newspapers stretched in wooden frames made of bent cane, and a bar at a prominent position.[11] In this form, the Viennese coffee house goes back to the Biedermeier era.[12] "Comfortable upholstered seats, marble, mirrors—clichés of the first class—[...] a social difference that can be overcome in four steps."[13]

11 Charlotte Ashby: "The Cafés of Vienna. Space and Sociality," in: Ashby et al. (eds.): *The Viennese Café and Fin-de-Siècle Culture*, 2013, 9–31: 9.
12 Ibid., 13.
13 Czech: "Wien 1 Frankziskanerplatz," op. cit.

In 19th-century Vienna, the café became the most important public space for the bourgeoisie. It also served as a social meeting spot, a venue of entertainment and intellectual, cultural and political discourse.[14] The coffee house was an institution with varied gradations, ranging from the elegant cafés in the inner city, where the upper middle class met, to those of the lower middle class in the outskirts, where the local neighborhood came together. Even if the cafés differed according to social affiliation, their basic orientation (unlike the English clubs) was nevertheless accessible to everyone. "It [the coffee house] is a sort of democratic club to which admission costs the small price of a cup of coffee. Upon payment of this mite every guest can sit for hours on end, discuss, write, play cards, receive his mail, and, above all, can go through an unlimited number of newspapers and magazines."[15]

The cafés acted as an entry point into a clique that drew a person's interest. There were so-called *Stammtische* (regulars' tables)[16] for certain guests, which were an informal platform on which news was quickly exchanged and from which it was disseminated. The regulars' tables were not exclusive, but relatively open to newcomers. The groups and affiliations were visible in the public space of the coffee house and recognizable for those interested. One knew who was meeting where and when. At the same time, the coffee house was a place with greater freedom than in otherwise socially very regulated life. If one did not want to talk to anyone, one did not have to; one could sit at a table undisturbed and read the newspaper. One could just as unabashedly pass the time. But established personalities also met in the coffee house and it offered the only opportunity for meetings between women and men without starting people gossiping; in short, it was the place of modern, liberal Vienna.

14 Ashby: "The Cafés of Vienna," op. cit., 16.
15 Stefan Zweig: *The World of Yesterday*, trans. Benjamin W. Huebsch and Helmut Ripperger, London, Toronto, Melbourne and Sydney: Cassell and Company, Ltd., 1947, 41.
16 Ashby, op. cit., 27.
17 Jeremy Aynsley: "Graphic and Interior Design in the Viennese Coffeehouse around 1900," in: Ashby et al. (eds.), op. cit., 158–177: 173.

"Kleines Café" had already been the name of the original venue. In relation to the history of the Viennese coffee house, it also has a strong symbolic meaning: Of the large bourgeois coffee house scene in Vienna with all its liberal and Jewish intellectuals, only a "Kleines Café" more or less remained—which, by the way, is still a meeting point for a liberal and alternative scene.

A typical technique of the shop sign in the 19th century, for cafés as well, was behind-glass painting.[17] Czech also used this for the KLEINES CAFÉ portal sign on Franziskanerplatz. As with later projects (e.g., Galerie Hummel, Musikalienhandlung Arcadia, Restaurant Immervoll/Pöschl), he designed sans serif capital letters, as were also used in the middle and later 19th century.

In 1974, all the house doors, including the church and the monastery door of Franziskanerplatz, were painted in different shades of green; the pale lime green chosen for the historic shop portal of the café (originally: the butcher's shop) was a shade not yet represented and during renovations always turns out somewhat differently.

As the work on the extension progressed, the entrance portal to the older part of the café was also renewed. The inner, orange-red door was there; the outer, light blue one was replaced by Czech. The new glazing bar forms an optically coherent rectangle in the middle across the casement. The roller shutter was integrated into a box that simulates an oversized beam profile.

The counter of the added room is, so to speak, the "extension" of that of the first, slightly deeper lying room, which is why it is lower and less prominent. As already noted, the barman stands at eye level with the visitors in the upper room who are sitting at the bar. This functional logic triggers an irritation in the perception; the room gains something "sinking" and thus unstable.[18]

The use of mirrors was also an established element in coffee houses. They served to "self-assure a self-confident bourgeoisie" that reflected itself in the mirror.[19] The mirrors in the Kleines Café are designed quite differently: only when one sits down does one see oneself in the mirror as well as the back of the heads of the people sitting opposite and the faces of those sitting next to them. By multiplying the number of people, the mirrors reduce the intimacy of the Kleines Café and at the same time make it possible to observe the other visitors inconspicuously.

While Czech was conceptualizing the extension of the Kleines Café, he first wrote about "transformation" as an architectural term. "It is remarkable how little of reality architects perceive. The city itself is the existent. It is stronger than anything one can invent in its place. It is not a matter of erecting a world on the basis of a plan: we have at hand a powerful built mass to which we can only make minor additions — to change, estrange, reinterpret, and perhaps regulate it. […] The more we comprehend it [the existent], the less we must stand in opposition to it, and the easier it will be to understand our decisions as a continuation of a whole. Transforming an existing building is more interesting than building a new one — because, in essence, everything is transformation."[20]

18   Rudolf Kohoutek wrote about Czech's architecture that on closer inspection it is not very comforting; "Hitchcock could have filmed everywhere in this place." Kohoutek: "When the background comes to the fore," in: *Hermann Czech. Options in Architecture*, 1987, 16. Peter Kubelka once described the Kleines Café to Czech as a "malicious establishment." ("boshaftes Lokal")
19   Marie Theres Stauffer: "Spiegel in Räumen von Adolf Loos," in: Ákos Moravánszky; Bernhard Langer; Elli Mosayebi (eds.): *Adolf Loos. Die Kultivierung der Architektur*, 2008, 173.
20   Czech: "For a Change" (1973), trans. Elise Feiersinger, in: Czech 2019, 109–115: 113–114.

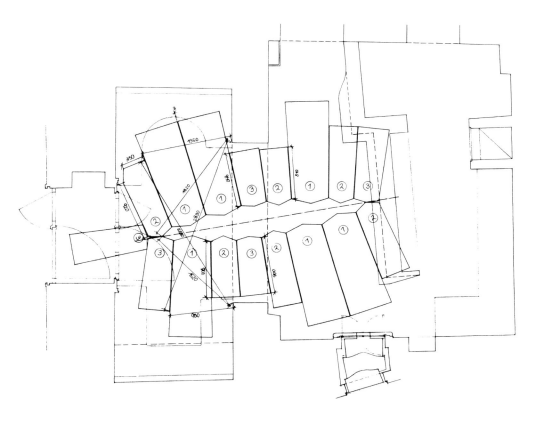

Kleines Café I, Additions 1977

In 1977, the floor in the lower part of the Kleines Café was renewed and high desks were built above the disconnected aluminum beer kegs. At that time in Vienna, the artist Karl Prantl suggested paving St. Stephan's Square with slabs made of discarded gravestones from Viennese cemeteries. Czech took up this idea for the floor of the Kleines Café: the slabs were laid according to their own logic, with as little loss of shape as possible, resulting in the now visible pattern. According to Czech, this opens different fields of association: the figure enclosed by the plates resembles a gap or fissure that symbolizes the theme of death already contained in the gravestones and creates a connection to Edgar Allan Poe. There is a study[21] on this by Marie Bonaparte, a student of Sigmund Freud, featuring the psychoanalytic topos of the "vagina dentata," a vagina with teeth, which can be related to sexual fears. A completely different association connects Hermann Czech with the

21 Marie Bonaparte: *Edgar Poe. Eine psychoanalytische Studie.* With a preface written by Sigmund Freud, 1934.

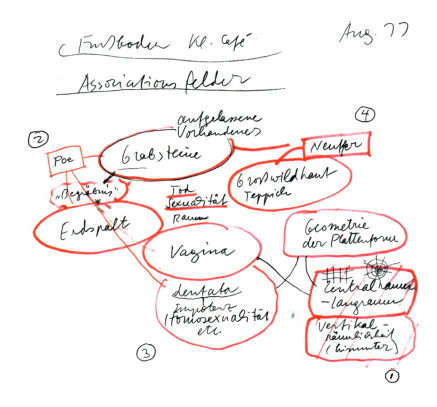

original co-owner Hans Neuffer, who took part in hunts in Africa several times. The shape reminded Czech of the skin, the fur of big game, as it is sometimes used as a carpet. It is essential for him that the interpretations are followed up in the design process through associations that arise after the first conception. "Such layers of meaning do not engender the design; one does not come up with the images *in advance*. The process is just the opposite: while the gravestones are a chosen motif with a strong content, when set, due to their shape, a modular geometric figure comes about. It is only after this step that the full range of implications is considered — and now the questions are raised as to which effects are to be accepted, emphasized, or avoided. (Showing the inscriptions on the fronts of the gravestones, for example, is avoided because it would be flippant and lack critical meaning in this context.)"[22]

These diverse interpretations once again proved to Czech that architecture is associative.[23] For him, this is a property that, if used consciously, gives architecture a "richness" that "is far superior to all efforts to create plastic, sculptural form."[24]

22 Czech: "Can Architecture Be Conceived by Way of Consumption?" (2011), trans. Elise Feiersinger, in: Czech 2019, 229–247: 236–237.
23 Czech first recognized the associative content of building components when designing the single-family house in the Plischke Master School.
24 Czech: "Einige weitere Entwurfsgedanken" (1980), in: Czech 1996, 81.

The fields of association in Czech's sketch from the late 1970s are personal and individual. But if one relates the design of the floor to the history of the Viennese coffee house, connections to the Austrian history of the expulsion and murder of a large part of the well-known, mostly Jewish coffee house visitors and owners at the turn of the century and the interwar period come to mind.

In 1978, Hermann Czech designed a café in Salzburg, which, according to the client's request, was to resemble the Kleines Café. The spatial preconditions, however, were completely different: the restaurant consisted of a barrel vault partially closed off lengthways by a wall. For Czech, the idea of treating the space like that of the Kleines Café was completely impossible: He suggested the introduction of two rows of pillars—one of them almost at the level of the wall—to define the space, whereby Heinrich Tessenow's wooden columns in the Villa Böhler in St. Moritz played a role. However, the client rejected the proposal and insisted on the implausible copy of the Kleines Café, which he then arranged to be carried out.

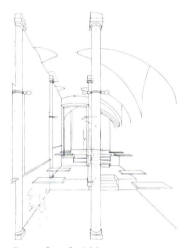

Design for café, Salzburg, 1978

Kleines Café

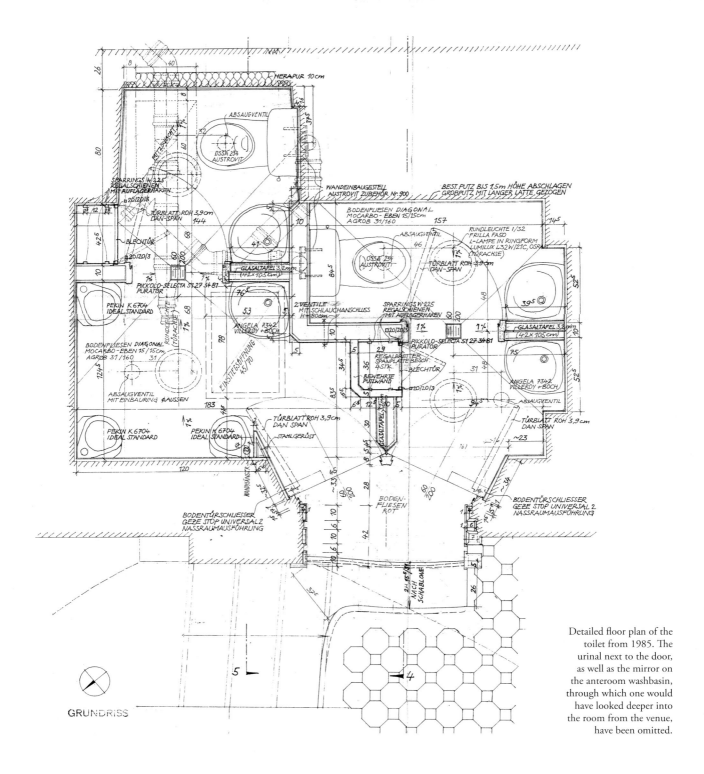

Detailed floor plan of the toilet from 1985. The urinal next to the door, as well as the mirror on the anteroom washbasin, through which one would have looked deeper into the room from the venue, have been omitted.

In the arch above the inserted toilet entrance there are actually four light bulbs instead of the otherwise mirrored ones.

Kleines Café, Toilet Installation 1985

When one of the small business premises surrounded by the Kleines Café became vacant, toilets were installed in 1985. Czech decided on a variant he had already implemented in the Salzamt Restaurant: a washbasin with a mirror in the anteroom and in the toilet. "The mirrored situation really exists on the other side." For the very top step—freely lying at a right angle— leading from the seating area to the toilets, Czech considered a detail of the same situation from Michelangelo's Ricetto staircase in the Laurentian Library in Florence, but rejected it again because of the risk of tripping. The applied solution is a simple rounding.

The closing words of Czech's documentary about Loos (1970) could also characterize the Kleines Café: "An architecture that is not based on ornamentation but on spatial effects does not become obsolete. It remains an expression and background for the contradicting tendencies of modern man: comfort, representation, irony."[25]

The Kleines Café is still in operation; only the surfaces are renewed from time to time.

[25] Czech: *Ins Leere gesprochen. Der Architekt Adolf Loos*, documentary film 1970, ORF archive.

Antiquarian Bookshop Löcker
originally Antiquarian Bookshop Löcker & Wögenstein

Period of origin: 1973/1977/1979
Address: Annagasse 5, 1010 Vienna
Clients: Erhard Löcker and Walter Wögenstein
Project team: Paul Katzberger

The publisher and antiquarian Erhard Löcker[1] and Hermann Czech have been friends for many years, with the antiquarian bookshop being their first joint work. They subsequently collaborated on a number of book projects: *Das Looshaus* (Czech, Mistelbauer, 1976), *Zur Abwechslung* (Czech, 1977), *Josef Frank 1885–1967*, the catalog for the Frank exhibition, compiled and edited by Johannes Spalt and Hermann Czech, or *Eine Muster-Sprache*, the German-language edition of Christopher Alexander's *A Pattern Language* edited by Czech, were published by Löcker Verlag. Czech advised Löcker on the selection of reprints of important architectural and historical publications, supervised the new editions and extended his advice to their appearance. The result was the facsimile reprints of Heinrich Kulka's first retrospective, *Adolf Loos – Das Werk des Architekten* (1979), of Otto Wagner's *Die Baukunst unserer Zeit* (1979) or of Josef Frank's *Architektur als Symbol* (1981), the latter supplemented with an extensive register of terms and edited by Czech.

Work at the Löcker & Wögenstein antiquarian bookshop in downtown Vienna began at the same time that Czech was writing his essay "Zur Abwechslung" ("For a Change").[2] In the section "Multi-layeredness" he quotes Josef Frank's request to "design our surroundings as if they had originated by chance."[3] And he himself writes: "But our model, the existent, did not originate 'by chance' [...], but as the result of innumerable, intelligible motivations of earlier individuals. Correspondingly, we can attain diversity if we allow all our motivations to flow into every design and follow up on all the ramifications and thought processes [...]."[4]

1 Visit to the antiquarian bookshop and interview with Erhard Löcker on December 13, 2012. Walter Wögenstein (d. 1982) was a partner in the antiquarian bookshop and publishing house in the early years. Since 1978 and 1982, the companies have solely been run under the name Löcker.
2 Czech: "For a Change" (1973), trans. Elise Feiersinger, in: Czech 2019, 109–115.
3 Ibid., 114.
4 Ibid., 115.

Selected Projects

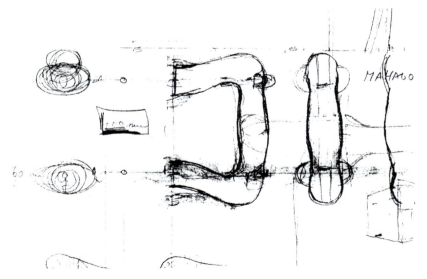

Antiquarian Bookshop Löcker

The showcase compartment simulates a wide-spanned "hall" with little columns.

Adolf Loos: Goldman & Salatsch men's fashion salon, 1901

Such possible "thought processes" can be traced when setting up and furnishing the antiquarian bookshop: There is a niche with a lower ceiling in the shop's salesroom. Czech placed a bookshelf under the cantilever, which looks like a load-bearing support. Loos executed a similar element in the men's fashion salon Goldman & Salatsch on Graben. At the same time, the shelf forms a frame and, together with another low shelf on the floor, creates a kind of window for the desk area behind it, which is thus shielded from the sales area.

In the cellar of the antiquarian bookshop there were still oak barrels from Löcker's father, in which red wine was originally stored, which is why the wood is colored red. The cladding of the plan cabinet in the salesroom, selected by Löcker from a practical point of view, with the wood of the wine barrels—the material found in the cellar—and its "extension" with a flat glass showcase as a horizontal display point to the principle also formulated in the text "For a Change": "The aim is a congruence of all considerations in a result that is definite but transparent and allows the multi-layered network of relationships to carry on."[5]

Ibid., 115.

Stone floor plate size 50/51 cm to achieve an irregular joint pattern. This results in single and double displaced tile spacers (the latter as empty square spaces). The non-displaced tile spacer occurs only once (at the start of laying); a rapport is not possible.

In the conception of the stone floor in the antiquarian bookshop, Czech's attitude that one must consciously construct chance also became manifest. The characteristic of "chance" could not be achieved through the carelessness or arbitrariness of the architect—this would correspond to the irrational tendencies in architecture criticized by Czech—but the appearance of chance can only be constructed through precise considerations, as is the case with the English landscape garden that depicts nature or, in the case of an actor, who portrays spontaneous reactions.

By diagonally laying the stone floor slabs measuring 50/51 centimeters, which were not cut into a square, Czech achieved an irregular, seemingly random effect that evens out or conceals the structure of the non-rectangular spaces. In the seating area, the slabs made of Solnhof natural stone were replaced by wooden parquet in the same dimensions.

One of the highly set ground floor windows, which serve as the bookstore's shop windows, features shelves irritatingly distorted rearwards; the atrium, which connects the other rooms with the business premises, was covered with a steel and glass construction that was supposed to look like a "net," but with a greatly simplified design. The existing bay window was built into the spatial structure; its stone consoles were exposed, the courtyard floor was grouted with asphalt and coated red. The all-glass entrance door subsequently received a wooden handle that is easy to grasp, despite the unfavorable spacing of the existing glass boreholes. And Hermann Czech also adapted the toilet in the antiquarian bookshop: The washbasin is in a corner of the room; two mirrors are attached above it at right angles so that one can see one's unreversed, not mirror-inverted, face.

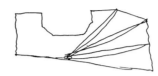
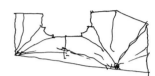

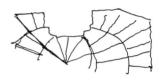

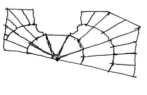

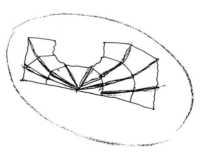

Antiquarian Bookshop Löcker

Wunder-Bar

Period of origin: 1975–1976
Address: Schönlaterngasse 8, 1010 Vienna
Clients: Monika Pöschl, Eva Gerl
Project team: Elsa Prochazka

Models of the ribbed profile

1 Czech: "Wunder-Bar, Wien 1975–1976," unpublished, Czech Archive, and interview on December 4, 2008.
2 Czech: "Mehrschichtigkeit" (1977), in: Czech 1996, 79–80: 80.

The Wunder-Bar is located in a Baroque house, the ground floor of which features irregular barrel and cove vaults. Hermann Czech wanted to bring "precision" into the spaces. He was always interested in Gothic beyond any religious connotation, not only, like Ernst A. Plischke, for constructive reasons, but also because of its association values: "Gothic always was a popular style because it is easily recognized."[1] Czech thus inscribed the three rooms with Gothic ribs, a style characteristic that contradicts the low ceiling height, but at the same time the geometric location of the ridges of imaginary cross vaults. "Such considerations are concrete and unrepeatable."[2] First constructed as a cardboard model on a 1:1 scale, later milled in wood, the ribs now define the rooms. At first, they were intended to be continuous and closed at the crown. For cost reasons, they were finally only executed from the corners as pieces reaching into the vault, which suffices for the architectural definition.

Czech also used mirrors in the Wunder-Bar, but in different arrangements. He made a distinction between illusion mirrors, which create the effect of another room, and "real" mirrors, framed on the wall, which the viewer immediately recognizes as such. The spatially illusionistic mirrors were mounted in the area of the toilet doors, which are uncomfortably close to the bar, so as to defuse this closeness.

The power outlets initially installed on the walls at a height of 1.8 meters turned out to be too low for the required upper edge of the mirror. Czech solved the problem by adjusting the shape of the mirror frames instead of moving the outlets so that the lamps are also visible in the mirror.

The benches were upholstered with the profile already tested and proven in the Kleines Café. They received turned wooden feet, the different shapes

of which correspond to "female and male calves." As in the Löcker & Wögenstein antiquarian bookshop, diagonally fitted mirrors were mounted in the toilets. They are adjusted exactly at right angles so that one can see oneself in the correct unreversed direction. André Heller came up with the name "Wunder-Bar." Czech accepted the name solely on the condition that it did not appear anywhere.

In 1977, Czech elaborated upon the term "multi-layeredness"[3] from the text "For a Change." The idea that a transformation is more interesting than a new building continues: "Of two buildings of the same quality, the older one is superior to a contemporary one—simply because of the infeasible characteristic of age." Because buildings are "time machines"—a comparison coined by Wolfgang Mistelbauer—which get a new layer applied with every renovation, every new use. The multi-layeredness that arises when one allows all motivations to flow into the design creates an overdetermination. For the user, the overdetermination acts as an indeterminacy that gives him/her leeway. This leeway—according to Czech—is what Josef Frank meant when he demanded "that we design our surroundings as if they originated by chance."[4]

3 Czech: "For a Change" (1973), trans. Elise Feiersinger, in: Czech 2019, 109–115: 115f.; "Pluralism" (1977), trans. Michael Loudon, in: Kenneth Frampton (ed.): *A New Wave of Austrian Architecture*, 1980, 60.
4 Frank: "Accidentism" (1958), trans. Christopher Long, in: Frank 2012, Vol. 2, 372–387: 385.

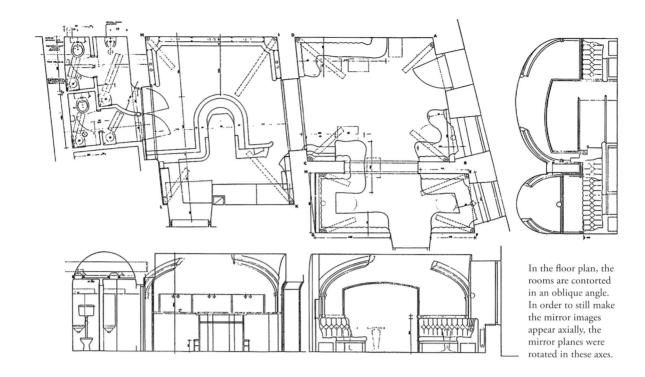

In the floor plan, the rooms are contorted in an oblique angle. In order to still make the mirror images appear axially, the mirror planes were rotated in these axes.

Czech's approach to this design is similar to that of the Kleines Café I insofar as he also used a "fake" element here. He calls his conception "eclectic," a "short cut to associations that were otherwise inaccessible." Whereas an Alberti cornice defined the space in the Kleines Café, in the Wunder-Bar it is the cut-off Gothic ribs, painted as if an old version had been exposed in places.

The Wunder-Bar is located on Schönlaterngasse, a narrow, winding street with Baroque town houses in the very center of Vienna. The Alte Universität (Old University), which traces back to a Jesuit college, and the Heiligenkreuzerhof ensemble are in the immediate vicinity.

From the 16th to the 18th century, Vienna developed from a "Gothic burgher city to a Baroque royal seat."[5] The narrow, Gothic gabled houses were demolished, the plots merged, and Baroque tenement houses, aristocratic palaces, churches and monasteries erected. The bourgeois class of merchants and tradespeople was pushed more and more into the suburbs by the nobility and court.

5   Hans Bobek; Elisabeth Lichtenberger: *Wien. Bauliche Gestalt und Entwicklung seit der Mitte des 19. Jahrhunderts*, 1966, 23–25; Ferdinand Opll; Karl Vocelka; Peter Cendes: *Wien: Geschichte einer Stadt. Teil 2. Die frühneuzeitliche Residenz (16.–18. Jahrhundert)*, 2003.

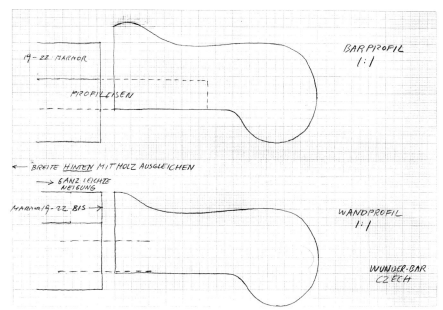

The profiles (in German "Lümmelborde") on the bar and wall desk also enable a stable grip from below (if they are not affected by chewing gum residue).

With the use of the Gothic ribs, Hermann Czech also refers to the medieval origins of the buildings on Schönlaterngasse. In a way, the view of Adolf Loos and Josef Frank is disavowed here: Both saw the only source of usable elements in Roman antiquity, because they correspond to a universal language that everyone knows.[6] "We have recognized that the ancient forms (forms in their broadest meaning) are the only and self-evident ones whose symbols we grasp and that the thought process that led to their creation is our tradition."[7] With "forms in their broadest meaning," Frank meant the basic stance according to "the organic design of inanimate material" under the premise of seeing "man as the measure of all things." In this sense, he also criticizes the Romanesque and Gothic, epochs in which the focus was not on people but on the Church with its rules and people had no choice except to search for the infinite: "Thus everything grew toward the sky, for the ground was crowded. For the first time, the longing for the infinite and intangible was given form, and its symbol is the tower in the narrow street whose peaks are lost in gray mist, or vaulting whose ribs disappear in twilight and incense. Yet we are disenchanted when the cathedral comes

6   See Loos: "Architektur" (1909), and Frank: *Architektur als Symbol* (1931).
7   Frank: *Architecture as Symbol* (1931), trans. John Sands, in: Frank 2012, Vol. 2, 9–191: 173 (The Destruction of Form).

Mirrors in different roles: making the space illusionary and apparently applied simply to the wall

into full view and gentle sunlight seeps through open windows."[8] For Frank, the Renaissance was the first modern style ("redemption came from the fabled South"), which ended the errors of the Gothic: "This [the changes brought about by the Renaissance; author's note] was the outcome of the scientific, anti-metaphysical mode of thought. The mystical was no longer true, for the striving for mysticism arises, for the most part, from one's resolve not to think any further if one does not possess the courage to want to recognize truths."[9]

In the 18th century, Goethe first referred to Gothic as the "German" style.[10] In the 19th century, after the Wars of Liberation against Napoleon, this idea of identifying a united German nation with the symbol of the Cologne Cathedral was carried out further. The impressive Gothic spaces would extend beyond the mind and could only be explained by the superior spiritual intellectuality of the German.

Why did Czech use Gothic elements that seem to contradict his view (against the "irrational")? He points to the Gothic reception in France at the same time, for example, at Viollet-le-Duc, where it was not the religious or national, but the constructive connotations of the Gothic that advanced architectural thought (which also corresponds to Plischke's view), compared

8 Frank, ibid., 85 (Gothic).
9 Frank, ibid., 89 (Invention of a Style).
10 Liana Lefaivre; Alexander Tzonis: *Architecture of Regionalism in the Age of Globalization*, 2012, 59f. Lefaivre and Tzonis show that this construction of history has been historically refuted by German intellectuals; the Gothic originated in France.

to the productive role of the Renaissance—already since Semper—in the German-speaking world. In the Gothic style of the Wunder-Bar, the focus is on the associative effect and the spatial reinterpretation of the vault geometry.

The Czechian "Gothic" conveys further associations: the implied ribs look like truncated, damaged rubble, perhaps also resemble roots that could continue to grow like loops, and the "plump" benches on their "meaty calves" indicate a certain down-to-earth quality. This Gothic has lost all "spirituality." What Friedrich Kurrent said about Restaurant Ballhaus also applies to the design of the Wunder-Bar: "In my opinion, the bar was the first sign of 'postmodernism' before this term existed. Yes, a Viennese mannerism, because different things were brought together, pieced together [...] making the incompatible compatible was new!"[11] The design of the Wunder-Bar also shows clear aspects of irony, which represented a new element in relation to the world of thought influenced by Wachsmann. Hermann Czech describes his approach in "For a Change"[12] in the section "Irony" as follows: The individuality not previously conveyed in the section "Method" "reacts with irony; possibly out of uncertainty because its motives are not definite enough."[13] Czech's irony is based on this uncertainty; the joke is not at the expense of someone else, even if everyone can feel encouraged to laugh at themselves. What Freud said about humor applies even more to Czech's irony. For Freud, humor is an expression of the super-ego that comforts the ego in a hopeless situation. "Humor [...] not only signifies the triumph of the ego but also of the pleasure principle, which is able here to assert itself against the unkindness of the real circumstances."[14]

A well-known example of the use of ironic means in modern architecture is Venturi and Rauch's design of the Guild House (1960–1963) retirement home in Philadelphia, one of the first postmodern buildings. Venturi and Rauch placed the shiny replica of a television antenna above the parapet of the central axis of the entrance façade. On the one hand, it symbolized the fact that old people spend a lot of time in front of the television. On the other hand, it also symbolized the marginalized importance of architecture in relation to the new media. With Robert Venturi, irony is also an attempt to express criticism of society in architecture.[15]

11 Friedrich Kurrent: "Wolfgang Mistelbauer," in: idem: *Aufrufe Zurufe Nachrufe*, 2010, 179.

12 Czech: "For a Change" (1973), trans. Elise Feiersinger, op. cit., 112.

13 Ibid. Jerry Lewis said in a conversation with Martin Scorsese: "Comedy comes out of pain, comedy comes out of uncertainty," October 6, 2015, Museum of the Moving Image, New York.

14 Sigmund Freud: "Der Humor" (1927), in: idem: *Kleine Schriften I*, Kapitel 29 [http://gutenberg.spiegel.de/buch/kleine-schriften-i-7123/29]. English translation by James Strachey et al. in: Sigmund Freud: *Humor. The Standard Edition of the Complete Psychological Works of Sigmund Freud*, London: Hogarth, 1964, Vol. 21, 160–166: 163.

15 See Stanislaus von Moos: *Venturi, Rauch & Scott Brown*, 1987, 57ff.

Villa Pflaum
Addition, renovation, interior design

Period of origin: 1976/1977–1979/1981/1987/2004
Address: Greifensteinerstrasse 156, 3423 St. Andrä-Wördern
Client: Dr. Hannes Pflaum and his wife
Project team: Volker Thurm, Ingrid Lapaine

The large villa northwest of Vienna was built in 1849 for the banker Ludwig Pereira by Ludwig Förster and Theophil Hansen, both important architects of Vienna's Ringstrasse. Between 1977 and 1979, Hermann Czech implemented an extension that resulted out of a special situation:[1] The villa was used by the City of Vienna as a children's home for many years, while the owners only had two adjoining rooms that they wanted to convert into a holiday apartment. "May anything be added to such a building?" Hermann Czech asked. The villa is a regular square block in the plan, but in elevation it follows the ideal of a romantic castle which offers a different view from every angle. Added later, the winter garden dissolves the symmetry further since its window axes do not match those of the old structure.

In his first proposal, Czech designed a square wooden pavilion that docks onto the villa. In the second, finally executed design, he added two elements to the villa: a "dependent" one, "leaned" at right angles around the corner of the old building and an "independent" cube that inserts itself into the dependent, "softer" one. This concept was modified several times by Czech. The veranda now projects out of the soft structure; the cube is limited in the interior by a staggered support, which results in an open spatial system on the ground floor. The original exterior wall becomes the interior wall inside the leaning building, but its former function can still be felt, as the old, weathered stone of the corner pilaster strips and the window frame were exposed. To connect the dependent structure with the old building, only the transom height of the existing windows came into question: "This was the only way possible to maintain the light exposure and the only way the window division of the old building remains visible from all sides." The lower level of the addition resulted from this connection height. Its location blocks the driveway that originally led around the building,

---

[1] The following paragraph is based on Czech: "Motivenbericht zum Zubau Villa Pflaum in Altenberg," unpublished, Czech Archive, as well as an interview from December 4, 2008.

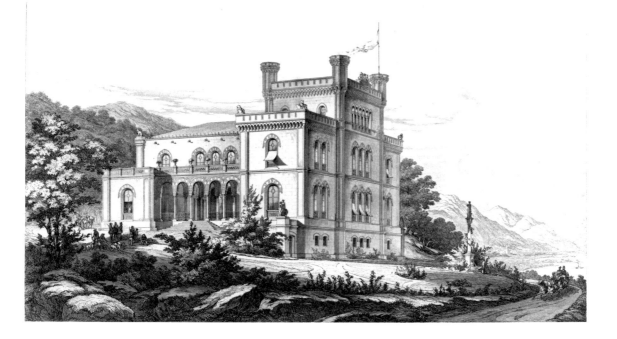

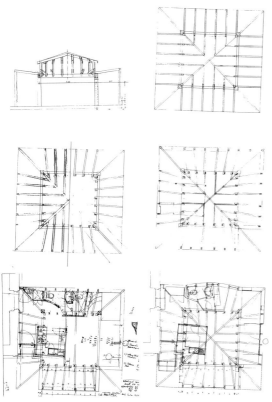

In the first project, the figure of the space was influenced by the material thickness of the beams.

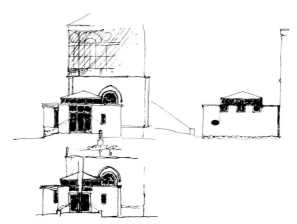

The first project: an independent, slightly twisted addition made of wood.

2 Czech: Project text, in: Ulrike Jehle-Schulte-Strathaus: "'In welchem Style sollen wir bauen?' Gedanken zur Stil-losigkeit von Hermann Czech," *wbw* 6/1996, 25.

3 Renate Wagner-Rieger: *Wiens Architektur im 19. Jahrhundert*, 1970.

4 Elana Shapira: "Jüdisches Mäzenatentum zwischen Assimilation und Identitätsstiftung in Wien 1800–1930," in: Claudia Theune; Tina Walzer (eds.): *Jüdische Friedhöfe. Kultstätte, Erinnerungsort, Denkmal*, 2011, 179.

5 A reference from Hannes Pflaum.

6 Bundesdenkmalamt (ed.): *Dehio-Handbuch. Die Kunstdenkmäler Österreichs. Niederösterreich, südlich der Donau*, Teil 2, 2003, 2745f.

creating separate entrances to the children's home and the new holiday apartment. Towards the entrance of the children's home, the addition has a closed, but not forbidding façade. "The structural diagram Förster and Hansen intended for the north façade is created in combination with the winter garden, which is now in the middle [...]."[2]

Villa Pereira was erected from 1846 to 1849 in the period of Romantic Historicism.[3] Historicism combined various styles as a kind of code for political and cultural values. In this building, the two architects melded a classicist style with Byzantine-Moorish elements for their client, the banker Baron Ludwig Pereira, which had to do with his Jewish origins, as well as his liberal attitude and position in the Habsburg Monarchy.[4] In 1860, the winter garden made of a glazed iron structure was added, presumably by Heinrich Ferstel. In 1886, the house, which is also mentioned in art-historical discourse as a model for Miramare Castle near Trieste,[5] was acquired by Moritz Pflaum.[6]

208 Selected Projects

In the text "Mehrschichtigkeit" ("Pluralism") published in 1977, Czech addresses the issue of monument preservation. According to his understanding, a restored building is also a building of our time: "Not only are the methods and insights of preservation themselves conditioned by their epoch, but the very fact that a building that was once used for a different purpose is now being put to new use adds a temporal layer."[7] He does not evaluate these different, sometimes contradicting layers, while monument preservation conversions are often about returning a building to an "original state." Czech recognizes a quality whose "aesthetic 'information density'"[8] comes about through the superimposition of historical layers. For the user, this creates the indeterminacy that Frank means with his "chance" comparison.[9]

7 Czech: "Pluralism" (1977), trans. Michael Loudon, in: Kenneth Frampton (ed.): *A New Wave of Austrian Architecture*, 1980, 60.
8 Ibid. Czech is referring to a term coined by Max Bense, which in this case is not qualitative but quantitative.
9 Ibid., 80.

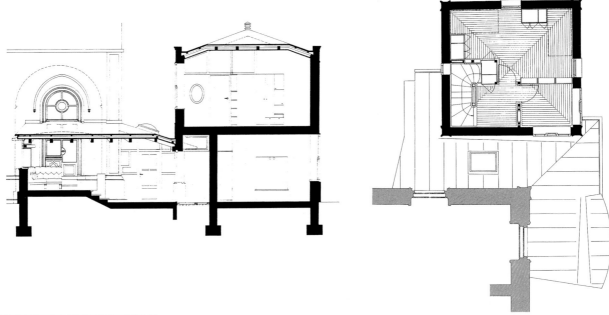

Adolf Loos, House Rufer, 1922

10   In an art-historical perception of the addition, this multi-layeredness is leveled to the phrase "stylistically adapted to the architecture." *Dehio-Handbuch*, op. cit.

For the extension, Czech added a new square to the villa's square floor plan, which in turn contains smaller squares. This stands in now solid construction in the orthogonal directional system of the villa, while the likewise square wooden pavilion of the first draft shows a slight rotation. In continuation of Hansen and Förster's design, Czech also appointed the addition cube with corner and cornice profiles. Here, however, the corner pilaster strips of the walls make their conceptual development from individual pillars clear; the one at the garden exit becomes an actual free-standing support, which is reminiscent of the "table" system of prefabricated construction methods of the 1960s. On the upper floor, too, this pillar stands freely at a right angle between larger windows, through which the symmetry of the smaller perforated windows is broken again. The relationship to the irregular historical elevation of the villa arises from multiple, also reciprocal overlays and reinterpretations.[10]

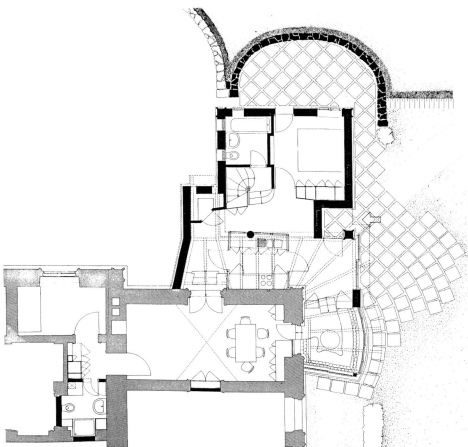

The cube is also the classic type of modernist house. Thus, the cube element of Romantic Historicism now overlaps with the contemporary one and its irregular perforated façade. This irregularity, in turn, has an unexpected relationship to the irregular elevation of the villa's historical form.

This complexity does not contradict the internal organization—but is rather derived from it. In the economy of a Loosian spatial plan, two floors in the addition are organized at one floor height of the villa. The bathroom is reached from a landing after the first three steps of the stairs. This enables the bathtub to be lowered into the higher-lying floor. The bathroom is lit through three windows in unusual positions: One sits very low and affords a view from the bathtub, the other two are high in the wall and only serve to allow daylight to enter. Despite the view and daylight, the privacy of the bathroom is preserved.

Villa Pflaum

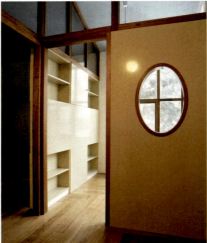

From 1981 on, after the City of Vienna had unexpectedly terminated the lease, Czech advised the Pflaum family on the planned overall use of the historic villa. As a result, what had been destroyed was not reconstructed, but exposed, and a new layer of living space was added by dividing the villa into several independent living areas for different branches of the family and equipping them with bathrooms.

The basis of the restoration was the rudimentarily preserved painting of several ceiling fields.

During the further conversion, the "re-possession" of the ground floor as of 2004, Czech exposed traces such as remnants of the ceiling painting. Irretrievably lost items were no longer reconstructed but remained visible in their damaged[11] condition. The central hall is once again a meeting point for all family members and a reception room for guests; this is followed by further living rooms and bedrooms and a spacious kitchen-cum-living

11 The villa was confiscated by the Russian occupation forces after the Second World War before it was used as a children's home. During this time great damage to the existing building occurred.

room. The newly built bathrooms feature gray-blue ceilings with a red border, the kitchen-cum-living room the opposite colors—a dark red, glossy ceiling with a green and blue-gray border. A new open fireplace twisted into the room and thus facing a seating area—a solution that already appears during the first renovation—forms a cozy corner. Globe lamps and lighting with black sheet metal shades on the outside are classic early 20th century types that forego "good form" in favor of the lighting effect.

As a new layer, Czech added a contemporary homeyness to the villa that borrows from the living culture of Viennese modernism, but also cites his own designs.[12]

12 See also Czech: "Mehr Licht" (1964), in: Czech 1996, 19–21: 19, 20.

The structure of the new southern front now corresponds to that of the original northern front.

Villa Pflaum

House M.

Period of origin: 1977–1981
Address: Kranichgasse 7, 2320 Schwechat
Client: M.
Project team: Gustav Deutsch, Ingrid Lapaine, ÖBA: Wilhelm Koczy

Adolf Loos: Renovation of the Mandl House, 1914–1915

1 Czech: "Haus M., Schwechat 1977–81" (1982), unpublished, Czech Archive.
2 Czech: Project text, in: *wbw* 6/1996, 29. English translation in: "M House," in: *Architecture and Urbanism* 16:11, 44–47: 47.
3 The term "spatial design" (*Raumplan*) does not come from Loos himself, but from his colleague Heinrich Kulka, who uses the word in his book about Loos. Heinrich Kulka: *Adolf Loos*, 1931. The book was published as a reprint in 1979 by Löcker Verlag in collaboration with Hermann Czech.
4 Czech: "Haus M.," op. cit. This quote is taken from the Adolf Loos essay "Josef Veillich" (1929), originally published in the *Frankfurter Zeitung* on March 21, 1929, in: Adolf Loos: *Trotzdem. 1900-1930*, Innsbruck: Brenner, 1931, rpt. 1984.
5 Ibid.

Despite its higher ridge height, the house takes up the roof shapes and proportions of the surrounding residential structures. "The classic architectural ideological dispute between the pitched roof and the flat roof is solved by their combination."[1] On another occasion, Czech characterized the house: "As if the father had added to the grandfather's house."[2] The two slightly sloping and curved outer walls facing the garden are a reaction to the shape of the plot.

Loos's "spatial design"[3] plays an important role in House M.: Czech interprets it in the sense that Adolf Loos transferred the spatial economy familiar in the design of a floor plan into the section and viewed Loos's prophecy, "man will one day succeed in playing chess on a three-dimensional board," as a challenge.[4] House M. is an attempt to apply this spatial design, in which each room is given the appropriate height, to the entire house and to transfer it to contemporary conditions (for example, with regard to the same height of the kitchen and dining room, and the omission of a maid's room). "[...] in such a design concept one feels it as discomforting if one leaves the space under stairs, under a seat—even if it is only cubic decimeters—unused for no reason."[5]

In addition to the spatial plan, the design references Loos in several aspects: In the way the staircases are organized and in the marking of the "more public," more representative rooms with a row of pillars. Another spatial thought lies in the structural concept: The house is supported by its outer walls and four pillars inside. The load-bearing outer wall with openings still seemed the most sensible to Czech for a relatively small house. This means that the spatial design appears in the house's outward effect to be only "hinted at, through various irregularities." The four supports stand as a regular square in the middle of the house. Between the dining room

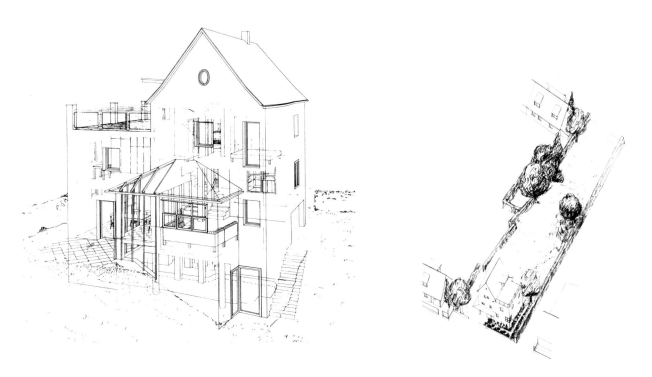

House M.

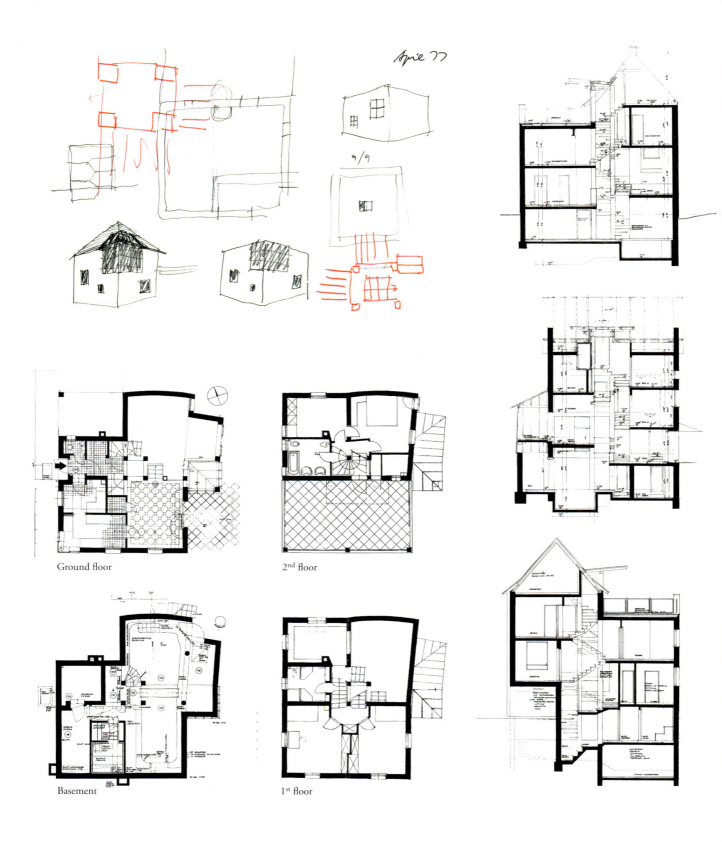

Ground floor
2nd floor
Basement
1st floor

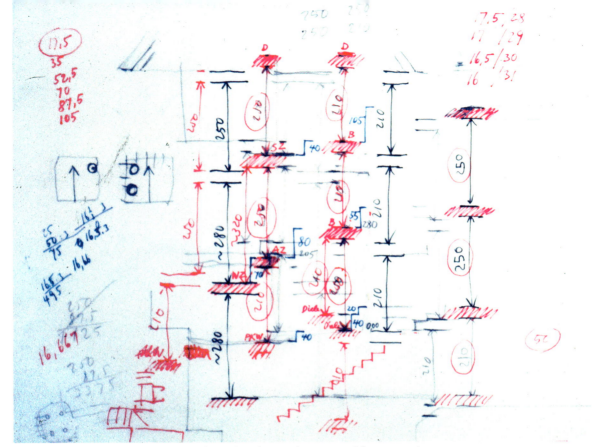

Sketch of the height positions, depending on the number of steps. Like in a musical fugue, every change has consequences for the whole context.

and living room, two of these supports, along with two others, now form a line of pillars. One of these supports is "fake" in that it has no load-bearing function. "The spatial value of this pillar front is exploited in several ways: one approaches it from the entrance, first laterally from behind, then takes the first small flight of stairs in front of this line of pillars into the dining room, and then ascends axially through the central opening into the living room."[6] The perception of the house from the outside is likewise based on a spatial concept—after all, it seems to consist of two rectangular, juxtaposed volumes. This idea becomes visible in the inner pillar front between the dining room and living room, which forms the dividing line between the two volumes. As with Loos, this creates various framed vistas.

6 Ibid.

Adolf Loos: Interior of the Rufer House, 1922

The staircase in House M. leads around the four pillars at the beginning, then between them, and finally turns around a single pillar on the last floor. It changes their character, but no valuation of superior or subordinate living areas arises. In the axis of the entrance one can see half into the lower floor and half into the main floor, but must turn right and now enters the first room of the house, the family dining room. After turning again by 90 degrees, one gets through the middle field of the line of pillars into the raised living area. The "monumental" character of this formation can be experienced—in the living room and in the dining room—while

Selected Projects

 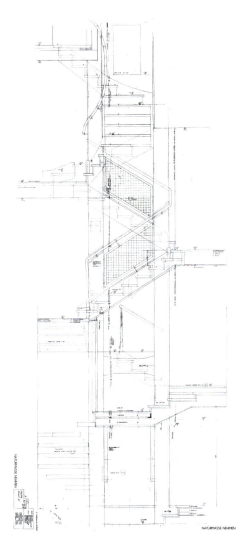

walking, as well as sitting. In this context, Czech mentions the concept of transparency used by Colin Rowe and Robert Slutzky, which refers not so much to the possible vistas, but to the ambivalent assignment of elements to different spatial contexts.[7]

From there, at a right angle, the further staircase to the upper floors begins, which, from a corner landing, first opens to a study, then to the first bathroom simply from a step that laterally widens (a medieval detail). At the end of the flight, it gives the impression that one is in a tenement house in which the two children's rooms take on the role of private apartments

7 Colin Rowe; Robert Slutzky: *Transparency* (1964), 1997 (4th edition).

House M.

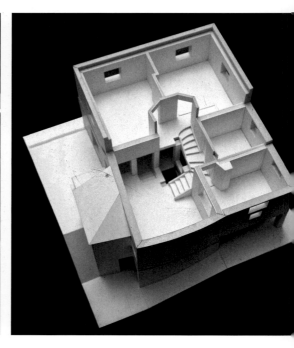

on a landing. On the next landing, the parents' bedroom level follows, in the further course of a spiral, again over widened steps, their bathroom and the terrace exit, and finally the loft at the top. The height of the rooms is therefore different, aligned depending on the common rooms or the other ones.

House M. is a new building. How can the "multi-layeredness" reflected by Czech be achieved in a new structure? In the text from 1977 he writes: "Historical depth is the model for other sorts of multi-layeredness: spatial polyvalence, the overlapping of different (even simulated) spatial concepts [...]."[8] When Czech began designing House M. in 1977, the first edition of his collected texts, *Zur Abwechslung*, had just been published by Löcker & Wögenstein.[9] In the foreword he defined his understanding of architectural theory as philosophical and programmatic. The philosophical aspect is—backward-looking—criticism of "bad theory," the programmatic aspect—future-oriented—as a decision-making aid and as "thinking towards design."

8 Czech: "Pluralism" (1977), trans. Michael Loudon, in: Kenneth Frampton (ed.): *A New Wave of Austrian Architecture*, 1980, 60.
9 Czech: *Zur Abwechslung. Ausgewählte Schriften zur Architektur Wien*, 1977.

Terrace exit with furniture storage depot

For Czech, the essential value of his essays lies not only in their historical aspects, but also in their "theoretical content." Looking back at his own texts since 1963, however, was sobering: "My discussion of Vienna was based on a hypothetical idea of a *Großstadt* (metropolis); now I doubt whether such an idea is at all viable in Vienna."[10]

The text "Mannerism and Participation" appeared for the first time in the publication. This is similarly programmatic as the text "For a Change" from 1973 and defines Czech's notion of architecture and its self-critical further development with the term "mannerism." For him, mannerism constitutes a conceptual approach to dealing with a development in architecture, an attitude towards architecture, which he actually rejects. It is an attempt to intellectually transform the inevitable in such a way that it can become an integral part of the design: "If you try to halt a development, you're always going to be on the wrong side. A realistic attitude must put up with these escalating changes, indeed, must expedite them."[11] What discourages Czech, according to his words, is the development of Vienna

10 Czech: "Vorwort," in: ibid., 7; as well as in: Czech 1996, 7.
11 Czech: "Mannerism and Participation" (1977), trans. Elise Feiersinger, in: Czech 2019, 119–124: 120.

into a "Greater Salzburg." The problem that preoccupies him is to design without becoming elitist or "aloof" or withdrawing to a position that no longer represents values. For him, architecture is irrevocably enlightening and humanistic, and he asks himself how it can be further thought: "Architecture can be representative and moving; it can represent a desired society different from the existing one and move us to bring it about. It can implement *freedom* and *self-realization*—either *directly*, as a concrete object, […] or *figuratively*, as expression […]. It must incorporate, in its essence, the external, the superficial that surrounds us; in its unity, all possible multiplicities. What attitude of mind is necessary to achieve this? First of all, one of intellectuality, of consciousness; further, a sense for the irregular and the absurd, that which breaks away from pre-established precepts: the attitude of mannerism. But this attitude of mind is simply the means with which to grasp some measure of reality. […] Mannerism is the conceptual approach of an acceptance of reality at its momentarily appropriate level; it grants the frankness and imagination that set even alien processes in

motion and tolerate them, without giving voice to the disingenuous fiction that architecture has given up its claim to produce a vision: to be open yet defined, meager yet comfortable."[12]

What effect does House M. have? "As if the father had added to the grandfather's house"—who was this "grandfather," who was the "father"? The surrounding houses were built in the early 1940s, the "grandfather" would then have to have been a National Socialist, or at least a follower. The "father" expanded the house with a flat-roofed extension. He contrasted the staid "grandfather" with a symbol of modernism—all in all, an image that corresponded to the political and cultural reality of the 1970s in Austria. In fact, the conception of the pitched roof was made at the request of the client, who did not want to attract attention in the area with his house. Inside, however, hidden from the eyes of the neighbors, there is "modern living" with an open floor plan.

12 Ibid.,123f.

Galerie Hummel
originally Kunsthandlung Hummel

Period of origin: 1978–1980
Address: Bäckerstrasse 14, 1010 Vienna
Client: Julius Hummel
Project team: Eduard Hueber

"The second room seems to be older due to the floor, though much cosier because of the colours used for the wall scheme of the walls. It is simply not true that gallery walls must be white."[1] The entrance step looks like it has been worn out from years of use. In fact, the stone was custom made in this form. The spotlights to illuminate the changing exhibitions are set as if by chance—"like a skin rash"—in the vault, near the vault "folds." The writing desk was placed in the front passage between the two rooms. In this way, it does not take up any gallery space and fulfils a security function: the gallery owner can cut off the visitor's path. The entrance door consists of three dissimilar parts: an openable door with a handle for entry in everyday use, a leaf that can be opened separately when larger objects are delivered, and a fixed frame element. All are designed differently in the frame profile.

1 Czech: Project text, in: Ulrike Jehle-Schulte-Strathaus: "'In welchem Style sollen wir bauen?' Gedanken zur Stil-losigkeit von Hermann Czech," *wbw* 6/1996, 14, and "Entwurfsprozess: Skizzen, Bauten, Projekte," *wbw* 6/1996, 50.

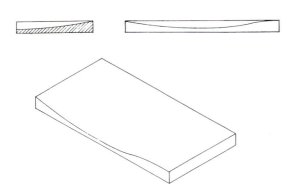

The floor slab near the entrance simulates centuries of wear and tear.

Selected Projects

Galerie Hummel

In 1980, Czech wrote under the heading "Associations": "All parts of the building speak; they themselves belong first of all to a world of thought or an epoch to which we react; through this or through similarities they trigger conscious or unconscious personal memories. They share how and why they were created; the constructive, economic and social conditions are contained in every architectural form. Architecture already has the real character of the 'object.' That is its wealth, which is far superior to all efforts toward three-dimensional, sculptural form."[2]

As in the Löcker Antiquarian Bookshop and in House M., the floor is made of bright natural stone, cut in squares, with a few colorful inclusions. The smoothed down granite step in the entrance area facilitates threshold-free access to the venue and, in its perceived wear and tear, signals a high number of visitors to the gallery—the association arises that going to a gallery is something normal.

2 Czech: "Einige weitere Entwurfsgedanken" (1980), in: Czech 1996, 81.

Various panel formats and edging differentiate the two rooms as older and younger, but also as more intimate and formal.

While working on Galerie Hummel, Czech and Johannes Spalt conceptualized an exhibition about Josef Frank for the University of Applied Arts.³ It featured a large selection of projects and a reconstructed wooden pavilion based on Frank's design. A compilation of selected texts by Josef Frank was initially republished in the exhibition catalog. During his Frank scholarship stay in Sweden (1969), Czech had, among other things, studied his fantasy designs—a selection of them appeared for the first time in the catalog.⁴ The drafts are explained with short texts; three considerations are also important in Czech's own projects: Czech remarks that House No. 3 was based on Le Corbusier's "Dom-Ino" principle; "foreign" spatial ideas thus constituted a design level. In House No. 9, Frank experimented with free forms by drawing "without reflecting on how it would look." In the exhibition catalog text, Czech contrasted Hugo Häring's approach, whose free forms were derived from studies of motion sequences. Frank's call to "design our surroundings as if they originated by chance"⁵ has a broader range of meanings that allows diverging considerations to be introduced. Accordingly, it is not a question of technically constructing a random effect, but rather of "simulating" it.

3 Spalt; Czech: *Josef Frank 1885–1967*, 1981.
4 Ibid., 218–235.
5 Frank: "Accidentism" (1958), trans. Christopher Long, in: Frank 2012, Vol. 2, 372–386: 385.

The passive leaf, the active leaf and the fixed part of the portal (from left to right) are not standardized, but set apart from one another.

Likewise "by chance," Czech placed the points of light in the vault of Galerie Hummel: They have nothing to do with the optimal lighting. But Czech emphasizes that one cannot do anything "without contemplating," and as soon as one picks up the pen, ideas and reflections arise. Therefore, he tried "with" contemplation to do something that looks random, like a "rash." In his essays, lectures, and conversations, Czech also mentions the "method acting" theory as a reference for this approach.[6] Afterwards, "the actor can observe himself during spontaneous reactions and learn to evoke the corresponding sensations by externally reproducing these reactions."

The design of Galerie Hummel's three door elements with their various frame widths is very atypical for architectural practice, where attempts are usually made to disguise differences to give preference to a more abstract order (three identical elements).

In letters about the fantasy designs, Frank several times used the Swedish word *krånglig*, which means "awkward," or "complicated." In doing so, he named a, for him, positive characteristic of his designs that met his demand

6 "Method acting" goes back to Konstantin Stanislavski and the Moscow Art Theater in the 1920s, as well as further refinement by Lee Strasberg.

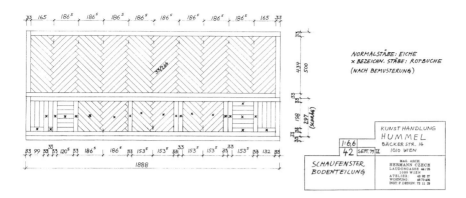

The slanted parquet slats in the shop window spell out the name of the art dealer.

of designing our surroundings "as if they originated by chance." In 1980, Czech also described a kind of complexity that arises from the incongruence resulting from the application of different—in each case well-founded—design criteria. "When designing, we proceed with systems in which we summarize the requirements (set or our own). None of the systems is completely sufficient, [...again and again] we have to come up with another system." The progressing series of design decisions will "remain noticeable in the modifications of the systems and their superimpositions. The result can still be superficially simple if all the superimpositions are congruent—on closer inspection they will reveal their complexity by vibrating."[7]

7 Czech: "Einige weitere Entwurfsgedanken," in: *Design ist unsichtbar*, 1980, 395–404: 399; also Czech 1996, 81. op. cit. Robert Somol and Sarah Whiting describe this vibration of an ambivalent design result decades later in a much-cited article ("Notes around the Doppler Effect and Other Moods of Modernism," 2002), but illustrate it according to Czech "with one unsuitable comparison: Christian Doppler's discovery concerns changes in one criterion: the wavelength—corresponding to the relative speeds of the observer and the emitting object; different wavelengths do not overlap, especially not different criteria." Unpublished notes, ca. 2010, Czech Archives. Robert Somol; Sarah Whiting: "Notes around the Doppler Effect and Other Moods of Modernism," in: *Perspecta* 33, 2002, 72–77; German (abbreviated): *ARCH+* 178, 2006, 83–87.

Galerie Hummel

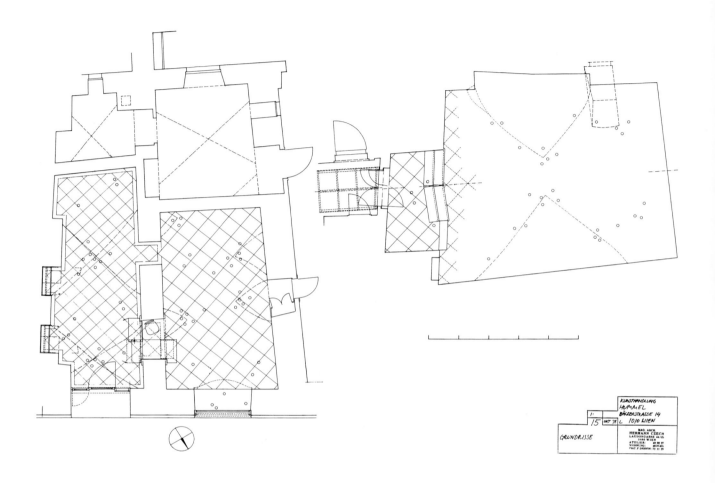

8 Czech: "For a Change" (1973), trans. Elise Feiersinger, in: Czech 2019, 109–115: 115.

Czech attempts to translate Frank's demand into the rationality of a design process, as he wanted to demystify Frank's original model as early as 1973: "But our model, the existent, did not originate 'by chance' or by some dark process of growth, but as the result of […] motivations of earlier individuals."[8]

A worktable with a pivotable component stands in the passage.

House S.

Period of origin: 1980–1983
Address: Seemüllergasse 29, 1170 Vienna
Client: S.
Project team: Peter Stiner, Walter Gruß, Gerhard Lindner, engineering: Peter Kramer
ÖBA: Heinrich Hausladen

Parquet boards from a demolition with a diagonal and half-diagonal pattern

1 Czech: "Haus S., Vienna, 1980–1983," undated, unpublished, Czech Archive; almost verbatim in: Ulrike Jehle-Schulte-Strathaus: "'In welchem Style sollen wir bauen?' Gedanken zur Stillosigkeit von Hermann Czech," *wbw* 6/1996, 24.

House S. is a "residential house for a physicist and a psychotherapist with adjacent psychotherapeutic practice."[1]

On the south-facing sloping site, the swimming pool and a stand of trees were a given. Towards the street to the north, the house splits into two structures, one taking up the direction of the street, the other that of the swimming pool. A group of trees fills the space between these two parts of the house. Towards the garden, the house forms a closed front with "shifted symmetry." The connecting link between the two wings is a round tower in which the library is located and whose star parquet pattern defines the 22.5-degree angle between the buildings. The different directions follow the comfortable sequence of movements in the floor plan.

Czech conceived the house to be elongated and narrow; "it develops like a backdrop in the east-west direction." In this way, almost all rooms are illuminated from the north and south. In the longitudinal direction, the diverse vistas, which also include trees, make the house appear large. The room heights in the tower are just over two meters; the main residential floor in the middle is accessible without differences in level; on the other two floors the room heights develop upwards and downwards from the central tower room via short flights of stairs. The staircase next to the tower divides the house into two wings, with the living and dining room and kitchen on the residential floor, as well as separate areas for the parents' and children's bedrooms on the top floor.

Czech mentions Adolf Loos as a reference for the preoccupation with ceiling heights. For the arrangement of two rectangular structures with a cylinder in between, he cites the scheme of Viennese Baroque palaces ("at

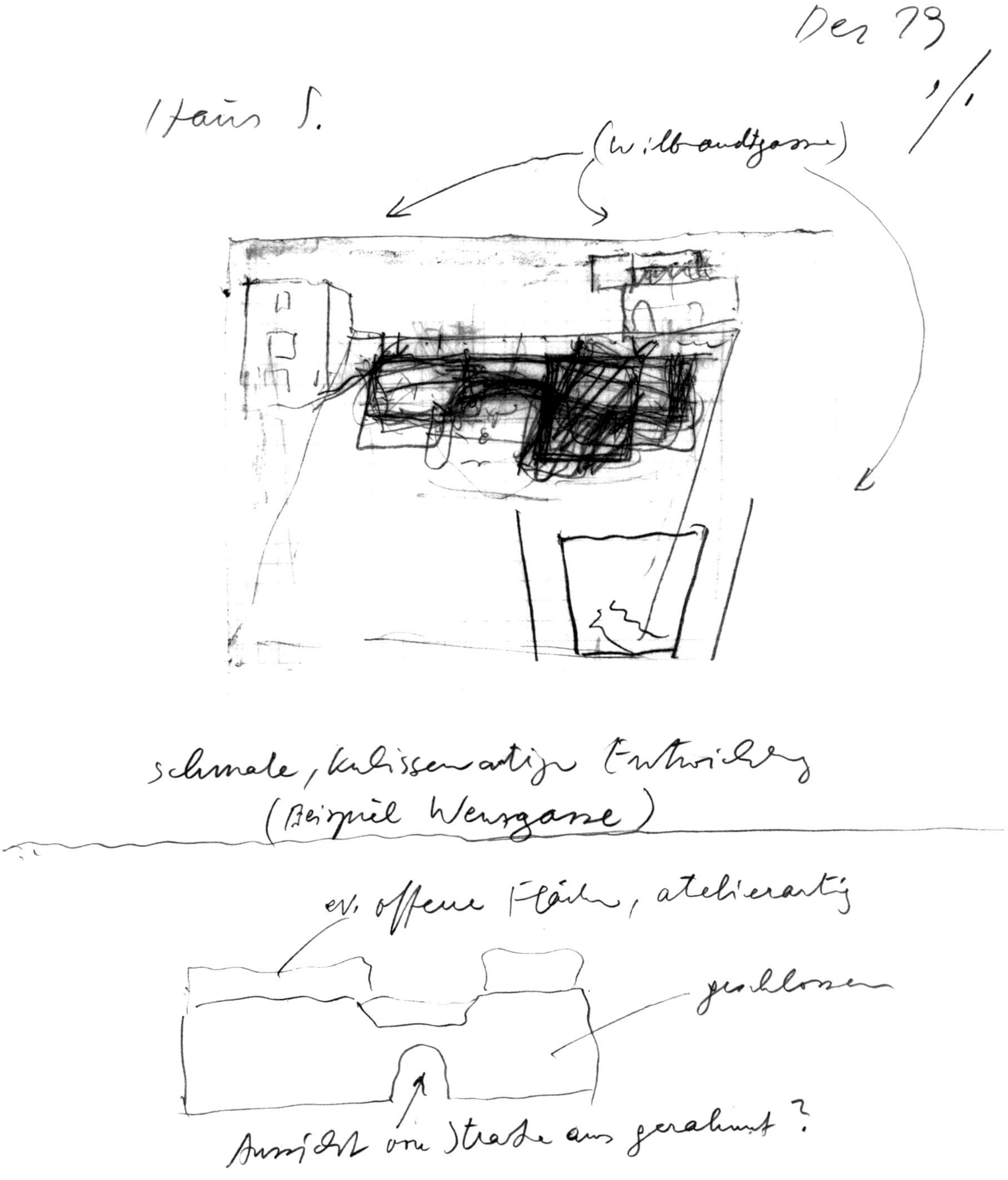

Haus S. Dez 79

(Wilbrandtgasse)

schmale, kulissenartige Entwicklung
(Beispiel Wengasse)

ev. offene Fläche, atelierartig

geschlossen

Aussicht von Straße aus gerahmt?

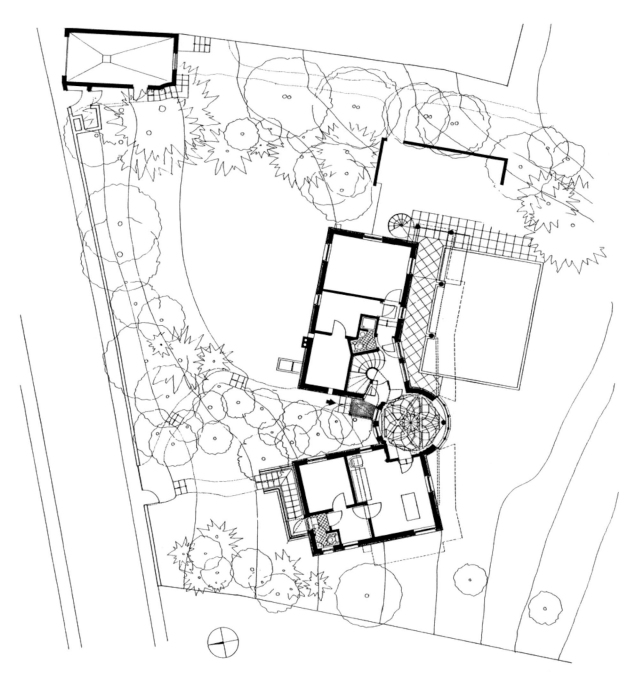

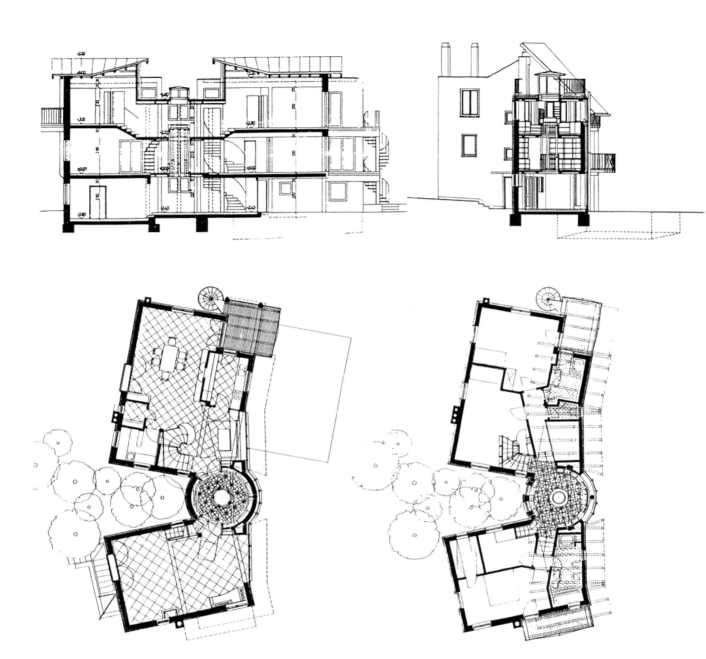

House S.

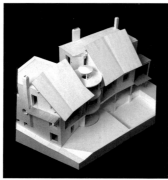

2   *Forum Design* exhibition, Linz, June 27 to October 5, 1980, conceptualized by Helmuth Gsöllpointner, Angela Hareiter, Laurids Ortner and Peter Baum.

3   The three direct quotes in this paragraph are taken from Czech: "S House" *a+u* 16:11 No. 554 (2016), 70–75: 74.

a very much reduced scale") and the library tower "would surely not have come into existence without John Soane." The wooden columns used in the library originate from Czech's contribution to the *Forum Design* exhibition in Linz.[2] At the client's request, the house is designed to use solar energy. To attach the solar collectors, a pitched roof is placed or cut into the flat roof towards the south, which corresponds to the optimal angle for solar energy use. A storage wall is placed into the circular tower. All windows are equipped with internal shutters or external Venetian blinds to regulate the solar heat radiation or the nocturnal heat losses. Czech adopted the requirements for the use of solar energy "into a conventional architectonic vocabulary, which that way is, however, expanded and enriched by unusual effects,"[3] as he himself describes. In the living room he used an element also employed by Josef Frank, namely a fireplace combined with an oval window facing west. This enables one to see into the fire and into the sunset at the same time.

For House S., Czech establishes references not only to Loos's spatial plan, but also to John Soane. On the main floor, the spatial plan is only noticeable through the different room heights; the entire longitudinal extension lies here at a floor level. In the early stages of this design, Czech also worked on projects such as the Josef Frank exhibition, conceived and designed jointly with Johannes Spalt, and the reprint of Frank's book *Architecture as Symbol*, with a register of terms compiled by Czech.

Friedrich Achleitner describes House S. as follows: "This house seems to me to be a successful and perhaps unintentional paraphrase of the Frank House on Wenzgasse. The central element is the library tower, which is surrounded by stairs. Everything is compressed in this tower, architecture and education, food for the eyes and the brain. One perceives the 'wings,' the room groups on the right and left, all the more freely. They appear open, unpretentious, permeable. Self-evidently in contact with the outside

world and with one another. Czech opines that the floor plan would have an affinity to a Baroque castle or chateau floor plan. That's true. But Fischer refracted by Frank. I didn't know that if one elongates the Frank House on Wenzgasse, a stair tower would pop out and a Baroque floor plan would emerge. Incidentally, House S [...] conveys freedom to House M [...], in the sense of Frank, as if a lot had already been the case."[4]

With Frank, the space assigned to the stairs is the hall, a space that had an essential function as a ground floor reception space in the upper-class residential buildings of the prewar period and served as a lounge between the bedrooms on the more private upper floors.[5] Frank's House Beer also provides vistas along the access path from the residential floor to the upper floor. Czech replaced the hall with a library room.

In the Baroque floor plans[6] he mentions, the round space is the center of the complex, where the main entrance is also located. The adjoining wings

4 Friedrich Achleitner: "Franks Weiterwirken in der neueren Wiener Architektur," in: *UM BAU* 10, 1986, 121–131: 127.
5 In Frank's smaller Swedish houses, the "hall" continues to be called this, but is spatially reduced to an anteroom or a hallway that serves as a divider to the other rooms.

Change of direction and round spaces: Dicopa Office (1975)

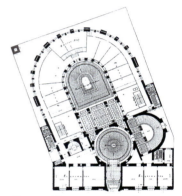

Change of direction and round spaces: Otto Wagner's Länderbank in Vienna, 1882–1884

are arranged at flat angles. The round shape of the tower at House S. also resulted from the question of how one can connect two different spatial directions via a mediating space. This configuration was used, for example, by Otto Wagner when building the Länderbank in Vienna. Czech sees the reference to John Soane, inter alia, in the spatial conciseness.

Frank's text "Das Haus als Weg und Platz" ("The House as Path and Place"), in which he explains House Beer, was reprinted for the first time in the Frank exhibition catalog in 1981.[7] In this essay, Frank called for the (residential) house to be designed like a city with streets, paths and places to rest. A particularly important element of this structure is the staircase, which also forms the center of House Beer. This leads through the house in such a way that the more public living spaces open by themselves and offer views of them. To indicate a change in the degree of privacy, the staircase is continued in the opposite direction to the private bedrooms.

6   At the same time (from 1981) Czech was working on a renovation of the Schwarzenberg Palace in Vienna. This corresponds to the mentioned Baroque configuration. In the Schwarzenberg Palace, a room with apses, which is vaulted by a dome, forms the center of the complex.
7   Frank: "Das Haus als Weg und Platz" ("The House as Path and Place") (originally in: *Der Baumeister* 8/1931), trans. Wilfried Wang, in: Frank 2012, Vol. 2, 198–209.

In this text, Frank vehemently opposed the rectangular living space as the most unsuitable one for living: "I believe that if one were to draw a polygon at random, be it with right angles or with obtuse ones, as a plan for a room, it would be much more functional than a regular rectangular one."[8] The rectangular room needs interior design to divide and structure it. It is the architect's job to create the rooms and not to furnish them; that should be left to the residents themselves. "It is a well-known fact that for good spaces it is quite irrelevant what kinds of furniture are being disposed in it, provided that they are not so large that they become architectural elements. The personality of the inhabitant can develop freely. The space will emphasize those positions to which every square and road is to be assigned."[9]

8 Ibid, 201.
9 Ibid., 207.

A year prior to Czech's commission for House S., he participated in the aforementioned *Forum Design* exhibition in Linz. The exhibition took place in a 600-meter-long temporary hall designed by Haus-Rucker-Co with borrowings from Joseph Paxton's Crystal Palace from 1851. The avant-garde of Austrian and international architects, designers and artists were invited to the exhibition. "The term design should be examined in its comprehensive meaning: its influence on the quality of life in general and on the identity of each individual in particular."[10] The best-known exhibit of the *Forum Design* was Christopher Alexander's Linz Café, a wooden pavilion temporarily built on a narrow side of the hall. These two works (hall and café) also embodied the transition phase between modernism, modernist criticism and the emerging "postmodernism."

10 Helmuth Gsöllpointner: "Design ist unsichtbar," in: *Design ist unsichtbar*, 1981, 7.

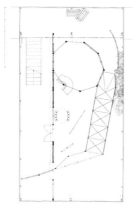

Change of direction and round spaces: Exhibition contribution *Forum Design* Linz 1980. Five of the nine wooden columns (different heights, different surfaces) are used in House S.

11 Czech: "Follow Me," in: ibid., 656f.
12 Czech financed the high-quality handcrafted wooden columns for the exhibition by using them in House S. and in Monika Pöschl's apartment.

Czech's concept for his exhibition contribution[11] was "to interest the visitor merely with architectonic means." He staged a "sequence of spatial experiences," which, like a Russian doll, led into smaller and smaller spaces and allowed the visitor to experience a space perceived as being inside, as an outside space in the next space. The highlight of this path was an oval room, the only one open to the exhibition hall and lit. It was formed by nine wooden columns and a fabric wreath attached above. As the last station to be entered, this type of space is repeated in an extremely reduced form, with a different geometric design and more precise formulation, and it is called "model space" by Czech. The conception corresponds to Frank's demands on the house as a path and place. The visitor is guided without being aware of it. No room has a right angle. The entire route is only given by architectural means and not by "furnishings." Unlike Frank, Czech also generated disturbance and confusion in the sequence of the spaces when they led to unexpected experiences and unsettled one's own body perception. The conception of the exhibition contribution called "Follow Me" by Czech is reminiscent of Lewis Carroll's Alice in *Alice in Wonderland*, who follows the white rabbit and unexpectedly finds herself in a world where different spatial principles apply. Czech had already used a similar concept for the Dicopa office conversion (1974–1975) in Vienna. There, the diversified interior design served to conceal a staircase soffit along a narrow corridor.

The floor plan configuration of House S. varies the loose arrangement in the *Forum Design* contribution in a geometrically stricter way, superimposed by further design considerations. The library room roughly corresponds to the oval room in the exhibition, while reusing five of its nine disparate wooden columns.[12] However, these do not form the actual space of the library but enclose the void in the middle and create an object similar to the "model space" of the exhibition. According to Frank's maxims, the stairs and library are organized as a structure of paths and squares, from which the rooms are accessed differently depending on their importance in the social structure of family life: The living rooms open directly to the library room, the bedrooms are connected via another staircase (parents) or a bridge (children). Between the library on the bedroom floor and the living room there is a separate, very narrow staircase that can be accessed like a secret passage via a set of cabinets. The different orientations of the two building wings are partially taken up in the respective other, for

55 cm wide, discreet connecting staircase between the living room and the sleeping area

example, in the children's rooms, which breaks through the otherwise strictly rectangular geometry of the rooms. From the balcony of the children's room there is another "secret staircase" in the form of a spiral staircase into the garden, which enables one to leave and re-enter the house unnoticed.

In the explanatory text "Einige Entwurfsgedanken" ("Several Design Thoughts") for his contribution to the exhibition in Linz, Czech wrote under the term "deformation": "When designing, we proceed with systems in which we define the requirements (imposed or own). None of the systems is entirely sufficient, at least at the 'edges' of the system we have to come up with another system. The design is a progressive series of decisions that remain noticeable in the modifications of the systems and their superimpositions. The result can still be superficially simple if all the superimpositions are congruent—on closer inspection they will reveal their complexity by vibrating."[13]

13 Czech: "Einige Entwurfsgedanken," in: *Design ist unsichtbar*, op. cit., 395–404: 399; partly also in: "Einige weitere Entwurfsgedanken" (1980), in: Czech 1996, 81.

The other four reused columns in Monika Pöschl's apartment (1980)

What Czech does not address in this project description is the fact that the library room also reflects the different personal backgrounds of the clients: One of the clients is a physician, the parents of the other client were communists and had to go into exile in London during National Socialism and came back to Vienna with the support of the Communist Party to help the reconstruction effort immediately after the end of the war. The view from the bottom floor through the void of the library tower is both: crystalline pattern and communist star, but at the same time it is reminiscent of the view through a kaleidoscope, colorful and open to new, fantastic spaces.

The book edges in the parapet create the dentil of the cornice profile.

House S.

Salzamt Restaurant

Period of origin: 1981–1983
Address: Ruprechtsplatz 1, 1010 Vienna
Clients: Monika Banićević-Pöschl, Tale Banićević, Denise Steiner-Herz
Project team: Paul Katzberger, Johann Gritzner

The restaurant is located on the ground floor of a house that had been built in the place of the former monopoly salt taxing authority, the Salt Office. By removing non-load-bearing transverse walls, a 17-meter-long, spacious dining room was created. Such a room, however, conveys the strongest impression from one end; from then on it can only get shorter. There is "no reason to go further" (at least spatially), as nothing new is to be expected and it becomes "weaker" the further one goes inside.

Czech's nearly imperceptible interventions enlarge the room in the middle: the floor slopes slightly towards the middle and rises again towards the back, barely visible to the eye, but unconsciously noticeable in terms of spatial awareness. The ventilation ducts are arranged on both sides in a longitudinal direction above the tables, but they are slightly bulged outwards in the horizontal. Along the two rows of tables there are staggered wooden columns with globe lights, each of which is arranged in a large, flat curve so that their distance in the middle increases. In the side niches along the window front, mirrors give the room additional depth.

The colors chosen for the sound-absorbing wall panels on the front sides were to be "as ugly as possible"—Czech wanted to come up with new color combinations in this way. Chandeliers made of colored glass were designed for the ceiling lighting in the dining room. These were gradually complemented by the client, Monika Banićević-Pöschl.

Adolf Loos: Café Museum, 1899

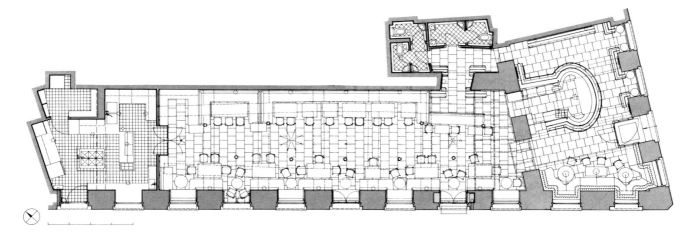

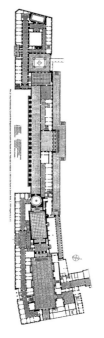

Albert Speer's former "New Reich Chancellery" in Berlin (1939) also had an inclined access (via a round room) to a long room due to a bend in Vossstrasse, which unconsciously increased the effect of the "marble gallery."

Access from the bar area to the dining room follows at an inclined angle. Czech ironically draws the comparison with Albert Speer's former New Reich Chancellery in Berlin: There, too, one enters the monumental corridor with a row of pillars on the way to the *Führerzimmer* not in the axis of the entrance, but at an inclined angle from a circular "mediating room."

Otto Wagner already used the circle to mediate between different spatial directions, for example, in the former Länderbank on Hohenstaufengasse in Vienna. In contrast to Speer and Wagner, however, there is no circular room in the Salzamt. Here, the elliptical bar takes on the "obscuration" of the changing direction of the room: the path into the dining room leads tangentially past the round counter edge and then bends in the direction of the dominant longitudinal axis. The bar itself can be almost completely occupied all around, and in addition to the described direct route into the dining room, there is a "secret route" on the opposite side of the counter, which necessitated a separate wall breakthrough and significantly enriches the overall spatial situation. From here, the main room can be entered from the side (or the toilet can be accessed via a "short route").

In 1985, Czech prepared the lecture "Ein Begriffsraster zur aktuellen Interpretation Josef Franks" ("A Conceptual Matrix for the Current Interpretation of Josef Frank") as a contribution to the Josef Frank Symposium organized by the Austrian Society of Architecture (ÖGfA)

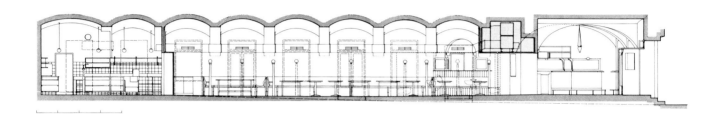

in Vienna.[1] After "For a Change," this is a key text from which Czech himself repeatedly quotes. It can be assumed that the conceptual origins for this contribution began during his Frank scholarship and the associated visit to the Frank Archive in Stockholm.[2] Czech discovered in Frank "an eye for actual life, drawing on everyday reality," in a line of thought by Otto Wagner and Adolf Loos. Wagner is about the relation to "real life," about "the exact and realistic conception of real urban life," while Loos is about "filter[ing] out the existing culture's viable elements."[3] Frank went beyond both judgmental positions and what applies for him is: "Anyone today who wants to create something that is alive must include everything that lives today."[4] For Frank, these ranged from "sentimentality and its excesses, tastelessness" up to "kitsch."

As early as 1970, Czech quoted Frank's statements about "kitsch," which he had taken from his unpublished writings, in "Der Loos-Gedanke,"[5]: "Every great work of art must border on kitsch. If people are so charmed by kitsch, then that at least is a genuine sentiment; they aren't putting on airs. And the work of art must speak to this true feeling and shape it into a meaningful form."[6]

In 1983, in a critical examination of Christopher Alexander's *Pattern Language*, Czech wrote: "Mustn't, on the contrary, a participation concept also include those whose hearts are full of malice? Mustn't an architectural concept be capable of taking in everything that surrounds us, the clichéd,

1 ÖGfA Josef Frank Symposium 1985, published in: *UM BAU* 10, 1986, therein Czech: "Ein Begriffsraster zur aktuellen Interpretation von Josef Frank" (1985), 105–120. Also in: Czech 1996, 111–122. English translation by Elise Feiersinger, "A Conceptual Matrix for the Current Interpretation of Josef Frank" (1985), in: Czech 2019, 151–181.
2 Since his trip to Sweden in 1969, Czech had intended for some time to write a book about Frank.
3 Czech: "A Conceptual Matrix…," op. cit., 159.
4 Ibid., 160.
5 Czech: "Der Loos-Gedanke" (1970), in: Czech 1996, 69–72.
6 Frank's published writings first appeared collectively in 2012; those unpublished during his lifetime are still awaiting publication. Quoted here in the text "A Conceptual Matrix for the Current Interpretation of Josef Frank" (1985), trans. Elise Feiersinger, in: Czech 2019, 151–181: 163.

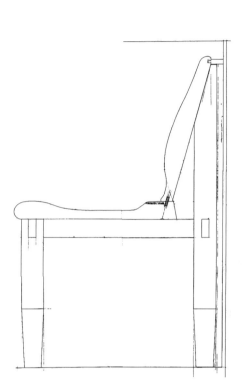

the dishonest, the ready-made? Mustn't it be capable in certain cases of doing without aesthetic judgment, which is a moral judgment? Mustn't there be some sense of the unexpected, the absurd, and that which contradicts the rules?"[7] Czech describes this approach with the term "mannerism."

The spatially effective interventions in the Salzamt are different from those in the Kleines Café (cornice) or in the Wunder-Bar (Gothic ribs). Czech pared the architecture down to the traditional, everyday furnishing elements (lights, ventilation ducts, framed mirrors, a continuous wooden bench) and repeated his own proven ones: the upholstered bench (in the bar area, not in the restaurant area), the mirrors with the spherical lights fitted into the frame, the rounded counter. Moreover, he worked

[7] Czech: "Christopher Alexander and Viennese Modernism" (1984), trans. Elise Feiersinger, in: Czech 2019, 135–148: 146. In this sense, one can perhaps understand Czech's reference to Albert Speer.

on everyday elements such as the globe lights—standard bathroom lights with porcelain sockets—by combining them with functional aspects to create objects that resemble three-dimensional assemblies: In the dining room, they became wooden columns tapering upwards with matching "capitals" and two rows attached to coat hooks. They generate a diffuse, soft, glare-free light which, due to the positioning of the columns, is not above the tables, as is often the case, but between them, so that seated guests—similar to the Kleines Café—have a light source just behind them and a little further in front.

The swiveling black sheet metal pendant lights in the bar area are typical workshop lights, as they had existed in the interwar period and as they were also used in the Wunder-Bar.

The bar with its weaker light intercepts the visitors at the entrance to then usher them, in a deaccelerated manner, into the dining room, which is effectually reinforced by the varying brightness between bar and restaurant. The users of Czech's architecture are not guided along an axis but find their way "into the light" by themselves after a brief irritation. They are aided by the wood-cladded underside of the paneling for the ventilation that is hung behind the door in the dining room: the darkly lacquered panels are structured by light-colored joint cover strips, with the strips attached directly above the passage picking up the direction of the bar area, while those drawn further into the room take up that of the dining room. The intersection of the two matrixes reflects these two "layers" and defines the threshold not as a border, but as a flowing transition.

Basement Remodeling in Palais Schwarzenberg
Restaurant, bar, hall, banquet kitchen and staff rooms

Period of origin: 1981–1984
Address: Schwarzenbergplatz 9, 1030 Vienna
Client: Karl Johannes Schwarzenberg
(largely demolished)
Project team: Walter Gruss, Harald Schönfellinger, Romana Ring, engineering: Peter Kramer ÖBA: Sepp Müller, Andreas Heinrich

The restaurant was located in the basement of the Schwarzenberg Palace, which had been built by Lukas von Hildebrandt from 1697 to 1704 and completed by Johann Bernhard and Josef Emanuel Fischer von Erlach. One of the most important Baroque complexes in Vienna, it is situated in the immediate vicinity of Belvedere Palace. At the time of the Czech renovation, the upper floors contained hotel rooms. The intervention in the basement solved several operational problems: The kitchen could be relocated and enlarged, the supply of the hall operations on the upper ground level was simplified and the hotel received additional lounge areas with an entrance, hall and bar that could be used together with the restaurant.[1]

For Czech, the starting point for the architectural conception was the building's structure, one by no means as clear as might have been assumed due to the uniform façade, but rather "disturbed or hidden" by multiple changes during the construction period and later alterations.[2] The redesign works out the structure of the existing substance, "even where irregularities reveal its historical layering."[3] However, Czech never intended to design a "Baroque" restaurant. "The architectural means of the present should be used—even when some of them are themselves historical clichés, like for instance crystal chandeliers. A contemporary concept of an elegant restaurant does not exclude a critical and ironical point of view which allows the clientele to feel comfortable but at the same time stimulated."[4]

The spatial circumstances dictated that the dining rooms should be accommodated in relatively small, demarcated halls. For Czech, this resulted in the task of still enabling the kind of intimacy and anonymity that one expects as a visitor to a restaurant, because "it is strange to have the feeling that you have to share your living room with someone." The

1 Czech: "Neu und Alt. Umbau des Restaurants im Palais Schwarzenberg," in: *wbw* 3/1985, 26–31: 26.
2 Ibid.
3 Czech: "Transformation Schwarzenberg Palais," in: *Architecture and Urbanism* 16:11, 60.
4 Ibid.

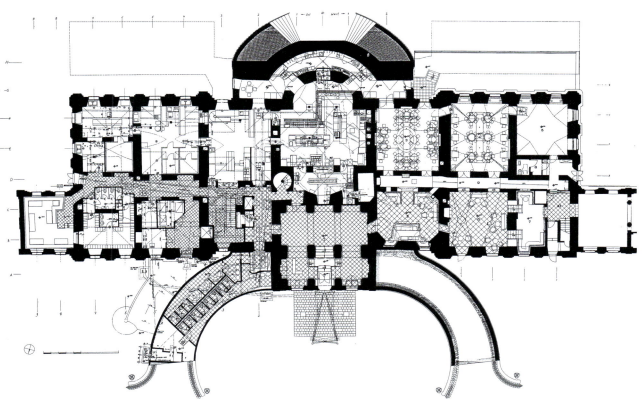

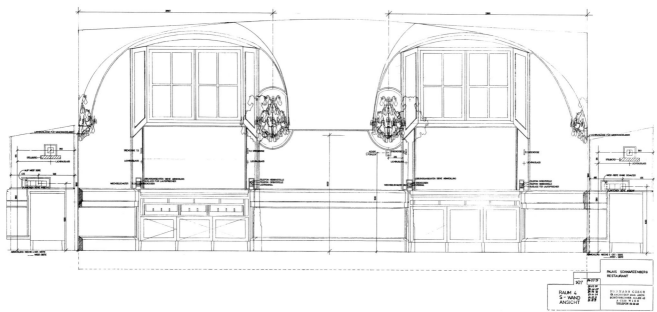

5 Czech: "Lower ground floor, Palais Schwarzenberg, Vienna, 1983–4," in: *Hermann Czech. Options in Architecture*, 1987, 8–11: 9.
6 Ibid., 10–11.

formation of two spatial conditions is particularly important here: light and acoustics.[5] So, in order to achieve the desired differentiation, Czech distributed several floor lamps in the space instead of illuminating it with a chandelier in the middle, as is often done in a room with a vault.[6] The resulting possible low height of the chandeliers enables an intimate atmosphere in some areas; its variable positioning in the space allows alternative groupings of tables. To counter the problem of possible glare, there are two "classic" options: enlarging the light-emitting surface with fabric or matt glass or using crystal glass chandeliers that multiply the points of light. Czech opted for the latter, combining the Baroque crystal chandelier type with internal light sources. Czech employed a variant of this floor lamp in the bar, but instead of the refraction of light through crystal glass, a bright fabric was used here.

Another measure to create the desired intimacy in the Schwarzenberg restaurant was muffled acoustics that Czech produced using carpets and textile wall coverings whose wood frame profiles accentuate the vault structure.

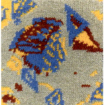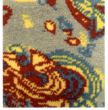

Fitted carpet in three colors based on a design by Christian Ludwig Attersee—the gray background corresponds to the color of Viennese standard dirt according to the information provided by the Austrian Textile Institute.

The design of a wall covering from Otto Wagner's Postal Savings Bank in different colors

The carpets were designed by the painter Christian Ludwig Attersee in three color combinations. The wall colors in the dining areas of the restaurant were a strong red or pink for the vaults and plinth areas, combined with the sand color or dark blue[7] of the wall coverings—a sedately striped textile design by Otto Wagner for the Postal Savings Bank in other color combinations.

7 It is also typical of Czech's colors that different people designate them with different colors.

In one of the rectangular picture frames in the corridor, a view into the bar through one of the oval frames there—technically possible because of the existing masonry cavities in the fireplace area.

In the bar, the vault is additionally painted glossy, making the color darker and reflecting the point-like light sources from the floor lamps. The green of the bar armchairs and the wooden wall friezes, which complement the red, enhances the effect, though the primary lighting mood is dominated by the warm red.

Czech designed two types of seating furniture for the restaurant, namely the restaurant chair and the previously mentioned armchair for the bar and hotel hall. A type from the early 19th century served as a model for the restaurant chair, as our idea of seating comfort arose at this time—and with which Baroque palaces were frequently furnished. A library chair by John Soane serves as the reference for the armchair.

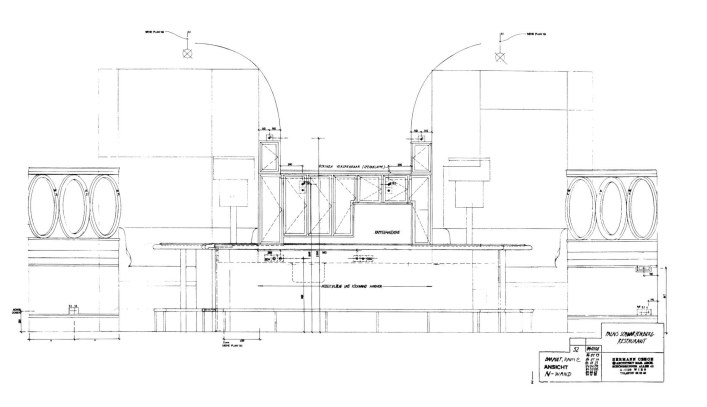

Armchair designs based on model types from the early 19th century, when our idea of a comfortable armchair was first emerging.

Basement Remodeling in Palais Schwarzenberg

Czech also designed the entrance area to the restaurant: the main entrance was located directly under the former stately entrance on the raised ground floor of the palace, which was accessed by two side ramps, and was formed by the less representative, comparatively low door into the basement. Czech countered this situation by designing an inviting canopy for a weather-protected driveway: a dematerialized steel structure with a clamped "sail"—elements that come from the study of Frei Otto and had already been processed in several designs such as the retractable roof over the Graben or in the Mödling shopping center project. In this case, he overlapped the modernist construction with references to the Baroque palace, such as the originally turquoise-gray color scheme and the general

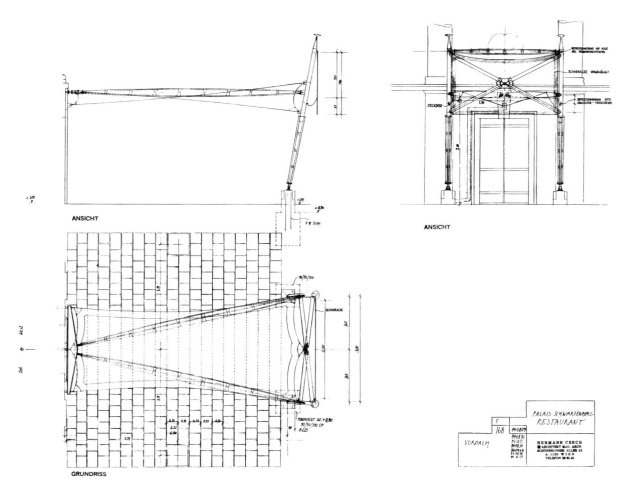

effect of the construction as that of a Baroque canopy stretched between ceremonial staffs.

The reception among contemporaries was quite critical. Friedrich Kurrent wrote in 1985 after a visit to the restaurant: "I felt as if I was seeing the fall of the monarchy a second time (when I missed it the first time). A beautiful requiem? Sometimes I have the feeling that Czech is about to overtake Loos *and* Frank *and* Venturi *and* Hollein on the left. Will that end well?"[8] Kenneth Frampton said in an interview in 1989: "I like particularly […] his polemical piece entitled 'No Need for Panic,' although what he has done since, in the Schwarzenbergpalast, has been enough to panic me."[9]

8   Friedrich Kurrent: "Frank und frei," in: *UM BAU* 10 1986, 85–93: 92.
9   Frampton interview in: *UMRISS* 1–2/1989, 9–13: 13.

Christopher Alexander: Linz Café, 1980

10 Czech: "Modernity and/or Urbanity. Presentation of personal work," in: *Texten. Colloquium Architectuur* "Modernisme en de Stad," 1986, 57–78: 76.
11 Czech: "Eine Einschätzung des Schwarzenberg" (2008), unpublished text, Czech Archive.
12 Christopher Alexander: *The Linz Café – Das Linz Café*, 1981.
13 Alexander et al.: *Eine Muster-Sprache. Städte Gebäude Konstruktion*, edited by Hermann Czech, 1995. English original: Alexander et al. *A Pattern Language: Towns, Buildings, Constructions*, Oxford and New York: Oxford University Press, 1977.
14 *A Pattern Language*, ix.
15 Alexander: *Linz Café*, op. cit., 64–65.
16 Alexander et al.: *A Pattern Language*, op. cit., 544.
17 Ibid., 644–647.
18 Ibid., 673–675.
19 Ibid., 1153–1156.

Czech sees his way of working as an eclectic "short-cut"; he used viable elements from the world of the trivial or even from architectural history instead of designing them himself to solve architectural problems in an economic way and to generate meanings and associations. For him, this reference to the past is to be read with critical and ironic undertones and in no way nostalgically. As an example, he cites the crystal chandelier, which can be seen as a cliché of "elegance." In this case, it is also the classic solution to the problem of glare that exists with low-lying lighting.[10] "It is a reflected architecture of defined individual decisions."[11]

Christopher Alexander designed the so-called Linz Café for the *Forum Design* exhibition in Linz in 1980, in which Czech also participated with an exhibition contribution. A documentation of the project with the translation of Alexander's English project description by Hermann Czech was published in 1981 by Löcker Verlag.[12] Alexander's claim when designing the Linz Café was to "make something which is simple, ordinary and comfortable." The visitor's well-being was the starting point for his considerations. For Alexander, the project offered the opportunity to use a selection of those "patterns" he had defined in *A Pattern Language*,[13] his "sourcebook of the timeless way."[14] Together with his staff at the Center for Environmental Structure at the University of Berkeley in California, he had defined "patterns" based on his own experience and in search of archetypal solutions. For the Linz Café, for example, the patterns "Main Entrance," "Tapestry of Light and Dark," "Sequence of Sitting Spaces" or "Warm Colors" were used.[15] In "Main Entrance" he demands: "… give it a bold, visible shape which stands out in front of the building."[16] For "Tapestry of Light and Dark" Alexander analyzes that it is important to create differently lit areas in a building, since spaces that are supposed to form an effective setting for a function are determined by their special light.[17] "Sequence of Sitting Spaces"[18] is about creating a sequence of more informal and more formal seating in a building. In "Warm Colors"[19] he states that one should choose the surface colors in such a way that they create a warm impression together with the natural, reflected and artificial light. Cold colors should only be used to highlight the warm ones.

One cannot directly compare these two projects—the Linz Café was a solitary new building, the Schwarzenberg Restaurant was built into existing premises, and while one served as an informal, temporary café for an audience of art and architecture enthusiasts, the other was an elite restaurant for an upscale public. Both, however, were designed under the premise of offering the visitor "well-being" and "comfort."

In his projects, Czech also works with solutions that incorporate the intuitive behavior of people and therefore often use historical or archetypal elements such as the design of an entrance or the way in which artificial light is deployed. Here is also a parallel to Josef Frank, who defined architecture as follows: "Yet the rules for the good house as an ideal do not change in principle and have only to be looked at afresh. How does one enter a garden? What does the route look like from the gateway? What is the shape of an anteroom? How does one pass the cloakroom from the anteroom to reach the living room? How does the seating area relate to the door and the window? There are many questions like this which need to be answered, and the house consists of these elements. This is modern architecture."[20] Alexander calls the answers to these questions "patterns" and regards them as universal and unchangeable. In contrast to this, Czech differentiates the answers or "patterns," overlaps them, makes them "multi-layered." In an interview in 1983, while working on the Schwarzenberg restaurant, Czech said: "The more experience one has, the more accurately one can assess the effects that certain design decisions involve; that means it will happen less seldom that an intrinsically logical design evokes completely uncontrolled, often ridiculous associations for others. Only then can the brittle matter of architecture be used as a language. Only then is it possible to accomplish the inconspicuous, normal, and self-evident that looks as if it has always been that way."[21]

Czech himself sees his work in Palais Schwarzenberg as an important example in relation to the architectural discourse of the then-current "postmodernism," as well as the concept of "atmosphere," which came into the discourse later.[22] In 2008, he fought against the threatened demolition of the premises in a statement: "The destruction of an existing building for no technical or functional reason also means an economic destruction of values, after which, in the unlikely most favorable case, one achieves the same quality through further increased effort. (Strictly speaking, the new solution would have to be *better* if the loss of the unfeasible quality of the relative age is to be compensated for.)"[23]

20 Frank: "The House as Path and Place" (1931), trans. Wilfried Wang, in: Frank 2012, Vol. 2, 198–209: 209.
21 Czech: "Was ist Ihre Kunst im speziellen?" (1983), in: Czech 1996, 91–94: 94.
22 Czech: "Eine Einschätzung…," op. cit., "At most in the result, but not in the methodical design process, 'atmosphere' plays a role."
23 Ibid.

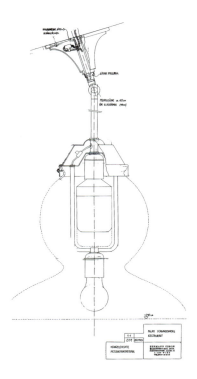

Conference space with wall paneling; lighting with variable luminous flux distribution: scattered light and downlight

In 2014, the premises were made accessible to the public again as part of the "Vienna Design Week" with accompanying artistic (Heinz Frank) and architectural (Hermann Czech) interventions under the title "Hermann Czech. Atmosphäre: Eine Illustration zu einem verfehlten neuen Theoriebegriff" ("Hermann Czech. Atmosphere: An Illustration of a Failed New Theoretical Concept").[24] On this occasion, Czech summarized his thoughts on the term "atmosphere." For him, it arises as the result of a design process (or later changes, e.g., as a result of an aging process), but cannot be defined in advance as a controllable goal. The user should remain free in his feelings. "On the other hand, an intention to want to control the 'atmosphere'—the effect on the user—amounts to manipulation, setting him or her not as an end, but as a means for other purposes, such as money or opinion making. 'Design' production of this kind renounces not only truthfulness, but also irony and sarcasm, and genuine communication altogether."[25] The understanding of architecture as language (communication) rather than as a means of producing atmosphere creates the scope for interpretation that language always contains.

24 The "Vienna Design Week" 2014 was curated by Lilli Hollein and took place from September 26 to October 5, 2014. See also: Archive 2014, www.viennadesignweek.at.
25 Czech: Text sheet in the "Vienna Design Week" 2014 exhibition.

The cornice on the wall is painted; only the perspective projection of a "tooth" on the corner of the wall is actually implemented.

Exhibition *Von hier aus. Zwei Monate neue deutsche Kunst* (*Up from here – Two months of new German art in Düsseldorf*)

Period of origin: 1983–1984, duration of the exhibition: 29.09.–02.12, 1984
Address: Halle 13, Messe Düsseldorf
Clients: City of Düsseldorf and Gesellschaft für aktuelle Kunst Düsseldorf e.V.
Concept: Kasper König
Project team: Franz Loranzi, Wolfgang Podgorschek, Ernst Jönke, ÖBA: NOWEA

Kasper König conceived and curated an exhibition with exhibits by 63 German artists in the 12,000 m², nearly square-shaped Halle 13 of the Messe Düsseldorf complex.[1] Czech was appointed as the architect after Ludwig Leo had turned down the offer. He decided to use the trade fair wall system only in suitable individual cases, but to provide open wall and room elements, which ultimately resulted in a city metaphor, and to generate the "genius loci," as Kasper König postulated, through a corresponding design process. "It was only decided in each case what could be kept with certainty, and in each case postponed what would obviously be subject to change. The series of decisions had to begin with the conditions of the hall and its infrastructure."[2] Before it was known which exhibits were to be shown and how they were to be presented, basic spatial decisions had been made: The food service available on one side of the hall was neglected, while two cafés were placed within the exhibition area.[3] The hall's largest delivery gate was used as an entrance and exit. From a separate entrance to the exhibition grounds, a ramp led from the outside to the inside through the gate to first lead visitors upwards at the entrance and thus give them an overview of the exhibition. Since the gate was not in the middle of the long wall of the hall, the ramp ran diagonally towards the center of the space. This axis continued to have an effect inside, albeit only abstractly; its "goal" could not be reached directly, but only indirectly, while there were "open aisles" in the transverse direction. To maintain an overview from the ramp, a decision was also made to reduce the height of the exhibition installations towards the center.

After two corner-forming walls had already established an inside-outside relationship, two opposing spatial types were made available for the presentation of the exhibits: the free-standing pavilion and a dense,

---

1 See Czech: "Zur Architektur der Ausstellung," project text, 1984, Czech Archive, published in: Kasper König (ed.): *Von hier aus. Zwei Monate neue deutsche Kunst in Düsseldorf*, exhibition catalog, 1984, and in: "Museum auf Zeit. Zur Ausstellung 'von hier aus,' zwei Monate neue deutsche Kunst in Düsseldorf, in: *wbw* 71/1984, Heft 12, 32–35. See also "'von hier aus.' Interviews mit Hermann Czech und Kasper König," in: *Displayer* 01/2007, hfg Karlsruhe.
2 *wbw* 71/1984, op. cit., 32f.
3 Interview… in: *Displayer*, op. cit.

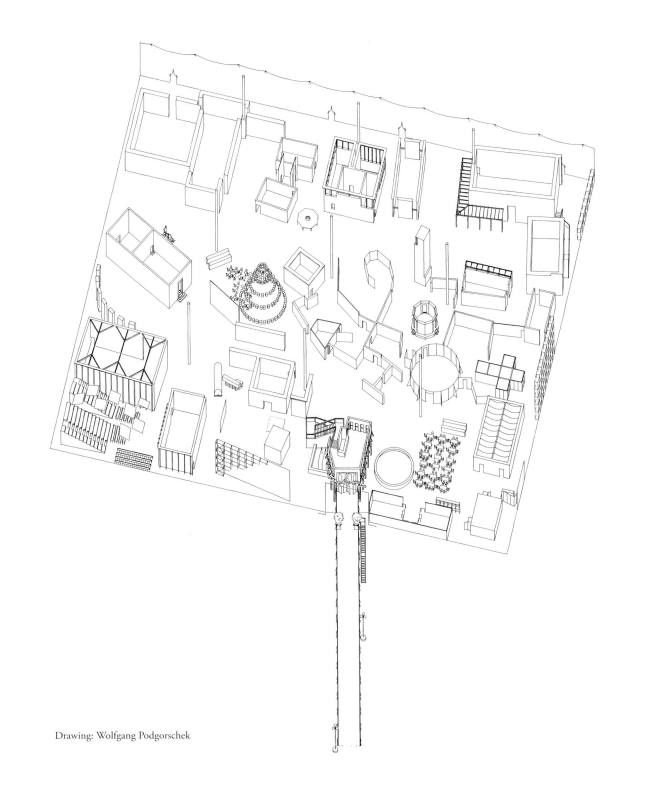

Drawing: Wolfgang Podgorschek

"settlement"-like arrangement of wall elements. The characteristics of the spaces were to be as diverse as possible, "for a variety of surfaces, from wallpaper to concrete formwork, lighting features ranging from intimate incandescent lamp lighting to pale work lighting in the hall, etc."[4] In this way it was possible to respond flexibly to the exhibits and the wishes of the artists. The "spaces" finally built were partly defined by the artists themselves, partly developed together with or designed for the artists. "The design problem has best been resolved if you can't say which spot is the best one. Perhaps it will become obvious that a seemingly random arrangement requires very precise considerations. Decisions that are really left to chance often lead to apparent intentions of which the planner has no idea."[5]

Czech had his first experience with a large-format exhibition as an assistant at the Institute of Design at the College of Applied Arts[6] in Vienna (1974–1980). The institute supported Hans Hollein, who was commissioned in 1974 to design the opening exhibition of the Cooper Hewitt Museum in New York as the new National Museum of Design

4 wbw 71/1984, op. cit., 33.
5 Ibid. Partial English translation, "Exhibition von hier aus Düsseldorf," in: *Architecture and Urbanism* 16:11, 52–57: 56.
6 Today it is called the University of Applied Arts.

for the Smithsonian Institution (Washington, DC) in 1976. Czech acted as project manager and years later edited a comprehensive publication on Hollein's exhibition concept.[7]

The newly founded museum had taken over a collection of mainly anonymous works from three millennia that had previously served as illustrative material for Cooper Union students. With the opening exhibition, the term "design" was supposed to overcome the restriction as an expression of "good taste" or "good form."[8] Hollein gave the show the programmatic name *MANtransFORMS*, thereby making it clear that for him the term "design" applied to everything that people "transform." The central idea behind the exhibition design was to convey this "message" to the public through various types of direct confrontation.[9] Reactions and associations were to be evoked in the visitors, thus stimulating their own thinking. Instead of presenting individual objects in linear historical contexts, "related topics and objects in situational contexts and supported by relationships of spatial arrangement" were shown.[10]

7 Hans Hollein: *MANtransFORMS. Konzepte einer Ausstellung. Concepts of an Exhibition*, 1989.
8 Lisa Taylor, then-director of the museum in the introduction in: ibid., 9–12: 10.
9 Hollein: "Aus dem Exposé vom September 1974," in: ibid., 17–21: 17.
10 Ibid.

Exhibition *Von hier aus. Zwei Monate neue deutsche Kunst* (*Up from here – Two months of new German art in Düsseldorf*)

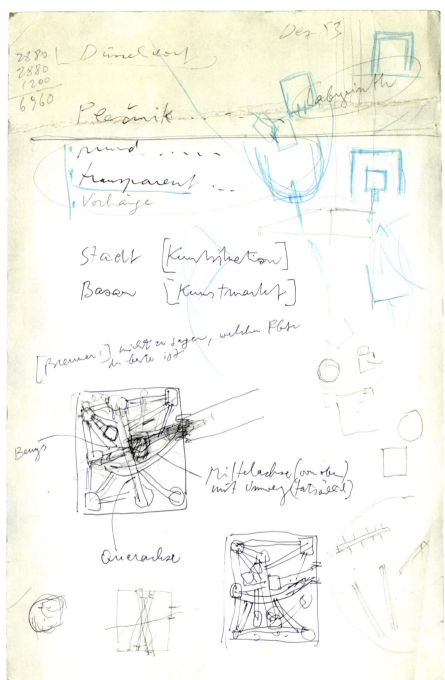

Selected Projects

Hollein refrained from imparting historical knowledge; selected object topics such as "hammers," "bread," "stars" or "a piece of cloth" symbolically stood for everything else made by people in order to communicate the concept of design in its entire cultural breadth.

Conceived together with Johannes Spalt on behalf of the University of Applied Arts, the second comprehensive exhibition Czech organized, as co-curator in this case, highlighted Josef Frank at the Museum of Applied Arts in 1981.[11] Here Spalt and Czech replicated a 1:1 scale garden house by Frank as a model and appointed it with his furniture. In the run-up to the exhibition, Czech had already prepared the reprint of Frank's most important written work, *Architecture as Symbol*, in Löcker Verlag and subsequently published it with a register of terms to mark this show. The two catalogs[12] appearing as part of the exhibition supplemented the only comprehensive theoretical text accessible again in book form at that time and were to long remain the only tangible information on the architectural and theoretical work of Josef Frank.

arbeitsgruppe 4, of which Spalt had been a member, had already conceived, designed and produced a series of pioneering exhibitions between 1955 and 1964—largely on their own initiative—the contents of which rank among the pioneering achievements in the rediscovery of modernism after 1945[13] and that were of particular importance for Czech. The architects of arbeitsgruppe 4 developed a system of modular picture panels in a careful, classic layout for their exhibitions. They vividly arranged pictures on these panels, forming a logical, sequential flow of information and, depending on the topic, combining them with models, furniture and handcrafted objects.

The rational, serial approach of arbeitsgruppe 4 to exhibition design was almost the opposite of that of Hans Hollein, which aimed at personal associations and treated each object individually. In *Von hier aus*, Czech melded both concepts by creating spatial experiences such as the entrance ramp or the urban structure-like organization. However, these are based on rational decisions such as the fact that there is no stringent order of the exhibits, but logical—and in some cases serial—sequences within the individual thematic areas. Czech has continued and further developed this approach over the course of his extensive exhibition work.

The exhibition designs of arbeitsgruppe 4 show parallels to the exhibition typology conceived by Otto Neurath for the Austrian Museum of Society and Economy in the 1920s.[14] Neurath developed free-standing

arbeitsgruppe 4: *Architektur in Wien um 1900* exhibition, 1964

Hans Hollein: *MANtransFORMS* exhibition: Presentation of "Bread," 1976

11 Johannes Spalt; Hermann Czech (eds.): *Josef Frank 1885–1967*, 1981.
12 Spalt; Czech, ibid.; and Spalt (ed.): *Josef Frank. Möbel, Geräte & Theoretisches*, 1981.
13 Gabriele Kaiser: "Bilanzen mit Ausblick," in: Architekturzentrum Wien (ed.): *arbeitsgruppe 4. Wilhelm Holzbauer, Friedrich Kurrent, Johannes Spalt 1950–1970*, 2010, 142–159: 144.
14 Nader Vossoughian: *Otto Neurath. The Language of the Global Polis*, 2011, 69.

Exhibition *Von hier aus. Zwei Monate neue deutsche Kunst* (*Up from here – Two months of new German art in Düsseldorf*)

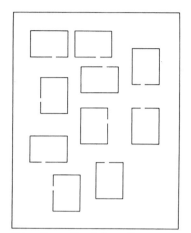

Rémy Zaugg: Sketch from: *Das Kunstmuseum, das ich mir erträume oder der Ort des Werkes und des Menschen* (*The Art Museum of My Dreams or A Place for the Work and the Human Being*), 1987

panels that were independent of the respective exhibition space, each with its own lighting. Commissioned by Neurath, Josef Frank designed a system of wooden exhibition boards that could easily be set up in different spatial configurations and were first used in 1927. For this exhibition, Frank organized the panels into a string of individual rooms accessed via a central aisle. In the middle there was a larger open area where models were displayed.[15] A simple, city-like spatial structure thus developed.

Czech's arrangement in *Von hier aus* seems much freer, enabling the impression of a random and chaotic arrangement of the displays and exhibits to arise at first glance. However, every formal decision is actually based on a reflection on the spatial conditions, according to the artists' wishes and in consideration of the curator's ideas. By superimposing these factors equally, Czech constructs a design on a rational, intellectual level "as if it had"—according to Frank—"originated by chance."

Czech's design shows an interesting parallel to the conception of the "ideal exhibition space" by the Swiss artist Rémy Zaugg around the same time. In a 1986 lecture entitled "Das Kunstmuseum, das ich mir erträume oder Der Ort des Werkes und des Menschen" ("The Art Museum of My Dreams or A Place for the Work and the Human Being"),[16] Zaugg summarized his thoughts: For him, it is the exhibition space that makes art possible in the first place; it already has a special relationship to the outside world and, depending on its quality, the art object can develop in it. In Zaugg's understanding, exhibiting means placing something in a special context and connecting things. For him, the ideal exhibition space is one in which people and the work of art can meet in a respectful way, and in a sketch he showed an exhibition space that consists of many small, independent spaces for each work of art.

15 Ibid., 72.
16 Rémy Zaugg: *Das Kunstmuseum, das ich mir erträume oder Der Ort des Werkes und des Menschen*, 1987.

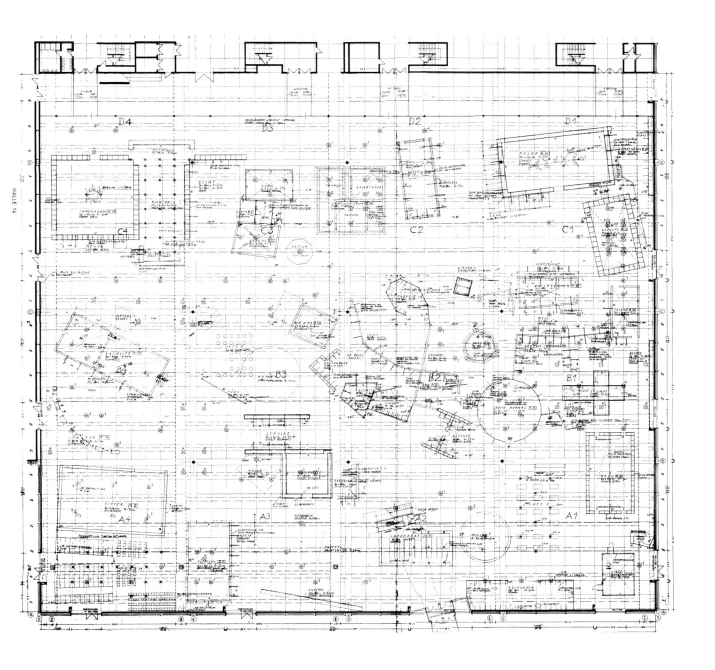

Exhibition *Von hier aus. Zwei Monate neue deutsche Kunst*
(*Up from here – Two months of new German art in Düsseldorf*)

Stadtparksteg Pedestrian Bridge

Period of origin: 1985–1986
Address: Stadtpark, 1010 Vienna
Clients: City of Vienna and Zentralsparkasse-Kommerzialbank of the Municipality of Vienna
Project team: Walter Michl, Wolfgang Podgorschek, Michael Loudon, engineering: Peter Kotzian, Alfred Pauser

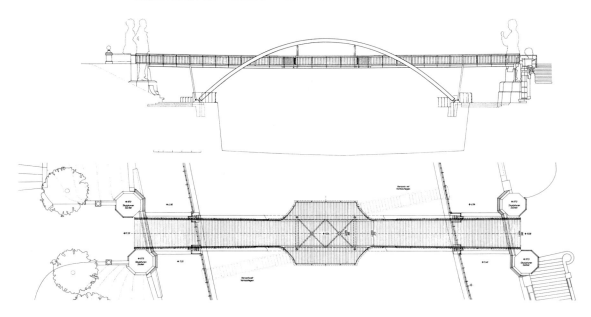

Otto Wagner: Vindobona Bridge, design, 1904

1 Czech: "Stadtparksteg" (2003), project description, https://www.nextroom.at, architecture online database.

A provisional structure since the Karolinenbrücke had been destroyed in 1945, the pedestrian bridge over the Vienna River in the Stadtpark was to be replaced.[1] Like the previous bridge, the new one now leads in the axis of Reisnerstrasse slightly diagonally across the river, but the construction was carried out orthogonally, so the route (especially near the "balconies") remains legible. The construction principle of the bridge was to result in the smallest possible area of silhouettes to obstruct the view in the direction of the river as little as possible. The bridge was made of steel; the railing and substructure are painted in the same shade of green (adapted from Otto Wagner) as the historic iron railings from the time of river regulation. The arches of the bridge were painted blue to blur with the sky, but contrary to Hermann Czech's intention, after a renewal of the paintwork, they are currently light gray.

The width of the bridge and the railings narrow almost imperceptibly towards the middle, which means that from the pedestrian perspective, the path to the middle seems longer, while from there to the other bank it seems shorter. Made of wooden planks, the walking area was designed with a slight sag of 25 centimeters to provide a good view from the banks ("analogous to the curved section of a theater floor"). In the design, four large-dimensioned figures were to be placed on top of the original, low-lying bridge supports to alienate the entire scale of the footbridge. Later, thoughts were made about putting up head sculptures by Franz West, which were ultimately positioned on the Stubenbrücke to the northeast of the footbridge, as Franz West wanted steel chains as an "inverted suspension" for the heads, which, however, would not have been technically possible with the Stadtparksteg. The new supports of the arch structure on the front quay were designed to also function as seating. Initially provisional due to the open question of sculptures, the connecting railings were completed around 2003 during a renovation of the front quay system by Manfred Wehdorn in a sensitive variant solution.

In 1983, Czech and the civil engineer Heinrich Mittnik took part in the competition for the new route for the Vienna River Valley metro crossing. The route of the Gürtel beltline railway in this area was to be relocated according to the specifications of the City of Vienna, which would have rendered Otto Wagner's existing route inoperable. Wagner's city gate-like bridge over the

Zeile (the never-built boulevard over the planned vaulted covering of the Vienna River) would have been destroyed or, at best, remained as a solitary relic. Czech's project, as well as Wilhelm Holzbauer's, were the only two to oppose the tender and intended to continue using the bridge; however, they were not taken into consideration in the competition result. Ultimately, after a long journalistic discussion and a change in the plan, which provided for the preservation and further use of the Otto Wagner structure, Wilhelm Holzbauer was commissioned to carry out the project because his solution stylistically imitated a Wagnerian railway building.

In the course of this competition design, Czech recognized that Wagner had made an advantage out of the formal problem of the bridge leading diagonally across the Vienna River Valley by "leaving" the disc-shaped central pillar under the orthogonal bridge with its portals in the direction of the river (namely of the planned boulevard), thus making the tension of the diagonally crossing directions even more visible.[2] An analogous idea came into play with the Stadtparksteg.

2 Czech: "Zur Wientalbrücke und andere Fragen der Architektur in der Stadt," in: Czech 1996, 100–104: 102. A more detailed account of the planning history in: Heinz Geretsegger; Max Peintner: *Otto Wagner*, supplemented edition 1983, 333–338.

If one walks along the Vienna River towards the Danube Canal, one comes to a third bridge, the Zollamtssteg, a pedestrian bridge designed by the architect Friedrich Ohmann.[3] A contemporary of Wagner whose attitude was more conservative than the latter, Ohmann planned the entire regulation of the Vienna River between the Stadtpark and the Danube Canal.[4] His work was characterized by a symbiosis of modern and traditional elements, whereby the reflection of a local reference was particularly important for him. Friedrich Achleitner used a picture of the Zollamtssteg in an article for the catalog for the exhibition *A New Wave of Austrian Architecture* in the spring of 1980 at the Institute for Urban Studies in New York. He illustrated his characterization of Viennese architecture as "a history of influences and their assimilation, a pluralist history of coexistence, confrontation and juxtaposition of different languages and mentalities, a history of the synthesis or combination of contradictory elements […] Austria has never been a country of architectural innovations."[5]

Czech's design shows clear parallels to the Zollamtssteg. The main girder is also an arch, and the middle of the bridge is also emphasized in terms of design: Ohmann narrows the space in the middle by having the railing jump in around the width of the arch construction, and spatially encloses it with two lanterns. Czech employs an extension in the middle, a lookout location which, with the design of the wooden handrail and the low height of the cross bracing, appears spatially contained and almost homey. An innovation—although not ostensible—arises by changing familiar elements.

The path over the Stadtparksteg is slowed down by various interventions—an altered perspective, a widening in the middle. Coming from the western part of Stadtpark, it continues the park's non-axial routing and becomes another "recreation space." To the east, the view leads into the depths of the Reisnerstrasse rising behind the Stadtpark, which results in a surprising perspective. In 1996, a sculpture by Donald Judd was erected on this axis on behalf of the Museum of Applied Arts under director Peter Noever, through which the path can now be continued. The oversized figures or heads proposed by Czech for the bridge reference similar bridge designs by Otto Wagner, for instance, on the Ferdinandbrücke built in 1905 with its four pylons.[6] In another design, the Vindobonabrücke, Wagner conceived four statues resembling guards. The "sunken" figures proposed by Czech would have had an unusual symbolic effect: Wagner's

---

3 The reference to the Zollamtssteg was also mentioned by Friedrich Achleitner as a "different repetition" in: Achleitner: *Österreichische Architektur im 20. Jahrhundert. Ein Führer in vier Bänden, Band III/1 Wien 1. – 12. Bezirk*, 2010, 84.

4 Pühringer: "Ohmann, Friedrich," in: *Neue Deutsche Biographie* 19, 1998, 492f.

5 Achleitner: "Comments on Viennese Architectural History: Motifs and Motivations, Background and Influences, Therapeutic Nihilism," in: Frampton (ed.): *A New Wave of Austrian Architecture*, 1980, 2–23: 3f. Works by Missing Link, Hermann Czech, Heinz Frank, IGIRIEN (Werner Appelt, Franz Eberhard Kneissl, Elsa Prochazka), Heinz Tesar and Rob Krier were shown at the exhibition.

6 Both designs by Otto Wagner are taken from the book by Geretsegger; Peintner: *Otto Wagner*, 1964.

optimistic worldview, in which stately symbols could still be used without a care, is no longer possible in Austria in 1985. The authorities have lost influence, yet they are still present, if perhaps only unconsciously. One of Czech's figures, sitting on the lower plinth, would not have towered over the passers-by; one would have encountered it at "eye level."

The detailed execution of the steel construction in the middle follows Otto Wagner, who also used standardly produced steel elements in a raw manner, with visible connections in addition to elements he designed and crafted. Czech used industrially produced profiles reduced to the structurally necessary minimum. In contrast to this, the handrail on the balcony-like enhancements is made with an elaborately ergonomically machined wooden profile. The walking area made of wooden planks relates to the historical crossings over the waters of the Stadtpark.

Friedrich Ohmann and Josef Hackhofer: Zollamtssteg, 1899–1900

Stadtparksteg Pedestrian Bridge

Residential Block Petrusgasse

Period of origin: 1985–1989
Address: Petrusgasse 4, 1030 Vienna
Client: Gemeinnützige Bauvereinigung "Wohnungseigentum"
Project team: Georg Übelhör, Michael Loudon, engineering: Herbert Endl,
ÖBA: Sepp Müller

Petrusgasse is located in the middle of Vienna's 3rd district and in the immediate vicinity of important municipal buildings of "Red Vienna" from the 1920s and 1930s, such as the Rabenhof housing complex with its over 1,000 apartments. However, the district is not a uniform typical working-class district, but has always been a mixed residential and commercial district with feudal sprinkles that now house embassies and consulates.

It was obvious to plan subsidized apartments with an appealing standard for an urban middle class for the "Gemeinnützige Bauvereinigung Wohnungseigentum," a non-profit building association.

With his first new apartment building, Czech builds upon his experience with adapting old apartments.[1] In his opinion, "housing" as a subject of modern architecture is outdated. The apartment with a particularly "clever" floor plan for the *Existenzminimum* (subsistence level) was put into perspective by the realization that it is possible to live well in many types of apartments and that the functionality of the floor plan is of secondary importance for the "quality of life." For Czech, the most striking feature of the old urban buildings in contrast to modern apartment floor plans is their "a-functionality": the layout of the apartment was determined by the constructive structure, the lighting and the access; the utilization of the rooms was largely negligible for their arrangement. When arranging the rooms, Czech tied into the living quality and flexibility of old-style apartments: "Rooms and spatial relations are not primarily determined by functions."[2] For Czech, it was important that the stories allow a certain variability of the apartment sizes despite the concrete shell construction. The small apartments in demand at the time can be combined to form larger units if needs change (walls that are not blackened in the floor plan correspond to the possible openings).

---

1 Czech: "Das Schweigen als architektonische Botschaft. Wohnhaus in Wien 3," in: *architektur aktuell* 135/1990, and English version of the text: "Apartment Building, Petrusgasse, Vienna, since 1985," in: *Hermann Czech: Options in Architecture*, 1987.
2 Czech: "Apartment Building, Petrusgasse, Vienna, since 1985," in: *Hermann Czech: Options in Architecture*, 1987, 5.

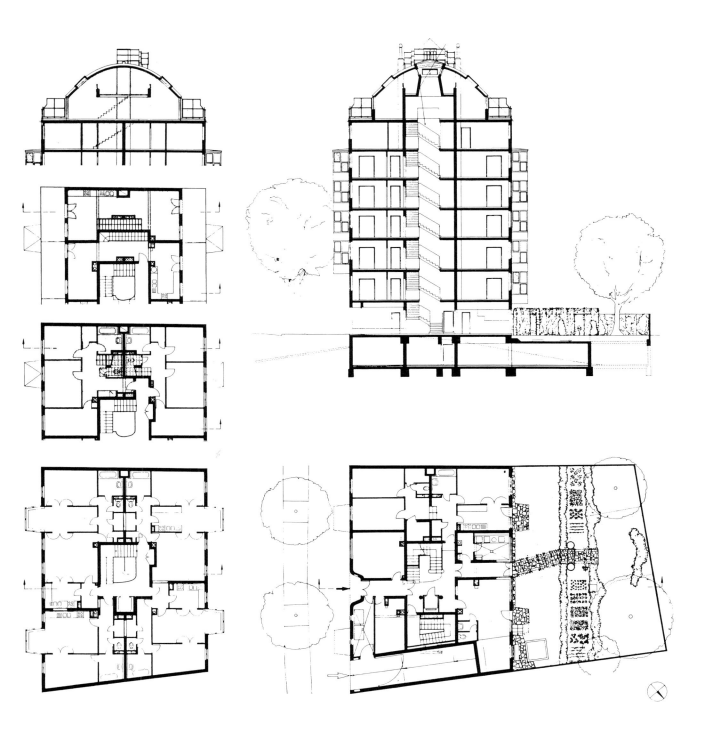

3   The "Neufert" is a standard reference work in the German-speaking architecture sector. Ernst Neufert: *Bauentwurfslehre. Handbuch für den Baufachmann, Bauherren, Lehrende und Lernende*, Berlin 1936 and Wiesbaden 2012 (40th edition).

4   Czech: "Das Schweigen…," op. cit. English translation in: Ulrike Jehle-Schulte-Strathaus: "'In welchem Style sollen wir bauen?' Gedanken zur Stil-losigkeit von Hermann Czech," wbw 6/1996, 27.

The façades on the street and in the courtyard are carefully elaborated. Following the incidence of light, the window sizes from bottom to top are lower and wider, according to the principles of Neufert.[3] The detailed execution of the plaster on the ground floor shows the horizontal grooves of an implied rusting to accentuate it towards the street; the plaster above, however, is extremely precise and without any added color pigments. Nonetheless, "its essential architectonic message consists in maintaining silence. Only in the long run—by change or interpretation—such a house may become the very expression of its contents."[4]

Czech does not only refer to apartments in old buildings regarding the neutrality of the spaces. Typical for this are the double doors between the rooms and an oriel in the living room. As in the classic old building, the double doors in the larger apartments on Petrusgasse are in one axis, so that when the doors are open one can look through all the rooms, which gives the apartment spaciousness and visual expanse. Nevertheless, all individual rooms can also be accessed through a corridor without any disruption.

The treatment of the street-side façade corresponds to that of old buildings with a more structured ground floor and the design that becomes lighter towards the top.

In the year before receiving the commission for Petrusgasse, Czech penned an essay for the Bolzano Chamber of Architects entitled "Adolf

Loos – Widersprüche und Aktualität" ("Adolf Loos – Contradictions and Topicality")[5] in which he redefined his stance on architecture by referring to Loos and Frank. As the basis of Loos's "design ethos," Czech analyzed Loos's image of modern life and modern people: "This image of modern life contains both the element of comfort and that of representation; it is a cosmopolitan, democratic, commercial culture, sustained by entrepreneurs and plumbers […], ennobled by the formal ideals of antiquity."[6] Czech calls this an "anti-formalist, 'bottom-up' stance." As another essential attitude of Loos, Czech emphasizes Loos's understanding of typology. For Loos, form is the product of a culture, not of an individual. "When Loos designs a men's fashion salon or a coffee house, he doesn't ask what this restaurant would have to look like in a different, yet to be created culture […]. He does not consider every detail from scratch.

5 Czech: "Adolf Loos – Widersprüche und Aktualität," in: *Mitteilungsblatt der Architektenkammer der Provinz Bozen*, 1984 and in other publications, latest version in: Podbrecky; Franz (ed.): *Leben mit Loos*, 2005, 17–25.
6 Ibid., 19.

Josef Frank and Oskar Wlach: Housing construction on Simmeringer Hauptstrasse, 1931

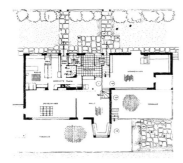

Josef Frank and Oskar Wlach: House Beer, 1931, living room with bay window

7   Ibid., 22. A partial English translation of this quote appears in Czech: "A Conceptual Matrix for the Current Interpretation of Josef Frank" (1985), trans. Elise Feiersinger, in: Czech 2019, 151–191: 190 and 159.
8   Ibid., 22f; Frank quotations from: *Architecture as Symbol* (1931), trans. John Sands, in: Frank 2012, Vol. 2, 9–191: 167.
9   Frank: "The People's Apartment Palace" (1926), trans. Brian Dorsey, in: Frank 2012, Vol. 1, 254–267.
10 Maria Welzig: *Josef Frank 1885–1967*, 1998, 96f.
11 Czech; Spalt: *Josef Frank 1885–1967*, 1981, 136.
12 For more information on the organization of the typical floor plans, see Eve Blau: *Rotes Wien. Architektur 1919–1934*, 2014, 213.

Anyone wishing to convey new ideas cannot simultaneously make use of a new language to do so. Loos was, of course, a lifestyle reformer, though his aim was not to create an ideal, parallel culture for outsiders, but rather to filter out the existing culture's viable elements."[7] To be able to apply Loos's thoughts, their further development through Josef Frank is of central importance for Czech. "Frank continues Loos's world of thought and prevents it from becoming doctrinal." His skepticism and tolerance lead him to demand that architecture embraces "the entire spirit of the time, along with all its sentimentality and its excesses, along with all its tastelessness […]."[8] Czech sees this as an ethic that lies in precisely grasping the concrete and not in fabricating an ideal world.

Josef Frank clearly took a position in the housing question in 1926 in the text "Der Volkswohnungspalast. Ein Rede, anlässlich der Grundsteinlegung, die nicht gehalten wurde." ("The People's Apartment Palace. A Speech to Mark the Groundbreaking That Was Never Delivered.").[9] He criticized the multi-story residential buildings of "Red Vienna" as monumental and backward, because they followed the type of the palace, both in the external design with oversized passageways, emphasized corners and other elements, as well as in the organization of the apartments. His contributions to the "Red Vienna" building program were conceived differently: Frank's aesthetic is a "'democratic aesthetic' of simplicity."[10] The façades are anti-monumental, the corners and central axes broken up by loggias.[11] The stories are uniform; none of them is highlighted. Balconies or loggias are regularly distributed across the façade. The structuring takes place through accentuated stairwells.

The floor plans of "Red Vienna" were largely predetermined by the City of Vienna. The rooms were often organized in a linear sequence, one room opened up the next—anteroom, kitchen-living room, room, chamber.[12] The combined kitchen-living room initially used was later replaced by a separate kitchen (work kitchen). Both were heavily criticized by Frank. The continuous suite of rooms would not correspond to modern living, but again put the bourgeois urge for representation before a contemporary living culture. For Frank, the latter consisted of the matching of lifestyle and living space. The most important room for him was the *Wohnküche*, the combined kitchen-living-room: It is where people live together, it is the public part of the apartment. The private (sleeping) rooms should be clearly separated from this and have their own entrances. Frank managed to organize the

floor plans of the apartments in his houses in such a way that the rooms are not in a row of doors, but are accessed from a main room (kitchen/living room) or the anteroom, despite the city's contrary specifications.[13] Moreover, Frank improved the lighting and ventilation of the apartments by organizing them so that most had at least one room facing the street and one facing the courtyard.[14]

The exterior design of Czech's house on Petrusgasse takes up Frank's stance towards this "'democratic aesthetic' of simplicity." However, Czech increased it to "silence." Its aesthetics do not allow any reference to the residents, the façade looks just as bourgeois as it is proletarian, at first glance average, inconspicuous; only at second glance does it reveal high-quality details. The windows, which become smaller and wider towards the top, actually provide every apartment the same incidence of light, regardless of the floor on which it is located. The oriels assigned to each apartment repeat Frank's façade design of the municipal housing on Simmeringer Hauptstrasse. In the floor plan, they repeat the bourgeois comfort of the oriel in House Beer. The residential floors of Loos's House on Michaelerplatz also represent a democratic aesthetic in their simplicity and the sameness of the windows. When Loos was asked to structure the façade more strongly, he replied with flower boxes in front of the windows, which again did not emphasize any story.

13 In terms of the internal organization of the floor plans, those of Frank differ significantly from the usual Viennese residential construction program.
14 Christopher Long: *Josef Frank*, 2002, 76.

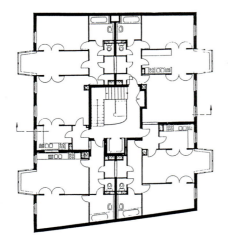

Conversion of the De Waal Apartment, Silbergasse, 1973

15 Blau: *The Architecture of Red Vienna*, op. cit., 202.
16 Czech; Mistelbauer: *Das Looshaus*, 1984 (3rd edition), plans: 20–22.

The floor plans in the House on Michaelerplatz are traditionally organized:[15] An elongated anteroom separates the representative rooms facing the street from the serving rooms facing the courtyard. The majority of the rooms can be accessed individually from this anteroom. The representative rooms are also connected to one another via an axis. In terms of the structural conception, the floor plan is entirely open and one could organize the apartments completely differently at any time without having to intervene in the structural statics of the house.[16]

Czech's floor plans combine the advantages of these different concepts: spaciousness without appearing monumental and restricting the furnishing, as well as separate accessibility in the larger apartments via an internal corridor. The kitchen and living room can be used as a common room, but can also be separated if necessary. The small apartments are equipped with combined kitchen-living rooms. Czech designed the construction in such a way that later changes, such as merging apartments, are possible.

One could interpret Czech's Petrusgasse floor plans as a superimposition of spatial configurations of bourgeois, metropolitan living from the Gründerzeit, for example, also that of Loos's House on Michaelerplatz with later considerations of the interwar period on more social and more modest forms of living such as Frank's house in the Werkbundsiedlung. The design of the common areas such as the entrance and staircase also links bourgeois elements with those of the reform movement in "Red Vienna." Classic light tiles with dark edge stripes and doormats embedded in the floor are combined with terrazzo tiles and a railing made of metal bars. The ceiling cornice—concealing gas pipes behind it—is painted a vivid yellow (a color which is mandatory for marking gas pipes) while the applied green, blue and wine-red tones can already be found on Otto Wagner's *Stadtbahn* railings and in the Kleines Café. Czech used the same industrially manufactured products for door fittings, door thresholds, the formation of the stairs and the round lights in the general areas: solid, comfortable, anonymous, everyday objects that are commonplace in Vienna.

Exhibition *Wien 1938 (Vienna 1938)*

Period of origin: 1986–1988
Address: Vienna City Hall, Volkshalle
Client: Historical Museum of the City of Vienna
Concept: Documentation Centre of Austrian Resistance
Project team: Franz Loranzi, Gerhard Riedling, Karin Tschavgova, Stephen Bidwell, Bernhard Denkinger, Ina Martin

The *Wien 1938* (*Vienna 1938*) exhibition took place in the Vienna City Hall to mark the 50th anniversary of the "Anschluss" between Austria and National Socialist Germany. The so-called *Volkshalle* (People's Hall) on the ground floor of the Vienna City Hall was chosen as the exhibition space. "The neo-Gothic hall of the Vienna town hall—itself an old German dream—becomes part of the information," wrote Czech about his concept.[1]

The Vienna City Hall was built from 1872 to 1883, like many city halls of that time, in the Neo-Gothic style, symbolically linking to the free cities of the Middle Ages. At the end of the 18th and beginning of the 19th century in Germany, Gothic was understood as a "German" style by a number of thinkers and poets such as Fichte, Herder, Schlegel, Goethe and Heine.[2] Under the impact of the Napoleonic Wars, the idea of a united German nation arose among intellectuals as well. The Cologne Cathedral became an important object of identification in this narrative. The Gothic architecture of the cathedral was interpreted as a German way, superior to other nations in its spirituality and religiosity, of translating the Christian faith into a building.

Josef Frank and Otto Neurath: Exhibition design, 1927

Josef Frank also designed an exhibition in the *Volkshalle* of the Vienna City Hall in 1927.[3] He conceived the exhibition for Otto Neurath's Museum of Society and Economy, which the City of Vienna had made available for this purpose. A member of the Vienna Circle, Otto Neurath wanted to contribute to the education of workers with his museum. The aim of the respective exhibitions was to make economic and social relationships understandable for working people with no academic qualifications through simple, rational graphic representations. Otto Neurath and the members

1 Czech: Project text, in: Ulrike Jehle-Schulte-Strathaus: "'In welchem Style sollen wir bauen?' Gedanken zur Stil-losigkeit von Hermann Czech," *wbw* 6/1996, 17.
2 Liane Lefaivre; Alexander Tzonis: *Architecture of Regionalism in the Age of Globalization*, 2012, 70–75.
3 On the following paragraph see Nader Vossoughian: *Otto Neurath. The Language of the Global Polis*, 2011, 54–87.

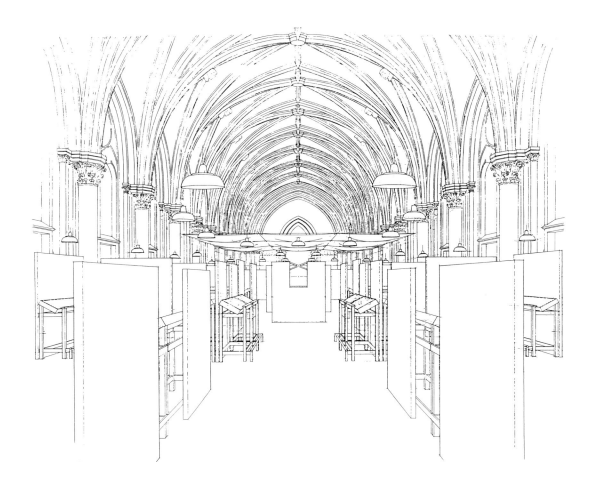

of the Vienna Circle wanted to convey a "scientific world conception" free of prejudices and superstitions to the broadest possible sections of the population. They regarded it as a contribution to the emancipation of the individual and to the democratization of society as a whole. For the exhibition, Josef Frank designed wooden panels with lights on the upper edges, which he grouped into rooms. His design thus completely masked the strongly space-defining effect of the Gothic vaults.[4] Visitors to the exhibition were to feel at home in the rational world of science. In Vienna of the year 1938, however, when the National Socialists came to power, irrationality, prejudice and an emotionality that led to the negative triumphed. Frank and Neurath had already left the country in 1934, years before the "Anschluss."

4 Ibid., 72.

Exhibition *Wien 1938 (Vienna 1938)*

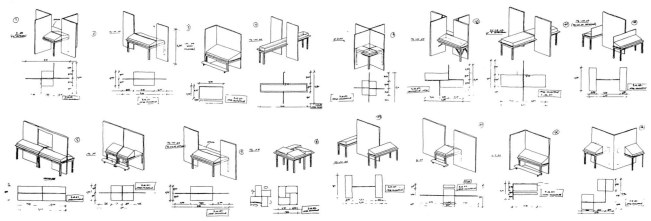

Variants of the spatial relationship of different levels of information

In the *Vienna 1938* exhibition, Czech incorporated the Neo-Gothic design of the space directly into his concept. The upper part of the space with the ogival vaults remained free of any design; "inconspicuous" insertions such as lighting and its fascia strips were removed. Below it was a horizontal dividing line made of cross-tensioned wires on which black workshop lights in a typical industrial design from the 1920s were mounted. Among these were the panels of the exhibition, arranged in a labyrinthine manner. In this way, Czech contrasted the ideal of the German notion of an ethically and spiritually superior people, united in a common state, symbolized by the Neo-Gothic as an "old German" style, with the nightmare into which the supposed ideal had developed.

The material selected by a total of 23 curators under the direction of the *Dokumentationsarchiv des österreichischen Widerstandes* (Documentation Centre of Austrian Resistance) consisted mainly of written documents and photographs. Agreement was soon reached on the concept of placing these documents in the foreground and dispensing with other object categories such as weapons, bombs, insignia, stamps, everyday objects, etc. The only representational exhibits were uniforms from the numerous Nazi organizations and prisoners' clothing, each with headgear, on standing dolls—but without heads—in vertical display cases.[5]

The exhibition was designed with different levels of information so that when going through it more quickly, one could perceive and read

5 For more about the exhibition concept, see also: Ulrike Jehle-Schulte-Strathaus: "'In welchem Style sollen wir bauen?' Gedanken zur Stil-losigkeit von Hermann Czech," *wbw* 6/1996, 17, 49.

In the "Mass Events" area the red of the swastika flag is used; in the subsequent "Terror" area the black is used.

the large-sized, vertically arranged images and texts on the roughly 25 sub-topics. One level below, individual topics were illustrated and explained. The highly informative original documents (appeals, forms, police reports, court judgments, correspondence from authorities, prisoner letters, etc.) were displayed in small, horizontally arranged reading cases underneath. By no means was the visitor to feel obliged to read all these documents. However, if one "got stuck" on a topic, one could delve deeper into the reading; the reading cabinets were equipped with bars and footrests for leaning against and resting upon.

Exhibition *Wien 1938* (*Vienna 1938*)

Rudolf Schilbach: Prof. Dr. Kurt Knoll, Rector of the University of World Trade, in the uniform of an SS-Standartenführer, oil on canvas, 1943

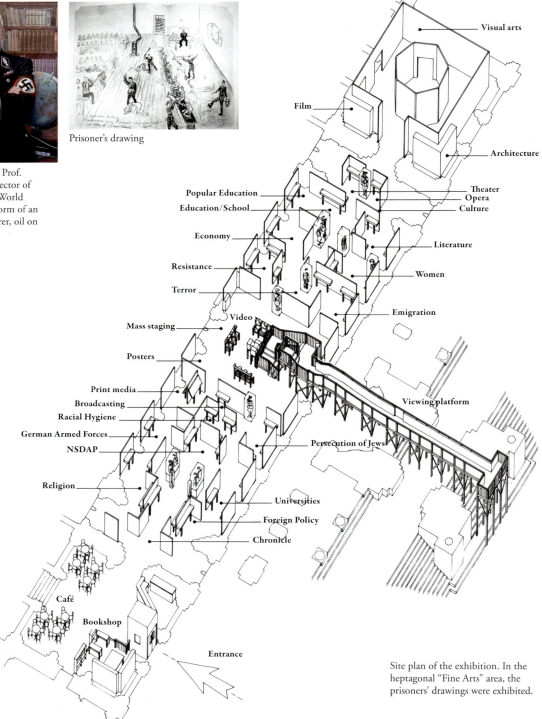

Prisoner's drawing

Site plan of the exhibition. In the heptagonal "Fine Arts" area, the prisoners' drawings were exhibited.

The only colors used were the red and black of the swastika flag: red, e.g., as the background of the panels about the mass events, black on the "reverse sides," where it was about terror and persecution.

In the middle of the exhibition, Czech designed a wooden installation that led over steps and a gangplank to a balcony outside the City Hall tower, from which one looks out over the Rathausplatz (formerly Adolf-Hitler-Platz) from the perspective of a speaker, albeit at eye level with the audience. Hitler had given a speech from a balcony two floors above, constructed ad hoc for that occasion, on April 9, 1938, the day before the referendum on Austria's annexation to the German Reich.

At one end of the exhibition space, a square hall contained examples of representative Nazi painting—from a portrait collection assembled back then of historical and contemporary personalities claimed by Nazi ideology, which is kept in today's Wien Museum. The still popular "quality" of this art was juxtaposed with the role of art as a witness of the times: with prisoners' drawings, some of which were improvised on slips of paper, documenting their torments, in a heptagonal room figure inserted in the center of the hall.

Exhibition *Wien 1938* (Vienna 1938)

Unexecuted poster design by Franz Merlicek

Czech also suggested hanging a swastika flag with inverted colors (black flag with red swastika) on the City Hall tower, which has a device for mounting a flag almost 40 meters long. He also presented the draft of an exhibition poster by Franz Merlicek:[6] the black-and-white photo of a man with his hands in his coat pockets; from his clothes and hat it could not be determined whether the photo had been taken in the 1930s or in the present; behind the man, however, his shadow showed his arm stretched out in the Hitler salute. The first proposal was rejected by the city politicians (with the not unjustified reference to possible ambiguous black-and-white photos), the second by the—predominantly left-wing—exhibition committee as "too bold." Especially the second proposal would have transposed the exhibition theme into the present as a poster.

Of the reactions to the exhibition, Czech was particularly concerned with that of the American communications scholar Alan G. Gross.[7] He criticized the fact that the exhibition surely left the Austrian past in the past. According to Gross, it inadvertently repeated the historically outdated way of seeing Austria as the first victim of Nazi Germany and of ascribing responsibility for the events exclusively to an external "force" instead of also attributing it to Austria and its people. On the other hand, for Gross, only Czech's lookout gangplank, his rejected proposals for the inverted flag and the poster design by Franz Merlicek pointed in a direction that would have given current anti-Semitism the presence it deserves.[8] In contrast to the local Viennese press, which did not know what to do with it, he interpreted the viewing platform as a link between the events of that time and today. The walkway "peopled the now empty square with the ghosts of Viennese cheering their new Leader, Adolph Hitler."[9] Gross saw the gangplank as a symbolic structure that led visitors to the exhibition straight into a shameful past of empty promises.

6 In the 1980s he was a partner in the Demner und Merlicek agency and one of Austria's most successful commercial artists.
7 Alan G. Gross: "Presence as Argument in the Public Sphere," in: *Rhetoric Society Quarterly*, Vol. 35, 2/2005, 5–21.
8 Ibid. Gross erroneously refers to Czech as the author of the poster design, 10.
9 Ibid., 13.

Unexecuted proposal for a swastika flag with reversed colors on the city hall tower

Exhibition *Wien 1938* (*Vienna 1938*)

Exhibition Design *Wunderblock: A History of the Modern Soul*

Period of origin: 1988–1989,
duration of the exhibition: April 27–August 6, 1989
Address: Riding Hall in the Former Court Stables, Messepalast Vienna
(today: MuseumsQuartier, Halle E+G, Museumsplatz 1, 1070 Vienna)
Client: Wiener Festwochen
Exhibition concept: Jean Clair, Cathrin Pichler, Wolfgang Pircher
Project team: Gilbert Blumenthaler (?), Rudolf Gitschthaler, Elke Krasny, Franz Loranzi, Ina Martin, Gerhard Riedling, Harald Schönfellinger, Gerold Steiner, Karin Tschavgova, Ingo Vavra, Torsten Warner

In 1989, on the occasion of the fiftieth anniversary of Sigmund Freud's death, the Wiener Festwochen,[1] along with the curators Jean Clair, Cathrin Pichler and Wolfgang Pircher, conceived the exhibition *Wunderblock. Eine Geschichte der modernen Seele* (*Wonderblock: A History of the Modern Soul*). Hermann Czech took over the design of the exhibition, which was to be held in the then-unrenovated spaces of the Winter Riding Hall in the former Imperial Court Stables (today: Halle E+G MuseumsQuartier). In terms of content, the exhibition attempted to show an intellectual history of the modern conception of the soul as a scientific object of research and as a theme in art from the beginning of the 18th century to the beginning of the 20th century. Scientific works in the form of apparatuses, books and documents were displayed alongside the works of important artists with paintings, sculptures and graphics.[2] The name "Wunderblock" ("Mystic Writing-Pad") is borrowed from a text by Sigmund Freud from 1925: "Notiz über den 'Wunderblock'" ("A Note Upon the 'Mystic Writing Pad.'") In this text, he compares the so-called "Wunderblock" ("mystic writing-pad"), a wax-coated writing tablet that can erase what is engraved on it by mechanically removing the wax, with how human memory works. Like the mystic writing-pad, this is always receptive like a blank sheet of paper, but at the same time what has been experienced remains, similar to what has been written, in the depths of the wax layers of the mystic writing-pad.[3]

---

1 The Wiener Festwochen (Vienna Festival) is a cultural festival in Vienna that has existed since 1951 and takes place annually.
2 N. N. "Jean Clair/Cathrin Pichler/Wolfgang Pircher: *Wunderblock. Eine Geschichte der modernen Seele*," *KUNSTFORUM International*, Bd. 101: *Bild und Seele*, 290f. See also: Jean Clair, Cathrin Pichler, Wolfgang Pircher (eds.): *Wunderblock. Eine Geschichte der modernen Seele* (exhibition catalog), Wiener Festwochen, Vienna: Löcker, 1989.
3 N. N. "Jean Clair/Cathrin Pichler/Wolfgang Pircher: *Wunderblock. Eine Geschichte der modernen Seele*," *KUNSTFORUM International*, Bd. 101: *Bild und Seele*, 290. See also Sigmund Freud: "A Note Upon the 'Mystic Writing-Pad,'" in: James Strachey (ed.): *The Standard Edition of the Complete Psychological Works of Sigmund Freud: Volume XIX (1923–1925) The Ego and the Id and Other Works*, trans. James Strachey, London: Hogarth Press and The Institute of Psycho-Analysis, 1961, 227–232.

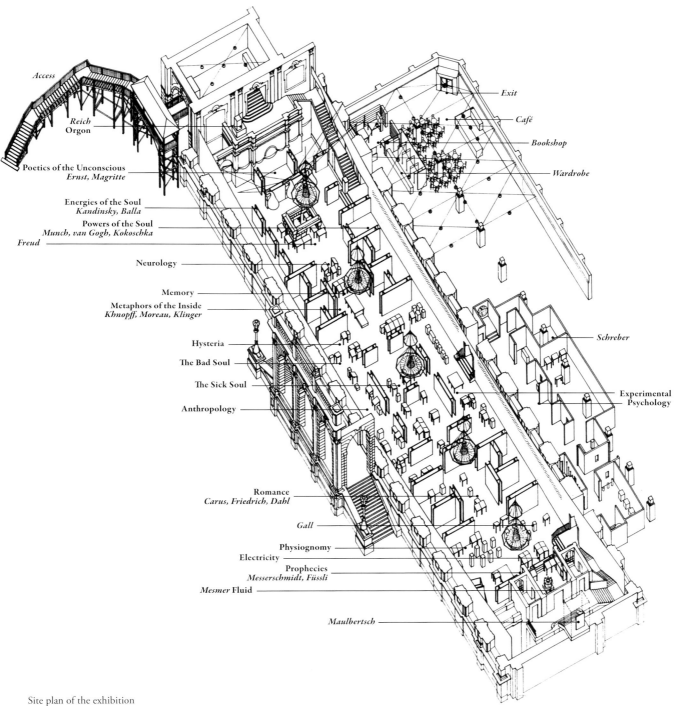

Site plan of the exhibition

In order to get to the exhibition, one had to "enter" via a wooden stairway designed by Czech through the skylight of the archway of the passage to the side of the Riding Hall. In this way, visitors entered the hall space in the longitudinal axis from above. The former Imperial Riding Hall features a portico in the middle of the façade. However, this never functioned as an entrance, as one would expect, but served as a grandstand at imperial equestrian events in the courtyard of the complex. For this reason, too, Czech designed a new, articulated entrance. The wooden construction seemed provisional and "undesigned." The raw timber structure is filled in with the usual crosses for timber skeleton constructions. These "X" infills are used by Czech on many projects at different scales. They were structurally derived from arbeitsgruppe 4 at the Pastoral Care Center in Steyr-Ennsleite, and Czech utilizes them constructively, but also as a motif. The timber structure ended with a platform in front of the entrance, which was covered with a hipped gabled roof and reminiscent of a surveillance tower—a bit like how Freud in *The Interpretation of Dreams* describes the path from the unconscious via the preconscious to the conscious with the guardian of censorship in between.

For Czech, the roof in front of the new entrance served as a meeting place for guided groups. Due to the symmetrical arrangement above the passage, it could continue to be used. Coming from the entrance, one set foot in a gallery located at one end of the long side of the 13-meter-high space of the former Riding Hall. In the first space, still above the passage, was the ticket counter, behind which the semicircular window of the original opening was placed. After the exhibition, it was reinstalled in its original location so that it did not have to be stored elsewhere. Looking out from the gallery, one had an initial overview of the entire exhibition and gained an impression of the diversity and "branchings" of the trains of thought and conceptions of the modern soul in science and art. The exhibition "began" with Wilhelm Reich's Orgone Accumulator and "ended" in the gallery across the street with an apparatus by Franz Anton Mesmer (both "useless" gadgets in retrospect given the current state of science), so it initially went counter-chronologically. Behind the Mesmer apparatus on the back wall hung a picture by the Baroque painter Franz Anton Maulbertsch, which referred to the pre-modern history of the soul as religious.

The long, hall-like exhibition space was divided by free-standing wall elements covered with linen fabric in various colors (linen colors, gray-blue, red) in such a way that one never saw axially through the entire space, working one's way from theme to theme but, at the same time, a certain

freedom of access routes remained. The works of art were presented on these walls, while scientific topics introduced in showcases and by apparatuses placed freely on pedestals. The showcases made of wood, both natural and lacquered in colors (blue, green, red), were a further development of those from the exhibition *Vienna 1938*. They were designed so that one could comfortably lean against them if one wanted to delve into an area of the exhibition. Text panels were attached to the showcases by means of hinges, which could be folded up for reading (also to convey the fact that one doesn't have to read everything).

The exhibition contribution dedicated to Sigmund Freud was the only one designed as a kind of spatial showcase in the longitudinal axis of the hall. Formed on the outside by display cases, on the inside a selection of small figures from Freud's collection of antiquities was displayed above the showcases, with photographs placed above them. The individual showcases were arranged in a slightly shifted manner; the entire spatial configuration seemed irregular and thus visually conveyed the complexity and occasional contradictions of Freud's findings. In need of renovation, the side walls of the hall were obscured by textile coverings that hung on ropes stretched over the 90-meter length of the hall. The temporary ventilation pipes, whose outlets were incorporated into the fabric, were routed behind this construction. The existing five large chandeliers were upgraded with steel rings equipped with spotlights to illuminate the exhibits.

Top left: To illustrate the function of a measuring instrument, not a human cranium, but rather a gypsum replication of one was inserted.

Top right: Freely suspended cones equipped with loudspeakers provided locally restricted acoustic information.

Bottom left: Café

Bottom right: Perception experiments were shown in adjoining rooms.

4 Czech: "Entwurfsprozess: Skizzen, Bauten, Projekte," *wbw* 6/1996, 49.

Commencing with objects created at the beginning of the 20th century, the exhibition worked its way back to the 18th century. In order to get to the exit, one had to walk through the exhibition again in the opposite direction, i.e., according to the chronology. "On the way back, now in normal chronological sequence, the old question of *where the soul is located* is raised and traced up to Sigmund Freud's *A History of the Modern Soul*,"[4] as Czech describes his exhibition concept. Through a no longer existing wooden hall attached to the rear of the Riding Hall, in which the café and shop were housed for the duration of the exhibition, one reached the outside again at ground level behind the building complex. The café was furnished with various designs of black lacquered bentwood chairs typical of fin-de-siècle Viennese coffee houses and freely arranged tables with white stone slabs and black steel bases. Posters hung from the walls and pillars, and a network of black cables fitted with black tin lamps, typical for workshop lighting in the interwar period, stretched across the tables. The

The showcase dedicated to Sigmund Freud could be entered. Its spatial configuration is not free of inconsistencies.

café could also be visited independently of the exhibition via the exhibition exit, which then functioned as the entrance to the café. This also provided barrier-free access to the exhibition. Czech had already employed the black metal lights in several projects with a wide variety of applications, such as his own office or the Salzamt Restaurant. When designing the *Vienna 1938* exhibition,[5] he used the lights, also extended across the space on cables, to illuminate the exhibition panels. The design of the café, with the typical furniture of Viennese coffee houses from the interwar period in combination with the workshop lights in an exhibition on the anniversary of Freud's death, provokes further associations: Freud's expulsion in 1938, the persecution of the Jewish population under National Socialism, the Viennese coffee house as a meeting place for Viennese intellectuals, where people of Jewish origin were disproportionately represented, and the cynical reference of National Socialist propaganda to the value of manual labor.

5   See project description, p. 290.

Brunner Gasse Residential Block

Period of origin: 1989–1994
Address: Franz-Kamtner-Weg 1–9, Brunner Gasse, 2380 Perchtoldsdorf
Client: Municipality of Perchtoldsdorf, Lower Austria
Project team: Harald Schönfellinger, engineering: Reinhard Klestil,
ÖBA: PAG Consult Alfred Grekowski

1 Czech: Project description, in: Ulrike Jehle-Schulte-Strathaus, "'In welchem Style sollen wir bauen?' Gedanken zur Stillosigkeit von Hermann Czech," *wbw* 6/1996, 33.

The settlement on Brunner Gasse consists of "villa-like buildings with several flats."[1] Each apartment has its own garden with direct access; from the first-floor apartments it is via an outside staircase. The attic apartments have terraces. The private open spaces do not overlap. Covered parking spaces for each house are integrated into the respective ground floor. The shell construction allowed the future tenants to be involved in the planning process of the apartment floor plans until a relatively late stage in the implementation. Even the window sizes could also be determined within a defined maximum opening. "The objective was to create equivalent flats," but not identical ones. Every apartment thus has its own advantages. "In fact, it is not possible to decide which flat is best." Only solutions that would have been unreasonable for future tenants, such as "trapped" spaces, were excluded. Anton Brenner's "four-family house" was a reference project for the design. A former student of Josef

Frank, Brenner had been committed to social housing all his life. Among other things, he also took part in the conception of the Frankfurt kitchen and had also planned two houses in the Vienna Werkbundsiedlung. The four-family house was to serve as a transition from the dense development in the city to the open development in the country. Each of the four dwellings had its own entrance and was conceived to have a special benefit in order to guarantee the equivalence of the apartments.[2]

The roof addition corresponds to the maximum utilization of the local building regulations, in that the void of the pitched roof area, combined with a dormer window permitted on the top floor, was made into useful space. However, this attic room had to be financed by the future tenants themselves and 13 of the 14 prospective tenants opted for this room. For Czech, this conception of the top floor also had the advantage that it could be spatially experienced in this way with its slope.

In 2009, Czech referred to the work in a symposium on the subject of "Die Architektur der neuen Weltordnung" ("The Architecture of the New

Anton Brenner: *Das Vierfamilienhaus* (*The Four-Family House*) 1951. Each apartment has its own entrance from the outside and access to a part of the garden. "A plan of this kind, which is to provide for equivalent apartments, is only properly resolved when it is extremely difficult to find the most advantageous apartment."

2 Anton Brenner: *Der wirtschaftlich durchdachte Plan des Architekten: Grundrisse – Ansichten von Bauten – Innenarchitekturen – städtebauliche Lösungen – alte und neue Pläne und Bauideen*, Vienna: Verlag Ertl, 1951, 41.

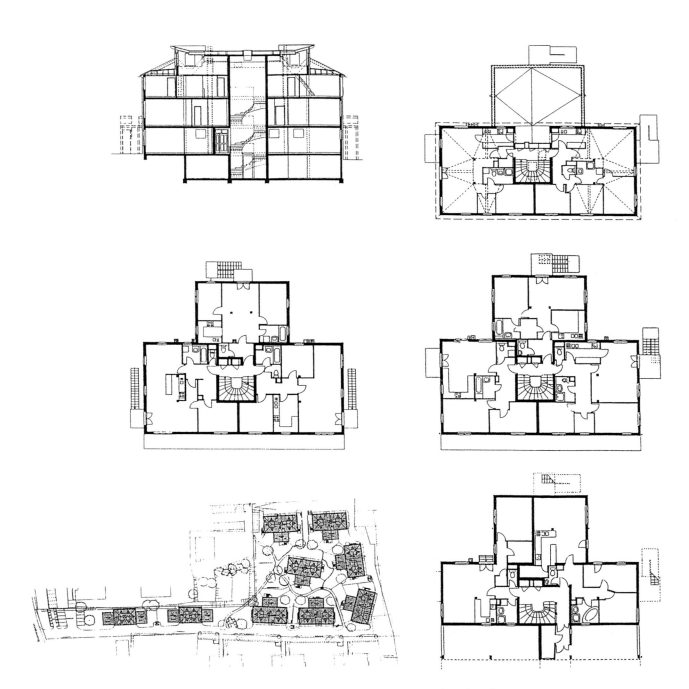

Floor plans of an attic, two upper floors and a ground floor, each according to the tenant's wishes

306   Selected Projects

NORDANSICHT

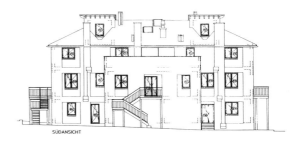

SÜDANSICHT

WESTANSICHT

OSTANSICHT

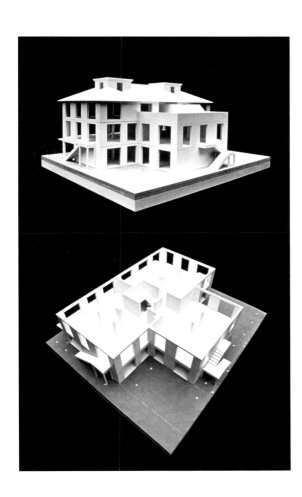

"A casual appearance, which the architect would not succeed in creating, arises from individual rational decisions."
(Hermann Czech)

Brunner Gasse Residential Block

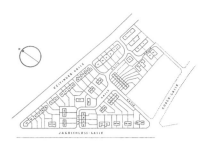

Josef Frank: Werkbundsiedlung site plan, 1932

Josef Frank: House in the Vienna Werkbundsiedlung, 1932

3   Czech: "Can Architecture Be Conceived by Way of Consumption?" (2011), trans. Elise Feiersinger, in: Czech 2019, 229–247, 240.
4   Ibid., 240–241.
5   Czech: "A Conceptual Matrix for the Current Interpretation of Josef Frank" (1985), trans. Elise Feiersinger, in: Czech 2019, 151–181.
6   Frank: *Architecture as Symbol* (1931), trans. John Sands, in: Frank 2012, Vol. 2, 9–191: 168, quoted in: Czech 1996, 113. English translation quoted in "A Conceptual Matrix for the Current Interpretation of Josef Frank" (1985), trans. Elise Feiersinger, in: Czech 2019, 151–181: 159.
7   Czech: "A Conceptual Matrix…, 157.

World Order") with the term "critical kitsch."³ "A casual appearance" is created "through rational decisions" (namely that the tenants were able to intervene in the design and help determine the window sizes)—and further: "The design submits to the aesthetic local codes but sidesteps them at the same time, so that they fail in comparison to the reason-based advantages." Czech recognizes the building codes of the conservative community (construction type, building height, roof form, dormers, etc.) as "motifs which are utilized in an attempt to create a predetermined atmosphere." If the building regulations are now "appropriated impartially or even demonstratively, analyzed and, in many cases rationalized contradictorily, the result is not so much a double-coding that preserves the illusion of an intact world. Rather, the productive use of the motifs gives a jolt to their consumption and makes people identify with their environment on a new level."⁴

As already described, Czech summarized his attitude towards Frank in 1985 in the text "Ein Begriffsraster zur aktuellen Interpretation Josef Franks" ("A Conceptual Matrix for the Current Interpretation of Josef Frank"),⁵ which also explains his own conception of architecture. It begins with a reference to the differences between the Stuttgart and Vienna Werkbundsiedlung, the initiator and artistic director of which was Josef Frank. The aim of the Wiener Werkbundsiedlung was to create a more diverse modern architecture. Frank had therefore only invited architects such as Adolf Loos, Josef Hoffmann, Hugo Häring, André Lurçat, Gerrit Rietveld, Richard Neutra or Gabriel Guévrékian, who had not been there in Stuttgart because, from the standpoint of the rigid representatives, they were regarded more as forerunners and outsiders of modernism. Frank directed his criticism towards the dogmatic industrial aesthetics of the Bauhaus and its concept of reforming life along with the construction method. He wanted to offer an alternative, a modern and at the same time comfortable form of living, because for him the house "through its existence […] has to gratify people and contribute in all its parts to their [the tenants'] delight."⁶ According to Czech, Frank finally formulated his "Copernican step toward a non-doctrinaire, inclusive architecture," prepared in the 1930s and 1940s, in the 1958 essay "Accidentism."⁷ Czech quotes from Frank's text that "every human being needs a certain degree of sentimentality to feel free" and from Frank's criticism of functionalism, which forbids people to do so. At the end he repeats Frank's demand,

which Czech had been thinking about since the first Frank reception in the 1960s, namely, "that we should design our surroundings as if they originated by chance."[8] Czech attempts to interpret Frank's formulation "originated by chance": It could not be a question "that design decisions are to be left to chance," but that a broader range of meanings manifested itself in it: "**As if it had always been that way**. This aspect refers to **the existing**, namely the historical as well as the contemporary. **How it is always done**. The **normal**. This even encompasses an aspect of practical value (the **right thing**). **As it originates by itself**. The **spontaneous**, the **natural**. Without effort, through usage: perhaps by its user. The **self-evident**, the **unobtrusive**—or maybe not?"[9]

For Czech, Frank's call goes beyond an autonomous, rational, "exclusive" architecture to an "inclusive" one that enables "a shared commitment" and an "ability to reach a consensus." "Frank's formulation leads to a dialectic

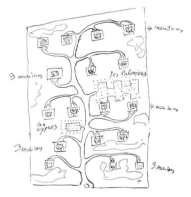

Le Corbusier: Project for the periphery of Buenos Aires; Villa Savoye is repeatedly arranged in a settlement structure.

8 Ibid., 161.
9 Ibid., 162 (emphasis in the original text).

Brunner Gasse Residential Block 309

In the required competition façades, clichés of self-construction are used; of course, they are still façades designed by architects. *Wohnen Morgen* (*Living Tomorrow*) competition together with Werner Appelt, Franz Eberhard Kneissl and Elsa Prochazka (IGIRIEN working group), as well as Rolf Wessely and Adalbert Singer, elevations and site plan, 197

Otto Wagner: Administration building for the Nussdorf weir and lock system, 1899 – the roof attachment served as an observation station.

10 Ibid., 163.
11 "Typical Plan," in: Koolhaas; Mau: *S,M,L,XL*, 1995, 335ff.
12 Frank: "On the Development of the Werkbundsiedlung" (1932), trans. Roderick O'Donovan, in: Frank 2012, Vol. 2, 226–233: 233.

in which architecture is firmly grounded in the ideal and the real, and the personal and the general: For if he appears to take architecture away from the commitment of planning systems and surrender it to arbitrariness, in reality he takes it away from the arbitrariness of the planner and provides it with the commitment and credibility of real life."[10]

In the Brunner Gasse residential building, it was left to the future users to determine the position of the windows within a precisely defined framework. In this way, a conceptual chance, instead of an arbitrary one, emerged from the hand of the architect, who arranges window openings according to formal criteria. Czech had already dealt with the question of integrating the user in the façade design in the *Wohnen Morgen* (*Living Tomorrow*) competition in which he participated in 1975 together with Werner Appelt, Franz Eberhard Kneissl and Elsa Prochazka (IGIRIEN working group), as well as Rolf Wessely and Adalbert Singer. In the project drafted at the time, the houses were imagined as demarcated objects; the construction principle of each house could have been implemented in different materials by the respective user. However, the approval of the material could only lead to the use of components from the building supplies store, which was shown in schematic façade drawings and perceived by the jury as provocative.

So that the future users could determine the floor plans themselves in Brunner Gasse, the supporting structure—as in the Loos House and previously in the American "typical plan" (Koolhaas[11])—was formed by the load-bearing outer walls, the load-bearing access core and the supports placed freely in the space. The roof addition utilizes the otherwise unusable remaining space in the specified roof pitch and realizes the dream of a "tower room" for the residents of the upper apartments, which is normally reserved for castle owners. In addition to this logical chain of decision-making in the design, the resulting house shape shows unexpected parallels to Otto Wagner's administration building near the Nussdorf Weir.

Josef Frank wrote in the introduction to the publication on the Vienna Werkbundsiedlung, which he was the initiator and artistic director of: "Only someone who approaches the design of a small house without prejudices and takes account only of the functional requirements is in a position to build and furnish in an entirely rational, that is to say modern, way."[12]

Brunner Gasse Residential Block

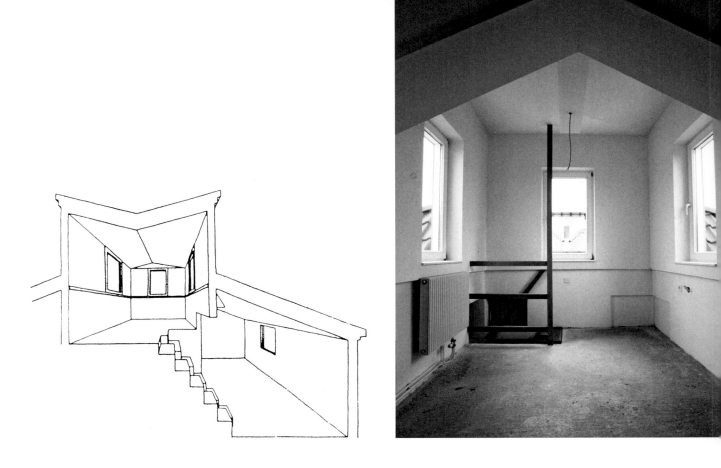

13 Otto Kapfinger; Adolf Krischanitz: *Die Wiener Werkbundsiedlung. Dokumentation einer Erneuerung*, 1985, 55.

14 Iris Meder: "'Natur und Architektur werden hier ineinandergeschoben.' Haus und Garten in der Wiener Werkbundsiedlung," in: Nierhaus; Orosz, op. cit., 96–101: 96f.

15 Ibid., 96.

The conception of the outdoor spaces was based on the idea of "combining house and garden, architecture, apartment and nature into an entity."[13] In the Werkbundsiedlung, this thought is expressed in a variety of ways in which the interior and exterior spaces are connected. The transition from architecture to nature is designed very consciously from the start of planning. The architecture of the house dissolves in the garden into the primary elements that define the architecture: fortified floor, protective wall, shielding roof using natural stone, trellises and pergolas. Josef Frank's notion of the garden was derived from English country house construction.[14] Together with Oskar Strnad, he took the view that the house should be overgrown by nature. "The goal was for the house to merge harmoniously with its surroundings, characterized by changeability, improvisation, coincidences and, according to Frank's definition, disorder."[15]

Selected Projects

Czech connected apartments and gardens with wooden additions, balconies and external stairs, some of which were combined so that the upper floor balcony functions as a covered outdoor area for the ground floor. The open spaces assigned to the tenants are separated from the common outdoor spaces with hedges and today, more than twenty-five years after completion, offer a self-evident image of the overgrowth and the individual expression "without effort, through usage: perhaps by its user" (see Frank's open space concept for the Viennese Werkbundsiedlung), without creating a dissonant contrast to the architecture. The color scheme of the houses—light gray and bold pink—and the green of the plants tie in with the colors of the vineyards in the area: light gray the ground, green the leaves of the vines in summer, and red-pink in autumn.

Atelier Czech, Singerstraße

Period of origin: 1986–1989
Address: Singerstrasse 26A, 1010 Vienna
Project team: Franz Moser, Walter Michl

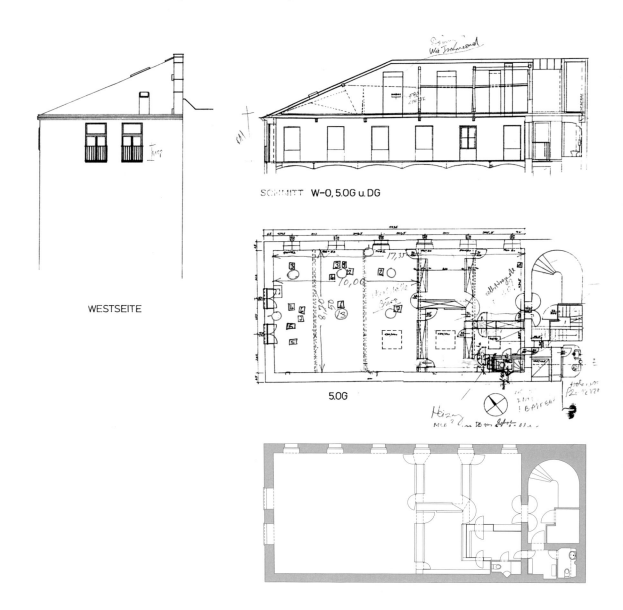

Marcel Duchamp: "porte paradoxale," 11 Rue Larrey, Paris 1927

Selected Projects

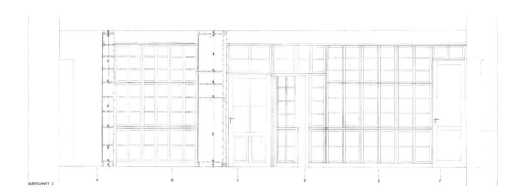

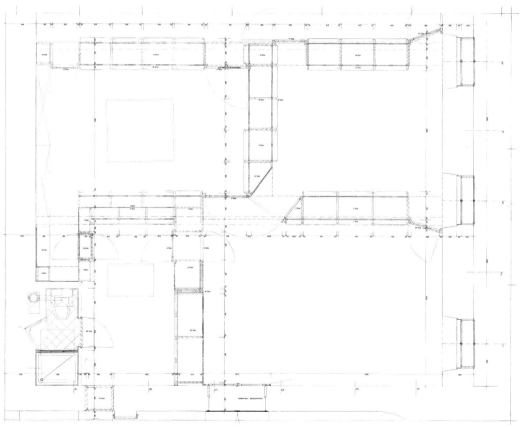

Transparent subdivision of a loft story (in the former State Printing House from 1820/40); at the same time protection of the library from dust. According to Czech, he owes the realization, as well as their livelihood during this time, to his partner Monika Kaesser.

Atelier Czech, Singerstraße

Atelier Czech, Singerstraße

Arcadia Music Shop
with Stephan Seehof

Period of origin: 1989–1990
Address: Kärntnerstrasse 40/State Opera, 1010 Vienna
Client: Erhard Löcker

The Arcadia Music Shop space on the ground floor behind the arcades on a side of the Vienna State Opera had been used for temporary exhibitions before the integration of the shop. But August Sicard von Sicardsburg and Eduard van der Nüll had already planned shops there in the original design.

 Czech continues this task in line with the original concept. The large arched windows behind the arcade front give the impression of a story, but conceal a mezzanine utilization through cloakrooms above an existing false ceiling. This is now covered by dark reflective glass. On the lower part of the outside shop windows, Czech placed slanted, enameled glass signs bearing the name "Arcadia," which serves for optimal visibility from a greater distance. A pragmatic solution typical for Czech is that the script is cut off at the two business entrances. The remaining lettering "AR–IA" calls forth associations with the sung "aria" and thus both with the location, namely the State Opera, and with the goods offered in the music shop.

 The narrow salesroom, elongated parallel to the façade and connected to another room by several openings in the rear longitudinal wall, received several layers of furnishings: hanging lights with green shades, a floor in the complementary color red, wooden shelves and boxes, and a picture gallery of composers and musicians above. The box-like furniture with neatly arranged CDs and records move like magnetic particles around the pillars of the façade structure standing in the space.

Czech did not want linear, uniform, office-like lighting, but rather a separate, specific one for each area. The suspension lamp with green glass shade chosen for this purpose is a standard product normally used as a single

1. The *Adolf Loos* exhibition was organized by the Graphic Art Collection of the Albertina Museum together with the Historical Museum of the City of Vienna (and with the Loos House as the third exhibition location) and shown from December 2, 1989 to February 25, 1990. A committee of seven people was entrusted with the conception and implementation: Hermann Czech, Friedrich Kurrent, Hans Puchhammer, Burkhardt Rukschcio, Roland Schachel, Anton Schweighofer and Johannes Spalt. Catalog: *Adolf Loos*, edited by Burkhardt Rukschcio, 1989.
2. Czech: "Transformation" (1989), trans. Elise Feiersinger, in: Czech 2019, 185–191.

lamp. The number of lights now installed irregularly and at different heights corresponds to the required illuminance. For Czech, it wasn't a matter of creating something original, but of solving a specific problem.

Completed in 1869, the Vienna State Opera is one of the most important cultural buildings on the Ringstrasse. It embodies the spirit of the quality of the 19th-century metropolis repeatedly emphasized by Czech. An intervention in this substance is also an engagement with the idea of this metropolis.

In 1989, a major Adolf Loos retrospective took place in Vienna. Czech was on the exhibition committee[1] and had been involved in its conception since 1985. For the catalog he wrote the text "Der Umbau" ("Transformation").[2] He had already formulated the architectural meaning of the term *Umbau* ("transformation") in 1973: "Transforming an existing building is more

interesting than building a new one—because, in essence, everything is transformation."³ And in 1977 he wrote: "Reuse and renovation reinterpret what already exists and opens our eyes to ambiguity and complexity."⁴ In 1985, he named transformation as the central theoretical architectural topic.⁵ "Is something new and different set against the existing, or is it a continuation of the existing with other (or even the same) means? It seems that the transformation must contain both, and that the continuation of the existing consists in the formation of a new entity on a higher level."⁶ For Czech, "in essence, everything is transformation," because every design is about the relationship to what is already there.

In a text on the subject of Loos penned in 1989, Czech defined transformation as a fundamental constituent element of the city. "The nineteenth-century metropolis is an opus at different scales."⁷ On the largest scale it is a network of traffic circulation, then an addition of built

3 Czech: "For a Change" (1973), trans. Elise Feiersinger, in: Czech 2019, 109–115: 114.
4 Czech: "Pluralism" (1977), trans. Michael Loudon, in: Kenneth Frampton (ed.): *A New Wave of Austrian Architecture*, 1980, 60.
5 Czech: "Wohnbau und Althaus" (1985), in: Czech 1996, 106–109.
6 Ibid., 109.
7 Czech: "Transformation" (1989), trans. Elise Feiersinger, in: Czech 2019, 185–191: 186.

Arcadia Music Shop

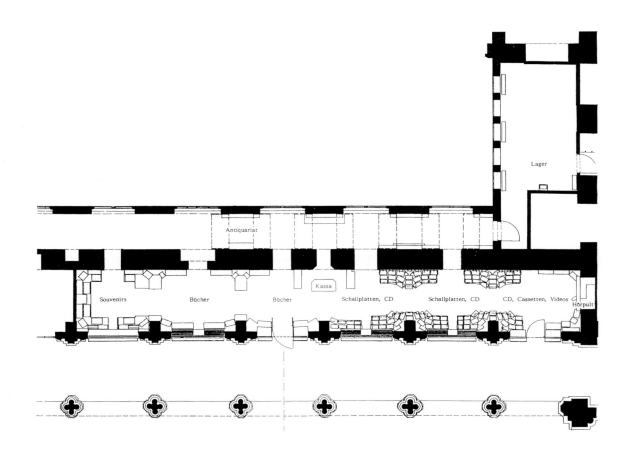

structures, and on the smallest scale the individual use is formed. "Order arises through the decisions in the larger scales, variety through the decisions in the smaller scales."[8] Since the various scales possess different time frames, "without the process of transforming, urban life would be utterly inconceivable."[9] In Adolf Loos, Czech recognized an architect for whom transformation plays an elementary role; for Czech, Loos's transformations are new, fully valid works. Loos no longer followed the hierarchy of urban scales in a straight line, but rather his transformation "approaches the building's 'substance' by calling it into question—but certainly not by eliminating it."[10] Loos's interventions on the existing structure "are not interpretations, but rather reinterpretations, not instances of fitting out a building, but transformations."[11] Czech named three different figurations of Loosian transformation: the addition of

8 Ibid., 186.
9 Ibid., 187.
10 Ibid.
11 Ibid.

Selected Projects

new spatial layers, the removal of a load-bearing wall with the inclusion of the necessary support structure in the new spatial configuration, and the insertion of an additional floor in the form of a gallery. All of these figurations exist—partly already in the building fabric—in the Arcadia Music Shop.

Czech states that the quality of architecture is that it "only speaks when it is questioned."[12] The answers that Czech's architecture gives, the associations it triggers, confront me, the questioner, with my own subjectivity. Due to my intensive preoccupation with the era of Viennese modernism, the naming "Arcadia" and the lettering "Aria" left over by the door's interruption provoke further associations in the context of 19th-century Vienna that Czech himself was not aware of: Arcadia is a landscape in Greece historically associated with the myth of a golden age and a happy shepherd people who live without hardship in the idyllic surroundings. Founded in Hellenism, this myth reemerged in the Baroque and Renaissance periods. By contrast, "Aria" (in the German spelling) is, among other things, the ancient name of a region in Central Asia ("Arya" in English), the home of the Aryans. As is known, they were usurped by the National Socialists as a mythical people of a noble race. The Vienna State Opera also emerged as a symbol of the liberal Viennese bourgeoisie, a social class largely shaped by assimilated Jewish entrepreneurs. Directly opposite the Opera arcades stands the Palais Todesco, the first residential building of a Jewish family in Vienna which they were allowed to build themselves as property owners after Jews had been granted legal equality. Ludwig Förster and Theophil Hansen designed and built it between 1861 and 1864. Sophie von Todesco ran a salon in this house, which Johann Strauss and Hugo von Hofmannsthal, among others, visited. Palais Todesco incorporates Hellenistic elements in its design.[13] Hellenism symbolized an epoch of peaceful coexistence between Jewish and non-Jewish citizens in Greece and, in terms of style, established at the same time a connection with European-Christian architecture, which referred to antiquity.

The Vienna State Opera, along with its orchestra, the Vienna Philharmonic, was "Aryanized" immediately after Austria's "Anschluss" to Germany. All Jewish musicians were dismissed, some expelled, and some deported. Seven out of the sixteen Jewish members did not manage to escape in time and were murdered.[14]

12 Czech: "Pluralism" (1977), trans. Michael Loudon, op. cit., 60.

13 See Elana Shapira: *Assimilating with Style: Jewish Assimilation and Modern Architecture and Design in Vienna – The Case of "The Outfitters" Leopold Goldman and Adolf Loos and the Making of the Goldman & Salatsch Building (1909–1911)*, Dissertation, University of Applied Arts Vienna, 2004.

14 There is a historical review of the Vienna Philharmonic during the National Socialist era under the direction of Oliver Rathkolb, see https://www.wienerphilharmoniker.at/de/orchester/geschichte/nationalsozialismus. Bernadette Mayrhofer; Fritz Trümpi: *Orchestrierte Vertreibung: Unerwünschte Wiener Philharmoniker. Verfolgung, Ermordung, Exil*, 2014.

Block Development at the U3-West Ottakring Turnaround

Period of origin: 1990–1997
Address: Paltaufgasse, Ottakringerstrasse, Weinheimergasse, Thaliastrasse, 1160 Vienna
Client: Bauträger Austria Immobilien
Project team: Georg Übelhör, Bogdan Szwajnoch, engineering: Alfred Pauser

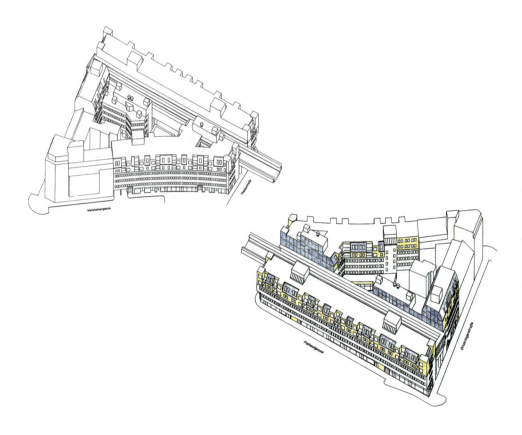

1 Czech: Project text (1991), unpublished, Czech Archive.

"The reason for the redevelopment of the block area is the subway turnaround facility. This cause simultaneously represents the main characteristic of the development. The subway is not hidden or denied, but drawn upon as the identification of this block. This building will probably remain the only one in Vienna into which the subway will visibly enter as an elevated line."[1]

Czech had initially been entrusted with the "surface design," namely planning measures in the vicinity of the stations during the general planning of the U3-West line. This gave rise to the idea of developing the turnaround facility and subsequently commissioning a development study. Czech proposed a mixed-use block development with shops, offices, apartments and an underground car park.[2] The block continues the urban characteristic of the area. The route is slightly tilted and an arcade-like projection is designed along Paltaufgasse to gain usable depth on this side of the development. On the Thaliastrasse side, the protrusion results in a symmetrical division of two structures with the subway line in the middle.

Adolf Loos: Hotel design for Paris, 1924

2 Development study "Blockbebauung Paltaufgasse" (January 1991), Czech Archive.

Block Development at the U3-West Ottakring Turnaround

Shops to be accessed through a two-story passage leading through the block were planned on the ground floor. On the one hand, this passage represented a sensible route towards the subway station. On the other hand, it should "be remembered as lying underneath the subway line due to the positioning of the subway line supports." The nearly one-story difference in height between Thaliastrasse and Ottakringerstrasse was to be compensated for by an even slope, which also forms an orienting structure in the city topography. Ultimately, however, the planned passage area was added to the rentable area, thus destroying the idea of its commercial diversity.

Selected Projects

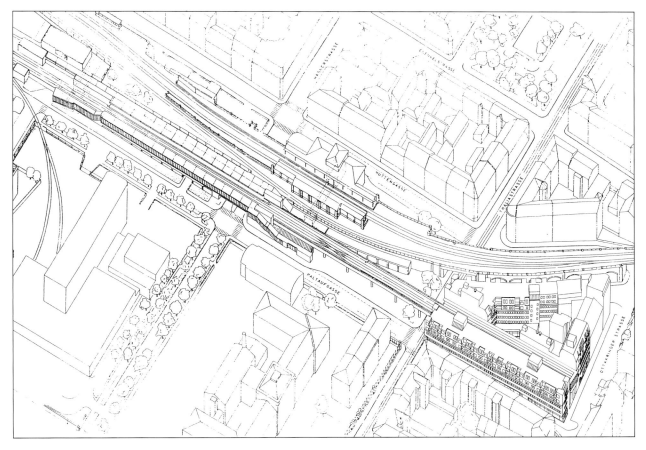

In the development study, as well as in a project description[3] he later compiled, Czech preceded his design with an isometric drawing showing the turnaround facility in its immediate vicinity to a bridge and station on the suburban line as part of Otto Wagner's metropolitan rail network. As an author in *Die Furche* and in later texts, Czech had already campaigned for the preservation of the metropolitan railway facilities in the 1960s and pointed out their importance as a structuring and designing element of Vienna and the perception of Vienna as a 19th-century metropolis.[4]

In 1963, he already stated: "The generous, optimistic conception of a metropolis and a generous approach to the challenges it poses gave rise to a

3 Czech: Project description, in: "Entwurfsprozess: Skizzen, Bauten, Projekte," *wbw* 6/1996: 56.

4 Czech: "Die Stadtbahn wird unterschätzt" (1963); "Otto Wagners Verkehrsbauwerk" (1968), also in: Czech 1996, 24–31; "Die Sprache Otto Wagners" (1974), also in: ibid., 73–76. English translation by Michael Loudon, "The Work and Diction of Otto Wagner," in: *a+u* (Tokyo) 7/1977, 45–66. Elise Feiersinger's English translation of "Otto Wagners Verkehrsbauwerk" and parts of "Die Stadtbahn wird unterschätzt" appear in "Otto Wagner's Vienna Metropolitan Railway" (1963/68), in: Czech 2019, 19–38.

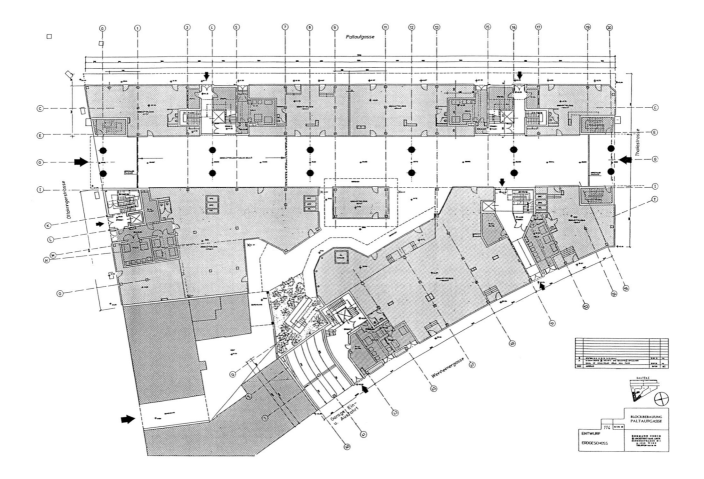

railway system that is at present not only not outdated, but, on the contrary, is still our most modern."[5] The design achievement of the *Stadtbahn* is, for Czech, that at the same time it gives the city its image and that the buildings "merge with their anonymous background." "Real life in the metropolis" is where "it [architecture] has to stand the test," wrote Czech in 1974.[6]

Sixteen years later, in "Elemente der Stadtvorstellung" ("Elements of Urban Conception"), the "Gründerzeit metropolis," with its notion of the big city, is still the most viable conceptualization of the city for him. Its unbeatable quality is its principle of "the abstraction of functions and, with it, the capacity for a mix. Instead of the four functions of living/working/leisure/transport, which modern urban planning seeks not only

5 Czech: "Otto Wagner's Vienna Metropolitan Railway" (1963/68), trans. Elise Feiersinger, in: Czech 2019, 19–38: 24.
6 Czech: "Die Sprache Otto Wagners," op. cit., 75. English translation by Michael Loudon, "The Work and Diction of Otto Wagner," in: *a+u* (Tokyo) 7/1977, 45–66: 63.

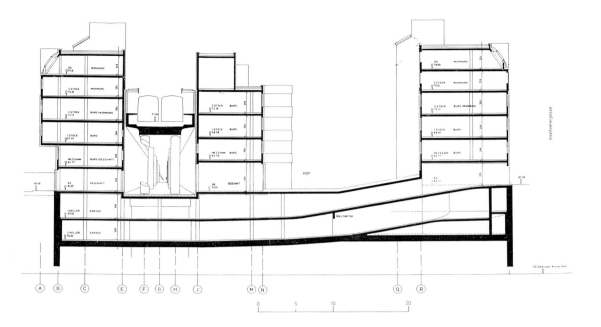

to analyze, but also to separate, the historical city knows only the much more elementary distinction between built fabric and traffic."[7] The space that remains between the built volume is at the same time the traffic area. This forms a public space; it is not an end in itself, but serves locomotion and access to the buildings.

Czech's project for the development of the turnaround corresponds to this conception of the metropolis of the traditional Gründerzeit city. Movement on foot (= public space), work (shops/offices) and living are layered on top of each other, a concept employed, for example, in 1912 by the architects Hoppe, Schönthal and Kammerer for the Westermann houses on Dorotheergasse. The arches under Wagner's *Stadtbahn* were occupied by shops and craftsmen and the routes to and from the *Stadtbahn* stations were designed as commercial passages. A further development of this concept by Czech is the superimposition of the transportation structure with residential and office use and its integration into an urban block of houses. He had already worked on this topic extensively during his studies at the Plischke Master School with the draft for the Schottenfeld urban redevelopment project. Even then, Czech, contrary to the fashion

Entertainment palace, diploma thesis, 1971

7 Czech: "Elements of Urban Conception" (1990), trans. Elise Feiersinger, in: Czech 2019, 195–209: 198.

Block Development at the U3-West Ottakring Turnaround

333

A high passage was planned under the structure; however, the area was also rented out, which required a ceiling for independent access to the supports.

The view of the Gallitzinberg Hill from the depths of Thaliastrasse would have been largely lost if the turnaround facility had been enclosed.

8   Czech: "What Will Happen to the Existing City?" (1967), trans. Elise Feiersinger, in: Czech 2019, 65–70: 67.

of the utopian settlement models at the time, spoke up for a further adaptation of the existing city. In 1967, he wrote: "It is pointless to want to produce a metropolis. The metropolis already exists. Urban planning does not involve creating something new, but setting up new relationships in the existing."[8] And, contrary to Roland Rainer's conception of the "dispersal and de-mixing" of the existing city, he advocated for a new mix of functions and a densification of the existing. In his diploma thesis (1972), Czech drew upon a group of building blocks in the existing city (Taborstrasse) to transform and expand them into an "entertainment palace" with a superimposition of the most varied of urban functions.

The subway line characterizes the building from the outside and inside. The supporting structures of the line remain visible inside. At Czech's prompting, the bridge of the line above Thaliastrasse was not enclosed, thereby preserving the characteristic view of Gallitzinberg Hill over the length of Thaliastrasse.

Although the public shopping arcade was not implemented in the turnaround facility project, the idea of this passageway remains noticeable

within the retail spaces. The structure of the track above is visible in the sales areas through the concrete supports, the arrangement of which is ultimately based on the use of the underground car park and is decisive for their organization. In the sporting goods store, the store operators even use the structure as an orientation element in the form of a running track marking.

With its gate building corners and the crenellated roof end, the block's outer design is reminiscent of apartment blocks in "Red Vienna." In Czech's case, however, the plasticity is justified: The gate structures mark the entrance to the turnaround facility with the necessary fire protection distances between the windows and the railway line; the crenellated roof edging creates equivalent outdoor and indoor spaces for the apartments on the top floor. In its closedness and anonymity, this building could also be seen as a late interpretation of a block from Otto Wagner's "metropolis perspective."

MAK Café and Thonet Chair

Period of origin: 1991–1993
Address: Stubenring 5, 1010 Vienna
Client: MAK – Austrian Museum of Applied Arts, Director Peter Noever
(Czech's MAK Café was demolished in 2005; the premises were subsequently rebuilt several times.)
Project team: Margarita McGrath, Thomas Roth, Tilman Wetter

"This interior results from the strategic use of the existing, of thought, and of geometry. More important than what it talks about is what it remains silent about. It works, but there is nothing to be seen — a nuisance for any creator of forms. What remains of Adolf Loos's concept of modernity is that it cannot be about style, not even about contemporary style." Czech added two quotes from Adolf Loos to this project description: "Good architecture can be described; it need not be drawn. The Pantheon can be described. Secession buildings cannot." "*One may only* do something *new* if *one can* do it *better*."[1]

What is this space being silent about? And if one may only do something new if one can do it better—which of the existent does the design refer to?

In the 19th and early 20th centuries, the coffee house in Vienna was an essential place of public life and its design a topic in the architectural discourse of the fin de siècle.[2] The design of the café followed the discussion about the design of the living spaces and showed some parallels.[3] Around 1900, there were cafés in the style of historicism, the interiors of which resembled sumptuous aristocratic salons. They served a broad middle class as a meeting place of the family, as a substitute for their own, not so spaciously and elegantly furnished living spaces. From 1900 onwards, Art Nouveau coffee houses appeared with the typical concept of a *Gesamtkunstwerk* (a total work of art). With the design of the Café Museum in 1899, Adolf Loos consciously took a contrary position in this discourse. He borrowed from the atmosphere and the expression of the first coffee houses of the Biedermeier period. Towards the end of the 19th century, the Biedermeier underwent a re-evaluation in intellectual circles as a cultural golden age; the

1 Czech: Project text, in: *architekturjournal wettbewerbe* 173/174, 1998, 48. The reason for this was Czech's application for the Loos Prize (State Prize for Design) – "for financial reasons. A prize that one has to submit for is not appreciated by me anyway. I then received the 'Audience Award' given in connection," Czech mentions in passing.
2 See Jeremy Aynsley: "Graphic and Interior Design in the Viennese Coffeehouse around 1900," in: Charlotte Ashby et al. (eds.): *The Viennese Café and Fin-de-Siècle Culture*, 2013, 158–177.
3 See Richard Kurdiovsky: "The Cliché of the Viennese Café as an Extended Living Room," in: ibid., 178–198.

Selected Projects

Biedermeier coffee house was romanticized as a place of cultural life and set against the over-commercialized contemporary cafés.[4]

Adolf Loos's Café Museum soon gained popularity among the artists and became a meeting place for the avant-garde. There were two fixed artists' tables: a musicians' table with Franz Lehár, Alban Berg and Oscar Straus, and a table for the writers and painters with Franz Werfel, Roda Roda, Robert Musil, Christian Morgenstern, Albert Paris Gütersloh, Gustav Klimt, Egon Schiele, Oskar Kokoschka and others. Peter Altenberg, Karl Kraus and Adolf Loos also frequented the café themselves.[5] Years later, Loos proudly wrote: "When I finally had the chance to create an interior […] the response was very hostile. That was twelve years ago when I did the Café Museum in Vienna. The architects called it 'Cafe Anarchism.' But my Café Museum still stands today while all the modern joinery of the thousands of others has long since been consigned to the junk room."[6] Café Capua, designed by Loos in 1913, pursued the direction he had started in Café Museum. Here he used elements that he also employed in private living spaces: marble-clad walls and a classicist frieze (he used the same for the renovation of House Duschnitz in Vienna in 1915, for example). Café

Adolf Loos: Café Capua, 1913

4 See Ashby: "The Cafés of Vienna: Space and Sociability," in: ibid., 9–31.
5 See Hans Veigl: *Wiener Kaffeehausführer*, 1994.
6 Loos: "Architecture" (1909), trans. Michael Mitchell, in: Adolf Loos: *On Architecture* (Studies in Austrian Literature, Culture and Thought), Riverside, CA: Ariadne Press, 2002, 73–85: 78.

Capua, like Café Museum, became a stomping ground for intellectuals and artists associated with Adolf Loos.

At the Loos exhibition in 1989, co-curated by Czech, Johannes Spalt designed two exhibition booths,[7] showing both cafés Loos had realized in Vienna by means of a montage of original furniture in the foreground in front of photos of the cafés in the background. Café Capua was spatially similar to the MAK Café: a large, high, rectangular space characterized by a dominant ceiling construction—in Café Capua by a grid-like glass ceiling, in the MAK Café by an ornamented stucco ceiling.

The Museum of Applied Arts, in whose premises Hermann Czech designed the MAK Café, is the successor institution of the Austrian Museum of Art and Industry and is still located in the Neo-Renaissance building specially designed by Heinrich Ferstel in 1871.

7 Johannes Spalt: *Johannes Spalt*, 1993, 241.

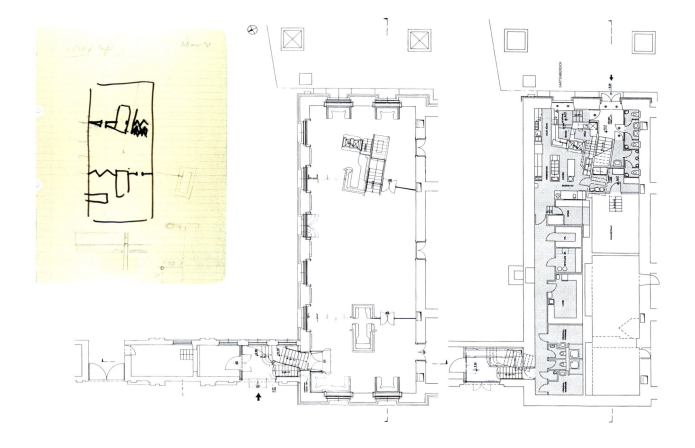

Around 1900, the museum was an important place in the discourse on living. Museum director Arthur von Scala[8] exhibited English furniture there for the first time in Vienna, which Loos recognized in 1898 in the article "Das sitzmöbel" ("Chairs").[9] Scala supported the Arts and Crafts movement in England and campaigned for an end to historicism and a similar movement in Austria. For this purpose, he won over Otto Wagner as a member of the board of trustees, and Josef Hoffmann and Kolo Moser as teachers for the arts and crafts school attached to the museum. He became a pioneer of *Jugendstil* (Art Nouveau) and the Wiener Werkstätte, which, however, developed their own forms instead of orienting themselves towards the English models according to Scala's wishful thinking. In his text, Adolf Loos placed himself in conscious opposition to the Secession, which had just been founded, and to the development that was to take its

8 Edwin Lachnit: "Arthur von Scala," in: *Österreichisches Biographisches Lexikon 1815–1950*, Vol. 10, 1994, 9.
9 Loos: "Das sitzmöbel" (June 19, 1898), in: Loos 1962, 48–54.

MAK Café

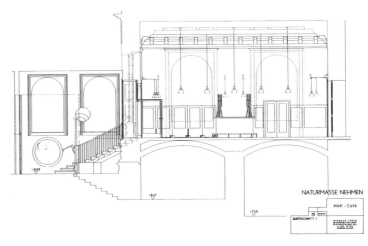

Josef Frank: Tea salon, 1930

course with the establishment of the Wiener Werkstätte in 1903 when he postulated: "Everything that an earlier period has already produced, insofar as it is still useful today, can be imitated." And he demanded: "either imitate or create something that is totally new."[10] What he ruled out were attempts to express new ideas in old styles or to want to "modify" an old work. In a later text, he restricted this prohibition of changing what already existed, insofar as he said that changes to what already existed are only allowed if they bring an improvement—as quoted by Czech at the beginning.

In 1930, Josef Frank designed a tea salon for an exhibition of the Austrian Werkbund, also held at the Austrian Museum for Art and Industry.[11] That same year he assumed management of the Austrian Werkbund with the aim of establishing an opposing standpoint to the German Werkbund. Frank rejected its dogmatic and moralizing attitude towards modern architecture. Instead, he wanted to show an alternative way of modern architecture, in which comfort was the top priority and the taste and wishes of the residents were to be taken seriously and not prescribed from above. "This puritanical ideal is frequently advanced again today because it provides the possibility of positing an absolute [...]. Morality in architecture is one of those evils that appears today at the moment it is threatened elsewhere. This undermining of morality is one of the

10 Loos: "Der neue Stil und die Bronze-Industrie" (May 29, 1898), in: Loos 1962, 26–32: 28. English translation, "The New Style and the Bronze Industry," available at https://thispublicaddress.com/2016/03/02/the-new-style-and-the-bronze-industry (accessed March 19, 2021).
11 Christopher Long: *Josef Frank 1885–1967*, 2002, 121.

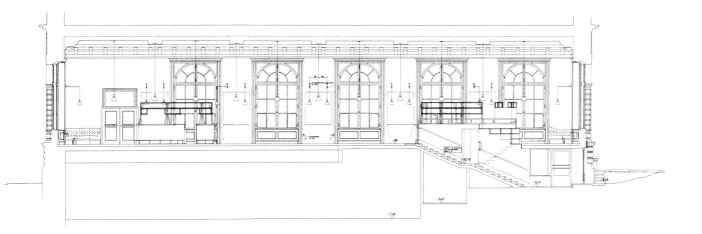

finest achievements of our time. It would be completely out of touch with life to now put the chastity commissions of the eighteenth century in charge of façades and chairs," wrote Frank in 1931.[12] The 1930 Werkbund exhibition was the first public event to take this new position. Dedicated to the subjects of travel and tourism, the show featured examples of products from Austrian manufacturers and several model rooms designed by various Austrian architects.

Frank's tearoom was designed with an unusual lightness at the time: Thonet chairs and tables lacquered in light green, a red-stained grand piano[13] designed by himself, and light folding walls made of wood stood loosely positioned in a room whose walls were painted in various pastel tones. The literary figure Soma Morgenstern commented: "Frank's tearoom appeals in a self-evident completeness, in a solemn unity of form. Color on color, delicate and light, creates an atmosphere of peaceful serenity in which all of the new *sachlich* doings are extinguished, and at the same time a new, humane style is fostered."[14]

In the museum building, which is historically essential for the history of architecture, Czech implemented his ideas of the coffee house. The existing elements of the intended hall in the northern part of the building, such as the heavily ornamented and colorfully painted stucco ceiling, the

12 Frank: *Architecture as Symbol* (1931), trans. John Sands, in: Frank 2012, Vol. 2, 9–191: 93.
13 Otto Kapfinger researched the history of this Bösendorfer grand piano by Josef Frank in the course of the major Josef Frank exhibition at the MAK in 2015–2016, designed and guest curated by Hermann Czech, and presented it to the public in a lecture on February 28, 2016.
14 Soma Morgenstern (1930), quoted in Long: *Josef Frank*, op. cit., 121.

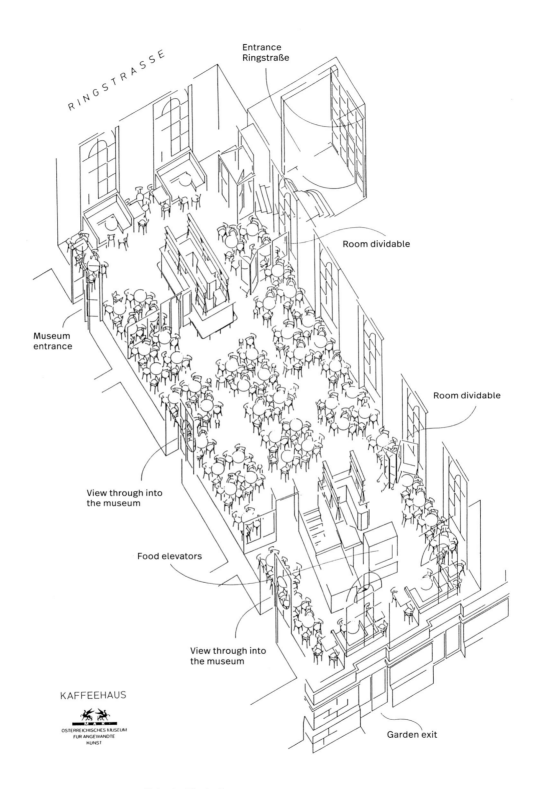

large window openings, and the historic parquet floor, remained decisive for the space. They were complemented and emphasized by the white painted walls and the white chairs and tables (with white tablecloths in the restaurant part) evenly distributed in the room. Necessary furnishings such as the two bars, the sideboard or room dividers were placed in the room as light, wooden elements with a reduced design. Technically new elements for lighting and ventilation were made of metal, whereby industrially manufactured products often found in workshops were selected as standard.

The lighting fixtures consisted of pendant lights which, due to their even distribution in the room and the chosen height, enabled the tables to be regrouped and arranged freely. There were smaller metal lights suspended from rotatable consoles along the walls.

Christoph Grafe describes the MAK Café as follows: "Czech introduced an entrance by opening up the existing panelling in the rustica of Ferstel's connecting passage between the museum and the applied arts school building […]. This door gave access to a vestibule with a freestanding flight of stairs, set in an angle departing from the orthogonal geometry of the building and lit by a large lamp of frosted glass as used on one of Vienna's modern bridges across the Danube. Inside, Czech revived the bench positioned against the niches of the windows on the short sides of the café room, relating to the exterior, the boulevard and the garden in a fashion that is deeply embedded in the tradition of the Viennese Kaffeehaus. On the internal wall facing the museum, small round windows allowed a glimpse of the adjacent exhibition spaces, rendering the café into a showcase display of informal sociability and giving a highly controlled, theatrical presence to the museum, as if viewed through a looking glass.

Exploiting these elements which epitomized the qualities of the *Kaffeehaus*, its comfort and festive tranquility, and reworking them into a contemporary interior full of subtle visual relationships, the MAK café established itself as a social institution. The intelligence of the architectural solutions suggested that Viennese traditions, which only too often are monopolized by the tourist industries, could indeed be reinvented and made productive for contemporary urban culture."[15]

In summary, it can be said that Hermann Czech's MAK Café pays homage to the Viennese coffee house—without any undertones.

15 Grafe: "MAK Café," in: Grafe; Bollerey (eds.): *Cafés and Bars – The Architecture of Public Display*, 2007: 199. The publication ensued despite the already completed demolition and with reference to it.

Thonet Chair

Czech also designed his own chair in two versions for the MAK Café, with and without armrests. The objective was "to achieve the most comfortable and light chair possible using bentwood technology."[16] For this reason, he used what had been the cheapest and most popular model in Viennese inns for a long time as the starting form, presumably a factory design from the 1920s. Czech made it more comfortable according to our current sitting habits, "the backrest is a little more inclined and a little wider."

Adolf Loos: Café Museum chair, 1899

The bentwood chairs[17] from Thonet belonged to the typical furnishings of the Viennese coffee house. What made them so common was their light weight and moderate price as an industrially produced piece of furniture. Loos only used the bentwood chair for his coffee house furnishings; in his private living quarters he preferred classic English chairs that were more comfortable, larger and heavier. In contrast to other Viennese cafés, often furnished with niches made of U-shaped benches, Loos completely dispensed with this typical element. His Café Museum and Café Capua are each large, open spaces in which groups cannot isolate themselves in alcoves from the rest of the visitors. With this design, Loos gave preference to open exchange and the visibility of all people in the room.

For the seating of the Café Museum, Loos resorted to models No. 248 and No. 30 from the Kohn company.[18] Thonet's competitor at the time, this firm also manufactured bentwood furniture. In terms of design, there were great parallels in Loos's chair design to the widespread model No. 14, the simplest and cheapest one produced by Thonet. Loos altered the shape to make the chair more comfortable for use in a coffee house. He replaced the round bentwood profiles with elliptical ones, which saved wood and made the chair even lighter and therefore more moveable without any loss of stability. The color scheme was unusual: Loos opted for red-stained beech wood instead of the usual mahogany or rosewood tint.

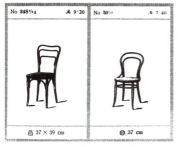

J. & J. Kohn: Catalog page with Loos models

Czech also used a common Thonet model as a prototype for the chair in the MAK Café, even if the bentwood technology is no longer one of the cheapest because of the high proportion of manual labor. For him there was no reason for a new design; he saw it as his task to choose one that had proven itself. He changed it to make it more comfortable to sit on, and thus closer to "real life." The chairs are painted white, but not at the foot ends, in

16   Czech: "Komfort und Modernität," in: *Architektur Jahrbuch* 1997, 34.
17   Cf. Kurdiovsky: "The Cliché...," op. cit., 189.
18   Eva B. Ottillinger: *Adolf Loos. Wohnkonzepte und Möbelentwürfe*, 1994, 127.

Thonet chair model 383

order to prevent the paint from unsightly chipping in the more heavily used lower part. As already described, their backrests are wider and more inclined for better seating comfort. Even if the modifications to the armchair are based on rational considerations, they still lend it a high degree of gracility and elegance.

Winter Glazing of the Vienna State Opera Loggia

Period of origin: 1991–1994
Address: Vienna State Opera, Opernring 2, 1010 Vienna
Client: Vienna State Opera, Georg Springer (General Secretary of the Austrian Federal Theaters)
Project team: Manfred Haas, Thomas Roth, engineering: Peter Kotzian

Temple of Amon, El Chārga oasis, west of Luxor, 500 BC

1 Czech: Project text, in: Ulrike Jehle-Schulte-Strathaus: "'In welchem Style sollen wir bauen?' Gedanken zur Stil-losigkeit von Hermann Czech," *wbw* 6/1996, 34.

In lectures, Hermann Czech also shows pictures of the temporary enclosure of an archaeological excavation site in connection with the winter glazing, the effect of which is reminiscent of that of the Opera loggia and reveals different layers of time.

Open in the summer, the loggia of the Vienna State Opera on the Ring is closed off during the winter months by means of Czech's glass construction, whereby its temporary character can be felt. Czech writes: "The glazing is not on one level only; on the one hand, it forms a recess behind the sculptures and on the other one bulges at the ledge to allow for free movements. This creates complex, sagging, net-type glass levels."[1]

Winter Glazing of the Vienna State Opera Loggia

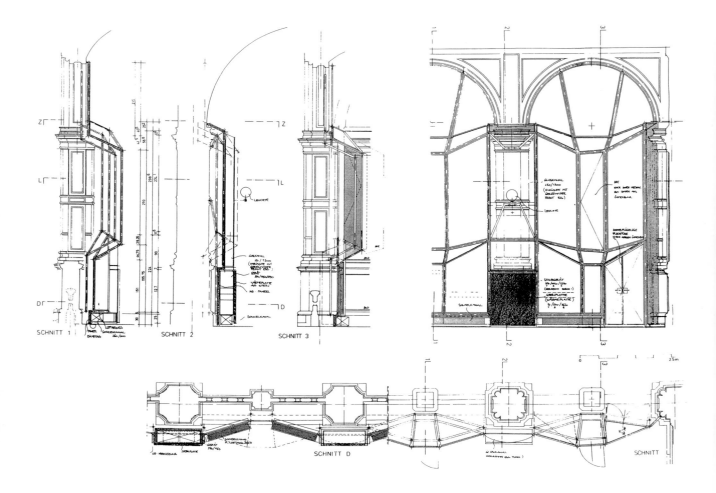

Since his participation in the Summer Academy in Salzburg with Konrad Wachsmann, where he also met Frei Otto in 1959, Czech had been interested in rope and net constructions, had conceived several "convertible" tensile canopies (Graben, Mödling shopping center) and designed a net-like steel construction with glazing for the courtyard roofing of the Löcker & Wögenstein antiquarian bookshop.

In its contrariety, the technical character of the steel and glass construction of the loggia glazing emphasizes the human expression of the bronze figures. The graceful statues are reflected in the glass and appear protected by their "own space" with its roof.

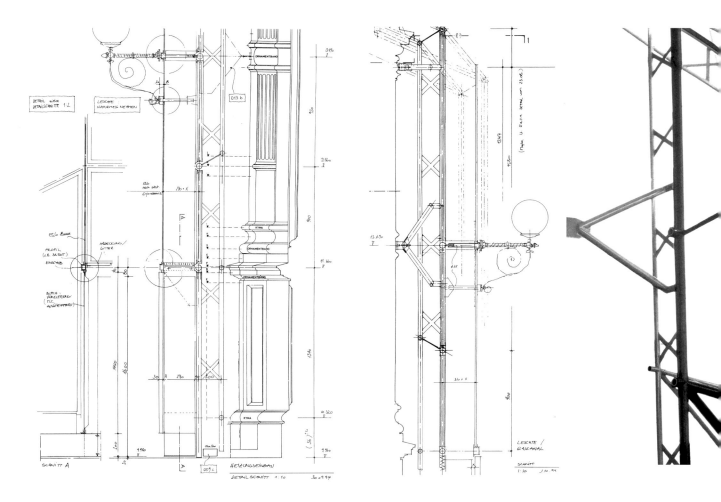

The double steel bar construction chosen for the loggia glazing of the opera makes it look light and gracile. The X between the crosspieces has the clear structural function of a connection, whereby the crosspieces only gain the necessary flexural strength as holders for the glass panes. Moreover, the X is a motif that has a meaning in Czech's biography as an architect. An X as a load-bearing construction in concrete was used by arbeitsgruppe 4 together with Johann Georg Gsteu when designing the Pastoral Care Center in Steyr-Ennsleite in 1961. Czech repeatedly names this building as defining for his architectural conception.[2] The X-pillar at the Pastoral Care Center was created on the basis of the rational and

2   For example, it was among the references selected by Czech for Valerio Olgiati's contribution to the 2012 Venice Architecture Biennale. Valerio Olgiati: *The Images of Architects*, Chur 2013.

Winter Glazing of the Vienna State Opera Loggia

arbeitsgruppe 4 with Johann Georg Gsteu: Ennsleite Pastoral Care Center, 1961

Design of the Salzburg beer pub, 1978–1980

structural spirit of the Wachsmann seminars, but at the same time contains a certain figurative character and symbolism that goes beyond the pure rationality of the construction. Czech used the X—quite ironically and decoratively—as early as 1979 when designing a restaurant in Salzburg in the wooden construction of the partition walls between the seating groups: He applied the Ennsleiten X—reduced to a scale of 1:25—and defined the construction as an ornament. The X can also be found in a tea table design by Josef Frank, shown in the catalog compiled by Czech and Spalt for the Frank exhibition in 1981.[3] A closer look at van der Null and Sicardsburg's Opera façade likewise reveals an X in the ornament of the pillars. This multi-layered and double or multiple meaning of an element is typical of Czech's designs. The special thing about this multiple meaning is that there is no point in reading out a "correct" or "true" meaning—each one has its own story and justification.

3 Czech; Spalt: *Josef Frank 1885–1967*, 1981, 61.

Winter Glazing of the Vienna State Opera Loggia

Rosa Jochmann School

with Wolfgang Reder

Period of origin: 1991–1994
Address: Fuchsröhrenstrasse 21–25, 1110 Vienna
Client: City of Vienna, Kallco property developer, Winfried Kallinger
Project team: Martin Cikhart, Thomas Roth, Bogdan Szwajnoch, engineering: Gerhard Hejkrlik

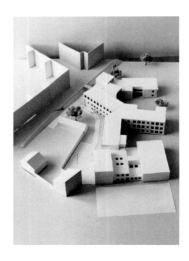

1 Czech at a lecture at RWTH Aachen on December 3, 2012.
2 Czech in an interview with Mikael Bergquist, corrected text, Czech Archive.
3 Walter Chramosta: *Rosa Jochmann Schule, Wien 11. Hermann Czech*, Vienna 1994, 4–8.
4 Czech: Project text, in: Ulrike Jehle-Schulte-Strathaus: "'In welchem Style sollen wir bauen?' Gedanken zur Stil-losigkeit von Hermann Czech," *wbw* 6/1996, 23.

During its completion, Czech described the school as "the most conventional new school building in Vienna." The architecture was not supposed to represent something that did not correspond to the state of school pedagogy, "…was not supposed to simulate a type of school that is only partially being considered today."[1] Czech did not question the educational concept of teaching children in closed classrooms with a fixed size of 7 by 9 meters. It would be pointless for him to simulate an openness that does not exist in the system. Instead, the given structure was to be designed in such a way that students and teachers feel as comfortable as possible in these rooms.[2] In his opinion, this is the most serious possible stance to not remain on the surface in the work.[3]

The property lies on the edge of the terrain. Czech makes use of this topographical situation by opening the main entrance on the first floor with a walkway, thereby mitigating the three-story building. The school is conceived as a combination of hall and corridor school. "Two to three classrooms with rooms to be divided or integrated are accessed by way of short, naturally lighted corridors with cloak room niches."[4]

One enters the school via the mentioned walkway on the middle floor in the middle of the U-shaped component and arrives directly in a wide, two-story hall with a large window front facing the schoolyard. Grouped around the hall are the library, the teachers' room, the principal's office and the doctor's room, as well as corridors branching off to the classes, which are structured by cloakroom tables and recessed doors. On the upper floor, the hall is enclosed by a gallery with access to classrooms. As on the entrance floor, corridors lead to further classes to the north and east. Directly adjacent to the hall, they are only available in the gallery area

on the upper floor. The basement houses the kitchen, dining room and multi-purpose room, while the gym, as a place of considerable attractive force, lies at the eastern end of the building.

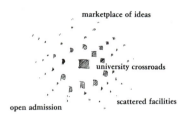

Christopher Alexander: Pattern 43, 1977 (University as a Marketplace)

5 Alexander et al.: *A Pattern Language. Towns. Buildings. Construction*, 1977; German edition: *Eine Muster-Sprache*, 1995.
6 Czech: "Christopher Alexander and Viennese Modernism" (1984), trans. Elise Feiersinger, in: Czech 2019, 135–148.
7 Ibid.,137.

Since 1984, Czech had been working with several translators for Löcker Verlag on the German edition of Christopher Alexander's *A Pattern Language*.[5] For him, there are many parallels between Alexander's way of thinking and that of Loos and Frank.[6] He attributes to both positions the aim "to sustain the perennial quality of architecture, to reinstate a disrupted continuity, to create buildings in which people can be themselves, and all that on the basis of the knowledge of concrete needs and their spatial patterns."[7]

In Pattern Number 43, Alexander describes the layout of a university and suggests organizing it like a marketplace: "Physically, the university marketplace has a central crossroads where its main buildings and offices are, and the meeting rooms and labs ripple out from this crossroads— at first concentrated in small buildings along pedestrian streets and then gradually becoming more dispersed and mixed with the town."[8] Although the elementary school has different proportions than a university and the structure described takes place in a building, the organization of the school can be read analogously. Czech virtually interweaves the school building with its outside space: the main entrance with the bridge faces

The directional change of the lights avoids beam-shaped shadows.

the closed residential development in the south; classrooms with their colored window frames are oriented towards the public playground to the west; the outdoor spaces of the school open to the undeveloped landscape to the north; and towards the closed firewalls of the buildings adjoining to the east Czech also completes the school with windowless walls (short sides of the gymnasium).

Despite its sober, standardized furnishings, the Rosa Jochmann School looks astonishingly homey inside. In 1953, arbeitsgruppe 4 designed the so-called *Wohnraumschule* ("Living Space School").[9] This school was organized around a common "living space," whereby the community experience was to be the focus. The closed classrooms were reserved as "thinking cells" for abstract lessons. All other activities such as handicrafts, singing and storytelling were to take place in the common "living space." The radical idea of arbeitsgruppe 4 for the 1950s was to think of school as a part of living. This left a lasting impression on Czech.[10] The organization of the Rosa Jochmann School could also be seen as the implementation of the concept of the living space school within the requirements of the municipal school authorities. Organized along corridors, the classrooms

8 Alexander et al.: "43 University as a Marketplace," in *A Pattern Language*, 231–235: 234.
9 Johannes Spalt: *Johannes Spalt*, 1993, 28–29.
10 Czech emphasized this several times in discussions about arbeitsgruppe 4; in his design for the Rosa-Jochmann-School, however, he himself made no reference to the Living Space School.

Rosa Jochmann School

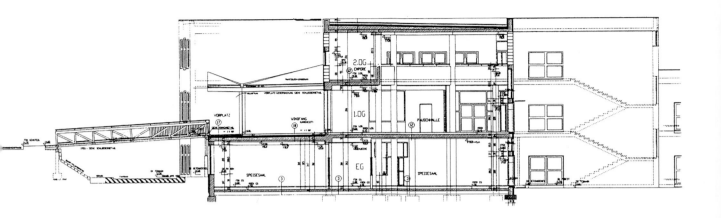

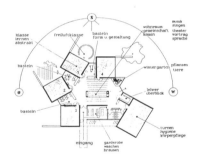

arbeitsgruppe 4: Living Space School project, 1953

nonetheless extend to more public, living-room-like areas (hall, dining room, playgrounds). All rooms are designed to be cozy in their own special way: the classrooms with wooden floors, contrasting colored ceilings and the large window openings with traditional window divisions. The colored ceilings are surrounded by a wide, rough frieze that has a sound-absorbing effect and, in contrast to this, is smooth and shiny in the middle section. This arrangement fulfills the requirements of a classroom, but at the same time gives the room a spacious and homey feeling. The middle window of each class is imperceptibly larger than the other two, which emphasizes the spatial center of the class and does not focus on the wall with the blackboard. The lighting—common office lighting fixtures that distribute uniform, glare-free light—are not arranged in a grid or in rows, but rather twisted towards one another, which in turn moderates the directionality of the room. Classic globe lamps and the ground-level view of the garden, which serves as a playground, lend the cafeteria the character of a dining room in a residential building. Czech equipped the entrance hall with a chandelier made up of fluorescent tubes in different shades of white and a ceiling made of sound-absorbing wooden panels that spread around the chandelier in a net-like pattern. Despite the austerity of the raw materials (fluorescent tubes, perforated wooden panels), the entrance hall of the school is reminiscent of a living culture in which the central hall was a natural part of living and life.

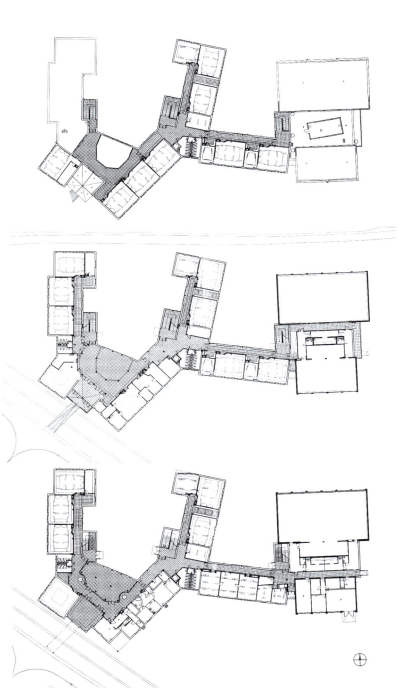

Rosa Jochmann School

Urbanization of Oranienburg

1st ranked expertise project, not carried out
Period of origin: 1992–1993
Address: Barracks of the Sachsenhausen Concentration Camp
Client: City of Oranienburg

Oranienburg is a small town north of Berlin, where the Sachsenhausen concentration camp was located as of 1936.[1] It was the first planned concentration camp of the National Socialists and, due to its proximity to the "Reich Capital" of Berlin, held a special position. The SS used it for training purposes and as a model; in 1938, the administrative headquarters of all concentration camps in Germany were relocated there. Subsequent to the prisoner camp, a system of administrative buildings, SS barracks and settlement houses for members of the SS was built. After the end of the war, the entire facility continued to be utilized until 1950 by the Soviet secret service as "Special Camp No. 7." Starting in 1956, the GDR regime converted the prisoner camp area into a memorial, which opened in 1961.

The subject of the expertise for the "urbanization of Oranienburg" was not the area of the former prisoner camp, i.e., the memorial, but of the former SS barracks that followed it. These were used from 1950 to 1989 by the National People's Army (NVA) of the GDR and also structurally expanded. After the *Wende* ("Turnaround") in 1989, the buildings partially housed the tax office and police headquarters of Oranienburg.

This "unfortunate continuity"[2] from SS barracks, to NVA barracks, to police headquarters prompted an initiative by LEG (Landesentwicklungsgesellschaft für Städtebau, Wohnen und Verkehr) des Landes Brandenburg mbH (State Development Corporation for Urban Development, Housing and Transport of the State of Brandenburg)—under the direction of Rainer Graff—on which the city decided in 1991 to release the site for a city expansion, for an "urbanization"—that is, by no means for exclusive residential construction. The basic consideration of the expert jury,[3] who also prepared the tender, was to make the barracks area, still a "blind spot"

---

[1] Czech: "'Wo Lager war, soll Stadt werden.' Das Gutachterverfahren Oranienburg 1992–1993," in: *Erbe verweigert. Österreich und NS-Architektur, Österreichische Zeitschrift für Kunst und Denkmalpflege, LXI*, 2007, Heft 1, 68–81. Reprint (text and notes added, image section shortened) in: *Ästhetik und Kommunikation*, 143, 2008, 54–68. For the history of the location, see also the Sachsenhausen Memorial and Museum homepage (<stiftung-bg.de>).

[2] Quoted from the tender text in: Czech: "'Wo Lager war, soll Stadt werden.'...," op. cit., 69.

[3] The jury consisted of the architects Bruno Flierl, Hardt-Waltherr Hämer, Otto Steidle, Benedict Tonon, the historian Annette Leo and the historian, theoretician and planner Dieter Hoffmann-Axthelm.

Memorial and barracks around 2001, still largely in the same condition at the time of the expertise procedure

in the city's topography due to its current use, part of the city and thus to raise the city's awareness of the adjacent memorial, "not by a peripheral housing estate, but with all urban functions, not following the area around the castle."[4] The call formulated by Dieter Hoffmann-Axthelm, "where camp was, there city shall be,"[5] was a conscious analogy to Freud's "where id was, there ego shall be." "Thus, the concentration-camp memorial relocated *within* the town would be a confession to the *entire* past and an offensive method towards a long-term, 'inclusive' memory."[6]

The draft essentially made a proposal about how the incriminated buildings, which also symbolize the Nazi crimes, could be dealt with. Czech saw the process and his project as a further, albeit "experimental" contribution to the problem of memorial sites, namely that "in view of the former concentration camp in a developing small town, informal commemoration confronted with everyday life could establish itself and remain."[7] The pending "monument preservation decision [was] to be won not only because of the content to be evaluated, but also *in itself* methodologically solely from the evaluation of interventions through urbanistic, architectural designs."[8]

Czech's project proposes a new geometric order for the urban structure that is now being added: "The new construction and development runs—not least due to the need to establish links to the northern and north-western town districts—diagonally to the former orthogonality of the barracks. This geometry represents the time layers between its former utilization [...]. In the north, the streets join the road running along the former concentration-camp wall with its entrance to the memorial [which then again corresponds to the historic entrance to the concentration camp—note by the author], which is thus visually present. The large axes of the barracks facilities are, however, destroyed or integrated into much smaller spatial relationships; the old entrance to the barracks area is left to the right. Only individual aspects such as the direction of a building or a line of trees still show that they belong to the older—incriminated—building plan."[9] The two new parallel streets form the main feature of the design.[10] They are accompanied by denser longitudinal buildings, adjoined by a ridge-like development (both typologies with mixed use), the density of which decreases towards the outside and in between, and which merges into three green zones via terraced houses. The function of the incriminated buildings would result from the zoning of the adjacent new development. Envisaged in the project is a more consumption-oriented

---

4   Czech: "Ein Gutachten," in: Czech 1996, 139–143: 140.
5   From the tender text.
6   Czech: Project text, in: "Entwurfsprozess: Skizzen, Bauten, Projekte," *wbw* 6/1996, 62.
7   Czech: "'Wo Lager war, soll Stadt werden.'...," op. cit., 81.
8   Ibid., 70.
9   Ibid., 76, caption under the isometric overview plan from the Czech project. English translation in the project text in: "Entwurfsprozess: Skizzen, Bauten, Projekte," *wbw* 6/1996, 62.
10 For a description of the project, see: Czech: "Ein Gutachten," op. cit., 141f, as well as: "Entwurfsprozess: Skizzen, Bauten, Projekte," *wbw* 6/1996, 62f.

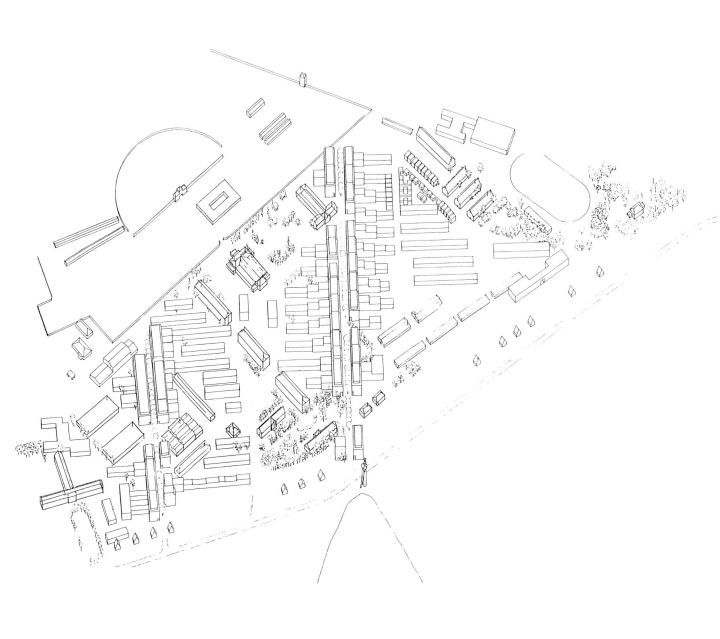

use in the eastern street and a more production-oriented one in the western street. "However, since both streets are intended for mixed use with offices and apartments, there may also be a trade-off," for example, through a "development in sections."[11]

A total of six architects' offices received invitations to take part in the expert review process:[12] four German offices, Hermann Czech and Daniel Libeskind. The jury ranked Czech's project first, that of the "Baufrösche" office third and awarded Daniel Libeskind an "honorable mention."[13]

Daniel Libeskind garnered media publicity far beyond local borders for his design, which countered the terms of the competition. His proposal draws a landscape plan, or rather a piece of landscape art, over the entire site, which contains a new, wedge-shaped building structure for economic, social and cultural uses.[14] The existing buildings will be torn down, but their foundations will still be visible. With the exception of the "Hope Incision" of the new development, the area is partially flooded and partially forested. Libeskind therefore did not plan to use the existing buildings again. Beyond that, he spoke out vehemently against a *residential* use in new buildings; that would be tantamount to a "domestication" and "trivialization" of the site. In the emotional and polemical debate[15] effectuated by the media, which ultimately lasted several years, he repudiated the concept of "urbanization" envisaged by the tender and the jury's decision and equated it with "housing construction," which could easily be understood subliminally as commercial or political speculation. "By falsifying facts and concealing the motivations, Libeskind discredited the procedure that had not been decided for him and thus all the other parties involved."[16]

Libeskind's project was ultimately favored by the City of Oranienburg, but it was not implemented even after several revisions. "What was to be avoided—that the site is reused, but still forms a blind spot in the city topography due to its inaccessibility—[…] actually occurred."[17]

Besides all the polemics that sparked off this project, an essential question was whether it is morally justifiable to *live* in or next to such a historically burdened place. Czech clearly speaks out in favor of this—in the context of a holistic urban usage and an undeniable urban history. The classification of uses as "compatible with memorial sites" or "reprehensible" is ambivalent anyway for Czech: Almost every use can be coded as "good" or "bad." For him, the ethical question is how to deal with existing buildings. "My

---

11 Czech: "Ein Gutachten," op. cit., 141.
12 "Baufrösche," Kassel; Klaus Neumann/Heike Büttner/Georg Braun, Berlin; Daniel Libeskind, Berlin; Hermann Czech, Vienna; Dr. Kabus/Ralf Ludewig, Oranienburg; Karl-Heinz Birkholz/Diethelm Franke/Erich Gassauer, Potsdam.
13 Czech: "'Wo Lager war, soll Stadt werden.'…," op. cit., 71.
14 For Daniel Libeskind's project, see his own project description in: Libeskind: "MoUrning," in: idem: *Kein Ort an seiner Stelle. Schriften zur Architektur–Visionen für Berlin*, 1995, 135–140, 137–140.
15 On the debate, see also contributions from Peter Neitzke and Dieter Hoffmann-Axthelm in: *ARCH+* 117 and 118, as well as Czech: "'Wo Lager war, soll Stadt werden.'…," op. cit.
16 Czech: "'Wo Lager war, soll Stadt werden.'…," op. cit., 73.
17 Ibid., 81.

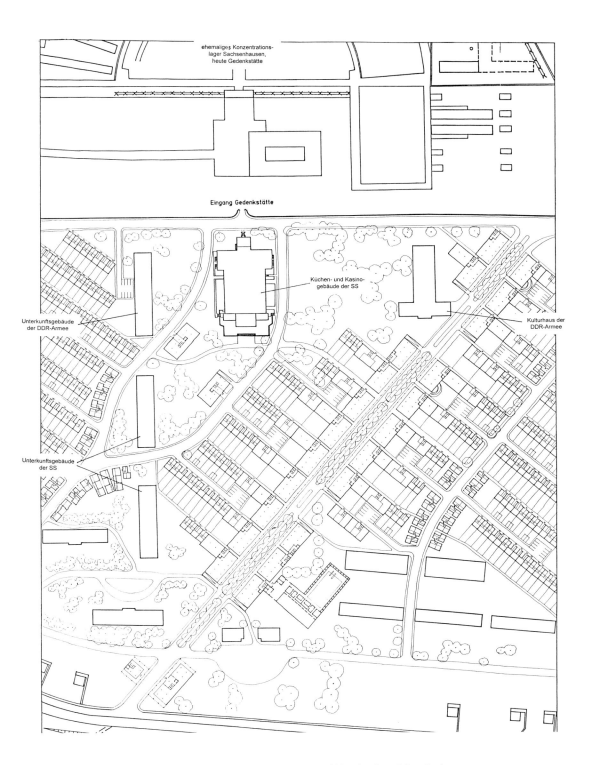

Urbanization of Oranienburg

project is decidedly based on the confrontation of the new development with the existing one. This visual juxtaposition and intertwining in its concrete appearance cannot be foreseen in every detail; in its planning version it has an open, even frivolous aspect. But it is precisely the openness with planning precision that defines the quality of an urban development.

Obviously, for us it is not—as in the late forties—primarily a matter of the knowledge of the Nazi crimes and the shock of this realization, but about the conveyed concern about how to 'deal' with these facts and to show this dealing. But decency is no less honorable than insight.

I now prefer a procedure that again allows experiences from this interaction—even those that cannot be foreseen. That is why I speak for a commemoration that arises in the confrontation with everyday life. Of course, it cannot be a 'prescribed' remembrance then. The commemoration of individual sites, to which one leads school classes and travelers, has its educational and political sense—but that already exists."[18]

Czech replies with architectural means, spatially linking the town via the new streets with the concentration camp memorial and "leaving" the existing structures "aside to the right." In doing so, he positions himself clearly in relation to the incriminated history of these buildings within the framework that architecture allows. For him, further decisions would go beyond architecture. In his 1971 essay "No Need for Panic," Czech made a distinction between what, in his opinion, architecture can and cannot do: "Architecture is overestimated. Fifty years ago people were convinced that modern architecture could cure tuberculosis. Now that tuberculosis really has vanished, architects feel called upon to solve problems of greater scope."[19] And this text ends with these sentences: "Architecture is not life. Architecture is *background*. Everything else is *not* architecture."

Nevertheless, architecture has an effect on "life" and the structure proposed in Czech's project could bring about a "bottom-up" culture of remembrance; dealing with the everyday confrontation with history, with the structures that have fallen out of the geometry and the former concentration camp that is on their own doorstep would then be a matter for the new residents and the city. Visitors to the concentration camp memorial would perceive it as part of the city, which could open additional levels of reflection.

18   Czech: "Ein Gutachten," op. cit., 142.
19   Czech: "No Need for Panic" (1971), trans. Elise Feiersinger, in: Czech 2019, 106.

The site after ca. 2002: The buildings erected after 1945 were demolished, thereby removing the traces of subsequent use by the NKVD (Soviet Secret Service) and NVA (GDR Army).

Furnishing of the Swiss Re Centre
with Adolf Krischanitz, in cooperation with Marcel Meili and Markus Peter

Period of origin: 1998–2000
Address: Rüschlikon, Switzerland
Client: Swiss Reinsurance Company, Zurich
Project team: Thomas Roth

1. Marcel Meili, Markus Peter: "Swiss Re Rüschlikon. Centre for Global Dialogue," trans. Maria E. Clay/Kimi Lum, in: idem et al.: *Swiss Re Rüschlikon. Centre for Global Dialogue* (= aka Werkdokumente 20), 2001, 38–43: 39.
2. Ibid.

Following a competition victory, the architects Marcel Meili and Markus Peter built a seminar center in Rüschlikon near Zurich for the Swiss reinsurance company Swiss Re. The property lies on Lake Zurich and already had a neo-Baroque villa with a park and gardener's house erected on it: "[…] Here classical and landscape elements converge in an odd, indefinable relationship, and the unusual refusal to recognize the rest of the surroundings and the lake lend the complex an extraordinary, somewhat aloof charm."[1] Meili and Peter described the required spatial program as "a sort of retreat from today's secular, global society."[2] In this meditative location overlooking the lake, people want to meet to reflect, discuss and teach about the risks of modern society. The seminar center with hotel and restaurant was to incorporate the existing buildings. Meili and Peter decided to place the largest building volume, the seminar and hotel building, at the previously undeveloped end of the property, next to the small gardener's house, and to add the restaurant with suites above to the villa. The park area thus stretches between the villa and the seminar building as the most important open space in the configuration. This arrangement enriches the often more important part of the events, namely the breaks between the official lectures, the time for informal exchange and unhindered internal discussions, with the element of movement. The seminar participants "stroll" in the park in conversation between the seminar rooms, the restaurant, the bar and the guest rooms.

The commission awarded to the architects Meili and Peter also included the complete furnishing. However, they refrained from continuing their architectural stance down to the last details. "We imagined it would be interesting to have the quiet and austere rooms interpreted by other architects who designed the furnishings according to

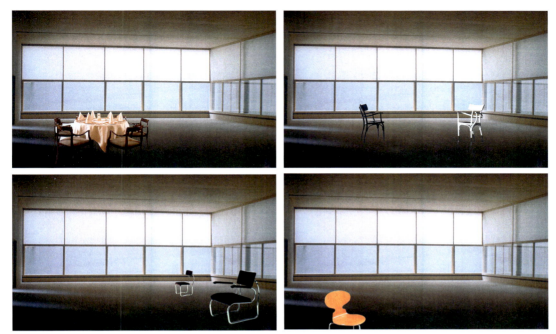

Examination of the juxtaposition of furniture that is "older" or "younger" than the building.

their own ideas."[3] Hermann Czech and Adolf Krischanitz applied together for the international tender and, in a selection process carried out by Meili and Peter with the clients, received the commission to appoint all the rooms with the exception of the villa. This was designed inside (also for reasons of monument protection) by Günter Förg as part of an art project. Curtain fabrics and carpets were designed by the Viennese painter and textile artist Gilbert Bretterbauer.

Czech was responsible for furnishing the restaurant, the three suites and a café, and set up a bar in the gardener's house. Krischanitz designed the flexible furniture for the Forum and Foyer, as well as the furnishing of the two types of hotel rooms in the seminar building. Elements from both architects can be found in the walkway and in the library. "In a controlled consensus, we split up the tasks: other than for a single piece of furniture—the group of sofas in the library—we didn't linger over team design work."[4] Krischanitz and Czech had already introduced a notion of the "flicker of contradictory 'design' worlds"[5] at the first presentation: through montages of different types of furniture in model photos of the

3 Ibid., 43.
4 Czech: "Approximate Line of Action," trans. Charlotte Eckler and Lisa Rosenblatt, in: *Marcel Meili, Markus Peter: 1987–2008*, 2008, 434–441: 438.
5 Ibid.

Furnishing of the Swiss Re Centre

building by Meili and Peter. A difference can result from the associative time characteristics of an intervention: Furniture types can, for example, be "younger" (as in Czech's renovation of Palais Schwarzenberg) or "older" than the room furnished with it. Later attempts with modern furniture classics by Le Corbusier and Charles and Ray Eames in model rooms on a 1:1 scale showed "that these icons seemed cliché today and that they didn't go with the style of the architecture [...]."[6] Instead, the decision was made to design everything from scratch "based on the principle of creating furnishings that tended to be anonymous and altogether heterogeneous; not distinctly stylish, but not lacking character either; designed to meet high standards and at the same time ostensibly casual, as if only in passing: a non-designer atmosphere, but without the interchangeability of common furnishings."[7]

6 Otto Kapfinger: "The Complex Whole, Simply Put," in: Meili, Peter et al., *Swiss Re Rüschlikon. Centre for Global Dialogue*, 2001, 48–67: 66.
7 Ibid.

When appointing the guest rooms, Czech used elements of his own earlier restaurant plans. The bar in the gardener's house, which also forms a completely independent element spatially in the overall ensemble, is designed by Czech as a "world of its own": a glossy, lacquered ceiling in strong red, globe lights, a Murano chandelier, which, however, dangles from the small crane runway of the former gardener's workshop; as seating, the MAK chair in black, the wing armchairs and the chair with the upholstered backrest from the first theater café, the curved leather bench from the Wunder-Bar or the Salzamt Restaurant, illusions of openings created by mirror fields with likewise illusionary sliding windows above, oval window openings, a counter with a haptically comfortably profiled bar rail and behind it a combination of multiple symmetrical shelf elements. The globe lamps made of frosted glass are provided with openings upwards

Furnishing of the Swiss Re Centre

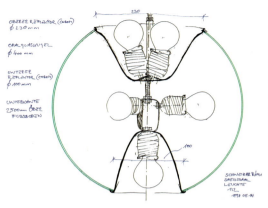 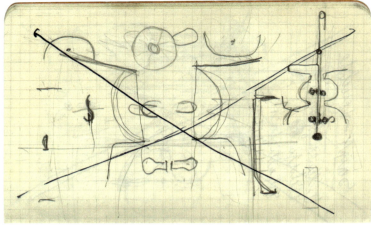

The idea of a lighting fixture with variable luminous flux distribution that has been pursued for decades.

8   Czech: "Approximate Line of Action," trans. Charlotte Eckler and Lisa Rosenblatt, *Marcel Meili, Markus Peter*, op. cit., 438.

9   Czech: "Die Sprache der Verführung," in: *SvM. Die Festschrift für Stanislaus von Moos*, 2005, 150–157: 155.

10 Otto Kapfinger: "The Complex Whole, Simply Put," in: Meili, Peter, et al., *Swiss Re Rüschlikon. Centre for Global Dialogue*, 2001, 48–67: 64.

and downwards, so that in addition to the uniformly diffuse light they also emit light directly upwards and downwards. The chairs and armchairs were also alternately distributed around the table by Czech in the bar and appear very physical—almost like a group of different animals gathering around a watering hole. "I definitely followed my recipe for diversity from 1973, 'allow(ing) all our motivations to flow into the design …follow(ing) up all the ramifications and thought processes, rather than imitating some harebrained recipe or sticking to some flat discipline.' […] in my own designs, something (consciously) operatic also happened."[8] In the other guest rooms, Czech remained more reserved, but again combined his own existing designs. When furnishing the restaurant, Czech used the restaurant armchairs from Palais Schwarzenberg, with wooden parts stained in dark wine red, but in a modified, stricter shape (the legs are—"in the lower half, where they do not add anything to comfort"[9]—straight and no longer curved), plus glossy black glass table surfaces with light wooden frames. The positions of the globe lamps with downlight openings are matched to possible different table arrangements. This "corresponds 'coincidentally' to the changing rhythms of the window divisions and the non-grid pattern of the ceiling divisions by Meili, Peter."[10] The armchairs reappear in the bar near the restaurant, as well as in the café in the gallery area, but here in combination with a small round armchair. Again, the

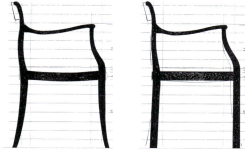

The Schwarzenberg Restaurant armchair and its Swiss variant

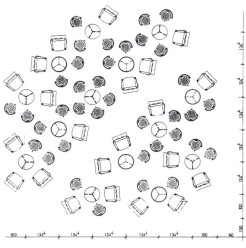

Very heavy and very light seating combined in the café

Furnishing of the Swiss Re Centre

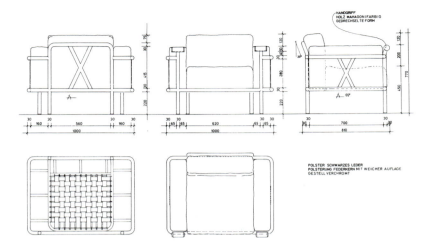

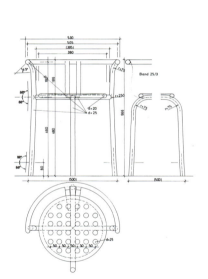
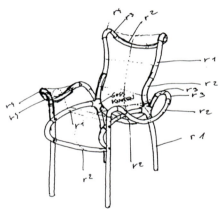

furniture is not set up in a grid (to be precise: the tables already are), but rather look more like a herd of animals. Such an arrangement creates unusually close relationships with chairs at other tables, which is ideal for informal communication in a seminar group during a break.

For the presidential suite, Czech designed a reading armchair, actually a one-off prototype, in which a high-strength net is stretched over a frame (here made of bentwood) so that the body does not touch the frame anywhere, but only the net, including the armrests and the critical front edge of the seat.

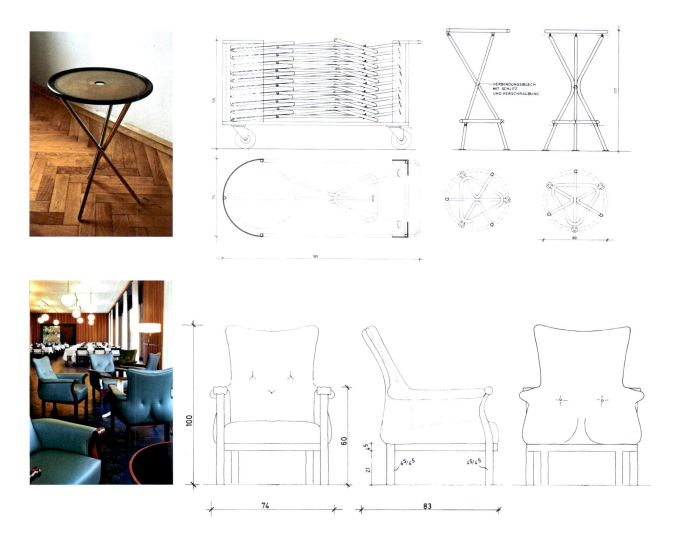

Josef Frank argued a number of times against the cubic shapes of chairs and against the use of tubular steel as a material.[11] For him, the comfort of an armchair depended solely on its shape. "Although the entire world knows that the chair is not a prism because it belongs fundamentally to sitting, conforming inversely to the human body and is thus rounded, constant experiments are nevertheless undertaken to make it and all domestic implements conform with the cube in order to re-attain the unity that was once considered stylish in furnishings."[12] Today, one would call a modernist design classic "stylish furnishing."

11 Inter alia, Josef Frank: "What Is Modern?" (1930), trans. Nader Vossoughian, in: Frank 2012, Vol. 1, 404–431.

12 Frank: *Architecture as Symbol* (1931), trans. John Sands, in: Frank 2012, Vol. 2, 9–191: 131.

Sofa design together with Adolf Krischanitz

Marcel Meili and Markus Peter commented in retrospect: "The interventions by Hermann Czech, Adolf Krischanitz, Gilbert Bretterbauer, and Günther Förg generate their own atmospheres. The complex thus avoids being leveled out by one specific signature."[13]

Czech is critical of the use of the term "atmosphere." In 2008, he wrote a text for a book about the work of Marcel Meili and Markus Peter.[14] In this, he addressed the current tendencies towards understanding architecture as the creation of atmosphere[15] and spatial moods. This differs fundamentally from his approach of understanding architecture as "background." Of course, every background also has an atmosphere, the creation of which is not at the beginning of the design process, but rather the result. "But the theme of architecture was architecture itself, even if it had ready a rich field of associations—through to a true eclecticism. Life could unfold *before* it, and in the best case, lean *on* it. I do not view the work of Meili and Peter any differently. The design is consciously conceived from the aspect of production, as a series of decisions. The first questions are dedicated to underlying thoughts, criteria, and parameters; the result, at most, is subject to monitoring the impression it mediates."[16] For Czech, thinking about architecture in terms of effect, atmosphere and mood means conceiving "architecture by way of consumption" and seeing the user as a "consumer" (see also Elisabeth Nemeth's essay in this book).

13 *Marcel Meili, Markus Peter*, op. cit., 255.
14 Czech: "Approximate Line of Action," trans. Charlotte Eckler and Lisa Rosenblatt, in: *Marcel Meili, Markus Peter*, op. cit.
15 The term "atmosphere" refers to its understanding by the German theorist Gernot Böhme. See: Gernot Böhme: *Atmosphäre* 1995 and *Architektur und Atmosphäre* 2006.
16 Czech: "Approximate Line of Action," trans. Charlotte Eckler and Lisa Rosenblatt, in: *Marcel Meili, Markus Peter*, op. cit., 438f.

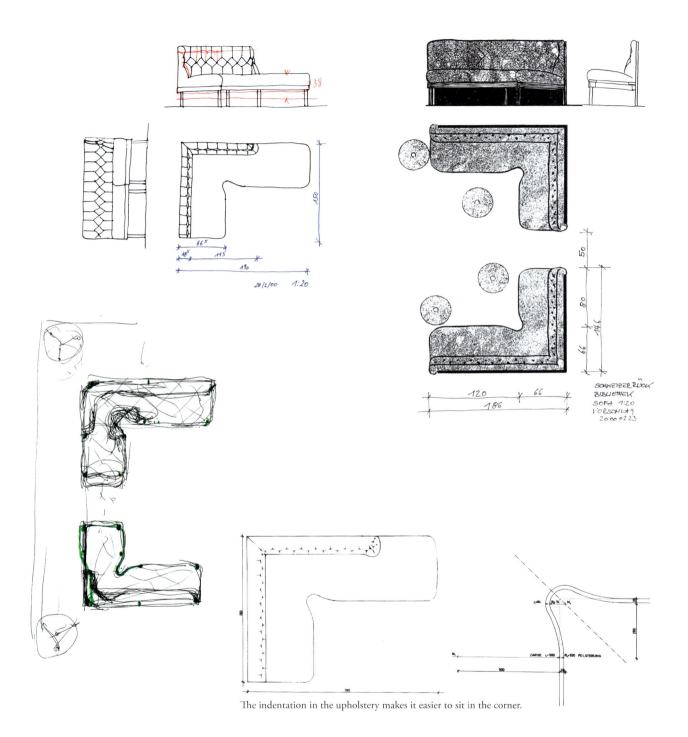

The indentation in the upholstery makes it easier to sit in the corner.

Furnishing of the Swiss Re Centre

"Area of Tolerance"
Exhibition contribution on the occasion of the 7th Architecture Biennale
with Sabine Götz

Project period: 2000
Location: Austrian Pavilion, Giardini della Biennale, Venice
Curator: Hans Hollein: "Area of Tolerance. For Peace, Freedom of Art – Against Racism and Xenophobia"

In 2000, Hans Hollein curated Austria's contribution to the 7th Venice Architecture Biennale as commissioner. His topic was "Ausländer lehren, entwerfen und bauen in Österreich" ("Foreigners teach, plan and build in and for Austria"). During the preparations for the exhibition in Austria, a government coalition made up of conservatives and right-wing populists was sworn in. Hollein then added a clear response to the exhibition: He invited international and Austrian architects to design, as a statement, an "Area of Tolerance"—possibly for the Ballhausplatz square, where the official seats of the Federal Chancellor and the Federal President face each other. Due to the regular demonstrations that took place there, this square had mutated into a real and symbolic place of resistance against the new government. Ben van Berkel, Zaha Hadid, Adolf Krischanitz, Greg Lynn, Thom Mayne, Jean Nouvel and Hermann Czech received invitations.

In terms of urban space, the Ballhausplatz is not a closed square; rather, it opens to the Volksgarten and Heldenplatz. Czech's suggestion was to place a 40 x 20-meter field surrounded by a six-meter-high, transparent fence in front of this opening. The volume corresponds to the "cages" used in many spots in Vienna as ball playgrounds for young people living nearby. Czech did not "close" the square with a building, but with a transparent volume.

    The contribution to the Biennale itself consisted of two posters that only differed in their captions. Both showed realistic simulations of the empty cage: "This is a playground." was the headline for the first poster, "This is a jail." for the second. The playground designation makes reference to the name Ballhausplatz as the location of the building in which imperial ball games were once played. A playground/sports field is traditionally a

This is a classical problem of urban design: to define and enclose a square with a transparent building volume of 40 x 20 x 6 meters.

— Don't overestimate the role of architecture.

This is a playground.

Youth in play can be loud and disturbing.

— Ballhausplatz is named after the one time hall for ball games of the Imperial Court.

This is a jail.

At any time there are 200-400 deportees being held in custody in Vienna.

Original Photographs:
Österreichische Nationalbibliothek
Georg Riha (BMLV Zl. 13.088/760-1.6/85)

Visualization:
Wolfgang Beyer, Vienna

"Area of Tolerance"

place associated with tolerance, as it is important to treat the opponent with respect in the game and, if necessary, to accept being outplayed. Young people who use a playground are often noisy too, which requires tolerance from their surroundings. The jail or prison camp designation pointed to the constant number of two to four hundred deportees being held in police custody in Vienna at that time. Both references were briefly explained. As a conclusion, the phrase "Don't overestimate the role of architecture." stood between the two posters.

"Architecture is overestimated," Hermann Czech wrote in the 1971 essay "No Need for Panic."[1] This text was a response to Hans Hollein's 1968 manifesto "Everything Is Architecture." Back then, Czech stated that architecture was overestimated in terms of its ability to resolve non-architectural issues. At the same time, however, he also argued that architecture is "*under*estimated." In any case, in the then-rampant slogan "'environment' this continuously overturning nonsense has crystallized: the arrogance to believe that architecture can save the world, and the modesty to believe that this can be achieved by rounding off all corners."[2] The essay concludes with the realization that architecture has no other role "apart from standing there and keeping quiet. Architecture is not life. Architecture is *background*. Everything else is *not* architecture."

With his contribution to the exhibition, Czech repeats his criticism of the claim—ascribed to Hollein—of architecture, in this case, to bring about a solution to the socio-political problem of a lack of tolerance towards those who think differently. At the same time, however, his contribution also showed that architecture can certainly add to socio-political criticism. In this work, Czech's partner, the psychoanalyst Sabine Götz—as in other conceptual insights—has a constitutive part.

Such a "cage" on Ballhausplatz would have raised the interesting question of which interpretation would have been closer to the members of the federal government: the playground or the jail? Czech himself later said that the intervention was not architecture, but a statement by means of architecture that would not be immediately understood in the built state—then, namely, it would actually be either a playground or a prison camp.

1 Czech: "No Need for Panic" (1971), trans. Elise Feiersinger, in: Czech 2019, 106.
2 Ibid. – Rounded corners were a formal trend of the decade, from building structures to plan graphics.

"Area of Tolerance"

Hadersdorf Model Housing Estate

Period of origin: 2000, 2006–2007
Address: Friedhofstrasse 169, 1140 Vienna
Clients: ÖSW, GSG
Project team: Andreas Mieling, Sven Kremer, engineering: Gmeiner/Haferl

1 Märkli
2 Krischanitz
3 Kollhoff
4 Steidle
5 Peter Meili
6 Diener
7 Tesar
8 Dudler
9 Czech
10 Krischanitz

1 Johann Christoph Bürkle (ed.): *Mustersiedlung Hadersdorf. Neues Wohnen in Wien*, 2009. Besides Hermann Czech, the participating architects were: Diener & Diener Architekten; Max Dudler; Hans Kollhoff; Adolf Krischanitz; Peter Märkli; Marcel Meili, Markus Peter Architekten; Steidle Architekten; Heinz Tesar; landscape planning: Anna Detzlhofer.

The Hadersdorf model estate[1] was created on the initiative of Adolf Krischanitz together with the Lafarge-Perlmooser cement company. He developed the master plan and invited eight colleagues from three countries, including Hermann Czech, to each design a model house. Krischanitz wanted to explore the possibilities of a free-standing, multi-family apartment building in connection with the desire for a single-family house in the countryside and an urban densification under economic land consumption. Moreover, the potential of concrete as a building material was to be tested and demonstrated in the construction method.

When designing his model house, Czech, unlike most of his colleagues, chose a conventional wall construction made of concrete with a plastered thermal insulation composite system. The corners of the outside were rounded to make the "softness" of the cladding visible. In exchange, the partially colored concrete was to have remained visible on the inside of the construction. For cost reasons and because of doubts about the exploitability of the apartments, this was not executed in this way. The exposed concrete pergolas on the terraces indicate the volume that is not "built over" and optically close off the open space of the settlement at the upper edge without forming a barrier.[2]

Czech describes Krischanitz's master plan (in a positive sense) as "unwieldly": "The buildings and outdoor spaces have an ambiguity that must be appropriated over time [...]."[3]

2 Project text by Hermann Czech in the publication on the estate, ibid.
3 Czech: "Can Architecture Be Conceived by Way of Consumption?" (2011), trans. Elise Feiersinger, in: Czech 2019, 229–247: 238.

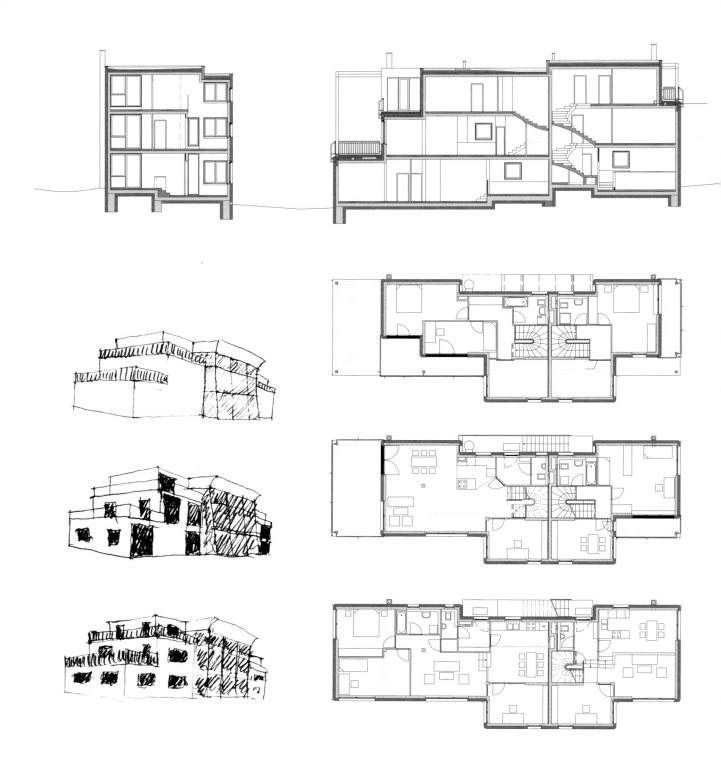

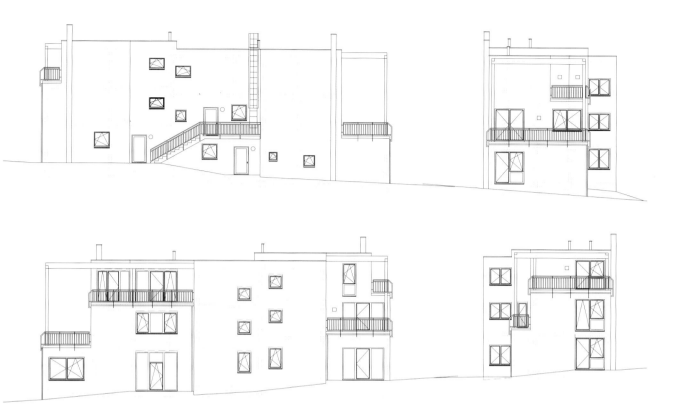

Inside the house there are three apartments organized completely differently. Apartment 3 extends over three floors, forms smaller, differentiated spaces around the stairs in terms of height, proportions, lighting and views, and provides a variety of perspectives between the levels. Apartment 1 is a spacious apartment on one level that exploits the gently sloping terrain to create two different room heights. Apartment 2 has two floors: one floor is almost entirely taken up by a large kitchen-living room, above which the bedrooms can be found. A space across both levels makes a connection.

In 1998, Czech wrote: "'Current' tendencies of architecture seem to me to be characterized by a disruption in the relationship between abstraction and concreteness. On the one hand, architectural thought largely relates only to the concrete object. The abstraction step towards the planning context—however this should be redrafted—is dispensed with. The real context is left up to the investor; ideologically it is replaced by philosophical axioms detached from the matter. On the other hand, architecture largely

seeks innovation not in the alienation and transformation of what is already there, but in constructions and materials abstracted as much as possible from contexts (which, of course, sometimes assume separate existences in a downright rustic concreteness—not ailed by any thought). I see false abstraction and false concreteness not so much as moral criteria, but more as artistic ones. Because the architectural intervention is only strong when it is binding; arbitrariness ends in redundancy and boredom."[4]

The abstract level in Czech's house design is the relationship to the neighborhood, formed from different types of single-family houses and typical for the periphery of the 20th-century metropolis. Czech was the sole participant to use the same building elements also found in the houses in the area: full thermal insulation, large and small windows, terraces, and an attached staircase. The concrete level relates to the application of these elements in the design, the way they are deliberately used makes the difference to the neighborhood: The properties of full thermal insulation and its ease of processing are recognizable as such at the rounded corners and utilized in the design. The windows are precisely set into the façade depending on the requirements: small kitchen windows so that visitors can be spotted early, windows of bathrooms and toilets so that one cannot see in from the outside, and the patio doors so that every apartment receives its assigned outdoor space which is as private as possible. The outside staircase is plain, downright banal. No access to an apartment becomes a designed "entrance stairway."

4 Czech: "Konkret, abstrakt," in: *wbw* 11/1998, 38–43: 38.

Hadersdorf Model Housing Estate

Hotel Messe Vienna
originally Messehotel

Competition
Period of origin: 2002–2005
Address: Messestrasse 2, 1020 Vienna
Client: Universal International Operator: Austria Trend Hotels & Resorts
Project team: Anna Marija Dufils-Meniga, Andreas Mieling, Thomas Roth, Valentin Scheinost, Georg Übelhör, Ola Kopka
Partner and consultant services: Achammer, Tritthart & Partner

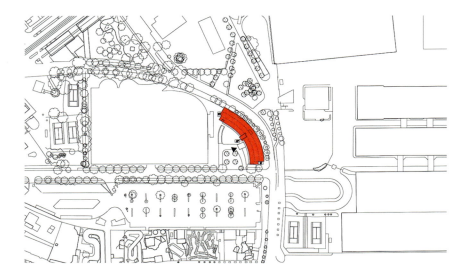

When Czech won the invited competition for the Hotel Messe (a hotel next to the Vienna fairgrounds), the future development of the exhibition area was still unclear.[1] His primary urban planning considerations were therefore: "The hotel is a characteristic individual object of the area; its foyer and guest rooms must form a noticeable location between the exhibition center and the parking deck. What is required is not a 'drumbeat-like' surprise, but a profound peculiarity that one remembers once one has seen the building—and once one has been inside."[2] The chosen urbanistic figure is a curved and inclined structure, positioned in such a way that it makes optimal use of the property (the lot borders on a bend in the east) and is recognizable from all important viewing directions. Czech also sees the curved shape of

1 The Vienna University of Economics and Business campus opposite the hotel was first opened in 2013.
2 Czech: Hotel Messe Wien, "Projekttext," Az W, 2006, https://www.nextroom.at.

Selected Projects

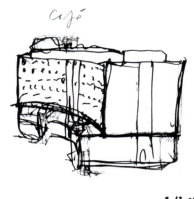

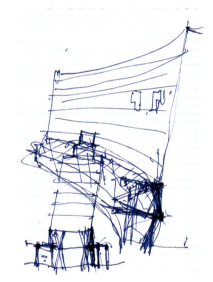
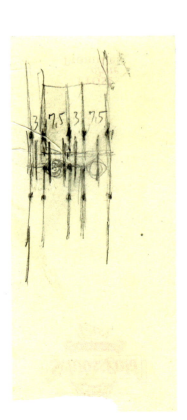

the building, which is slanted outwards by 3.6 degrees, as a reference to the *Wurstelprater* amusement park in the immediate vicinity. The façade is clad in a horizontal subdivision with wider, untreated or narrower, dark-coated corrugated aluminum sheets. These were mounted in their production widths, whereby the number of floors, which does not correspond to a multiple of the sheet width, is obscured. The light, untreated sheets will weather over time; the dark ones retain their original color, which is why they optically "frame" the untreated ones and the façade does not get a blotchy look.

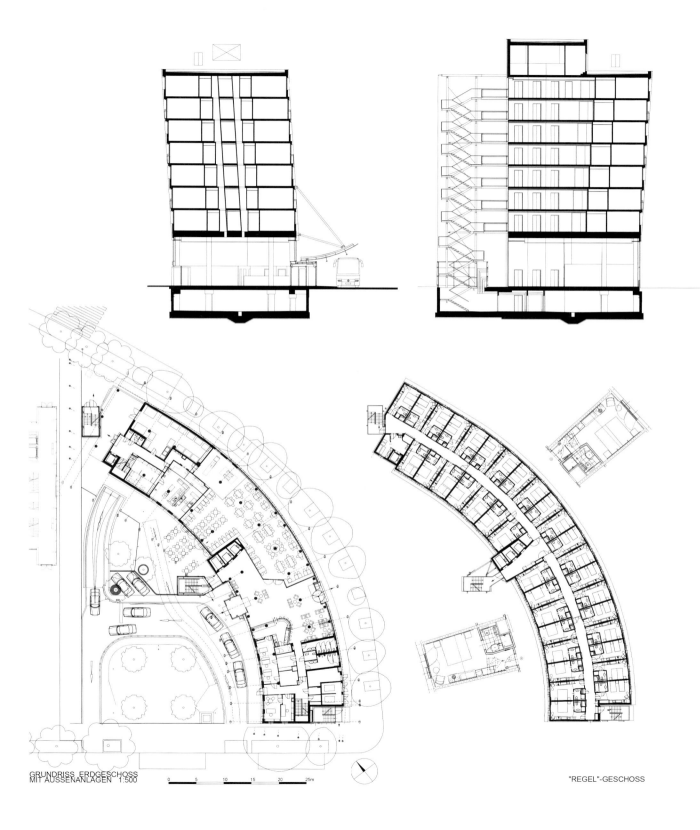

GRUNDRISS ERDGESCHOSS
MIT AUSSENANLAGEN 1:500

"REGEL"-GESCHOSS

Adolf Loos: House for Josephine Baker, 1927–1928

Otto Wagner: Design for a Hotel Vienna, 1910

The façade design of the base zone follows the intention to visually articulate the closed areas visible from the entrance to the fair. Since the client could not accept Czech's suggestion to use this zone as a billboard, he resorted to a floor pattern by the classicist architect Leo von Klenze, which he had designed for the Munich Glyptothek, because it is geometrically simple and has a complex visual effect. The pattern avoids the lifelessness of a closed wall on the street front facing the exhibition center, which does not contain the main entrance with the right of way, but service rooms; however, the importance of the adjoining glass façade of the hotel lobby with the side entrance is retained. Czech does not consider this pattern to be

Selected Projects

ornamentation, like the kind often used extensively in recent façade design. The difference for him is that ornaments can be left out, but patterns "with specific roles in the conception of specific perceptual interrelations" cannot. The use of a "pattern" (in the literal sense) by Klenze on the base façade of the Messe Hotel creates a "pattern" (in the sense of Christopher Alexander).³ It distracts from the closed walls of the adjoining rooms. Otto Wagner made a design for a hotel on Ringstrasse in 1910. Here, too, the ground floor is highlighted with a pattern, a striped one, which also obscures the structure of the building. Wagner made the ground floor with the striped pattern seemingly higher; the pattern covers the first floor.⁴

The two-story hotel lobby is particularly important: the inclined supports mediate between the support grid of the garage below and that of the rooms above. Standing exactly in the axes of the opposite entrances, the two supports are meant to slow down movement into the lobby and thereby make it a pleasant lounge space. The (escape) staircases are on the outside of the building.

3 Whereby Czech does not understand Alexander's term "pattern" as a "rule." In the afterword to the German translation of Christopher Alexander's *A Pattern Language*, he wrote: "The pattern language is not a 'pattern book,' although it can be used as such in a first approximation. The patterns are not 'rules,' but structures of arguments." Alexander et al.: *Eine Muster-Sprache*, 1995, 1265.

4 Heinz Geretsegger; Max Peintner: *Otto Wagner 1841–1918. Unbegrenzte Großstadt* (1964), 1980, 156, Fig. 160.

Through the various interventions, the actual spatial impression of the small rooms is enlarged: They have French windows, the table lamp also shines on the ceiling as general lighting. The luggage rack is located under a fold-up extension of the table. The open clothes closet is only 1.5 meters high—the eye level of an average-sized adult is above it—and the closet does not obstruct the view into the room; the floor below is also openly visible.

Like the Wunder-Bar, the bathrooms have corner mirrors. Depending on cultural preferences, there are rooms with a shower or a bathtub. The hotel is adorned with photographs by Margherita Spiluttini and Seiichi Furuya—extensive, wallpaper-like images in the foyer and restaurant, and in smaller, framed formats in the rooms.[5]

Czech designed an armchair for the lobby, around which a lengthy legal battle broke out, since he was accused of plagiarism. It involved a

5   Conception together with Monika Faber, who at the time was chief curator of the Albertina Vienna's photo collection.
6   Czech: "Fauteuil 'Messehotel.' Zu einer behaupteten Urheberrechtsverletzung" (2008), draft commentary, unpublished, Czech Archive.

critical modification of the LC2 by Le Corbusier, Pierre Jeanneret and Charlotte Perriand. At first glance, Czech's fauteuil differs from the usual LC2 design in several points: The tubular profiles are larger and painted light green instead of chrome. The leather cover is not black, but green-gray. "These accidental changes alienate Le Corbusier's design, but allow it to shine identifiably through."[6] The most important change in content, however, is the addition of two wooden handles on the front edges of the side upholstery, which, as with classic armchairs, enable them to be grasped and make it easier for the sitting person to get up. This alteration purposely contradicts Le Corbusier's design and its material ideology in relation to tubular steel, which Czech puts into perspective with the "touch-friendly wooden handle." "Compared to the naive and clichéd use of the original today as an expression of 'modernity,' the design takes a critical and ironic position."[7]

7 Ibid.

Hotel Messe Vienna

In 2003, Czech wrote a piece entitled "Komfort – ein Gegenstand der Architekturtheorie?" ("Comfort – A Matter for Architectural Theory?")[8] For him, this question can be clearly answered in the affirmative, everything else would result in an "inferior architecture concept." The function—and with it the comfortably fulfilled function—is for Czech the "material of architecture" and not an annoying mandatory requirement from outside. "The 'function' is not specified in the design, but always *first conveyed in the design*."[9] According to Czech, comfort was a comprehensive concept of early modernism. Architecture was to make life easier, and people were to be able to fulfill themselves, freed from ineffective work through technology and freed from ornaments and all cultural debris. In fact, as Czech analyzed, many contemporary designs are uncomfortable— the chair is not comfortable, the handle hurts when using it, the cup makes one soil oneself—meaning that modernism has largely not met its requirements. In the reductionist design approach of modernism, he also recognized a moral-ideological aspect that wanted to bring the user to asceticism instead of offering him or her comfort. Out of respect for the user, Czech advocates comfort as a criterion for good architecture, but does not want this to be misunderstood as a lack of criticism of the client's wishes. "Of course, architecture is not only committed to the user; and it can undoubtedly have emancipatory traits and see further than the client."[10]

Czech already quoted Otto Wagner in 1974 on the hotel construction issue in the text "Die Sprache Otto Wagners" ("The Work and Diction of Otto Wagner") with a request for the design of the hotel room.[11] This was to resemble a sanatorium room rather than a living room. According to Wagner, "comfort and cleanliness" were the most important characteristics. A feeling of luxury was to be evoked by real material objects.

Czech's design includes a new element atypical of the modernist tradition, namely humor. For example, at one end of the access corridors to the room floors, the windows in the front wall are twisted into the façade according to the slope of the building, so that one does not know at first whether one has looked correctly or whether the floor is moving. Hotel staff refer to the window as the *Schweizerfenster* ("Swiss Window") after the nearby "Schweizerhaus," a popular restaurant from which one traditionally does not leave in a sober condition. Alongside mannerism, humor is another way for Czech to deal with reality.[12]

8 Czech: "Komfort – ein Gegenstand der Architekturtheorie?," in: *wbw* 3/2003, 10–15.
9 Ibid., 14.
10 Ibid., 15.
11 Czech: "Die Sprache Otto Wagners" (1974), in: Czech 1996, 73–76: 73. English translation by Michael Loudon, "The Work and Diction of Otto Wagner," in: *a+u* (Tokyo) 7/1977, 45–66: 45.
12 Czech: "Architektur, von der Produktion her gedacht," *Hintergrund* 41, 2009, 37.

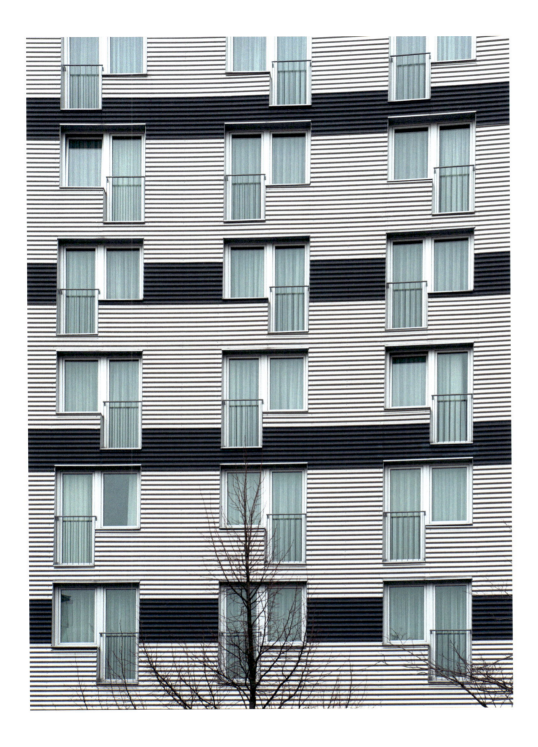
Hotel Messe Vienna

"Housing for Generations" Am Mühlgrund
Housing for Generations with Adolf Krischanitz and Werner Neuwirth

Period of origin: 2007–2011

Address: Zieritzgasse 10, 1220 Vienna

Client: EBG (non-profit single and multi-family residential building cooperative)

Project team: Andreas Mieling, Thomas Roth; engineering: Helmut Schöberl, Klaus Straka, landscaping: Anna Detzlhofer

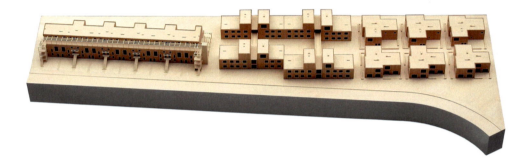

The Am Mühlgrund residential construction concerned an expert opinion addressing the topic of "multi-generational housing." Living concepts were sought "for all generations—taking into account the needs in the different phases of life."[1] The offices of Hermann Czech, Adolf Krischanitz and Werner Neuwirth jointly participated—in this case, "all generations" were already represented in the project team. Certain construction and equipment elements such as the wooden façades were designed together, but the spatial concepts differ between the three architects.

What makes Hermann Czech's component special is the formation of a story section with a room height of 4.1 meters. This height takes advantage of the Viennese building regulations, which allow a building height of 7.5 meters with a staggered story, but prevent a third full floor. Normally, this maximum construction height is not maxed out for two stories. Czech invoked this rule, however, and thus enabled the user to implement an individual additional level as a "gallery for a seating,

1 Tender text from Wohnfonds Wien, 2007.

sleeping, playing, working place, etc." The gallery then divides the space into a room height of two meters each. This can be utilized in practice, but according to the building code it is lower than the prescribed room height, meaning that the area gained does not count towards the usable living space, which is decisive for the rent. "Moreover, the unusual height constitutes a special spatial quality from the start." Czech mentions as particularly important the fact that the users can also appropriate the open spaces in front of the apartments; the architecture has to withstand this sometimes defacing appropriation. The number of apartments is not definitely fixed; it can range between 15 and 30, since—depending on the requirements—both vertical and horizontal groupings of apartments are possible via defined openings in the reinforced concrete bulkheads of the supporting structure.

2   See Czech: "Die Sprache der Verführung," in: *SvM. Die Festschrift für Stanislaus von Moos*, 2005; Czech: "Architektur, von der Produktion her gedacht," *Hintergrund* 41, 2009; Czech: "Kann Architektur von der Konsumtion her gedacht werden?" (with excerpts from "Schau schää," 1964 and "Architektur, von der Produktion her gedacht," 2009), in: Faschingeder et al. (eds.): *Die Architektur der neuen Weltordnung*, 2009.

3   Czech: "Kann Architektur von der Konsumtion her gedacht werden," abstract for his lecture at the 11th International Bauhaus Colloquium, Weimar 2009, Czech Archive. English translation by Elise Feiersinger, "Can Architecture Be Conceived by Way of Consumption?" (2011), in: Czech 2019, 229–247: 231.

4   Czech: "Architektur, von der Produktion her gedacht," in: *Hintergrund* 41, 2009, 37.

For several years, Hermann Czech has been concerned with the question of whether architecture is becoming a consumer good or already is, and how one can conceptually respond to this.[2] He sees the current phenomena of interpreting the news value of star architecture as a quality criterion and splitting architectural achievements into individual specialist areas as the entry of architecture into a culture industry. "A common characteristic of many of these phenomena might very well lie in the temptation to conceive architecture not by way of production, but to conceive it by way of consumption instead — and the question arises as to whether this is possible without deceiving consumers and oneself.[3] He pursues the consideration of whether a critical design potential can be gained from these strategies with the help of the theoretical approaches of differentiated modernism. "Is it possible to place the recipient not as a mere means, but as an addressee of a truthfulness, even if it is a cynical one?"[4]

The environs around Am Mühlgrund, which was built in a dried-up meadow, are characterized by modest single-family houses and farms. A low-level determinacy, which first gradually disappears through the connection to the subway network and the associated larger-scale urban planning, gives the area a certain "do-it-yourself character" which—at least so far—has left a lot of room for personal initiative. Czech also offers this initiative to the residents of his component. The ground floor apartments have two entrances, meaning that one of the two rooms can be accessed separately. Tenants can build smaller extensions in the private gardens

The architecture has to endure unforeseen participatory user realization (as opposed to inside) on a case-by-case basis—as the "suffering of defacement."

without disturbing the overall impression of the residential complex. These appropriations are predetermined by the type of design and the execution of the entrances, canopies, gutters, etc., and therefore do not contradict the architecture.

Is it possible to gain critical design potential with the methods of differentiated modernism? In 1923, Adolf Loos had planned a terraced residential building for the City of Vienna, which Hermann Czech was already intensively dealing with during his student days.[5] The terrace house represented the connection between the housing estate and the multi-story building construction favored by the City of Vienna and was intended to combine the benefits of the one- to two-story housing estate with the higher density of the multi-story apartment block. Loos's terrace house design is accessed via external stairs and terraces. "These raised terraces could also be called raised streets; each apartment has

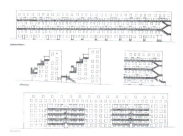

Adolf Loos: Terrace house, 1923

5 See Czech study paper on the terrace house, article in *Die Furche*, "Terrassenhäuser," 1966, and introductory, historical project overview by Czech in the *Neue städtische Wohnformen* catalog, 1967.

"Housing for Generations" Am Mühlgrund

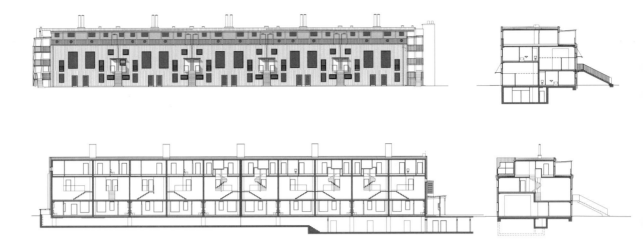

its own separate covered entrance, for sitting out and relaxing in the evenings."[6] Furthermore, for Loos, a floor-to-floor separation of living and sleeping areas based on the English model was a quality criterion that he was missing in the Viennese apartment buildings. In his opinion, it increases people's self-esteem when they feel like they are living in their own house.[7] The City of Vienna spoke out against the terrace house. They wanted to strengthen the community in a residential courtyard and prevent the more individual meeting points in the stairwells and corridors of the multi-story apartment blocks by making connections as small as possible. Communal life was to only take place in the (politically controllable) outer space of the courtyard.[8] The terrace house would have run counter to this intention.

This attitude reflects a conflict within the social democracy of the time, namely that between proponents of the low-rise construction and those of the multi-story construction. This conflict must be viewed in connection with the Viennese settler movement, which arose out of a self-organized movement in the face of the extreme housing and food shortages immediately after the First World War. The movement stressed personal initiative and assistance in building the houses and received support or direction from leading left-wing intellectuals such as Otto Neurath, Adolf Loos, Josef Frank and Margarete Lihotzky. Respect for people as individuals and their claim to self-fulfillment were the top priorities in the conceptual considerations.[9]

6 Loos: "Die moderne siedlung" (1926), in: Loos 1962, 402–428: 428. English translation quoted in: Kurt Lustenberger, *Adolf Loos*, London: Artemis, 1994, 136.
7 Ibid., 136.
8 Kristian Faschingeder: "Die Korrektur: Loos' unbekannter Gemeindebau," in: Moravánszky et al. (eds.): *Adolf Loos. Die Kultivierung der Architektur*, 2008, 201.
9 See Wilfried Posch: "Josef Frank, eine bedeutende Persönlichkeit des österreichischen Kulturliberalismus," in: *UM BAU* 10, 1986, 21–38.

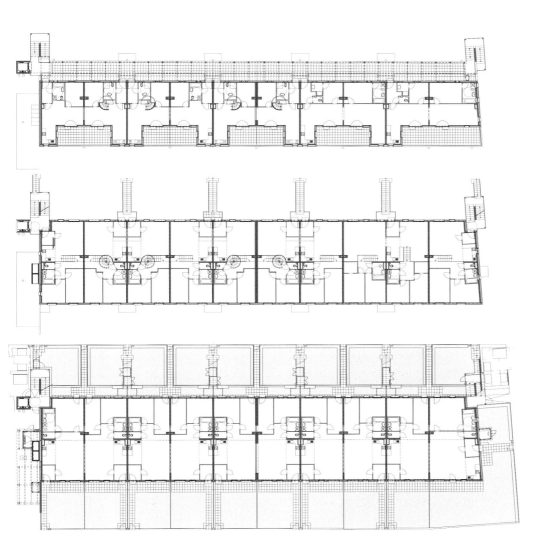

In 1922, a year before Adolf Loos designed his terrace house, a development took place that gave preference to the compact apartment building and which Kristian Faschingeder describes as follows: "In addition to the differences of opinion within the Social Democratic Party […], a politically motivated law separating the Social Democratically-ruled capital from the conservative surrounding area was to prove decisive: The ÖVSK (Austrian Settlement and Allotment Garden Association), which had formed the umbrella organization for the various settlement initiatives in 1921, had

sought to extend the urban area to the foot of the Semmering Mountain. However, any basis for this plan was removed by the *Trennungsgesetz* (Separation Act), which made Vienna its own federal state on January 1, 1922—without expanding the urban area." This meant that the building areas were spatially limited and the City of Vienna decided primarily to erect multi-story buildings to remedy the housing shortage.[10]

For Hermann Czech, the terrace house constituted a logical continuation of the Viennese settlement movement in a denser urban space. In 1966, he already stated that "the freedom in choosing an apartment is not so great as to be able to meet these requirements by changing residence."[11] What was meant was the division into single-family houses for families and multi-story houses for single people, which was common in the 1960s. Forty years later, he carried out these conceptual considerations for the Am Mühlgrund apartment building.

10 Faschingeder: "Die Korrektur: Loos' unbekannter Gemeindebau," in: Moravánszky et al. (eds.): *Adolf Loos. Die Kultivierung der Architektur*, 2008, 201.
11 Czech: "Terrassenhäuser," in: *Die Furche*, 18 June 1966.

Rooftop Extension Günthergasse

Period of origin: 2007–2010/2011–2015
Address: Günthergasse 2, 1090 Vienna
Clients: Stephanie Pflaum and Philipp Schüller
Project team: Andreas Mieling, engineering: Walter Brusatti, ÖBA: Johann Unterrainer

The house of this roof extension is located at the convergence of Günthergasse and Rooseveltplatz, diagonally behind the Votive Church, in an urban block laid out by Heinrich Ferstel. "The buildings and fronts of Rooseveltplatz roughly correspond to Heinrich von Ferstel's notions about the framing of the Votive Church [...]. Due to later changes to the tower and roof additions, the large structural elements are further differentiated and partially obscured."[1] The house façade itself displays an ambivalent symmetry: While the house portal is in the middle of the seven window axes, two axes protrude on the right as a risalit,[2] whereby a second symmetrical axis of the recessed five axes is formed to the left of the central axis. The design of the new dormer on the top floor takes up this ambivalence of the façade. "The relationship on both axes allows a more scaled resolution of the volume. Such an ambivalent solution is sought." Czech implemented this idea with a dormer with an arched window in one axis and a dormer with a rectangular window in the other. The dormers then "merge" into one in the concrete execution, whereby both retain their geometric individuality.

Since the historical attic construction only permitted parapet heights of more than 1.2 meters, Czech activated one of the skylights in the floor area for a wider view.

Directly adjoined at an obtuse angle, the house on Rooseveltplatz is one story lower and possesses a backdrop-like attic extension in the roof zone in the form of an ornamental gable, which, when viewed from the square, pushed itself in front of the existing sloping firewall of the roof to be expanded on Günthergasse. The steeper, higher roof of the extension would have generated an even more disruptive firewall and further "coarsened" the structural relationship between the two adjoining houses. Czech therefore planned an incision at this point in the form of a roof terrace

1 This and the following quotations from: Czech: "Dachausbau Günthergasse," description for submission to the advisory board (which had to agree to the fact that the roof incision was not permissible for a terrace), 2008, Czech Archive.
2 This narrow risalit at the blunt corner to the front of the square, i.e., at the eastern end of Günthergasse, corresponds to a counterpart (at the left side house) at the western end, at the corner of Schwarzspanierstrasse.

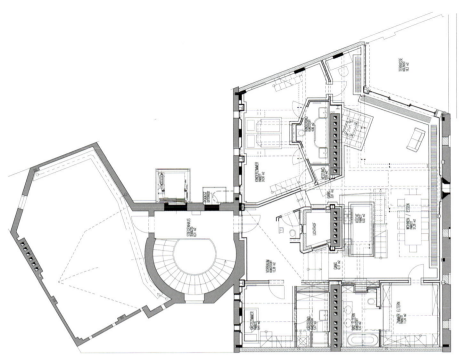

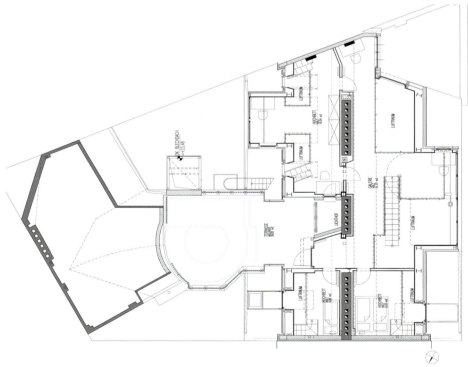

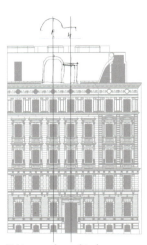

Taking up the ambivalent axis division of the stock

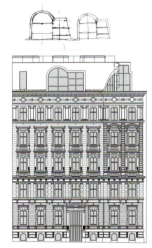

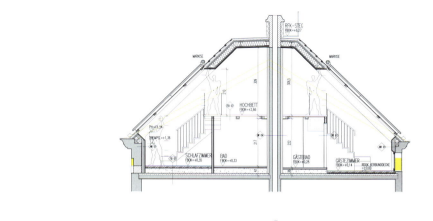

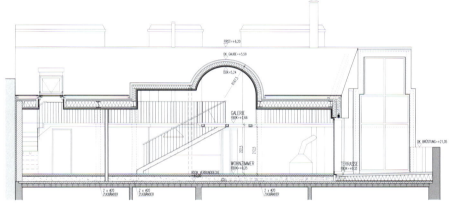

Rooftop Extension Günthergasse

with ridge-high rear glazing. "The projected incision in the roof creates a further 'backdrop' element behind the historic decorative gable parallel to the front of our house. This makes the two development directions clearer. Instead of a coarser one, the result is a more informative perception of details." Conversely, from this terrace, the ornamental gable with its detailed structure forms the foreground of the view to the Votive Church. The terrace follows the width of the existing recess in the house façade and thus leaves the eaves edge open in this area, which corresponds to the section visible from Rooseveltplatz, even with a steeper roof.

The vertical division of the apartment inside into a main level and a gallery level resulted from the building code, which did not allow two floors here. The apartment now consists of the open living space with an integrated kitchen and three separate rooms (bedroom and children's room), each with

its own bathroom. All spaces extend over both levels. The room height under the gallery is as low as possible at 2.13 meters (lower edge of the beam) to 2.27 meters (lower edge of the floor). However, these low areas alternate with the very high open voids to structure pleasant and differentiated living areas.

The gallery-level structure consists of a support grid made of white-painted I-beams, which is attached to the ceiling via flat steel suspensions. In this way, no supports will obstruct the lower level. Located between the flat steel suspensions is the railing construction formed by further flat steel profiles, a net for fall protection and a handrail made of round wood. This construction uses industrially manufactured components and materials to realize the separate perceptions of comfort. The floor covering of the gallery is a bright red linoleum, in the children's room a lime green one.

3 Frank: "The House as Path and Place" (1931), trans. Wilfried Wang, in: Frank 2012, Vol. 2, 198–209.
4 Alexander: A City is Not a Tree; German text: "Eine Stadt ist kein Baum," in: *Bauen+Wohnen* 7/1967, 283–290.

In the apartment, Czech varied tried-and-tested elements from his own drafts: the living room is centered on an open fireplace; set diagonally—depending on the position of the terrace wall—it turns towards the seating area. In the children's room, the shared bathroom in the middle of the space, accessible from both sides, divides it into two areas. Two staircases—one for each child—lead to the gallery level; these "samba stairs" have staggered steps and integrated shelves. Elements from Czech's plan for "a room for a little girl" in the Klemmer Apartment (1971–1972) are reincorporated: the children's room intrinsically functions like a small house or a maisonette with separate living and sleeping areas.

The unusual thing about the apartment's organization is that each room has its own access from/to the lower and from/to the upper level (the children's room even has two entrances on each level—one for each child), providing countless possibilities of movement through the apartment. This arrangement literally radicalizes Josef Frank's description of the house as "path and place."[3] The spatial sequence is extended by two terraces, of which one (on the street side) is assigned to the lower one and the other to the upper one (on the courtyard side). Both terraces are the "extreme ends" of the apartment.

While in House Beer, which was the reason for writing the essay "The House as Path and Place," Frank leads a path from the entrance through the various rooms and levels to the roof terrace, Czech spans a net of various path options, interrupted by numerous square-like expansions, between the terraces in the Günthergasse apartment. The "most prominent" place in the middle of the apartment is in front of the arched window in the dormer.

Czech's organization of the apartment shows parallels to Christopher Alexander's description of the city as a network structure.[4] In his 1965 essay A *City is Not a Tree*, Alexander differentiated between the structure of the "natural," grown, living city, which he described with the term "semilattice," an order that is not hierarchical, but contains cross-connections, and criticized the dogmatic "modern" structure of the city, which he compared with a hierarchical tree structure: In order for life to develop at all, it needs a complex structure that allows cross-connections.

Exhibition *Josef Frank: Against Design*

Period of origin: 2012–2015, duration of the exhibition: 16.12. 2015–12.6. 2016
Address: MAK – Austrian Museum for Applied Arts/Contemporary Art,
Stubenring 5, 1010 Vienna
Client: MAK
Concept with Sebastian Hackenschmidt
Project team: Gerhard Flora, Thomas Roth, Nina Holly, ÖBA: Michael Wallraff

In 2015, Hermann Czech, together with Sebastian Hackenschmidt, the responsible curator of the museum, put together a comprehensive solo exhibition[1] on Josef Frank. Czech's concept consisted in not only showcasing Frank's diverse oeuvre, but also understanding the fundamental design ideas behind it and comprehensively re-contextualizing them.[2] This analytical approach had already underlaid the basis for Czech's contribution to the 1985 Josef Frank Symposium in Vienna.[3]

Czech also provided the design of the exhibition. The 40 x 38-meter space set aside for this on the upper floor of the MAK is almost square, but surrounds an inaccessible void of the ground floor, so that an angular "U" remains as an exhibition area, from which a narrower "U" is separated by an inner row of pillars. Czech used this configuration for the chronological arrangement of the Frank exhibits in the broad exterior area, as well as for a parallel, narrow reference zone with comparisons and analogies of other architectural positions in the interior area.

The entrance to the exhibition room from the main building is in a corner of the "U" and the visitor entered the exhibition, so to speak, at the Viennese high point of Frank's career in the interwar period, into which his role in Viennese social housing and his furniture store *Haus & Garten* falls.

The inner reference zone with comparisons to Frank's work and theoretical considerations began with the various Viennese architecture teachers Otto Wagner and Karl König, and ranged from Leon Battista Alberti (Frank's dissertation topic) to Rem Koolhaas. First there were comparisons of actual time references, influences and opposites, for example, of Adolf Loos and Josef Hoffmann, of the settlement concept and the superblocks in Viennese municipal housing in the interwar period and via Hugo Häring, Gio Ponti and Bernard Rudofsky, to Ernst Plischke and arbeitsgruppe 4, etc.

---

1. In 1981, a large Frank exhibition took place at the same museum (then the Austrian Museum of Applied Arts), organized by the University of Applied Arts, curated and designed by Johannes Spalt and Hermann Czech. – After the Second World War, Friedrich Kurrent and Johannes Spalt made Frank known again in Vienna with a small but comprehensive exhibition in 1965 at the Austrian Society for Architecture premises (at that time Blutgasse, Vienna I).
2. Czech; Hackenschmidt: "Josef Frank: Against Design," trans. Eva Ciabattoni, in: Thun-Hohenstein et al. (eds.): *Josef Frank. Against Design*, 2015, 14–27: 15.
3. Czech: "A Conceptual Matrix for the Current Interpretation of Josef Frank" (1985), trans. Elise Feiersinger, in: Czech 2019, 151–181.

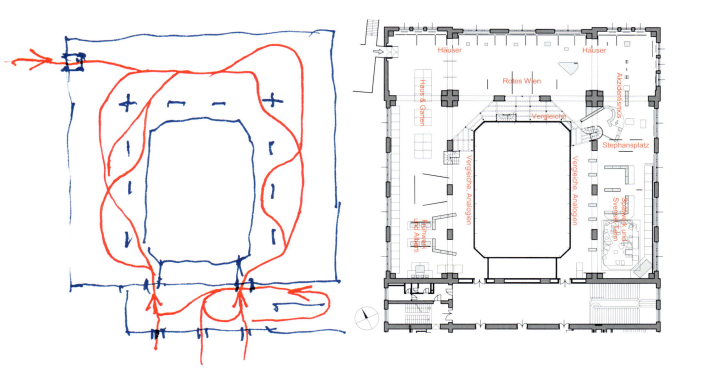

In the further course, however, personalities and positions whose or which actual influences are improbable or due to time constraints impossible, such as the Situationist International, Team Ten with Alison and Peter Smithson, Herzog & de Meuron and Rem Koolhaas, were drawn upon. With the *Raumplan* (spatial plan), the *picturesque* or *participation*, the comparisons also included important terms for Hermann Czech and his work.

In the 1985 essay "Begriffsraster zur aktuellen Interpretation Josef Franks" ("A Conceptual Matrix for the Current Interpretation of Josef Frank"), comparisons and differences to Christopher Alexander and Robert Venturi, among others, as well as the derivation from Adolf Loos, were already discussed.[4] In 2008, a preliminary remark in a reprint stated: "Josef Frank's interpretation was 'current' in 1985; […] But it would also be fruitful to measure viable positions of the last decade like that of Rem Koolhaas or those of Jacques Herzog and Pierre de Meuron, that is, a cynical truthfulness or an artful profundity, against Frank and vice versa. Frank's 'kitsch' and its productive role could be seamlessly replaced by

4   Ibid.

Exhibition *Josef Frank: Against Design*

'trash' or 'junkspace,' and the concept of the 'generic city' is not far removed from Frank's city planning watercolors."[5] Czech, however, regarded the understanding of the difference in each case to be as instructive as the comparison.[6] At a discussion[7] held in House Beer on the topicality of Josef Frank, discussion leader Dietmar Steiner discerned the difference between Koolhaas and Frank in that the former meant the positive allocation of the terms in a purely provocative way, while Frank had a deeply humanistic attitude. In contrast, Czech does not see Koolhaas's "cynical truthfulness" in any way as unproductive.

A wooden gallery was installed along one side of the inner gallery, to which three staircases led: reconstructions based on designs by Josef Frank. None of these staircases was likely to be built because they no longer complied with applicable building regulations regarding safety in use and accessibility. A proper staircase was also planned; it would have been located next to the staircase of a residential building in Salzburg from 1926, which changes direction and thus the view three times in one flight of stairs between two terraces. With the same number of changes in direction, it would have taken up about twice the area "and would have been extremely boring."[8] "The dense spatial experience of an economic sequence of movements is lost."[9] Plaques on all three staircases of the exhibition pointed to the misunderstanding that the schematic disability-friendly approach is subject to: believing that if a solution is comfortable for the disabled, then it is comfortable for

5 Czech: "Ein Begriffsraster zur aktuellen Interpretation Josef Franks," in: Iris Meder (ed.): *Josef Frank 1885–1967. Eine Moderne der Unordnung*, 2008, 76–89: 76 (note). English translation by Elise Feiersinger, "A Conceptual Matrix for the Current Interpretation of Josef Frank" (1985), in: Czech 2019, 151–181.
6 Hermann Czech on a tour of the exhibition he led.
7 Salon discussion: "Josef Frank zufällig" ("Josef Frank Accidentally"), moderated by Dietmar Steiner as part of the event *Alles Frank! 2 Tage rund um die Villa Beer*, April 2–3, 2016.
8 As note 6. With the limitation of the number of visitors to the gallery, the authorities finally dispensed with these stairs.
9 Czech, wall text in the exhibition.

Selected Projects

everyone. "'Comfort' occasionally means something different for disabled and non-disabled people. (Sometimes 'accessibility' even creates obstacles for non-disabled people.) The justified provision for 'accessibility' in our time, i.e., for comfortable access for old and/or disabled people (for which a broken leg suffices) today requires a harmonization of—possibly also different—access routes."[10]

Josef Frank stated in his 1931 essay "The House as Path and Place" that the staircase is an essential element of the house and should be perceived as part of the living space. "It must be handled in such a way that one may never have the feeling, before getting to it or being on it, to have to make one's way forwards and backwards; one should always proceed."[11] The other two staircases reconstructed for the exhibition are, on the one hand, a staircase from the houses of the Ortmann workers' colony in Pernitz, which is executed particularly efficiently by winding steps into which—nevertheless—not curved, but straight stair boards are chiseled; on the other hand, the stairs in House No. 9 of the "13 Houses for Dagmar Grill" series (later also called "Accidental House" by Frank). For the latter, Czech added visualizations of the adjoining spaces created by Mikael Bergquist and Olof Michélsen on a 1:1 scale.

Josef Frank: Project for a house in Salzburg, 1926; replica of the stairs in the exhibition

10 Ibid.
11 Frank: "The House as Path and Place" (1931), trans. Wilfried Wang, op. cit., 201.

Exhibition *Josef Frank: Against Design*

Another method of making spatial connections in the exhibition visible was the positioning of the used hanging boards in relation to one another. For example, Frank's own living space in Vienna was presented in a closed manner on three-sided panels. Behind it, original pieces of furniture from the apartment could be seen in the exhibition. In other places, panels with pictures and graphics of a house "frame" its model. Exhibition objects thus depict spatial configurations in various ways.

At the beginning of the reference sheet drawn up by Czech, as already mentioned, there is Karl König, Josef Frank's teacher at the Technical University in Vienna. The panel assigned to König shows, among other works, the door handle of a house on Vienna's Kohlmarkt from 1897, probably an industrial product. It is completely unadorned; despite this reduction, the handle is hand- and therefore "ergonomically"-shaped, for which it was expressly praised by Loos. Opposite on the same panel, a (somewhat later) door handle by Otto Wagner with a vertical flat cross-section has also been reproduced. It fits Wagner's world of shapes, but is not very pleasant to touch. In the case of Rem Koolhaas, at the end of the reference sheet, a door handle with the name "open" is reproduced.

12 See: <oma.eu/news/oma-designs-open-a-new-door-handle-for-olivari>. Koolhaas designed the "open" door handle in 2015 for the Italian manufacturer Olivari.

According to the description,[12] it separates the spindle (axis of rotation) from the lever (handle), which is varied in many ways; the latter is always a piece of—here horizontal—flat steel, so only slightly more comfortable when pressed than Otto Wagner's. There is also a design for a door handle from Josef Frank, and here, too, the handle and spindle are separate. However, the decisive idea for Frank was to use it comfortably: The handle is made of wood, so it is warmer when one touches it, and rounded in a shape tailored to the hand. "The closer we come into contact with a piece of furniture, especially if we hold it in our hands, the more non-geometrical and organic it needs to be to adapt to our hand," wrote Frank in 1934.[13] The standard door handle in Czech's residential projects corresponds to that used by Karl König.

The sole reference in the Frank exhibition that comes from Hermann Czech's own work is his "Spatial City Planning" concept. Carrying on the topic of the terrace house, based on Frank's cigar-shaped, stepped terrace restaurant or on his draft for the UN building in New York from 1947, in which a high-rise complex is connected by several walkways between the individual high-rise buildings, innumerable connections

13 Frank: "Rooms and Furnishings" (1934), trans. David Jones, in: Frank 2012, Vol. 2, 288–305: 295 and 297.

in space are proposed in a totally built-up, hill-shaped volume. In this concept from 1969, Czech thought the expansion of the city and its development networks into the third dimension. "Grand *volumes* are generated; not merely larger versions of slabs, towers, or other building types, but *rampant, amoeba-like growing and roaming entities*—yet clearly distinguishable individualities."[14]

A central term in Frank's works is "chance," which for Czech, among others, constitutes a departure from rules: Instead of following abstract rules when designing, the aim is to find a concrete solution that reflects the situation under specific conditions. The title of the exhibition, *Against Design*, which Czech also conceived, should also be understood in this context. Frank fought against totalitarianism and formalisms of all kinds throughout his life. The exhibition wanted to show that—"nowadays—in a time of star architecture's newsworthiness on the one hand and the segmenting of architectural planning into consulting services on the other—Frank's culture-critical ideas turn out to be no less relevant."[15] "'Against Design' can actually only be a German title (almost like a sentence containing *Handy* [mobile phone] or *Beamer* [projector]—words that do not exist in this context in English). Design has a much broader meaning in English than in German; in English, one simply cannot be 'against design,' since that would mean being against any goal or intention. The German meaning of 'design,' on the other hand, is abridged from the English *industrial* (or *product*, *fashion*, etc.) design. And that should be made suspicious as a culturally detached métier."[16] Today's understanding of the term "design" in German can be equated with Frank's understanding of "decorative arts." "The decorative arts have not reduced their reach in recent years […], they have grown to include everything that is related—technology, industry, trade, handicraft: all have become decorative art […]. Transforming the world with the decorative arts is relatively simple because it is based on setting up a unified system that can be applied to the whole world and all objects; thus, such experiments are always being undertaken. Their basic principle is as follows: all that exists is bad, it must be reformed and, in particular, in such a way that it can be brought into a closed system. […] This is just the opposite of what I would characterize as modern. […] For in everything that is modern there has to be a place for all our time encompasses, and our time encompasses so much and so fully that we cannot bring in into anything approaching a unified form."[17]

14 Czech: "Spatial City Planning" (1969), trans. Elise Feiersinger, in: Czech 2019, 99–101:101.
15 Czech; Hackenschmidt: "Josef Frank: Against Design," trans. Eva Ciabattoni, op. cit., 15.
16 Hermann Czech in an interview with Axel Simon, in: *hochparterre* 3/2016, 12–15.
17 Frank: "What Is Modern" (1930), trans. Nader Vossoughian, in: Frank 2012, Vl. 1, 404–431: 407 and 409.

Exhibition *Josef Frank: Against Design*

Sigmund Freud Museum
Architecture and Exhibition Design
with Walter Angonese and Bettina Götz/Richard Manahl (ARTEC Architekten)

Period of origin: 2017–2020
Address: Berggasse 19, 1090 Vienna
Client: Sigmund Freud Privatstiftung
Project team: Gerhard Flora, Andreas Mieling, Thomas Roth and Gerda Polig (ARTEC)

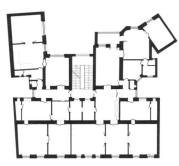

Ground plan mezzanine floor 1938

1   Hermann Czech: "Architectural Concept and Exhibition Design," trans. Elise Feiersinger, in: Monika Pessler and Daniela Finzi (eds.): *Freud. Berggasse 19 – Origin of Psychoanalysis*, Berlin: Hatje Cantz, 2020, 17.
2   Hermann Stierlin was a Swiss architect who settled in Vienna in 1886. From this time on he built a number of rental houses in Vienna, where he was also a building contractor in addition to his planning work. See Az W Architektenlexikon Wien 1770–1945, "Hermann Stierlin," accessed January 30, 2023, http://www.architektenlexikon.at/de/627.htm.

The former living and working spaces of the Freud family at Berggasse 19 in Vienna are an integral part of the newly adapted Sigmund Freud Museum Vienna. The family lived here for almost fifty years, from 1891 until they fled to London in 1938. A commemorative site for Sigmund Freud was opened in 1971 in a first part of the premises, which in the following decades developed into a museum with an archive, study library and research center for psychoanalysis.

"Berggasse 19 is a respectable, in certain details not unoriginal, apartment house dating to the high period of Vienna's *Gründerzeit*, but what makes it worthy of preservation is the past use of its mezzanine and *Hochparterre* (raised ground floor)."[1]

The house at Berggasse 19 was built in 1889/90 by the architect Hermann Stierlin[2] on the site of an older, lower structure. Sigmund Freud and his wife Martha moved into the east apartment on the mezzanine as the first tenants in 1891 and also used it as a consulting office. Over time, the family grew; the two had six children, and Martha Freud's sister, Minna Bernays, whose fiancé had died, moved in with them. As time went on, the family used several apartments in the house, in addition to the initial occupancy on the mezzanine: from 1896 to 1908 the apartment below on the raised ground floor as a consulting office and from 1908 the adjoining western apartment on the mezzanine. Even then, there were changes in the use of the rooms (consulting office and apartment) and changes in use by family members. When Sigmund Freud had to leave the house in 1938 at the age of 82, he was able to take nearly all of the furniture and furnishings with him into exile in London. After 1938, apartments in the building, as in others, were used as "collective apartments" for Viennese

Jewish women and men before their deportation and "Aryanized," i.e., passed on to non-Jewish people, mostly close to the National Socialist Party, who often lived in them until well after 1945.

In 1971, through the efforts of the Austrian psychiatrist Harald Leupold-Löwenthal,³ the first Freud commemorative site was opened in the mezzanine on the initiative of the Sigmund Freud Society, which was founded in 1968. At the end of the 1980s, the museum was expanded under the direction of Inge Scholz-Strasser and redesigned by the architect Wolfgang Tschapeller. Over the years, additional rooms in the house could be rented. In 2017, under the director Monika Pessler, a competition for the redesign of the museum was announced: on the one hand, this was to bring the technical standards up to the international level of a museum operation (visitor reception, café, cloakrooms, event space, library, escape routes, accessibility) and, on the other hand, propose a new concept of how the spaces could be conveyed as the "origin of psychoanalysis."

3   Austria Presse Agentur: "Psychoanalytiker Leupold-Löwenthal gestorben," Science.ORF.at, March 14, 2007, https://sciencev1.orf.at/news/147605.html. The Sigmund Freud Society has set itself the goal of making the life and work of Sigmund Freud and research results on psychoanalysis accessible to a broad public, see also: www.sigmundfreudgesellschaft.at, as well as www.freud-museum.at.

Mezzanine

1st floor

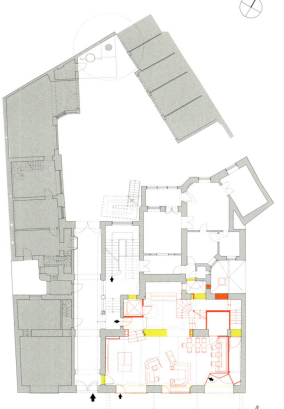

Ground floor and upper ground floor

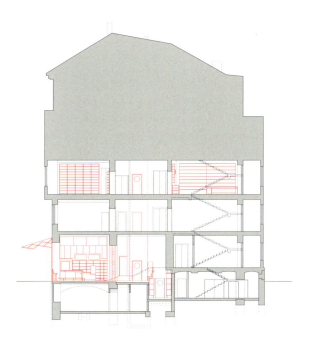

Selected Projects

The waiting room of Freud's consulting office, reconstructed in the 1970s. To show that the wall surface is not original, the part of it containing explanations is painted white.

In the competition, two of the invited offices joined forces to form a working group, Hermann Czech and Walter Angonese, who worked with ARTEC (Bettina Götz and Richard Manahl) as a local cooperation partner. Together they developed the basic concept; the construction of the museum was carried out jointly by the offices of Czech and ARTEC, and the exhibition design by Atelier Czech alone.[4]

Hermann Czech has been dealing with Sigmund Freud since his student days, in the early 1960s. During this time, he read, among other works, Freud's *Interpretation of Dreams* and *The Joke and Its Relation to the Unconscious*. He later underwent classical psychoanalysis himself. In House S., which Czech planned, he also designed the consulting rooms for the client, a psychoanalyst. In 1989, on the occasion of the 50th anniversary of Sigmund Freud's death, he designed the *Wunderblock: A History of the Modern Soul* exhibition as part of the Vienna Festival.[5]

4 Participation in museum conversion: Gerhard Flora, Andreas Mieling and Thomas Roth (Atelier Czech) and Gerda Polig (ARTEC), participation in exhibition design: Gerhard Flora.
5 See project description p. 298.

A closet installed by the Freuds, with a fake wall on both sides to disguise its depth. During an earlier museum renovation, part of the wall was demolished for an opening. Now the uncovered sidewall of the closet is visible, as are vestiges of the faux wall.

Compared to other commemorative sites, the Freud family's premises can no longer show any of their personal furnishings. "In 1938, Freud's family was expelled from its society—by this society; Freud was able to take his material possessions with him. […] All the commemorative site has to offer is the empty, authentic location: *Here it happened*—this is where Freud and his family lived, where the children grew up. And this is where psychoanalysis originated—not only through the work and case studies of Freud himself, but also through the participants in the Wednesday Psychological Society and through Anna Freud. But *there is nothing left*."[6]

Even before the Freuds moved to London, Edmund Engelman had documented the premises in a series of black and white photos. In 1997, Nada Subotinic used these images to reconstruct the floor plans and wall elevations of the rooms. Several pieces of original furniture and other items belonging to the Freud family have been donated to the museum over time,

6 Czech: "Architectural Concept and Exhibition Design," 17–23: 20–21.

mainly by Anna Freud. A reproduction of the interior would therefore have been technically possible to a certain extent, but the museum management deliberately decided against it, as Monika Pessler explains: "This void, which has existed in Freud's treatment room since his flight from the National Socialist regime, clearly represents the dark side of history. To reconstruct a 'world of yesterday' (Stefan Zweig) within these rooms – i.e. a world before the March 1938 Anschluss (annexation of Austria into Nazi Germany), as if Freud's forced exile in London never happened – would be to negate a significant part of Freud's history and, in doing so, negate ours."[7] Czech follows up the considerations methodically: A reconstruction would result in a laboriously produced surrogate and would detract from the actual subject of the exhibition. A symbolic rendition, i.e., reduced in any form, "would in any case have to be on a par with the methodological clarity of Sigmund Freud's texts."[8]

[7] Sigmund Freud Museum: "Freud, Berggasse 19," accessed on January 27, 2023, https://www.freud-museum.at/en/exhibitions-program/exhibition-details.
[8] Czech: "Architectural Concept and Exhibition Design," 17–23: 21.

The exhibition concept differentiates between two levels—"a museum with two types of contents": the level of the original spaces with the awareness of their historical use, as well as the actual exhibition material on the history of psychoanalysis and the Freud family. The separation of these two contents distinguishes the new exhibition design from the previous presentation and most commemorative sites. The room walls are reserved for information on the historical use of the rooms, furnishings and surfaces (with the conservation and restoration findings shown); the exhibition material not directly relating to the authentic rooms is arranged separately from the wall surfaces in free-standing showcases (similar to those that Czech had already developed for previous exhibition designs).[9] "Insofar, the authentic rooms in this building are a museum in and of themselves. This aspect can only be experienced at Berggasse 19, with an understanding of its spaces and their context. The exhibition avoids

9 Ibid., 22.

mixing media in its treatment of general information and place-bound aspects. They are, nonetheless, offered simultaneously and experienceable at the Sigmund Freud Museum as a unit—in some cases they are even drawn into slight relation with each other—but keeping them apart conceptually fosters the methodological clarity and comprehensibility of the content."[10]

Walls and ceilings had been opened for examination at certain points by conservators.[11] These open spaces are part of the exhibition and show the changing history of the utilization of the rooms. The remaining wall surfaces were painted in a neutral, yellowish white. In the area of the earlier tapestries or wallpaper, the white is slightly grayer to indicate this. By examining photo and film material as well as literature from the Freud Museum, historical fixtures from the time the rooms were used by the Freud family were found in the walls, such as a chimney pipe in Freud's treatment room or the cabling of a direct telephone line between Anna Freud's rooms and her friend Dorothy Tiffany Burlingham's apartment two stories above. A panorama composed of black-and-white photographs by Edmund Engelman is repeatedly presented on a stand similar to a sheet music holder. The few original pieces of furniture were placed in their original locations, but these were not supplemented by any further reconstructions. The sole exception is the waiting room; this room had already been reconstructed as part of the museum's earlier exhibition and was left as is, but with a corner painted white to suggest this fact.

All of the service facilities necessary for the museum to operate, such as the event space, museum ticket counter, shop and café, have been accommodated outside the authentic rooms of the Freud family. Only the additionally needed vertical circulation, consisting of an elevator and an escape stairs, occupies floor area that had been part of the historic uses, namely the former kitchen and a closet.[12] The platform area in the new escape stairs was covered with the broken tiles from the floors of the kitchen spaces. The new, non-authentic wall surfaces of the escape stairs are used to present the history of the building, particularly with the help of earlier research work by the Freud Museum, which documents the people who lived here at the time when the dwellings were used as collective apartments.

"The measures we implemented in these 'un-authentic' parts of the building are not based on decisions specifically related to historic preservation; they result from careful considerations that would be given

Uncovered intercom cable. There was an internal line to Anna Freud's friend Dorothy Burlingham, who lived on the second floor.

10 Ibid.
11 Determined by Hans Hoffmann and by the Riff OG team.
12 Czech: "Architectural Concept and Exhibition Design," 17–23:17.

to any renovation, which means being respectful of the existing fabric and sensibly reinterpreting it to bring about a new unified whole";[13] in particular, no reconstructions take place. In the ground floor façade, the later-created smooth plaster surface is reused. The opening sizes of the portals are retained; only the parapets are broken off and the new glazing is placed almost flush with the façade. Inside the visitor center behind it, with its museum ticket counter, café and shop, elements from Czech's architecture are actually reused, namely MAK Thonet chairs and aluminum sheet light fixtures (from the recent demolition of the Messehotel interior). The ceiling, a construction of plastered brick vaults on steel girders common at the time, is reinterpreted as a textile curtain with a new, shiny red color scheme with a green frame. The bar counters are painted a similar bold red, and a frameless mirror visually expands the space. The floor features light, polished screed.

For the exhibition, Czech further develops the classic spherical lamp, which he equipped with an additional downlight for the Swiss Re project.[14] It is modified with three busbars for spots; these can alternatively be used as power outlets for additional multimedia devices in the temporary exhibition rooms. It was important to Czech that the exhibition spaces continue to be equipped with centrally positioned ceiling lights, as is typical for living spaces of the time. In the new escape stairs, the globe lights are mounted so that they hang in a continuous line. During the conversions by Wolfgang Tschapeller at the end of the 1980s, the self-contained structural interventions were partially removed, repositioned or left as is, for example, the emergency staircase to the courtyard.

In *The Interpretation of Dreams*, Sigmund Freud reports on a dream of his own that takes place on the path in the stairwell between his private apartment on the mezzanine floor and the doctor's apartment on the upper ground floor: "The situation in the dream is taken from everyday reality. I occupy two flats in a house in Vienna, which are connected only by the public staircase. My consulting-room and study are on the upper ground floor and my living rooms are one storey higher. When, late in the evening, I have finished my work down below, I go up the stairs to my bedroom."[15] For Freud, the journey between apartments belonged to his everyday life. The staircase is historically the best-preserved part of the location. The Freud family, their guests and Freud's patients took the route through the hallway

Lighting fixture equipped with busbars for additional spotlights.

13 Ibid.
14 The lighting fixture was realized as an "Alva Spherical Luminaire" by Hermann Czech and Adolf Krischanitz together with the Austrian lighting company Zumtobel in a special series for several projects.
15 Sigmund Freud: *The Interpretation of Dreams*, translated and edited by James Strachey, London: Penguin Books, 1991, 336.

to the staircase. "This spatially distinctive path remains the main access to the museum, thus allowing visitors to experience the same."[16] A striking awning construction is stretched over the visitor center, which is extensively glazed in the house façade, and the escape exit of the museum, "because you don't expect a museum entrance under an awning."[17] The entrance to the museum still goes through the historic building entrance, which also serves as access for the other users of the building.

There is no predefined route through the museum, just as the Freud family took different routes in their everyday lives. "The path the visitors take is to a great degree open, but each should be able to quickly create his or her own mental map, in order to encourage moving back and forth throughout the exhibition."[18]

16 Czech: "Architectural Concept and Exhibition Design," 17–23: 19.
17 Conversation with Hermann Czech on November 4, 2022.
18 Czech: "Architectural Concept and Exhibition Design," 17–23: 23.

Appendix

Hermann Czech

Born in Vienna in 1936. Studied filmmaking at the Vienna Film School and architecture at the Vienna Technical University and the Academy of Fine Arts Vienna under Ernst A. Plischke; student under Konrad Wachsmann at the Salzburg Summer Academy. 1976–1991 correspondent for *a+u* magazine, Tokyo.
Architecture office in Vienna since 1979.

Teaching
Visiting professor at the University of Applied Arts in Vienna 1985–1986
at Harvard University, Cambridge, Massachusetts, 1988–1989 and 1993–1994
at the ETH Zurich 2004–2007
at the Vienna University of Technology 2008–2009 and 2013
at the Academy of Fine Arts in Vienna (Roland Rainer Chair) 2011–2012, as well as numerous national and international lectures

Solo Exhibitions
9H Gallery, London 1987
Architekturmuseum Basel 1996
Architekturforum Tirol, Innsbruck 1996–1997

Participation in the Venice Architecture Biennale in 1980, 1991, 2000, 2012 and 2023

Honors and Prizes
Josef Frank Scholarship 1969
Theodor Körner Prize 1972
City of Vienna Prize for Architecture 1985
Gold Medal of Honor for Services to the State of Vienna 1997
Honorary Prize of the State of Lower Austria for Architecture 1998
Berlin Art Prize 2001
Gold Medal of Honor of the Federal Capital Vienna 2007
RIBA International Fellowship 2014
Corresponding Member of the Bavarian Academy of Fine Arts 2016
Hans Hollein Art Prize for Architecture 2016

Buildings, Plans and Projects

(The selected projects presented in this book are highlighted; page numbers refer to the mention in the book or to the work presentation in *Werk, Bauen + Wohnen* (Zurich) – *wbw* 6/1996, as well as in *Architecture and Urbanism* (Tokyo) – *a+u* 16:11.)

1960	**School and shopping center** (Technische Hochschule project) [*wbw* 6/1996, 42; *a+u* 16:11, 33]
	Shopping center (Technische Hochschule project)
	Boutique Mischa, Vienna (with Klaus Bolterauer and Wolfgang Mistelbauer)
	Entertainment palace (Technische Hochschule project)
1961–1962	**Restaurant Ballhaus**, Vienna (with Wolfgang Mistelbauer and Reinald Nohàl; demolished) [55, 69, 79f, 122, 127, 128, 139, 154, 162–167, 176, 178, 205; *wbw* 6/1996, 21]
1963	**Shopping center with bar**, conditioning with light and acoustics (TH/Academy of Fine Arts project) [*wbw* 6/1996, 42]
	Single-family house (Academy of Fine Arts project) [85f, 190]
	House of pleasure (sketch) [88; *wbw* 6/1996, 45]
1964	**Exhibition space** (Academy of Fine Arts project: first in-class project) [85]
	Elementary school with courtyard (Academy of Fine Arts project) [88; *wbw* 6/1996, 43]
	Office building on Stephansplatz (Academy of Fine Arts project) [85, 87; *wbw* 6/1996, 46]
	Lake house (Academy of Fine Arts project) [*wbw* 6/1996, 24]
	Information stand (Academy of Fine Arts project)
1965	**Retractable roof over the Graben** (Academy of Fine Arts project)
1965	**Diving tower** (Academy of Fine Arts project) [85, 88; *wbw* 6/1996, 46]
1966	**Critical subway network design for Vienna** (planning with Friedrich Kurrent, Johannes Spalt, Hugo Potyka and Otto Steinmann) [104f; *wbw* 6/1996, 55]
	Terrace house (Academy of Fine Arts project)
1966–1967	**Mechanical bed/sofa for Wittmann** (competition project, 2nd place)
1966–1969	**Schottenfeld urban development project, terrace house** (Academy of Fine Arts project) [85, 176, 184; *wbw* 6/1996, 52]
1968–1969	**Summer house Josef Czech**, Vienna-Nussdorf, [55, 128, 168–175; *wbw* 6/1996, 14]
1968	**Alter Hofkeller**, extension (totally demolished)
	Subway and metropolitan railway network for Vienna (study) [105, 176; *wbw* 6/1996, 55]

	1969	Garden house (Academy of Fine Arts project)
		Children's boutique Luksics (project)
		Showroom Teppichhaus Inku (project)
		Spatial urban planning, *trigon* Graz (study; not accepted) [114f, 411f; *wbw* 6/1996, 28, 54; *a+u* 16:11, 33]
		Apartment Neuffer, conversion (project)
		Apartment Sailer, conversion (project)
	1970	**Kleines Café I**, Vienna, conversion and furnishing (lower space) [128, 134, 136, 176–180, 253]
		Mödling shopping center with pneumatic retractable roof (project) [176, 184, 342; *wbw* 6/1996, 44]
	1971	**Retractable roof over the Graben**, revision (Academy of Fine Arts project) [98–102, 176, 184, 262, 342; *wbw* 6/1996, 44; *a+u* 16:11, 42–43]
		Entertainment palace, revision of 1960 (diploma thesis) [129, 131f, 327f; *wbw* 6/1996, 43]
		Splendid Bar (project)
		Galerie Kalb (project) [*wbw* 6/1996, 21]
		Danube Canal (study with street project; Büro Windbrechtinger und Hufnagl)
	1971–1972	Children's room Klemmer, Vienna [170, 404]
	1972	High-rise concept beyond the central section of the Danube Canal (sketch) [*wbw* 6/1996, 57]
	1972–1974	Loft conversion Dertnig, Vienna (project)
	1973 and 1977	**Löcker & Wögenstein antiquarian bookshop**, Vienna [154, 194–199, 201, 228, 348; *wbw* 6/1996, 12, 45; *a+u* 16:11, 59, 80–81]
	1973	Trade fair stand Wittmann (project)
		Apartment De Waal, Vienna, conversion [288]
		Apartment Neuffer, bathroom (project)
	1973–1974	House Heilingsetzer, Schönbichl, conversion
		Danube Island Vienna (competition project) [*wbw* 6/1996, 57]
		Kleines Café II, extension (upper space) [10, 106, 182–188, 201f, 255, 259, 289; *wbw* 6/1996, 19, 48; *a+u* 16:11, 114–117]
	1974	Discotheque "Spiegel" (project)
	1974–1975	Dicopa office conversion, Vienna (destroyed) [241, 244; *wbw* 6/1996, 13]
	1975	Wohnen Morgen (**Living Tomorrow**), Neumarkt (competition; with Werner Appelt, Franz E. Kneissl, Elsa Prochazka, Adalbert Singer and Rolf Wessely) [*wbw* 6/1996, 28, 51]
	1975–1976 and 1978	**Wunder-Bar**, Vienna [49, 154, 200–205; *wbw* 6/1996, 19; *a+u* 16:11, 66–69]
	1976	Filmmuseum buffet and foyer (project)
	1976–1977	Graf hairdressing salon (project)
	1977	Ensemble theater (study)
		Kleines Café I, additions [150, 189–192]

1977	Housing construction on Rennweg (competition; with W. Appelt, F. E. Kneissl and E. Prochazka)
	Loos Bar, restoration (project)
1977–1979	**Villa Pflaum**, Altenberg near Vienna, addition [174, 216–225; wbw 6/1996, 25, 45; a+u 16:11, 122–127]
1977–1981	**House M.**, Schwechat near Vienna [170f, 174, 206–215, 228, 240; wbw 6/1996, 29, 53; a+u 16:11, 44–47]
1978	Café D., Salzburg (project) [191]
	Lights for Section N (project)
1978–1980	Bar on Priesterhausgasse, Salzburg (project) [344]
	Residential furnishings for Monika P. and Hanno P., Vienna [244, 246; wbw 6/1996, 18]
	Kunsthandlung Hummel, Vienna [154, 187, 226–233; wbw 6/1996, 50; wbw 6/1996, 14]
	Exhibition contribution "Follow Me," *Forum Design* Linz [243f; wbw 6/1996, 19]
1979–1981	House Neuwirth-Gallowitsch, Schwanberg, conversion (project)
	Exhibition concept and design *Josef Frank 1885–1967*, Austrian Museum of Applied Arts (MAK) (with Johannes Spalt) [229, 239, 273, 350, 414]
1980	Exhibition participation *A New Wave of Austrian Architecture*, Institute for Architecture and Urban Studies, New York (organized by Adolf Krischanitz) [17, 280]
	Exhibition contribution for *The Presence of the Past*, Architecture Biennale Venice [15]
1980–1983	**House S.**, Vienna [174, 234–247; wbw 6/1996, 24; a+u 16:11, 70–75]
1981	Großes Haus, Stuttgart, audience spaces (expertise review)
	Villa Pflaum, Altenberg near Vienna, space utilization concept
	Restaurant in Palais Schwarzenberg, Vienna, space utilization concept
1981–1982	Perchtoldsdorf, market square, monument to the Turkish invasion (project) [wbw 6/1996, 31]
1981–1983	**Salzamt Restaurant**, Vienna [193, 248–255, 369; wbw 6/1996, 46]
1982	Perchtoldsdorf, lighting of the market square [wbw 6/1996, 47]
	House Bleckmann, Salzburg, staircase and attic (project)
	Housing construction Vienna-Essling (study; with Johann Georg Gsteu, Roland Hagmüller and Adolf Krischanitz)
	Villa Kammerer I, conversion (project)
1982–1983	Apartment Schwarzenberg, Vienna
	Vienna River Valley crossing subway line Otto Wagner Bridge, Vienna (competition project; with Heinrich Mittnik) [278f; wbw 6/1996, 54–55]
1982–1984	**Palais Schwarzenberg**, Vienna: basement remodeling (partially destroyed) [149, 154, 241, 256–267, 368, 370; wbw 6/1996, 20, 47; a+u 16:11, 60–65]
1983	Alte Pumpe youth center, Berlin (winning project of an expertise procedure; not realized) [wbw 6/1996, 58]

1983–1984 **Exhibition design *von hier aus. Zwei Monate neue deutsche Kunst***, Messegelände Düsseldorf (concept: Kasper König) [268–275; *wbw* 6/1996, 8, 15, 50; *a+u* 16:11, 52–57]

1984 **Bleckmann mill**, conversion (project)

Europaplatz U3/U6 subway lines, Vienna (study)

Apartment Monika Kaesser, Vienna, door installation

1985 **Kleines Café II**, toilet installation [193]

Schatzkästchen (*Treasure Box*) exhibition design (presentation of Austria abroad) (project) [*wbw* 6/1996, 17]

Apartment Monika Banićević, Vienna, bathroom [in: *wbw* 6/1996, 13]

Villa Kammerer II, conversion (project)

Tower with camera obscura, Potsdamerstrasse, Berlin (project; initiated by André Heller)

Fauteuil Museum (study)

1985–1986 **Antiques shop Monika Kaesser**, Vienna, doorway, Wien, Portal [*wbw* 6/1996, 26]

1985–1987 **Stadtparksteg pedestrian bridge**, Vienna (competition; 1st place; realized) [276–281; *wbw* 6/1996, 30; *a+u* 16:11, 96–99]

1985–1988 **General planning of U3-West** (architecture), Vienna [*wbw* 6/1996, 56]

1985–1989 **Residential block Petrusgasse**, Vienna [282–289; *wbw* 6/1996, 27; *a+u* 16:11, 26–27]

Conception and exhibition design *Adolf Loos*, Albertina Vienna (with Friedrich Kurrent, Hans Puchhammer, Burkhardt Rukschcio, Roland Schachel, Anton Schweighofer and Johannes Spalt) [318, 332]

1986 **Casino Winkler**, Salzburg, addition (expertise project) [*wbw* 6/1996, 59]

Pavilion at the Palm Garden, Frankfurt (initiated by André Heller) [*wbw* 6/1996, 26; *a+u* 16:11, 76–77]

Elevator additions Winarskyhof, Vienna (competition project)

Apartment Monika Banićević, Vienna, cabinet installation

1986–1988 **Exhibition design for *Vienna 1938***, City Hall Vienna (concept: Documentation Centre of Austrian Resistance) [47, 290–297; *wbw* 6/1996, 17, 49; *a+u* 16:11, 136–139]

1986–1989 **Atelier Czech Singerstraße 26A** [314–321; *wbw* 6/1996, 12, 49]

1987 **Exhibition design and concept** *Hermann Czech. Options in Architecture*, 9H Gallery, London

Nightstand/stool

Villa Pflaum, entrance (project)

La Roche library, Vienna (study)

1987 **"Causeuse" loveseat**, contribution to the travelling exhibition *Vienna Furniture*, organized by Adolf Krischanitz, Vienna–Paris–Helsinki

Palais Schwarzenberg, Vienna, conversion of the western courtyard wing (project)

Exhibition design *Aging*, Kunsthalle Wien (project)

1987–1988 **Kurhaus-Restaurant**, Baden-Baden (destroyed) [*wbw* 6/1996, 20; *a+u* 16:11, 25, 28–31]

1988 **House Monika Kaesser**, Eisenberg, conversion and addition [*wbw* 6/1996, 32]

1988	Trigon Museum Graz (competition project) [*wbw* 6/1996, 61]
	Vimpex Office, conversion (project)
1988–1989	Exhibition design **Wunderblock. *A History of the Modern Soul***, Reithalle im Messepalast, Vienna (concept: Jean Clair, Cathrin Pichler and Wolfgang Pircher) [298–303; *wbw* 6/1996, 16, 49; *a+u* 16:11, 132–135]
1989 und 1990–1994	**Residential block Brunner Gasse/Franz-Kamtner-Weg**, Perchtoldsdorf [298–313; *wbw* 6/1996, 33, 51; *a+u* 16:11, 88–91]
1989	**Arcadia Music Shop in the Vienna State Opera** (with Stephan Seehof) [187, 322–327; *wbw* 6/1996, 34]
	Hotel, Ljubljana, (competition project)
	Settee Reichmann (study)
	Palais Schwarzenberg, Vienna, west ramp
	Porsche sales and service (study)
	Palais Schwarzenberg, Vienna, conversion of eastern court wing (project)
	Palais Schwarzenberg, Vienna, hotel entrance door
	Nitsch Library, Prinzendorf (project)
1989–1990	Rautenweg heating plant (project) [*wbw* 6/1996, 35]
1990 and 1992–1997	**Block development at the U3-West Ottakring turnaround**, Vienna-Ottakring [328–335; *wbw* 6/1996, 56; *a+u* 16:11, 108–109]
1990	Changing room house, Schwarzenberg tennis court (project)
	Palais Schwarzenberg apartments, upper floor main building (project)
	Palais Schwarzenberg, parking lot kiosk
	Coca-Cola office building (sketch)
	Supermarket Sutterlüty, Lustenau (competition project)
	Arcadia, Marble Hall desk, Vienna State Opera
	Danube Canal workshop
	Loft conversion Fletzberger, Vienna (with Irmgard Frank)
	Residential development St. Peter East, Salzburg (competition project) [*wbw* 6/1996, 51]
	Apartment Demner, Vienna, conversion
1990–1991	House Banićević, Henndorf, conversion [*wbw* 6/1996, 32]
1991–1993	**Café in the Museum of Applied Arts (MAK Café)**, Vienna (destroyed) [10, 336–345, 369; *wbw* 6/1996, 21, 48; *a+u* 16:11, 83–87]
	Thonet chair [338f; *wbw* 6/1996, 46]
1991–1994	The GEHEN shop, Cologne [*wbw* 6/1996, 26]
	Winter glazing of the Vienna State Opera Loggia [154, 346–351; *wbw* 6/1996, 34–35; *a+u* 16:11, 36–41]
	Elementary school Fuchsröhrenstrasse (Rosa Jochmann School), Vienna-Simmering (with Wolfgang Reder) [352–357; *wbw* 6/1996, 22–23; *a+u* 16:11, 92–95]

1992	Park & Ride study (with Alfred Pauser) [*wbw* 6/1996, 28]
	Haus Schwarzenberg, Dřevič, conversion [*wbw* 6/1996, 13]
1992 and 1993–1997	Bank Austria customer center, Vienna, conversion (destroyed) [*a+u* 16:11, 113]
1992–1993	**Urbanization of the site of former SS barracks of Oranienburg** (1st ranked expertise project; not realized) [47, 358–365; *wbw* 6/1996, 62–63]
1993	Urban development study Michelbeuern, Vienna (expertise project) [*wbw* 6/1996, 60]
1993–1994	**Donau-City residential development**, Vienna (2nd rank in an expertise project) [*wbw* 6/1996, 61]
1994 and 1996–1997	Employment office Vienna-Liesing (by Ernst A. Plischke), reconstruction and new usage [*wbw* 6/1996, 58]
1994	Roof superstructures for the Gloriette in Vienna (project) [*wbw* 6/1996, 59; *a+u* 16:11, 110–111]
1995	Surgical department of the Salzburg State Hospital (with competition project; with Georg Übelhör)) [*wbw* 6/1996, 60]
1995–1996	XIX Triennale di Milano, frame designs of international contributions
1996	Exhibition concept and design *Hermann Czech. Das architektonische Objekt*, Architekturmuseum Basel
1996–1997	Exhibition design *Schubert 97*, Historical Museum of the City of Vienna (concept: Otto Brusatti) [*a+u* 16:11, 50–51]
	Sales branch and main warehouse IKERA/Wein & Co, Vienna-Donaustadt (partially destroyed)
1998–1999	House Schwarzenberg, Turrach, conversion
1998–2000	**Swiss Re Centre**, Zürich-Rüschlikon, furnishing (with Adolf Krischanitz) [366–375; *a+u* 16:11, 78–79]
1998–2001	Vienna-Hütteldorf train station, conversion (winning expertise project; not realized)
1998–2003	Residential construction Geblergasse, Vienna
1998–2010	Theatercafé, Vienna (partially destroyed)
1999	"Grünes Gewölbe," Dresden, refurbishing (expertise project)
	Casino/Hotel in Lugano, (international expertise project)
1999–2003	Apartment Oetker, top floors and tower of an old building (from 16th century), Vienna, conversion [*a+u* 16:11, 104–105]
2000	Gasthaus Immervoll (later Pöschl), Vienna [187]
	Extension of the U2 subway line in Vienna (project of the 2nd competition phase; with ARTEC Architekten)
	"Area of Tolerance," exhibition contribution on the occasion of the 7th Architecture Biennale Venice, Austria Pavilion (curator Hans Hollein) [376–379; *a+u* 16:11, 32]
2000–2007	**Cement house of a model estate of international architects**, Vienna-Hadersdorf (initiated by Adolf Krischanitz) [380–385]
2001	High-rise study of the object Europaplatz 1 of the Austrian Federal Railways (ÖBB), Vienna
2001–2002	High-rise study Innsbruck (with further authors)

2002	**Saturn high-rise for IBM**, Donau-City, Vienna (project)
2002, 2003–2005	**Hotel Messe Vienna** [159, 386–395; *a+u* 16:11, 120–121]
2003–2004	**Bundestheater box offices**, Vienna, furnishing
2004–2005	**Weinhaus PUNKT**, conversion (old building from the 16th century), Kaltern/Caldaro [*a+u* 16:11, 118–119]
2004–2007	**Urbanihaus** (residential house 13th century/Baroque), Vienna, conversion [*a+u* 16:11, 100–103]
	Villa Pflaum, Altenberg near Vienna, transformation
2006–2008, 2009	**Volksoper Vienna**, balcony and gallery buffets and canteen (with Thomas Roth)
2007–2010, 2011–2015	**School yard**, Vienna, top floor conversion
2007–2011	**"Housing for Generations" Am Mühlgrund**, Vienna-Stadlau (with Adolf Krischanitz, Werner Neuwirth) [396–403; *a+u* 16:11, 128–131]
	Rooftop extension Günthergasse, Vienna [174, 404–411; *a+u* 16:11, 106–197]
2008	**Austrian Parliament Vienna**, transformation of the National Council Chamber (competition project)
2010	**Volksoper**, Vienna, transformation of the entrance foyer, cashiers' hall (with Thomas Roth)
2010–	**Attic conversion House Rychlik**, Bad Vöslau
2012–2015	**Exhibition design *Josef Frank: Against Design***, MAK Vienna, concept (with Sebastian Hackenschmidt) and layout [412–419]
2012–2016	**Residential development Buchleitengasse**, Vienna (with Adolf Krischanitz)
2013–2014	**Renovation of the Austrian Parliament Vienna** (bidder project; with Adolf Krischanitz and Werner Neuwirth)
2013–2015	**Exhibition design *The Vienna Circle***, University of Vienna (concept: Karl Sigmund and Friedrich Stadler) [*a+u* 16:11, 48–49]
2013–	**2 residential buildings on the eastern part of Steinhof** (after a mediation process; with Andreas Mieling)
2014–2015	**Exhibition design *Der Schatten der Avantgarde***, Folkwang-Museum, Essen (concept: Kasper König, Falk Wolf)
	Extension of the Wien Museum (competition, with ARTEC Architekten)
2015–2016	**Exhibition design *Július Koller One Man Anti-Show***, mumok Vienna (Concept: Daniel Grúň, Kathrin Rhomberg and Georg Schöllhammer)
2015–2016	**Buffet CinCin**, Vienna
2015–2019	**Hotel extension Erlhof**, Zell am See (with Andreas Mieling)
2017	**Exhibition design *Július Koller One Man Anti-Show***, Museion, Bozen/Bolzano, (takeover, concept: Daniel Grúň, Kathrin Rhomberg and Georg Schöllhammer)
2017–2020	**Sigmund Freud Museum Architecture and Exhibition Design**, Berggasse 19, conversion (competition, 1st rank; with Walter Angonese and Bettina Götz/Richard Manahl – ARTEC Architekten) [420–429]
2020–2022	**Interior design Josephinum**, Vienna (with Gerhard Flora)
2021–2023	**Austrian contribution to the 18th Architecture Biennale Venice**, (with AKT)

Significant Assistants at Atelier Czech 1979–2018

Reem Almannai
Heike Barth
Stephen Bidwell [290]
Petra Bohle
Alexandra Bohrn
Heidrun Breindl
John W. Cahill
Martin Cikhart [352]
Bernhard Denkinger [290]
Gustav Deutsch [206]
Anna Marija Dufils-Meniga [386]
Christoph Elmecker
Gerhard Flora [412]
Irmgard Frank
Anette Freudenberger
Lorna Fürst
Rudolf Gitschthaler
Johann Gritzner [248]
Walter Gruß [234, 256]
Eva Gschwindl
Manfred Haas [346]
Krista Höller
Nina-Flora Holly [412]
Eduard Hueber [194]
Paul Katzberger [248]
Franz Eberhard Kneissl

Doris Koglbauer
Ursula Konzett
Ola Kopka [386]
Elke Krasny
Sven Kremer [380]
Ingrid Lapaine [206, 216]
Magdalena Leutzendorff
Gerhard Lindner [234]
Franz Loranzi [268, 290]
Michael Loudon [276, 282]
Timothy Love
Ina Martin [290]
Margarita McGrath [336]
Srećko Merle
Walter Michl [276, 314]
Andreas Mieling [380, 386, 396, 404]
Franz Moser [314]
Susanne Nowak
Susanne Obkircher
Bert Pepler
Wolfgang Podgorschek [268, 276]
Elsa Prochazka [200]
Jana Raudnitzky
Wolfgang Reder [246]
Gerhard Riedling [290]

Romana Ring [256]
Thomas Roth [336, 346, 352, 366, 386, 396, 412]
Valentin Scheinost [386]
Harald Schönfellinger [256]
Karin Schweitzer(-Zinggl)
Liane Siebert
Astrid Stadtmüller
Susanna-Maria Stein
Peter Stiner [234]
Karin Sumereder
Romana Szczurowsky
Bogdan Szwajnoch [328, 352]
Volker Thurm(-Nemeth) [160, 216]
Karin Tschavgova [290]
Georg Übelhör [282, 328, 386]
Torsten Warner
Tilman Wetter [336]
Walter Zschokke

Writings by Hermann Czech

*(with page numbers, preceded by alternative title) = (re)published in: Czech 1996

Single Publications and Book Contributions

"Am Stephansplatz," 1963; [first publication: 1977] * 11

"Übertrieben," 1965; [first publication: 1977] * 23

"Umweltgestaltung," 1965; [first publication: 1977] * 46–47 (co-editor:) *Neue städtische Wohnformen* (exhibition catalog), Vienna: ÖGfA, 1967

"Was geschieht mit der bestehenden Stadt," in: *Neue städtische Wohnformen* (exhibition catalog), Vienna: ÖGfA, 1967

Das Looshaus (with Wolfgang Mistelbauer) self-published, Vienna, 1968

"Heinz Frank," in: *Heinz Frank* (exhibition catalog), Vienna: Löcker & Wögenstein, 1975; * 105

"Manierismus und Partizipation," 1977; [first publication:] * 89–91; also in: Gerd de Bruyn; Stephan Trüby (eds.): *architektur_theorie.doc Texte seit 1960*, Basel, Boston and Berlin: Birkhäuser, 2003, 243–244; "Mannerism and Participation," in: *A New Wave of Austrian Architecture*, 1980, 60; as well as in: *The Presence of the Past*, 1980, 132 [Engl./Ital.] and in: Elise Feiersinger (ed.): Hermann Czech: *Essays on Architecture and City Planning*, Zurich: Park Books, 2019, 119–124

Das Looshaus (with Wolfgang Mistelbauer), book edition, Vienna: Löcker & Wögenstein, 1976; 2nd revised edition, 1977; 3rd ed., Vienna: Locker, 1984; excerpts in: *der aufbau* 4–5/1964; *Bau* 1/1970; *a+u* 1/1978 [Engl./Jap.]; *9H* 2/1980 [Engl.]; (exhibition catalog) *Adolf Loos*, Paris, 1983

Czech 1996 – *Zur Abwechslung. Ausgewählte Schriften zur Architektur. Wien*, Vienna: Löcker & Wögenstein, 1977/1978; expanded new addition with afterword by Arno Ritter, Vienna: Löcker, 1996

"Man kann alles verwenden, was man verwenden kann," in: *Österreichische Beiträge zu einem modernen Wohn- und Lebensstil*, edited by Rudolf Dirisamer, Vienna: Zentralsparkasse der Gemeinde Wien, 1978, 81

(Editor:) Heinrich Kulka: *Adolf Loos. Das Werk des Architekten*, reprint of the 1931 edition, Vienna: Löcker, 1979

(Editor:) Otto Wagner: *Die Baukunst unserer Zeit*, reprint of the IV. edition from 1914, Vienna: Löcker, 1979

"No Need for Panic," "For a Change," "Mannerism and Participation," "Pluralism," "The Little Café," "Inner City Expansion," "Spatial City-planning," in: *A New Wave of Austrian Architecture*, preface by Kenneth Frampton, IAUS cat. 13, New York: Institute for Architecture and Urban Studies, 1980, 58–81 [Engl.]

(Author and co-editor with Johannes Spalt:) *Josef Frank 1885–1967* (exhibition catalog), Hochschule für angewandte Kunst, Vienna: Löcker, 1981

"Einige Entwurfsgedanken," in: *Design ist unsichtbar* (exhibition catalog), Forum Design Linz, Vienna: Löcker, 1981, 395–404; "Einige weitere Entwurfsgedanken" * 81

"Follow Me," in: *Design ist unsichtbar* (exhibition catalog), Forum Design Linz, Vienna: Löcker, 1981, 656–657

(Editor and compiler of index:) Josef Frank: *Architektur als Symbol. Elemente deutschen neuen Bauens*, reprint of the 1931 edition, Vienna: Löcker, 1981; 2nd revised edition. 2005; reprinted in: Frank 2012, Vol. 2, 9–191 [Ger./Engl.]

(Editor and translator:) Christopher Alexander: *The Linz Café/Das Linz Café*, New York and London: Oxford University Press/Vienna: Löcker, 1981 [Ger./Engl.]

"Zur Architektur der Ausstellung," in: *von hier aus. Zwei Monate neue deutsche Kunst in Düsseldorf* (exhibition catalog), Düsseldorf, Cologne: DuMont 1984, 1, 9

"Wohnbau und Althaus," in: *Wiener Wohnbau Wirklichkeiten* (exhibition catalog), Künstlerhaus Wien, Vienna: Compress, 1985, 52–55; * 106–109

"Spurensicherung" [Loos-Bar], in: *Wiener Bauplätze. Verschollene Träume – angewandte Programme*, edited by Peter Noever/Österr. Museum f. angewandte Kunst (exhibition catalog), Vienna: Löcker, 1986, 123–131

(Editor:) Josef Frank: *Architettura come simbolo*, Bologna: Zanichelli, 1986

Projekttext [Wohnbau Petrusgasse], in: *Werkstatt Metropole Wien – Band 1: Lücken in der Stadt*, edited by Dietmar Steiner, Vienna: Edition Atelier, 1987, 11–13

Hermann Czech. Options in Architecture (exhibition catalog), 9H Gallery, London: 9H Gallery, 1987 [with project texts on Residential Block Petrusgasse and Restaurant Schwarzenberg; Engl.]

"Der Umbau," in: *Adolf Loos* (exhibition catalog), Albertina, Vienna: Löcker, 1989, 159–172; * 125–127; also in: *Umbau* 29/2017, 10–13 [text impaired by layout]; "Verbouwing/Transformation," in: *OASE* 92, 2014, 14–16 [Dutch/Engl.]

Projekttexte, in: Otto Kapfinger; Franz E. Kneissl (eds.): *Dichte Packung. Architektur aus Wien*, Salzburg and Vienna: Residenz, 1989, 15, 27, 51, 89, 111, 155, 183, 187, 195, 203, 219, 237, 245

"Elemente der Stadtvorstellung" [with excerpts from "Wohnbau und Althaus," 1985 and "Der Umbau," 1989], in: Hannes Swoboda (ed.): *Wien – Identität und Stadtgestalt*, Vienna: Böhlau, 1990, 205–218; * 131–138

(Text quotations in article:) "Hermann Czech," Biennale di Venezia 1991, *13 Austrian Positions*, Klagenfurt: Ritter, 1991 [Engl.]

"Urbanisierung des ehemaligen Geländes der SS-Kaserne Oranienburg," in: *Centrum. Jahrbuch Architektur und Stadt 1993*, edited by Peter Neitzke; Carl Steckeweh, Braunschweig and Wiesbaden: Friedrich Vieweg & Sohn, 1993, 88–91; "Ein Gutachten," * 139–143 [with excerpts from a letter to Ignatz Bubis]

"Selbstkritik der Moderne" [with excerpts from "Der Loos-Gedanke," 1970, "Zur Abwechslung," 1973 and "Ein Begriffsraster zur aktuellen Interpretation Josef Franks," 1985], in: Annette Becker; Dietmar Steiner; Wilfried Wang (eds.): *Architektur im 20. Jahrhundert. Österreich*, Munich and New York: Prestel, 1995, 114–119; * 144–148

(Editor, translation revision, afterword:) Christopher Alexander et al.: *Eine Muster-Sprache. Städte Gebäude Konstruktion*, Vienna: Löcker, 1995

"Nachwort des Herausgebers," in: Christopher Alexander et al.: *Eine Muster-Sprache. Städte Gebäude Konstruktion*, Vienna: Löcker, 1995, 1263–1268

Hermann Czech. Das architektonische Objekt = special issue *wbw* 6/1996 (collaboration, selection, project texts)

(Exhibition texts:) *Hermann Czech – Das architektonische Objekt*, Architekturmuseum Basel, 1996

"Gegen einen absichtlichen Regionalismus" (1993), in: *Bau–Kultur–Region. Regionale Identität im wachsenden Europa – das Fremde*, Kunsthaus Bregenz, aka 1, Vienna: Österreichischer Kunst und Kultur Verlag, 1996, 58–65

"Komfort und Modernität," in: *Architektur Jahrbuch 1997*, Deutsches Architekturmuseum, Frankfurt, Munich and New York: Prestel, 1997, 31–34 [Ger./Engl.]

"Cleaning the Tools for Design" [Engl. 1999, Ger. abridged] in: Tom Fecht; Dietmar Kamper (eds.): *Umzug ins offene. Vier Versuche über den Raum*, Vienna and New York: Springer, 2000, 286–287; "Affûter les outils conceptuels," in: *l'architecture d'aujour'dhui* 362, 2006, 46–51

"Architektur soll man sich merken," in: *Österreichische Architekten [Hermann Czech] im Gespräch mit Gerfried Sperl*, Salzburg: Anton Pustet, 2000

Area of Tolerance (exhibition texts and design), Architecture Biennale Venice 2000

"Das Lokal" [text stylistically and grammatically disfigured by publisher], in: Romana Schneider (ed.): *Le Bar du Paris Bar*, Tübingen and Berlin: Wasmuth, 2001, 17–20

"Das Objekt in der Stadt," in: *redesign DIANA: Generalsanierung der IBM Zentrale Österreich*, Vienna: Holzhausen, 2001

Hochhausstudie Innsbruck (with several co-authors, edited by Max Rieder), edited by Stadt Innsbruck – Stadtplanung and Architekturforum Tirol, Salzburg: Anton Pustet, 2002

"'Less' or "'More'?"/ "'Less' vagy 'More'?,'" in: Judit Lénvai-Kanyó (ed.): *Transitions. On the State of Architecture* (Symposium Volume), Budapest: TERC, 2002, 46–67 [Engl./Hung.]

"Das Arbeitsamt in Liesing und seine Wiederherstellung 1996–97" [with excerpts from "Das Arbeitsamt Liesing. E. A. Plischke 1930–31," 2000], in: *Ernst Anton Plischke. Architekt und Lehrer*, edited by Komitee 100 Jahre E. A. Plischke, Salzburg: Anton Pustet, 2003, 40–47

"Eine Strategie für das Unplanbare," in: *wildwuchs. Vom wert dessen, was von selbst ist*, Amt der Wiener Landesregierung, Vienna: MA22, 2003, 84–85

"Die Sprache der Verführung," in: Stanislaus von Moos; Karin Gimmi (eds.): *SvM. Die Festschrift für Stanislaus von Moos*, Zurich: gta, 2005, 150–157

"Cafés," in: Christoph Grafe; Franziska Bollerey (eds.): *Cafés and Bars. The Architecture of Public Display*, New York and London: Routledge, 2007, 94–96 [Engl.]

"Polemische Architektur/Polemic Architecture" [about the PAUHOF contribution], in: Bettina Götz (ed.): *Before Architecture/Vor der Architektur* (exhibition catalog), 11th International Architecture Exhibition, La Biennale di Venezia 2008, Vienna and New York: Springer, 2008, 72–74 [Ger./Engl.]

"Ungefähre Hauptrichtung," in: *Marcel Meili, Markus Peter 1987–2008*; 434–441; German/English edition: "Approximate Line of Action," Zurich: Scheidegger & Spiess, 2008; reprinted in German in: *Hochparterre* 10/2008, 21. Jg., 66–68

"Adolf Loos – Widersprüche und Aktualität" [expanded new version of the 1984 text], in: Inge Podbrecky; Rainald Franz (eds.): *Leben mit Loos*, Vienna: Böhlau, 2008, 17–25

"Primär mit Worten" (Hotel Messe Wien), in: Elke Krasny (eds.): *Architektur beginnt im Kopf. The Making of Architecture* (exhibition catalog), Architekturzentrum Wien; German/English edition: "Primarily with words [Hotel Messe Wien]," in: *The Force is in the Mind*, Basel, Boston and Berlin: Birkhäuser, 2008, 34–41

Untitled, in: Claudia Enengl: *Johann Georg Gsteu. Architektur sichtbar und spürbar machen*, Salzburg: Anton Pustet, 2010, 128

"Theorie als Denken zum Entwurf" [aus Schriften seit den 1960er Jahren]/Thinking About Design, in: András Pálffy; TU Wien (eds.): *Konzept und Entwurf/ Concept and Design*, Sulgen: Niggli, 2012, 266–269 [Ger./Engl.]

"Der Hoffmann-Pavillon/The Hoffmann Pavilion," in: Diener & Diener Architects with Gabriele Basilico: *Common Pavilions: The National Pavilions in the Giardini in Essays and Photographs* (exhibition catalog), 13th Architecture Biennale Venice, 2012, Zurich: Scheidegger & Spiess, 2012, 148–154 [Ger./Engl.]

"Kann Architektur von der Konsumtion her gedacht werden?" [with excerpts from "Schau schää …" 1964 and "Architektur, von der Produktion her gedacht" 2009], in: Kristian Faschingeder et al. (eds.): *Die Architektur der neuen Weltordnung/Architecture in the Age of Empire*, Bauhaus-Universität Weimar (= Tagungsband 11. Intern. Bauhaus Kolloquium Weimar 2009) 2011; reprinted together with: "Can Architecture Be Conceived by Way of Consumption?" / "Pode a arquitecura ser pensada a partir do consumo?," in: Yehuda E. Safran (ed.): *Adolf Loos: Our Contemporary / Unser Zeitgenosse / Nosso Contemporâneo* (exhibition catalog), GSAPP, Columbia University, New York/MAK Wien/ CAAA Guimarães, New York: GSAPP, Columbia University: 2013, 13–20/93–100/173–179; 232–235 [Ger./Engl./Port.]; "Can Architecture Be Conceived by Way of Consumption?" in: Hermann Czech: *Essays on Architecture and City Planning*, edited and translated by Elise Feiersinger, Zurich: Park Books, 2019, 229–247 [Engl.]

Top down – bottom up. Hermann Czech – Roland Rainer Chair 2012–13, Vienna: Akademie der bildenden Künste, 2013

"Plan und Bild. Mögliche Rollen im Entwurfsprozess," in: Annette Spiro; David Ganzoni (eds.): *Der Bauplan. Werkzeug des Architekten*, Zurich: Park Books, 2013, 267–269; published simultaneously in English: "Plan and Image. Possible Roles in the Design Process," in: *The Working Drawing. The Architect's Tool* [Engl.]

"Village Texture," in: András Pálffy (ed.): *Village Textures* (in the series: Pálffy Editions), Vienna: Schlebrügge, 2014 [Engl.]

(Co-editor with Christoph Thun-Hohenstein and Sebastian Hackenschmidt:) *Josef Frank. Against Design. Das anti-formalistische Werk des Architekten / The Architect's Anti-Formalist Oeuvre* (exhibition catalog), MAK Wien, Basel: Birkhäuser, 2015

"Josef Frank: Against Design" (with Sebastian Hackenschmidt), in: Czech, Thun-Hohenstein, Hackenschmidt (eds.): *Josef Frank. Against Design*, 2015, 14–27 [Engl./Ger.]

"Rückblick 2017" (on the German translation of "Otto Wagner's Vienna Metropolitan Railway," 1976), in: Alfred Fogarassy (ed.): *Otto Wagner. Die Wiener Stadtbahn*, Berlin: Hatje Cantz, 2017, 9–15

Czech 2019 – Czech, Hermann: *Essays on Architecture and City Planning*, edited and translated by Elise Feiersinger, Zurich: Park Books, 2019

Czech, Hermann: "Architectural Concept and Exhibition Design," trans. Elise Feiersinger, in: Monika Pessler and Daniela Finzi (eds.): *Freud. Berggasse 19 – Origin of Psychoanalysis*, Berlin: Hatje Cantz, 2020, 17.

Czech, Hermann: *Ungefähre Hauptrichtung. Schriften und Gespräche zur Architektur*, Vienna: Löcker, 2022

AKT & Czech, Hermann: *Partecipazione*, Vienna: Luftschacht Verlag, 2023

Articles in Magazines/Periodicals

"Die Stadtbahn wird unterschätzt," in: *Die Furche* 20/1963; [appended:] "Otto Wagners Verkehrsbauwerk" * 24–31

"Neuere Sachlichkeit" [Europagespräch 1963; interview with R. Neutra], in: *Die Furche* 26/1963; * 56–57; "Newer Objectivity," in: Hermann Czech: *Essays on Architecture and City Planning*, edited and translated by Elise Feiersinger, Zurich: Park Books, 2019, 41–46 [Engl.]

"Der ornamentlose Otto Wagner," in: *Die Furche* 31/1963

"Über Rudolf Schwarz und Kirchenbau," in: *Wort und Wahrheit* 12/1963, Freiburg; "Rudolf Schwarz" * 32–33

"Architekturstatistik," in: *Die Furche* 5/1964; "Maßstäbe" * 11–12

"Mehr Licht," in: *Die Furche* 7/1964; * 19–21; also in: *Bau*, 2–3/1968 ("Neue Konzeptionen aus Wien"), 26

"Schau schää …," in: *Die Furche* 17/1964; * 81–83

"Architektur um 1900" [exhibition by arbeitsgruppe 4], in: *Die Furche* 24/1964

"Architekturgespräch" [X. Intern. Kunstgespräch der Galerie St. Stephan zu Kirchenbau], in: *Die Furche* 29/1964

"Wohnbaukritik," in: *Die Furche* 37/1964; "Aufrüttelndes" * 12

"Ring rund um den Brei," in: *Die Furche* 43/1964; "Einst und heute" * 22

"Großstädtische Architektur," in: *Die Furche* 47/1964; 13–14

"Ein Wien der Zukunft" [exhibition by arbeitsgruppe 4], in: *Die Furche* 49/1964

"Vom Hietzinger Tempel" [abridged], in: *Die Furche* 50/1964; [unabridged] * 22–23

"Kritik an der TH," in: *Der Akademiker*, November 1964

"Wiener Architekturfragen," in: *Der Akademiker*, December 1964

"Spießer als Original" [review: Mord an Apollo by A. v. Senger], in: *Die Furche* 8/1965

"Weltausstellung 67," in: *Die Furche* 9/1965; * 53

"Angelo Mangiarotti," in: *Die Furche* 15/1965; * 47–48; "Angelo Mangiarotti" in: Hermann Czech: *Essays on Architecture and City Planning*, edited and translated by Elise Feiersinger, Zurich: Park Books, 2019, 49–52 [Engl.]

"Das Otto Wagner-Buch," in: *Die Furche* 16/1965; "Das Wagner-Buch" * 60

"Das Adolf Loos-Buch," in: *Die Furche* 24/1965; "Das Loos-Buch" * 59–60

"Le Corbusier," in: *Die Furche* 36/1965; "Le Corbusier/Fast ein Unbekannter" * 48–49

"Die Autobahnkirche bei Florenz," in: *Die Furche* 40/1965

"Ein Geschäft am Kohlmarkt," in: *Die Furche* 50/1965

"Architekturzensur," in: *Die Furche* 51–52/1965; * 14–17

"Architektur an der Wiener TH," in: *Blätter* 1/1965–1966; "Zum Jubiläum" * 49–52

"Stadtplanung nach Rainer," in: *Die Furche* 2/1966

"Architekturstudenten," in: *Die Furche* 10/1966

"Wo parken wir morgen?," in: *Die Furche* 22/1966

"Terrassenhäuser," in: *Die Furche* 25/1966

"Adolf Loos und Funktionalismus," in: *Die Furche* 25/1966; "Loos und Funktionalismus" * 58

"Der falsche Weg," in: *Die Furche* 31/1966; "Die Chance" * 34–36

"Heinrich Kulka – Überlieferer einer Architekturtradition," in: *Die Furche* 39/1966

Untitled [demolition of the Florianikirche], in: *Die Furche* 39/1966; "Stadtbild und Moral" * 36–37

"Zwei entscheidende Fehler," in: *Die Furche* 43/1966; [expanded text:] "Ein U-Bahnnetz als Entwurfsproblem" * 38–40

"Wegbereiter der Großstadt" [review of F. Hennings: *Das Josephinische Wien*], in: *Die Furche* 46/1966

"Gutes Architekturklima" [on the exhibition by Graz architecture students], in: *Salzburger Nachrichten*, 1 March 1966

"Amerikanisches Bauen," in: *Salzburger Nachrichten*, 6 April 1966; also: "Aus Amerika," in: *Zur Abwechslung*, Vienna: Löcker & Wögenstein, 1977, 48

"Kirchenbau des 20. Jahrhunderts" [on the church building exhibition at ÖBZ], in: *Salzburger Nachrichten*, 9 April 1966

"Karlsplatznachlese," in: *Die Furche* 1/1967; "Der Karlsplatz" * 44–45

"Josef Frank – Intellekt, Liebenswürdigkeit, Ironie" [obituary], in: *Die Furche* 3/1967

"U-Bahn-Diskussion," in: *Die Furche* 5/1967

"Zukunft und Architektur," in: *Die Furche* 9/1967

"Intellekt und Disziplin," in: *Die Furche* 21/1967

"Ein Urteil," in: *Die Furche* 35/1967; * 53–54

"Sehenswürdig" [abridged], in: *Die Furche* 36/1967; [unabridged:] * 18

"Bauernfang," in: *Die Furche* 38/1967

"Mißverständnisse," in: *Die Furche* 46/1967; * 61

"Fast ein Anschlag," in: *Die Furche* 49/1967

"Netz mit Lücken" [discussion about the Vienna subway planning Wiener], in: *Freiheit – Magazin des ÖAAB*, 26 January 1967

"Für eine neue Großstadt," in: *Politische Perspektiven* 10/1967; * 41–43

"Das Kolleg St. Josef in Salzburg-Aigen," in: *bauforum* 1967; "Das Kloster in Aigen" * 54–55

"Das Wiener U-Bahnnetz als Entwurfsproblem und Trends in der Bautechnik," in: *bauforum* 1–2/1968; *Architektur & Bau Forum* 192, January/February 1998, 32–35

"Zum Funkhaus-Wettbewerb," in: *bauforum* 5–6/1968

"Eine Welt erfrischend jung. Konvulsionen der Architekturtheorie," in: *manuskripte* (Graz) 25, 1969, 43–45; * 64–68; also in: *The Austrian Phenomenon. Architektur Avantgarde Österreich 1956–1973*, edited by Architekturzentrum Wien, Basel: Birkhäuser, 2009, 909–912, as well as "A World Refreshingly Young," in the English accompanying volume, *The Austrian Phenomenon. Architecture Avantgarde Austria 1956–1973*,

173–176, and in: Hermann Czech: *Essays on Architecture and City Planning*, edited and translated by Elise Feiersinger, Zurich: Park Books, 2019, 77–90 [Engl.]

"Räumlicher Städtebau" [contribution to *Trigon '69*, as well as to the Austrian Architecture Congress, Payerbach 1970]; * 84

Edition: *Loos–Hoffmann = Bau* 1/1970 (responsible for the Loos section)

"Wien 1 Franziskanerplatz," in: *Bauwelt* (Berlin) 43/1975, 1206

"Der Loos-Gedanke," in: *Bau* 1/1970; * 69–72; as well as: "The Loos Idea," in: *a+u* 5/1978, 47–54 [Engl./Jap.]

"Josef Frank," 1970, unpublished; imprint in: *Archetype* (San Francisco) IV/1980 [Engl.], as well as in: *Lotus International* (Milan) 29/1981, 108–110 [Engl./Ital.]

"Otto Wagners Verkehrsbauwerk," in: *protokolle* 71/1, 182–191; * 24–31; also in: Richard Reichensperger (ed.): *Vorfreude Wien. Literarische Warnungen 1945–1995*, Frankfurt: Fischer, 1995, 107–116

"Nur keine Panik," in: *protokolle* 71 /2; * 63; numerous reprints, inter alia, in: *Baumeister* 11 /1992; in: Vittorio Magnago Lampugnani et al. (eds.): *Architekturtheorie 20. Jahrhundert*, Ostfildern-Ruit: Hatje Cantz, 2004; "No Need for Panic," in: Stefan Gruber et al. (eds.): *Big!Bad?Modern: Four Mega-Buildings in Vienna*, Zurich; Park Books, 2015, 102–103, and in: Hermann Czech: *Essays on Architecture and City Planning*, edited and translated by Elise Feiersinger, Zurich: Park Books, 2019, 105–107 [Engl.]

"Zur Abwechslung," in: *architektur aktuell* 34, 1973; * 76–79; diverse reprints, inter alia, in: *archithese* (Zurich) 3/1982, 15–19; partial reproduction of the first printing with annotations by Isabella Marboe ("Reflexiv avantgardistisch") in: *architektur aktuell* 446, 5/2017, 156–157; "For a Change," in: *A New Wave of Austrian Architecture*, 1980, 59–60 and in: Hermann Czech: *Essays on Architecture and City Planning*, edited and translated by Elise Feiersinger, Zurich: Park Books, 2019, 109–115 [Engl.]

"Innere Stadterweiterung," in: *architektur aktuell* 42, 1974; * 85–88

"Die Sprache Otto Wagners," in: *protokolle* 74/1; * 73–76; as well as: "The Work and Diction of Otto Wagner," in: *a+u* (Tokyo) 7/1977, 45–66 [Engl./Jap.]

"Wien 1 Franziskanerplatz," in: *Bauwelt* (Berlin) 43/1975, 1206

"Otto Wagner's Vienna Metropolitan Railway," in: *a+u* (Tokyo) 7/1976, 11–20 [Engl./Jap.] and in: Hermann Czech: *Essays on Architecture and City Planning*, edited and translated by Elise Feiersinger, Zurich: Park Books, 2019, 19–38 [Engl.]; German: "Otto Wagners Wiener Stadtbahn" (revised translation) in: Alfred Fogarassy (ed.): *Otto Wagner. Die Wiener Stadtbahn*, Berlin: Hatje Cantz, 2017, 9–15

"A Newly Discovered Bank by Adolf Loos Restored in Vienna," in: *a+u* (Tokyo) 68/1976, 17–20 [Engl./Jap.]

"Preserving Modern Architecture – Otto Wagner's Vienna Postal Savings Bank," in: *a+u* (Tokyo) 72, 12:1976, 13–16 [Engl./Jap.]

"Mehrschichtigkeit," in: *Bauen+Wohnen* 4/1977; * 79–80; numerous reprints, as well as "Pluralism," in: *A New Wave of Austrian Architecture*, 1980, 60 [Engl.]; "Stratificazioni," in: *Gran Bazaar* (Milan) 5/1979, 113 [Ital.]

"Vienna: Complexity and Contradiction Stagnating," in: *a+u* (Tokyo) 8/1977 [Engl./Jap.]; Ger.: "Wien: Komplexität und Verhinderung," in: wbw 1–2/1982, 71–72

"Josef Frank," in: *Archetype* (San Francisco) IV/1980, 37–38

"Kärntner-American-Loos Bar. Studi per un restauro" and "Josef Frank: Die 13 Briefentwürfe für Dagmar Grill" [first publication without title and translation mistakes], in: *Lotus International* (Milan) 29/1981, 114–116 [Ital./Engl.]

"Standpunkte; Haus M., Schwechat N und Türkendenkmal, Perchtoldsdorf N," in: *archithese* (Zurich) 3-1982, 15–19

"Wien: Komplexität und Verhinderung," in: *wbw* 1–2/1982, 69. Jg., 71–72 [Ger., partially in Engl./Fr.]

"Haus M. Schwechat," in: *wbw* 1–2/1982, 69. Jg., 20–21 [Ger., partially in Engl./Fr.]

"Haus S.," in: *ARCH+* (Aachen) 73, 1984, 8

"Christopher Alexander und die Wiener Moderne," in: *ARCH+* (Aachen) 73, 1984, 63–65; * 95–99; "Christopher Alexander and Viennese Modernism" in: Hermann Czech: *Essays on Architecture and City Planning*, edited and translated by Elise Feiersinger, Zurich: Park Books, 2019, 135–148 [Engl.]

"Über die räumliche Wirkung von Spiegeln," in: *wbw* 6/1984, 71. Jg., 20–25 [Ger., partially in Engl./Fr.]

"Museum auf Zeit: zur Ausstellung 'von hier aus,' zwei Monate neue deutsche Kunst in Düsseldorf," in: *wbw* 12/1984, 71. Jg., 32–35 [Ger., partially in Engl./Fr.]

"Adolf Loos – Widersprüche und Aktualität," in: *Mitteilungsblatt Architektenkammer der Provinz Bozen*, 3/1984; diverse reprints and expansions [Ger./Ital.]

"Ins Auge sehen," in: *UMRISS* 2, 1985, 14–15; * 128–130

"Vorschläge zur Erstellung eines Ziel-, Bewertungs- und Arbeitskatalogs" [urban design of the Gürtel], in: *UM BAU* 9, 1985, 36–40

"Neu und Alt. Umbau des Restaurants im Palais Schwarzenberg," in: *wbw* 3/1985, 72. Jg., 26–31 [Ger., partially in Engl./Fr.]

"Ein Begriffsraster zur aktuellen Interpretation Josef Franks," in: *UM BAU* 10 [Josef Frank-Symposium der ÖGfA], 1986; * 111–122; various reprints, inter alia, in: Iris Meder (ed.): *Josef Frank. Eine Moderne der Unordnung*, Salzburg: Anton Pustet, 2008, 76–89; "Ett utkast till en modern tolkning av Josef Frank," in: Mikael Bergquist; Olof Michélsen (eds.): *Josef Frank – arkitektur*, Stockholm 1994, 42–53, "Ett sätt att förstå Josef Frank idag," in: *arkitektur* (Stockholm) 3/1986, 28–29 [Swed.]; "Per una interpretazione attuale di Josef Frank," in: Hermann Czech (ed.): Josef Frank: *Architettura come simbolo*, Bologna: Zanichelli, 1986, VII – XXIX [Ital.]; "A Mode for the Current Interpretation of Josef Frank," in: *a+u* (Tokyo) 11 /1991, 20–37 [Engl./Jap.]; "A Conceptual Matrix for the Current Interpretation of Josef Frank" in: Hermann Czech: *Essays on Architecture and City Planning*, edited and translated by Elise Feiersinger, Zurich: Park Books, 2019, 151–182 [Engl.]

"Modernity and/or Urbanity. Presentation of personal work," in: *Texten. Colloquium Architectuur* ("Modernisme en de Stad"), 1986, 57–78

"Architektur und Kaffeehaus," in: *Space Design* 11/1988; * 123–124

"On Rigour," in: *9H* (London) 8, 1989, 72–73

"15 Jahre Zeitschrift 'wettbewerbe,'" in: *wettbewerbe* 113/114, 1992; * 138

"Das Schweigen als architektonische Botschaft. Wohnhaus in Wien 3," in: *architektur aktuell* 135, February 1990, 93–96

"Volksschule der Stadt Wien 'Rosa-Jochmann-Schule,'" in: *Zement Beton* 1/1995

"Selbstkritiker der Moderne: Josef Frank," in: *Der Architekt* 1/1996, 27–30

"Alles ist Umbau" [reprint with text excerpts from 1973, 1977, 1983, 1985, 1990], in: *wbw* 3/1998, 85. Jg., 4–11 [Ger., partially in Engl./Fr.]

"Konkret, abstrakt," in: *wbw* 11/1998, 85. Jg., 38–43 [Ger., partially in Engl./Fr.]

"Detail ist immer etwas anderes "("Le détail est toujours autre chose"), in: *l'architecture d'aujourd'hui* (Paris) 322, 1999, 56–59

"Das Arbeitsamt Liesing. E. A. Plischke 1930-31," in: *UmBau* 17, 2000, 68–75

"Ornament or Complexity" ("La forme d'une idée"), in: *l'architecture d'aujourd'hui* (Paris) 333, 2001, 94–95 [Engl./Fr.]

"Denkmal als Hindernis. Die ehemalige Reithalle ist das Übel. Sie ist es, die das Wiener Museumsquartier im Innersten nicht zusammenhält," in: *architektur aktuell* 10, 2001, 59–61

"Haus 9" [with plans], in: Architekturzentrum Wien (ed.): *hintergrund* 16/2002, 64–67 (= Sondernummer: 9=12 Neues Wohnen in Wien)

"Komfort – ein Gegenstand der Architekturtheorie?" [with excerpts from "Komfort und Modernität" 1997 and "Das Lokal" 2001], in: *wbw* 3/2003, 90. Jg., 10–15 [Ger., partially in Engl./Fr.]

"Hotel Messe Wien," in: ÖGfA 3/05, 6

"'Wo Lager war, soll Stadt werden.' Das Gutachterverfahren Oranienburg 1992/93," in: *Österr. Zeitschrift für Denkmalpflege* Jg. LXI, 1/2007 (= Tagungsband Erbe verweigert. Österreich und NS-Architektur), 68–81; also in: *Ästhetik und Kommunikation* (Berlin) 143, Winter 2008, 54–68

"Architektur, von der Produktion her gedacht," in: Architekturzentrum Wien (ed.): *Hintergrund* 41, 2009, 20–37 [= 16th Vienna Architecture Congress: The Making of Architecture]

Untitled, in: Architekturzentrum Wien (ed.): *Hintergrund* 46–47, 2010 (= Friedrich Achleitner 80), 38–39

Untitled / "A drawing's purpose in architecture…," in: Wesselenyi-Garay (ed.): *BorderLINE architecture*; 12th International Architecture Exhibition – La Biennale di Venezia, Hungarian Pavilion, Budapest: Mücsarnok/Hall of Art Budapest, 2010, 306–309 [Engl./Hung.]

"Vergabe einer geistig-schöpferischen Leistung. Umbau Parlamentssaal: ein Wettbewerbserfolg," in: *Architektur und BauFORUM* 15/2010, 1–2

(Selection and co-editor): "Feature Hermann Czech" = *a+u* 554, 16:11, 2016, 24–143, editor Christian Kühn [Engl./Jap.]

Films

Screenplay to the television film on Roland Rainer's city planning (with Jakob Laub), 1961

Otto Wagner, preparations for a (never realized) documentary film 1961–1963

Ins Leere gesprochen. Der Architekt Adolf Loos, documentary film, 35 mm, 20 min. 1970

Conversations and Interviews

"Was ist Ihre Kunst im speziellen?" [interview by Shinichi Eto; as well as House M., Villa Pflaum Addition], in: *Urban Housing* (Tokyo), Focus: New Wave in Vienna, 4/1983; * 91–94

"Zur Wientalbrücke" [conversation with Werner Korn], in: *Falter* 9/1983; * 100–104

"Ein Gespräch mit Hermann Czech" [by Markus Brüderlin], in: *Falter* 23/1984, 23

"Was bedeutet 'postmodern'" [survey response], in: *FORUM* 379–380, 1985, 29; * 110

"Theoretisch artikuliert sich die Wiener Szene nicht mehr. Wien – Graz" [interview by Leopold Dungl], in: *architektur aktuell* 125, 1991

"…so wie es war" [conversation with Franz E. Kneissl on the occasion of the Architecture Museum exhibition in Basel], in: *architektur aktuell* 192, 1996, 48–61

"Arena. Czech med täckning" [conversation with Mikael Bergquist], in: *Arkitektur* (Stockholm) 3/2000, 36–40 [Swed.]

"Lokaltermin in Wien" [conversation with Axel Simon], in: *archithese* (Zurich) 31_2001, 32–35

"Von der Elastizität des Holzes. Im Gespräch – Czech Eichinger Ritter," in: *zuschnitt* 5, March 2002, 20–22

"Die Ausstellung tappt in eine Falle" [interview by Matthias Dusini about The Austrian Phenomenon], in: *Falter* 16/2004, 22 and 5

"Sechs Statements zur Gegenwart und Zukunft der Entwurfsausbildung" [interview – response], in: *TransParent* 14, December 2005, 104–105

"Nein, um Gottes Willen, keinen Bezug zum Wein" [interview by Christoph Mayr Fingerle about the Weinhaus Kaltern], in: wein.kaltern GenmbH (ed.): *PUNKT*, Kaltern, 2006

Interview mit Hermann Czech, in: *Displayer* 01/2007, hfg Karlsruhe, 54–58

Interview "Architektur ist nicht das Leben," in: *a3 BAU* 11/2008, 24–26 (Mödling)

"'Bedingungen für das Verhalten von Gästen,' Hermann Czech im Gespräch mit Wolfgang Kos," in: *Im Wirtshaus. Eine Geschichte der Wiener Geselligkeit* (exhibition catalog), Vienna: Wien Museum, 2007

"'Er hat ihnen dort einen Gedanken hingebaut.' Hermann Czech und Adolf Krischanitz im Gespräch mit Bernhard Langer und Elli Mosayebi," in: Ákos Moravánszky; Bernhard Langer; Elli Mosayebi (eds.): *Adolf Loos. Die Kultivierung der Architektur*, Zurich: gta, 2008, 23–32

"Vienna: Gabriele Kaiser Talks to Hermann Czech about His Conversion of a Baroque Apartment Building into a Single Family House – Interview," in: *Architecture Today* (London) 189, 06-2008, 24–28, 31

"Alles in allem. Hermann Czech und Adolf Krischanitz im Gespräch/All Things Considered," in: *Adolf Krischanitz: Architektur ist der Unterschied zwischen Architektur/Architecture Is the Difference Between Architecture*, Ostfildern: Hatje Cantz, 2010, 204–213 [Ger./Engl.]

"Methoden der Verwirrung. Manuela Hötzl im Gespräch mit H. C."; in: *NiVo* (Niederurnen) 3/2014, 10–15; in the simultaneously appearing issues: "Ways to Cause Confusion"/"Méthodes destinées à susciter le désarroi" [Engl./Fr.]

"Mit dem Zufall planen" [interview by Christian Kühn], in: *Die Presse – Spectrum*, 9 January 2016

"Hermann Czech im Interview mit Axel Simon," in: *hochparterre* (Zurich) 3, 2016, 12–15

"Ich weiß nicht, was Wohnen ist" [conversation with Matthias Dusini], in: *Falter* 44/16, 31 October 2016

"Meister der Irritation" [interview by Wojciech Czaja], in: *Der Standard*, 12 November 2016

"'Von Dingen, die nach nichts ausschauen.' Ein Gespräch mit Hermann Czech, Wien," in: Tom Schoper: *Ein Haus. Werk – Ding – Zeug? Gespräche mit Gion A. Caminada, Hermann Czech, Tom Emerson, Hans Kollhoff, Valerio Olgiati*, Vienna: Passagen Verlag, 2016, 47–74

"'Das Phänomen Tür hat an gestalterischer Bedeutung verloren.' Hermann Czech und Arno Ritter diskutieren über die Tür, ihre Funktion, Gestaltung und Bedeutung in der Architektur," in: *zuschnitt* 68, December 2017, 14–15

"'Schluss mit der Wirklichkeit.' Walter Chramosta im Gespräch mit Hermann Czech," in: *Architektur & Bau FORUM* 11–12/2017, 6–7

Lectures and Interviews on the Internet

"A Palaver," Radio Orange FM 94.00, April 2006, conversation with David Pasek and Bernhard Frodl <o94.at> [November 2017]

"Lecture on 'Cafés' by Hermann Czech," 13 December 2007, 3 parts at: <https://www.youtube.com/watch?v=4Lig8Uc8_uk>, <https://www.youtube.com/watch?v=Z5sOkmSvfd4>, https://www.youtube.com/watch?v=jvZY8v-S85w> [November 2017]

"Hermann Czech. PORT_RE 11," in: *miesmagazin*, contribution by Arian Lehner, Dominik Kastner, Paula Brücke, 2012, <https://www.youtube.com/watch?v=YfHIJTzgZiU> [November 2017]

"Hermann Czech: Überlegungen zu Josef Frank und Against Design," MAK-Video 2016, at: <https://www.youtube.com/ watch?v=vsc3owJeIDc> [November 2017]

"Eröffnungsrede von Hermann Czech zur Ausstellung von Jakob Laub," Rondell Gallery, 8/2017, at:

<https://www.youtube.com/watch?v=Hda5o9HJzhg> [November 2017]

Articles on and Critiques of Hermann Czech and His Work

Achleitner, Friedrich: "Wiener Positionen," in: *UM BAU* 3, December 1980, 19–37

Achleitner, Friedrich: "Franks Weiterwirken in der neueren Wiener Architektur," in: *UM BAU* 10, August 1986, 121–131

Achleitner, Friedrich: "Hermann Czech. Laudatio," in: *Kunstpreis Berlin 2001*, Akademie der Künste, Berlin 2001; reprinted in: idem: *Wie entwirft man einen Architekten? Porträts von Aalto bis Zumthor*, edited by Eva Guttmann; Gabriele Kaiser; Claudia Mazanek, Zurich: Park Books, 2015, 39–44

Adam, Hubertus: "Im Zentrum ein Park. Marcel Meili und Markus Peter: Seminarraum und Gästehaus der Swiss Re, Rüschlikon, 1995–2000," in: *archithese* (Zurich) 31, 1/2001, 44–49

Bachmann, Wolfgang: "Wiener Klima. Aus einem Reisetagebuch," in: *Bauwelt* (Berlin) 76, 15 February 1985, 208–241

Bergquist, Mikael: "Svar på tilltal" ["Answers – Hermann Czech"], in: *Arkitektur* (Stockholm) 5/1996, 38–43 [Swed.]

Bizot, Jean François: "Die Wiener Krankheit," in: *Wiener*, November 1983, 22–27; simultaneously also in Dutch/Engl./Fr./Ital./Span.

Boeckl, Matthias: "Hermann Czech. Hotel Messe Wien, Austria," in: *architektur aktuell* 11.2005, 106–115 [Ger./Engl.]

Brooker, Graeme: *Key Interiors Since 1900*, London: Laurence King, 2013, 188–191 [MAK Café]

Brüderlin, Markus: "Märkischer Sand in Sandkasten" [*von hier aus*], in: *Falter* 23/1984, 22

Celsing, Johan: "The Robust, the Sincere," in: *Nordic Architects Write*, edited by Michael Asgaard Andersen, Abington and New York: Routledge, 2008, 390–399; Danish in: *Arkitekten* (Copenhagen) July 2010, 24–27

Chramosta, Walter: "Für den zweiten Blick," in: idem (ed.): *Rosa Jochmann Schule, Wien 11. Hermann Czech*, Vienna: Stadtplanung Wien MA19, 1994

Christoph, Horst: "Gegen die Klachel," in: *profil* 27, 30 June 1980, 50–51

Cladenby, Claes: "Wien genom tre," in: *Arkitektur* (Stockholm) 3 April 1986, 3–9 [Swed.]

Czaja, Wojciech: "Kein großes, weißes Rauschen" [Hotel Messe Wien], in: *Der Standard – Album*, 23 July 2005

Czaja, Wojciech: "Die nackte Wahrheit" [Model Estate Hadersdorf], in: *Der Standard – Album*, 6 October 2007

Domin, Maria: "Umbauten. Der Architekt Hermann Czech," in: *Wolkenkratzer* (Frankfurt) April–May 1984, 86–87

Elser, Oliver: "Hotel ist Hintergrund," in: *Frankfurter Allgemeine Zeitung*, 197, 25 August 2005, 34

Feller, Barbara: "Dichtes Wohnen am Stadtrand," in: *Deutsche Bauzeitung* (Stuttgart) 142, 6/2008, 16–18

Fischer, Holger: "Der Stillosigkeit ein Gesicht geben: Hermann Czech-Ausstellung in Basel," in: *Deutsche Bauzeitung* (Stuttgart) 130, 8/1996, 20

Fleck, Robert: "Zur ästhetischen Konstellation in Wien um 1968," in: idem: *Avantgarde in Wien*, Vienna: Löcker, 1982, 595–599

Floris, Job: "Notion on the Work of Hermann Czech," in: *OASE* (Rotterdam) 86/2011, 100–107 [Dutch/Engl.]

Froehlich, Dietmar E.; Williams Celeste M.: "Czech, Hermann 1936 – Architect, Austria," in: *Encyclopedia of 20th Century Architecture*, edited by R. Stephen Sennott, New York and London: Fitzroy Dearborn, 2004, Vol. 1, 337–340

Gassner, Robert: "Family Portrait with House / Familienbild mit Haus," in: *Candide – Journal for Architectural Knowledge* (Ostfildern) 1, December 2009, 117–140 [Ger./Engl.]

Gerngross, Heidulf: "Hermann Czech. Bauten und Projekte/Buildings and Projects = Buch XV – Hermann Czech," in: *ST/A/R* 07/2005, 113–120

Gijsberts, Pieter Jan: "Architectuur als Achtergrond: Theorie en Werk van Hermann Czech," in: *de Architect* (The Hague) 21, 11/1990, 60–71 [Dutch]

Gijsberts, Pieter Jan: "Umbau," in: *archis* (Doetinchem), April 1994, 38–43 [Dutch/Engl.]

Grafe, Christoph: "MAK Café, Vienna" (1993), in: *Cafés and Bars. The Architecture of Public Display*, edited by Christoph Grafe; Franziska Bollerey, New York and London: Routledge, 2007, 196–199 [Engl.]

Grimmer, Vera: "Change as a Principle. Generations-Housing on Mühlgrund, Vienna, Austria: Hermann Czech, Adolf Krischanitz, Werner Neuwirth," in: *Oris* (Zagreb) 18, 99/2016, 66–79 [Croat./Engl.]

Grimoldi, Alberto: "Critica di Adolf Loos e architettura contemporanea," in: *Ottagono* (Milan) 65, June 1982, 20–28 [Ital., partially in Engl.]

Grimus, Elisabeth: Hermann Czech: *Interventionen 1962–1984. Lokale in Wien*, Diploma Thesis, University of Vienna, 2008

Gross, Alan G.: "Presence as Argument in the Public Sphere" (on the historical exhibition Vienna 1938), in: *RSQ Rhetoric Society Quarterly* (Provo, UT) 35, No. 2, Spring 2005, 5–21

Grubbauer, Eva: "Das Konkrete als der besondere Fall bei Adolf Loos und Hermann Czech," in: *Das Konkrete und die Architektur*, 14. Jg., Heft 1, October 2009 <www.cloud-cuckoo.net>

Helsing Almaas, Ingerid: "MAK-Café. Hermann Czech," in: idem: *Vienna – Objects and Rituals = Architecture in Context*, Cologne: Ellipsis Könemann, 1997, 24–35 [Ger./Engl./Fr.]

Hrausky, Andrej: "Hermann Czech," in: *ab = arkitektov bilten* (Ljubljana) 70/1984, 30–33 [Sloven.]

Hubeli, Ernst; Luchsinger, Christoph: "Hermann Czech – Das architektonische Objekt," in: *wbw* 6/1996, 2–7 [Ger./Engl./Fr.]

Isasi, Justo F.: "Viena 9=12. Una Colonia Modelo"/ "Vienna 9=12. A Siedlung Prototype," in: *AV monografías 97, Vivienda urbana/Urban Housing*, 9_2002, 4–7 [Engl./Span.]

Jaehle-Schulte-Strathaus, Ulrike: "'In welchem Style sollen wir bauen?' Gedanken zur Stil-losigkeit von Hermann Czech," in: *wbw* 6/1996, 9–11

Kapfinger, Otto: "Hommage an das Alltägliche. Dargestellt am Beispiel eines Hauses von Hermann Czech in Schwechat," in: *Die Presse – Spectrum*, 10/11/12 April 1982

Kapfinger, Otto: "Wie ist das mit Josef Frank?," in: *archithese* (Zurich) 3/1982, 11–14, 54

Kapfinger, Otto: "Is it beautiful? Is it modern?," in: *Hermann Czech. Options in Architecture* (exhibition catalog), London: 9H Gallery, 1987 [Engl.]

Kapfinger, Otto: "Hermann Czech," in: *Wiener Festwochen* 1989, 50

Kapfinger, Otto: "Hermann Czech," in: *O. K.: ausgesprochen. Reden zur Architektur*, Salzburg and Vienna: Anton Pustet, Architekturzentrum Wien, 1999, 64–71

Kapfinger, Otto: "Hermann Czech zum 80er," in: *architektur aktuell* <https://www.architektur-aktuell.at/news/hermann-czech-zum-80er>, 9 November 2016

Kapfinger, Otto; Kneissl, Franz E.: *Dichte Packung. Architektur aus Wien*, Salzburg and Vienna: Residenz, 1989

Kohoutek, Rudolf: "When the background comes to the fore," in: *Hermann Czech. Options in Architecture* (exhibition catalog), London: 9H Gallery, 1987 [Engl.]

Kohoutek, Rudolf: "Weniger Humor, mehr Schmäh. Wiener Architektur-Avantgarden 1958–1973," in: Irene Suchy (ed.): *Schmäh als ästhetische Strategie der Wiener Avantgarden*, Weitra: Bibliothek der Provinz, 2015, 74–120

Krischanitz, Adolf: "Wiener Klima," in: *UM BAU* 3, December 1980, 4–6

Krischanitz, Adolf: "Hermann Czechs Arbeiten sind anders," in: *Kulturpreisträger des Landes Niederösterreich 1998*, St. Pölten, 1998, 28–29

Kühn, Christian: "Architektur nach 1945 – Entweder, oder. Oder dazwischen," in: *Parnass* 18/2001 ("Wegbereiter"), 96–105

Kühn, Christian: "Hochhaushoher Manierismus. Hermann Czechs Beitrag zur Typologie des Wolkenkratzers," in: *UmBau* 20, May 2003, 17–21

Kühn, Christian: "Wie im Wilden Westen" [Am Mühlgrund], in: *Die Presse – Spectrum*, 17 March 2012

Kühn, Christian (author and editor): "Hermann Czech and the Disappearance of Architecture," in: *a+u* (Tokyo) 554, 16:11, "Feature: Hermann Czech," 2016, 11–15, 16–23, 24–143 [Engl./Jap.]

Kurrent, Friedrich: "Hermann Czech 70," in: idem: *Einige Projekte, Architekturtexte und dergleichen*, Salzburg and Vienna: Müry Salzmann, 2016, 43–44

Lösel, Anja: "Hermann Czech, Ausstellungsarchitekt," in: *art* (Hamburg) 11, November 1986, 63

Mayer, Thomas: "Café Präsenz" [Theatercafé], in: *UmBau* 21, June 2004, 25–28

Menasse, Eva: "Seine Cafés sind immer voll: Der Architekt Hermann Czech" [Berliner Kunstpreis], in: *Frankfurter Allgemeine Zeitung*, 18 March 2001

Meyhofer, Dirk: "Stille Konzepte: Hermann Czech," in: *architektur & wohnen* (Hamburg) 2, 27 March 1985, 68

N.N.: "Hermann Czech," in: *Vogue* (Munich) 7/1984, 169

N.N.: "Hermann Czech: Salzamt; Palais Schwarzenberg; Haus S.," in: *Bauwelt* (Berlin) 76, 15 February 1985, 222–225

N.N.: "Hermann Czech," in: *l'architecture d'aujourd'hui* 09/1989, 111 [Fr.]

N.N.: "Oranienburg: 'Urbanisierung' eines ehemaligen Kasernengeländes," in: *Bauwelt* (Berlin) 84, 14–15/1993, 704–705

N.N.: "Schulgebäude Fuchsröhrenstraße, Wien," in: *Planen Bauen Wohnen* 151/1994, 64–65

N.N.: "Lapidare Zufälligkeiten: Zur Rosa-Jochmann-Schule von Hermann Czech (mit Wolfgang Reder)," in: *Architektur & Bauforum* 27, 167/1994, 115–121

N.N.: "Hermann Czech (1941, Vienne)"; in: *Dictionnaire de l'Architecture du XXème siècle*, Paris: Hazan/Institut Français de Architecture, 1996, 227–228

N.N.: "Exposition Schubert au Musée Historique de Vienne," in: *l'architecture d'aujourd'hui* (Paris) 05/1999, 58–59 [Fr.]

N.N.: "Ehemaliges Arbeitsamt in Liesing," in: *A+D Architecture and Detail* 6, 14/2000, 7

N.N.: "Raum Im Raum – Kinderzimmer in Wien (1971): Hermann Czech," in: *Baumeister* (Munich) 107, 3/2010, 58–61

N.N.: "Spuntini, Stuzzichini oder Cicchetti? Italienische Köstlichkeiten im Ambiente von Hermann Czech," in: *CUBE Magazin*, 4/2016, 58

nextroom – <https://www.nextroom.at> [Hermann Czech and various buildings]

Ring, Romana: "'Weil im Grunde alles Umbau ist.' Hermann Czech zum 80. Geburtstag: eine Textcollage," in: *Die Presse – Spectrum*, 4 November 2016

Ritter, Arno: "Warum? – Warum nicht?," in: Czech 1996, 151–154

Ritter, Arno: "In Ambivalenz. Eine gedankliche Annäherung an Hermann Czech," in: *wbw* 6/1996, 64–67

Safran, Yehuda E.: "Una camera per lei" / "A room of her own," in: *Ottagono* (Milan) 112/1994, 37–40 [Engl./Ital.]

Schumann, Ulrich Maximilian: "Czech, Hermann," in: *Lexikon der Architektur des 20. Jahrhunderts*, edited by Vittorio Magnago Lampugnani, Ostfildern-Ruit: Hatje, 1998, 72–73

Simon, Axel: "Seltenleer und Immervoll: Hermann Czech, Theatercafé, 1998 und Café Immervoll, 2000 Wien," in: *archithese* (Zurich) 31, 05/2001, 36–39

Simon, Axel: "Schwierige Architekten und intelligente Gasträume," in: *Hochparterre* (Zurich) 1–2/2005, 18. Jg., 61

Simon, Axel: "Räume mit Reserven: Weinhaus PUNKT und Bar zum Lustigen Krokodil," in: *Bauwelt* (Berlin) 97, 35/2006, 32–35

Simon, Axel: "Hotel Messe Wien," in: *Baumeister* (Munich) 103, 7/2006, 18–19

Sowa, Axel: "Stichwortgeber / Cue-Giver Hermann Czech," in: *Candide – Journal for Architectural Knowledge* (Ostfildern) 8/2014, 89–108 [Ger./Engl.]

Steiner, Dietmar: "An Amalgam of Adaption and Rejection: On the Continuity of Viennese Architecture," in: *9H* (London) 5/1983, 87–89 [Engl.]

Steiner, Dietmar: "Jedes Detail eine Geschichte. Wee Willie Winkie's World in Wien," in: *archithese* (Zurich) 4/1983, 3–10

Steiner, Dietmar: "Sie redet nur, wenn sie gefragt wird. Der Siegeszug einer neuen Wiener Architektur," in: *Die Presse – Spectrum* 9/10 April 1983

Steiner, Dietmar: "Der Besucher als Tourist, der Gast ein Künstler. Eine Düsseldorfer Kunstausstellung und das umgebaute Palais Schwarzenberg von Hermann Czech," in: *Die Presse – Spectrum* 27/28 October 1984

Steiner, Dietmar: "Unter der Bilderhaut. Versuch einer Einkreisung der 'Wiener Szene,'" in: *Bauwelt* (Berlin) 76, 15 February 1985, 242–244

Steiner, Dietmar: "Beyond Vienna," in: Wilfried Wang (ed.): *Emerging European Architects*, Cambridge, MA: Harvard University Press, 1988, 92–94 [Engl.]

Temel, Robert: "Mustersiedlung '9=12' in Wien-Hadersdorf/Model Estate '9=12' in Vienna-Hadersdorf," in: *architektur aktuell* 333, December 2007, 124–135 [Ger./Engl.]

Thalmann, Jay Renée: *Annäherung an die Wirklichkeit. Zum Architekturverständnis von Hermann Czech*, Master Thesis, gta, ETH Zurich, 2013

Thor, Clas: "Möten med Josef Frank" ["Encounter with JF"], in: *Wien – drömmarnas stad*, Stockholm: Ordfronts förlag, 1994, 181–189 [Swed.]

Thurn und Taxis, Lilli: "Museum für angewandte Kunst in Wien. Ein Geschmacksbildungsinstitut erneuert sich," in: *Baumeister* (Munich) 9/1992, 34–38

Thurnher, Armin: "Neu: Salzamt. Antworten an Hermann Czech," in: *Falter* 23/1983, 14

Ulama, Margit: "Lapidare Zufälligkeiten. Zur Rosa-Jochmann-Schule von Hermann Czech (mit Wolfgang Reder)," in *Architektur & Bauforum*, 167/1994, 115–121

Ulama, Margit: *Reflexion in Architektur. Neuere Wiener Beispiele*, Vienna: Löcker, 1995

Ulama, Margit: "Die Ambivalenz des Denkens. Hermann Czechs Architekturphilosophie und seine jüngsten Bauten in Wien/The Ambivalence of Thought," in: *architektur aktuell* 209/1997, 72–83 [Ger./Engl.]

Ulama, Margit: "Abseits der Moden. Das eigenwillige Œuvre des Wieners Hermann Czech," in: *Neue Zürcher Zeitung* 231, 6 October 1997, 27; reprinted in: idem: *Architektur als Antinomie. Aktuelle Tendenzen und Positionen*, Vienna and Bolzano: Folio, 2002, 131–135

Vah, Sarah (= Dietmar Steiner): "Architektur ist Hintergrund. Hermann Czech," in: *Wiener*, 10 October 1980, 28–33

Vass, Andreas: "Zu Hermann Czechs Text 'Der Umbau,'" in: *UMBAU* 29, 2017, 14–25

Waechter-Böhm, Liesbeth: "Aufbruch zur Unbeweglichkeit," in: *Die Presse – Spectrum*, 9 January 1993

Waechter-Böhm, Liesbeth: "Ein Finger mit Gymnastikraum" [new school construction in Simmering], in: *Die Presse – Spectrum*, 10 September 1994

Waechter-Böhm, Liesbeth: "Häuser mit Salettl. Wohnbebauung Brunnergasse in Perchtoldsdorf," in: *architektur aktuell* 171, September 1994, 18–22

Zschokke, Walter: "Nicht nur zur Abwechslung" [Oranienburg], in: *Die Presse – Spectrum*, 11 January 1997

Zschokke, Walter: "Zaubern mit Details" [Weinhaus Punkt], in: *Die Presse – Spectrum*, 28 June 2007

Zschokke, Walter: "Zeitgemässes Wohnen in Beton: Mustersiedlung mit zehn Mehrfamilienhäusern in Wien-Hadersdorf," in: *wbw* 4/2008, 22–29

Sources Used

A New Wave of Austrian Architecture, Preface by Kenneth Frampton, IAUS – Institute for Architecture and Urban Studies New York, Catalogue 13, New York: IAUS, 1980

Achleitner, Friedrich: Zeitungsartikel 1960–1970, Austrian National Library Archive

Achleitner, Friedrich: *Österreichische Architektur im 20. Jahrhundert. Ein Führer in vier (fünf) Bänden*, Salzburg and Vienna: Residenz, 1980–2010

Achleitner, Friedrich: "Franks Weiterwirken in der neuen Wiener Architektur," in: *UM BAU* 10, 1986, 121–131

Achleitner, Friedrich: *Aufforderung zum Vertrauen. Aufsätze zur Architektur*, Salzburg and Vienna: Residenz, 1987

Achleitner, Friedrich: *Die rückwärtsgewandte Utopie: Motor des Fortschritts in der Wiener Architektur?*, Vienna: Picus, 1993

Achleitner, Friedrich: *Wiener Architektur. Zwischen typologischem Fatalismus und semantischem Schlamassel*, Vienna: Böhlau, 1996

Achleitner, Friedrich: "Rund um die arbeitsgruppe 4," in: Pisarik; Waditschatka (eds.): *arbeitsgruppe 4*, 2010, 6–9

Adorno, Theodor W.: *Ohne Leitbild. Parva Aesthetica*, Frankfurt: Suhrkamp, 1967

Alexander, Christopher: *Notes on the Synthesis of Form*, Cambridge, MA: Harvard University Press, 1964

Alexander, Christopher: "A City is Not a Tree" (1965); Ger.: "Die Stadt ist kein Baum," in: *Bauen+Wohnen* 21, July 1967, 283–290

Alexander, Christopher: *Das Linz Café/The Linz Café*, Vienna, London and Cambridge, MA: Löcker/Oxford University Press, 1981

Alexander, Christopher et al.: *A Pattern Language: Towns, Buildings, Construction*, New York and London: Oxford University Press, 1977; Ger.: *Eine Muster-Sprache. Städte Gebäude Konstruktion*, edited and with an afterword by Hermann Czech, Vienna: Löcker, 1995

Alofsin, Anthony: *When Buildings Speak, Architecture as Language in the Habsburg Empire and Its Aftermath, 1867–1933*, Chicago: University of Chicago Press, 2006

Anderson, Stanford: "Sachlichkeit and Modernity, or Realist Architecture," in: Mallgrave (ed.): *Otto Wagner*, 1993, 323–360

arbeitsgruppe 4: *Wien der Zukunft* (exhibition catalog), Vienna, 1964

Ashby, Charlotte; Gronberg, Tag; Shaw Miller, Simon (eds.): *The Viennese Café and Fin-de-Siècle Culture* = Austrian and Habsburg Studies, Vol. 16, New York and Oxford: Berghahn Books, 2013

Aynsley, Jeremy: "Graphic and Interior Design in the Viennese Coffeehouse around 1900," in: Ashby et al. (eds.): *The Viennese Café and Fin-de-Siècle Culture*, 2013, 158–177

Bau 1963–1970, Vienna

Bauen+Wohnen 9/1965: Österreich baut, Zurich

Bauer, Ute: *Die Wiener Flaktürme im Spiegel der österreichischen Erinnerungskultur*, Vienna: Phoibos, 2003

Bayer, Konrad: "hans carl artmann und die wiener dichtergruppe," in: Weibel (ed.): *die wiener gruppe*, 1997, 33–39; Engl.: "hans carl artmann and the viennese poets," trans. Tom Eppleton, in: ibid., 32–39

Bedoire, Fredric: *The Jewish Contribution to Modern Architecture*, Stockholm: KTAV Publishing House, 2004

Beller, Steven: *Vienna and the Jews, 1867–1938. A Cultural History*, Cambridge, MA: Cambridge University Press, 1989, paperback edition 1990

Benedikt, Heinrich (ed.): *Geschichte der Republik Österreich*, Munich: R. Oldenburg, 1954

Berghaus, Günter: "Happenings in Europe," in: Mariellen R. Sanford (ed.): *Happenings and Other Acts*, London and New York: Routledge, 2005

Bergquist, Mikael; Michélsen, Olof (eds.): *Josef Frank – Architektur*, Basel: Birkhäuser, 1995

Bergquist, Mikael; Michélsen, Olof: *Josef Frank, Falsterbovillorna*, Stockholm: Arkitektur Förlag, 1998

Bergquist, Mikael; Michélsen, Olof (eds.): *Accidentism. Josef Frank*, Basel: Birkhäuser, 2005

Blau, Eve: "Isotype and Architecture in Red Vienna: The Modern Projects of Otto Neurath and Josef Frank," in: Judith Beniston; Robert Vilain (eds.): *Culture and Politics in Red Vienna* = Austrian Studies, Vol. 14, Leeds: Maney Publishing for the Modern Humanities Research Association, 2006, 227–259

Blau, Eve: *The Architecture of Red Vienna 1919–1934*, Cambridge, MA: The MIT Press, 1999; Ger.: *Rotes Wien. Architektur 1919–1934. Stadt – Raum – Politik*, Vienna: Ambra, 2014

Bobek, Hans; Lichtenberger, Elisabeth: *Wien. Bauliche Gestalt und Entwicklung seit der Mitte des 19. Jahrhunderts*, Graz: Böhlau, 1966

Boeckl, Matthias: "Zeichen und Wunder. Die magische Form als Erfolgsmotor einiger zeitgenössischer Architekturwegbereiter aus Österreich," in: *Parnass* 18/2001, 106–115

Bonaparte, Marie: *Edgar Poe. Eine psychoanalytische Studie. Mit einem Vorwort von Sigmund Freud*, Vienna: Internationaler Psychoanalytischer Verlag, 1934

Brandstaller, Trautl: "Friedrich Heer und 'Die Furche' 1946–60," in: Richard Faber et al. (eds.): *Offener Humanismus zwischen den Fronten des Kalten Krieges. Über den Universalhistoriker, politischen Publizisten und religiösen Essayisten Friedrich Heer*, Wurzburg: Königshausen & Neumann, 2005

Breicha, Otto; Fritsch, Gerhard (eds.): *Aufforderung zum Mißtrauen*, Salzburg and Vienna: Residenz, 1967

Brenner, Anton: *Wirtschaftlich planen – Rationell bauen. Das Wohnungsproblem in all seinen Abarten*, Vienna: Ertl, 1951

Bürkle, Johann Christoph (ed.): *Mustersiedlung Hadersdorf. Neues Wohnen in Wien*, Sulgen: Niggli, 2009

Chamberlain, Sigrid: *Adolf Hitler, die deutsche Mutter und ihr erstes Kind*, Giessen: Psychosozial-Verlag, 1991

Chramosta, Walter M.: "Für den zweiten Blick," in: *Rosa-Jochmann-Schule. Ganztagsvolksschule*, hg. v. Stadtplanung Wien MA 19, *Projekte und Konzepte* Heft 1, 1994

Clair, Jean; Pichler, Cathrin; Pircher, Wolfgang: *Wunderblock. Eine Geschichte der modernen Seele*, KUNSTFORUM International, Bd. 101: *Bild und Seele*, 290f. See also: Jean Clair, Cathrin Pichler, Wolfgang Pircher (eds.): *Wunderblock. Eine Geschichte der modernen Seele* (exhibition catalog), Wiener Festwochen, Vienna: Löcker, 1989

Clair, Jean; Pichler, Cathrin; Pircher, Wolfgang: *Wunderblock. Eine Geschichte der modernen Seele*, KUNSTFORUM International, Bd. 101: *Bild und Seele*, 290. See also Sigmund Freud: "A Note Upon the 'Mystic Writing-Pad,'" in: James Strachey (ed.): *The Standard Edition of the Complete Psychological Works of Sigmund Freud: Volume XIX (1923–1925) The Ego and the Id and Other Works*, trans. James Strachey, London: Hogarth Press and The Institute of Psycho-Analysis, 1961, 227–232.

Colomina, Beatriz; Buckley, Craig (eds.): *Clip, Stamp, Fold. The Radical Architecture of Little Magazines. 196X to 197X*, M+M Books, Media and Modernity Program, Princeton University, Barcelona: Actar, 2010

Colomina, Beatriz: "Sex, Lügen und Dekoration: Adolf Loos und Gustav Klimt," in: Safran (ed.): *Adolf Loos. Unser Zeitgenosse*, 2012, 81–92

Dahms, Hans-Joachim; Stadler, Friedrich: "Die Philosophie an der Universität Wien von 1848 bis zur Gegenwart," in: Katharina Kniefacz et al. (eds.): *Universität – Forschung – Lehre. Themen und Perspektiven im langen 20. Jahrhundert*, Vienna: V&R unipress, 2015, 115–127

Design ist unsichtbar, Österreichisches Institut für visuelle Gestaltung Linz, Vienna: Löcker, 1981 *die Reihe*, Band 1: Elektronische Musik, Vienna, 1955

Eisenman, Peter: "Aspekte der Moderne: Die Maison Dom-ino und das selbst referentielle Zeichen," in: idem: *Aura und Exzeß. Zur Überwindung der Metaphysik der Architektur*, Vienna: Passagen, 1995, 43–63

Enengl, Claudia: *Johann Georg Gsteu. Architektur sichtbar und spürbar machen*, Salzburg: Anton Pustet, 2010

Englert, Uwe: *Magus und Rechenmeister. Henrik Ibsens Werk auf den Bühnen des Dritten Reiches* (= Beiträge zur nordischen Philologie 30), Tubingen and Basel: Francke, 2001

Ermarth, Michael (ed.): *Kurt Wolff: A Portrait in Essays and Letters*, trans. Deborah Lucas Schneider, Chicago: University of Chicago Press, 1991

Europa-Gespräch 1963, Wiener Schriften, Heft 20, hg. v. Amt für Kultur, Volksbildung und Schulverwaltung der Stadt Wien, Vienna: Jugend & Volk, 1964

EXPORT, VALIE; Weibel, Peter: *Wien: Bildkompendium Wiener Aktionismus und Film*, Frankfurt: Kohlkunstverlag, 1970

Faschingeder, Kristian (ed.): *Die Architektur der neuen Weltordnung / Architecture in the Age of Empire*, Bauhaus-Universität Weimar (= Tagungsband 11. Intern. Bauhaus Kolloquium Weimar 2009), Weimar: Bauhaus-Universitätsverlag, 2011

Fecht, Tom; Kamper, Dietmar (eds.): *Umzug ins Offene. Vier Versuche über den Raum*, Vienna: Springer, 2000

Feuerstein, Günther: *Klub*, Veröffentlichungen des Klubseminars, 1963ff

Feuerstein, Günther: *Visionäre Architektur in Wien 1958–1988*, Berlin: Ernst & Sohn, 1988

Feuerstein, Günther: *Visionary Architecture in Austria in the Sixties and Seventies* (exhibition catalog), Biennale di Venezia, 1996, Klagenfurt: Ritter Verlag, 1996

Fleck, Robert: *Avantgarde in Wien. Die Geschichte der Galerie nächst St. Stephan 1954–1982. Band 1: Die Chronik*, Vienna: Löcker, 1982

Flick, Uwe: *Qualitative Sozialforschung. Eine Einführung*, Reinbek bei Hamburg: Rowohlt, 2007

Frampton, Kenneth: "Preface," in: idem (ed.): *A New Wave of Austrian Architecture*, 1980, 1

Frank, Josef: "Über die ursprüngliche Gestalt der kirchlichen Bauten des Leone Battista Alberti" (1910), in: Frank 2012, Vol. 1, 47–119 [Ger./Engl.]

Frank, Josef: *Architektur als Symbol*, edited and index compiled by Hermann Czech, Vienna: Löcker, 1981ff; Engl., *Architecture as Symbol*, trans. John Sands, in: Frank 2012, Vol. 2, 9–191

Frank 2012 – Frank, Josef: *Schriften / Writings, Veröffentlichte Texte in zwei Bänden*, edited by Tano Bojankin, Christopher Long and Iris Meder, Vienna: Metro/Löcker, 2012/2017 [Ger./Engl.]

Frank, Philipp: *Einstein. Sein Leben und seine Zeit* (Engl. 1947), 1949

Freud, Sigmund: *Humor. The Standard Edition of the Complete Psychological Works of Sigmund Freud*, trans. James Strachey et al., London: Hogarth, 1964, Vol. 21, 160–166

Freud, Sigmund: *The Interpretation of Dreams*, translated and edited by James Strachey, London: Penguin Books, 1991, 336.

Friedell, Egon: *Kulturgeschichte der Neuzeit*, 1931; Engl.; *A Cultural History of the Modern Age. Volume III. The Crisis of the European Soul: From the Black Death to the World War*, trans. Charles Francis Atkinson, New York: Alfred A. Knopf, 1932

Frei, Hans: "Neuerdings Einfachheit," in: *minimal tradition. Max Bill und die "einfache" Architektur 1942–1996*, XIX. Triennale di Milano 1996, 113–131

Galison, Peter: "Aufbau/Bauhaus. Logischer Positivismus und architektonische Moderne" (Engl. 1990), in: *ARCH+* 156, 2001

Geretsegger, Heinz; Peintner, Max; Pichler, Walter: *Otto Wagner 1841–1918. Unbegrenzte Großstadt. Beginn der modernen Architektur*, Salzburg and Vienna: Residenz, 1964; Munich: dtv TB, 1980

Göderitz, Johannes; Rainer, Roland; Hoffmann, Hubert: *Die gegliederte und aufgelockerte Stadt*, Tubingen: Wasmuth, 1957

Gorsen, Peter: "Der Wiener Aktionismus: Begriff und Theorie," in: Werkner (eds.): *Kunst in Österreich 1945–1995*, 1996

Graf, Otto Antonia: *Otto Wagner*, 7 Bde., Vienna: Böhlau, 1985ff

Gredlinger, Paul: "Serial Technique," in: *die Reihe*, Bryn Mawr, PA: Theodore Presser Company/Universal Edition, 1958, 38–44

Grosegger, Elisabeth; Müller, Sabine (eds.): *Teststrecke Kunst: Wiener Avantgarden nach 1945*, Vienna: Sonderzahl, 2012

Gross, Alan G.: "Presence as Argument in the Public Sphere," in: *Rhetoric Society Quarterly*, Vol. 35, 2/2005, The Journal of the Rhetoric Society of America, Department of English, Provo, UT: Brigham Young University, 5–21

Grüning, Michael: *Der Architekt Konrad Wachsmann Erinnerungen und Selbstauskünfte*, Vienna: Löcker, 1986

Grüning, Christa and Michael: "Konrad Wachsmann – Architekt Albert Einsteins und Pionier des industriellen Bauens," in: *Konrad Wachsmann: Holzhausbau. Technik und Gestaltung* (1931), Basel: Birkhäuser, 1995, 5–17

Hahlweg, Sabine: *Das Verhältnis von Kunst und Politik in Österreich am Beispiel der Wiener Gruppe*, Master's Thesis University of Vienna, 2009

Haller, Max (ed.): *Identität und Nationalstolz der Österreicher*, Vienna: Böhlau, 1996

Haller, Rudolf: *Fragen zu Wittgenstein und Aufsätze zur österreichischen Philosophie = Studien zur österreichischen Philosophie*, Bd. 10, Amsterdam: Rodopi, 1986

Haller, Rudolf: *Neopositivismus. Eine historische Einführung in die Philosophie des Wiener Kreises*, Darmstadt: Wissenschaftliche Buchgesellschaft, 1993

Hanisch, Ruth: "Vom Wienerwald zum Central Park. Wiener Wohnen im New Yorker Exil," in: Ottillinger (ed.): *Wohnen zwischen den Kriegen*, 2009, 131–140

Hintergrund 23 = The Austrian Phenomenon. Konzeptionen Experimente Wien Graz 1958–1973, Vienna: Architekturzentrum Wien, Edition Selene, 2004

Hintergrund 41 = The Making of Architecture, Vienna: Architekturzentrum Wien, 2009

Hintergrund 46–47 = Friedrich Achleitner 80, Vienna: Architekturzentrum Wien, 2010

Hollein, Hans; Walter, Pichler: *Hollein – Pichler – Architektur* (exhibition catalog), Vienna: Galerie St. Stephan, 1963

Hollein, Hans: *MANtransForms. Konzepte einer Ausstellung / Concepts of an Exhibition*, hg. v. Hochschule für angewandte Kunst, Vienna: Löcker, 1989

Hufnagl, Viktor; Windbrechtinger, Wolfgang and Traude (eds.): *Neue städtische Wohnformen* (exhibition catalog), Vienna: ÖGfA, 1967

Hufnagl, Viktor (ed.): *Österreichische Architektur 1960–1970*, Vienna: ÖGfA, 1969

Janik, Allan; Toulmin, Stephen: *Wittgenstein's Vienna*, New York: Simon and Schuster, 1972; Ger.: *Wittgensteins Wien* (1984), Vienna: Löcker, 1998

Jencks, Charles: *The Language of Post-Modern Architecture*, New York: Rizzoli, 1977

Johnston, William M.: *Österreichische Kultur- und Geistesgeschichte. Gesellschaft und Ideen im Donauraum 1848–1938*, Vienna: Böhlau, 1974

Johnston, William M.: *Der österreichische Mensch. Kulturgeschichte der Eigenart Österreichs*, Vienna: Böhlau, 2010

Jutz, Gabriele, Tscherkassky, Peter (eds.): *Peter Kubelka*, Vienna: PVS, 1995

Kaiser, Gabriele (ed.): *Ernst Anton Plischke. Architekt und Lehrer*, Salzburg: Anton Pustet, 2003

Kaiser, Gabriele: "Bilanzen mit Ausblick. Die Ausstellungen der arbeitsgruppe 4," in: Pisarik; Waditschatka (eds.) *arbeitsgruppe 4*, 2010, 142–159

Kaiser, Gabriele; Platzer, Monika (eds.): *Architektur in Österreich im 20. und 21. Jahrhundert*, Basel and Vienna: Architekturzentrum Wien, Birkhäuser, 2006; expanded new edition, Zurich: Park Books, 2016

Kampits, Peter: "Biedermeier und österreichische Philosophie," in: Warren Roe; (ed.): *The Biedermeier and Beyond*, 1999

Kapfinger, Otto; Krischanitz, Adolf: *Die Wiener Werkbundsiedlung. Dokumentation einer Erneuerung*, Vienna: Compress, 1985

Kapfinger, Otto: "Josef Frank – Siedlungen und Siedlungsprojekte 1919–1932," in: UM BAU 10, 1986, 39–58

Kapfinger, Otto; Kneissl, Franz E. (eds.): *Dichte Packung. Architektur aus Wien*, hg. v. Hochschule für angewandte Kunst, Salzburg and Vienna: Residenz, 1989

Kapfinger, Otto; Boeckl, Matthias: *Abgelehnt – nicht ausgeführt: die Bau- und Projektgeschichte der Hochschule für Angewandte Kunst in Wien 1873–1993; ein ebenso unbekanntes wie lehrreiches Kapitel der Wiener Kultur- und Architekturgeschichte; 125 Jahre Hochschule für Angewandte Kunst in Wien*, Vienna: "Stubenring 3" Verein Freunde der Hochschule für Angewandte Kunst, 1993

Kapfinger, Otto: "Transmodernity – Structuring the Void," in: Otto Kapfinger and Bert Lootsma: *TransModernity. Austrian Architects*, New York: Architectural Forum, 2001, Salzburg and Vienna: Anton Pustet, 2002

Kaplan, Jonathan C. *"Kleider machen Leute": Jewish Men and Dress Politics in Vienna, 1890–1938*, Master's Thesis, University of Technology Sydney, 2019

Keel, Daniel (ed.): *Denken mit Karl Kraus*, Zurich: Diogenes, 2007

Kirkham, Pat: *Charles and Ray Eames. Designers of the Twentieth Century*, Cambridge, MA: The MIT Press, 1995

König, Kasper (ed.): *von hier aus. 2 Monate neue deutsche Kunst in Düsseldorf* (exhibition catalog), Cologne: DuMont, 1984

Koolhaas, Rem; OMA; Mau, Bruce: *S, M, L, XL*, Rotterdam: 010 Publishers, 1985

Kos, Wolfgang: *Eigenheim Österreich. Zu Politik, Kultur und Alltag nach 1945*, Vienna: Sonderzahl, 1994

Koschel, Christine; Weidenbaum, Inge (ed.): *Ingeborg Bachmann: Wir müssen wahre Sätze finden. Gespräche und Interviews*. Munich and Zurich: Piper, 1983

Kraft, Viktor: *Der Wiener Kreis: der Ursprung des Neopositivismus*, Vienna: Springer, 1950

Krasny, Elke: *Architektur beginnt im Kopf. The Making of Architecture* (exhibition catalog), Architekturzentrum Wien, Basel: Birkhäuser, 2008

Kraus, Karl: *Die Fackel* (1899–1936)

Kraus, Karl: *Die letzten Tage der Menschheit. Tragödie in fünf Akten mit Vorspiel und Epilog* (1926)

Kraus, Karl: "Preface," trans. Michael Russell, in: *The Last Days of Mankind*, <https://thelastdaysofmankind.org/preface>

Kraus, Karl: "Heine and the Consequences," trans. Jonathan Franzen, in: Jonathan Franzen: *The Kraus Project: Essays by Karl Kraus*, New York: Farrar, Straus & Giroux, 2013, 3–114

Krischanitz, Adolf: *Architektur ist der Unterschied zwischen Architektur*, Ostfildern: Hatje Cantz, 2010

Kristan, Markus: *Die Sechziger. Architektur in Wien 1960–70*, Vienna: Album, 2006

Kubelka, Peter: "The Theory of Metrical Film," in: P. Adams Sitney (ed.): *The Avant-Garde Film: A Reader of Theory and Criticism*, New York: Film Culture/New York University Press, 1978, 139–159

Kühn, Christian (ed.): *Anton Schweighofer – der stille Radikale: Bauten, Projekte, Konzepte*, Vienna: Springer, 2000

Kühn, Christian: *Das Schöne, das Wahre und das Richtige. Adolf Loos und das Haus Müller in Prag*, Bauwelt Fundamente 86, Basel and Gütersloh: Birkhäuser and Bertelsmann, 2001

Kulka, Heinrich: *Adolf Loos. Das Werk des Architekten* (1931), reprint, Vienna: Löcker, 1979

Kurrent, Friedrich; Spalt, Johannes: "Unbekanntes von Adolf Loos," in: *bauforum* 21/1970, 29–48

Kurrent, Friedrich: "Frank und frei," in: *UM BAU* 10/1986, 85–93

Kurrent, Friedrich: *Einige Häuser, Kirchen und dergleichen*, Salzburg: Anton Pustet, 2001

Kurrent, Friedrich: *Texte zur Architektur*, Salzburg and Munich: Anton Pustet, 2006

Kurrent, Friedrich: *Aufrufe, Zurufe, Nachrufe*, Salzburg and Vienna: Müry Salzmann, 2010

Kuzmany, Marion: *Carl Auböck. 1924–1993. Architekt – Gestalten der modernen Welt*, Carl-Auböck-Archiv Wien, Salzburg and Vienna: Anton Pustet, 2009

Lavin, Sylvia: *Form Follows Libido. Architecture and Richard Neutra in a Psychoanalytic Culture*, Cambridge, MA: The MIT Press, 2004

Lefaivre, Liane: "Everything is Architecture. Multiple Hans Hollein and the Art of Crossing Over," in: *Harvard Design Magazine* 18, Spring/Summer 2003, Cambridge, MA, 2004

Lefaivre, Liane: *Rebel Modernists: Viennese Architecture Since Otto Wagner*, London: Lund Humphries, 2017

Lefaivre, Liane; Tzonis, Alexander: *Architecture in Europe since 1968*, London: Thames and Hudson, 1992

Lefaivre, Liane; Tzonis, Alexander: *Aldo van Eyck. Humanist Rebel*, Rotterdam: 010 Publishers, 1999

Lefaivre, Liane; Tzonis, Alexander: *Critical Regionalism. Architecture and Identity in a Globalized World*, Munich: Prestel, 2003

Lefaivre, Liane; Tzonis, Alexander: *Architecture of Regionalism in the Age of Globalization. Peaks and Valleys in the Flat World*, London and New York: Routledge, 2012

Lefaivre, Liane; Tzonis, Alexander: "The Narcissist Phase in Architecture," in: idem: *Times of Creative Destruction: Shaping Buildings and Cities in the Late C20th*, London: Routledge, 2017, 109–122

Libeskind, Daniel: *Kein Ort an seiner Stelle. Schriften zur Architektur – Visionen für Berlin*, Dresden and Basel: Verlag der Kunst, 1995

Lichtenstein, Claude; Schregenberger, Thomas (eds.): *As Found. Die Entdeckung des Gewöhnlichen. Britische Architektur und Kunst der 50er Jahre* (exhibition catalog), Baden: Lars Müller, 2001

Long, Christopher: "Wiener Wohnkultur: Interior Design in Vienna, 1910–1938," in: *Studies in the Decorative Arts*, Vol. 5, No. 1 (Fall–Winter 1997–1998), 29–51

Long, Christopher: *Josef Frank 1885–1967. Life and Work*, Chicago: University of Chicago Press, 2002

Long, Christopher: "The Origins and Context of Adolf Loos's 'Ornament and Crime,'" in: *Journal of the Society of Architectural Historians*, Chicago, Vol. 68, No. 2, July 2009

Long, Christopher: *The Looshaus*, New Haven, CT and London: Yale University Books, 2011

Long, Christopher: "Ornament Is Not Exactly a Crime: On the Long and Curious Afterlife of Adolf Loos's Famed Essay," in: Yehuda E. Safran (ed.): *Adolf Loos. Our Contemporary*, 31–48

Loos, Adolf: *Ins Leere gesprochen 1897–1900* and *Trotzdem 1900–1930*, Innsbruck: Brenner 1931

Adolf Loos (exhibition catalog), Galerie Würthle, Vienna 1961

Loos 1962 – Loos, Adolf: *Sämtliche Schriften 1*, edited by Franz Glück, Vienna and Munich: Herold, 1962

Loos, Adolf: *Spoken into the Void: Collected Essays 1897–1900*, trans. Jane O. Newman and John H. Smith, Cambridge, MA and London: The MIT Press, 1982

Loos, Adolf: "Ornament and Education," trans. Michael Mitchell, in: *Ornament and Crime: Selected Essays by Adolf Loos* Riverside, CA: Ariadne Press, 1998, 188

Loos, Adolf: "Architecture," trans. Michael Mitchell, in: Adolf Loos: *On Architecture* (Studies in Austrian Literature, Culture and Thought), Riverside, CA: Ariadne Press, 2002, 73–85

Loos, Adolf: *Gesammelte Schriften*, edited by Adolf Opel, Vienna: Lesethek, 2010

Loos, Adolf: "The New Style and the Bronze Industry," <https://thispublicaddress.com/2016/03/02/the-new-style-and-the-bronze-industry>

Lustenberger, Kurt: *Adolf Loos*, London: Artemis, 1994

Lyotard, Jean F.: *Das postmoderne Wissen. Ein Bericht (1979)*, Vienna: Passagen, 1986

Mach Ernst, *The Science of Mechanics*, trans. Thomas J. McCormack, Chicago: The Open Court Publishing Co., 1893

Mallgrave, Harry Francis: *Otto Wagner. Reflections on the Raiment of Modernity*, Santa Monica, CA: Getty Center for the History of Art and the Humanities, 1993

Mattl, Siegfried: "Autoritäre Modernisten und skeptische Avantgarde. Österreich um 1959," in: *Die Wiener Gruppe* (exhibition catalog), Kunsthalle Wien, Wolfgang Fetz, Gerald Matt, Vienna: Kunsthalle Wien, 1998, 14–19

Mayrhofer, Bernadette; Trümpi, Fritz: *Orchestrierte Vertreibung: Unerwünschte Wiener Philharmoniker. Verfolgung, Ermordung, Exil*, Vienna: Mandelbaum, 2014

Meder, Iris (ed.): *Josef Frank. Eine Moderne der Unordnung*, Salzburg and Vienna: Anton Pustet, 2008

Meili, Marcel et al.: *Swiss Re Rüschlikon. Centre for Global Dialogue*, Kunsthaus Bregenz, aka Werkdokumente 20, Bregenz: Kunsthaus Bregenz, 2001 [Ger./Engl.]

Marcel Meili, Markus Peter: 1987–2008, Zurich: Scheidegger & Spiess, 2008; simultaneously published in English

Mitscherlich, Alexander; Mielke, Fred: *Das Diktat der Menschenverachtung. Der Nürnberger Ärzteprozeß und seine Quellen*, Heidelberg: Lambert Schneider Verlag, 1947

Mitscherlich, Alexander; Mielke, Fred: *Wissenschaft ohne Menschlichkeit. Medizinische und eugenische Irrwege unter Diktatur, Bürokratie und Krieg*, Heidelberg: Lambert Schneider Verlag, 1949

Moravánszky, Ákos: *Die Architektur der Donaumonarchie*, Berlin: Ernst & Sohn, 1988

Moravánszky, Ákos; Langer, Bernhard; Mosayebi, Elli (eds.): *Adolf Loos. Die Kultivierung der Architektur*, Zurich: gta, 2008

Münz, Ludwig; Künstler, Gustav: *Der Architekt Adolf Loos*, Vienna and Munich: Anton Schroll, 1964

Nemeth, Elisabeth: *Otto Neurath und der Wiener Kreis: Revolutionäre Wissenschaftlichkeit als politischer Anspruch*, Frankfurt: Campus, 1981

Neufert, Ernst: *Bauentwurfslehre. Handbuch für den Baufachmann, Bauherren, Lehrende und Lernende*, Berlin: Bauwel Verlag, 1936, resp., Wiesbaden: Friedrich Vieweg & Sohn, 2012 (40th edition)

Nierhaus, Andreas; Orosz, Eva-Maria (eds.): *Werkbundsiedlung Wien 1932. Ein Manifest des Neuen Wohnens* (exhibition catalog), Wien Museum, Salzburg and Vienna: Müry Salzmann, 2013

Novy, Klaus; Förster, Wolfgang; Koch, Ernst (eds.): *Einfach bauen: genossenschaftliche Selbsthilfe nach der Jahrhundertwende. Zur Rekonstruktion der Wiener Siedlerbewegung*, Vienna: Picus, 1991

Oechslin, Werner: *Stilhülse und Kern. Otto Wagner, Adolf Loos und der evolutionäre Weg zur modernen Architektur*, Zurich and Berlin: gta/Ernst & Sohn, 1994

Oertel, Rudolf: *Die schönste Stadt der Welt: ein utopisches Buch*, Vienna: Wiener Verlag, 1947

Olgiati, Valerio: *The Images of Architects*, Lucerne: Quart, 2013

Opll, Ferdinand; Vocelka, Karl; Cendes, Peter: *Wien: Geschichte einer Stadt. Teil 2. Die frühneuzeitliche Residenz (16.–18. Jahrhundert)*, Vienna: Böhlau, 2003

Ottillinger, Eva B.: *Adolf Loos. Wohnkonzepte und Möbelentwürfe*, Salzburg and Vienna: Residenz, 1994

Ottillinger, Eva; Sarnitz, August: *Ernst Plischke. Das Gesamtwerk*, Munich: Prestel, 2003

Ottillinger, Eva B. (ed.): *Wohnen zwischen den Kriegen. Wiener Möbel 1914–1941*, Vienna: Böhlau, 2009

Parnass 18: Wegbereiter, Vienna: Parnass Verlag, 2001

Pelinka, Anton: "Zur Gründung der Zweiten Republik," in: Waechter-Böhm (ed.): *Wien 1945 davor/danach*, 1985, 21–22

Perloff, Marjorie: "Avant-Garde in a Different Key: Karl Kraus's *The Last Days of Mankind*," Critical Inquiry, Volume 40, Number 2, 2014 <https://criticalinquiry.uchicago.edu/Avant_Garde_in_a_Different_Key>

Pisarik, Sonja; Waditschatka, Ute (eds.): *arbeitsgruppe 4. Wilhelm Holzbauer, Friedrich Kurrent, Johannes Spalt, 1950–1970*, Architekturzentrum Wien, Salzburg and Vienna: Müry Salzmann, 2010

Plischke, Ernst A.: *Ein Leben mit Architektur*, Vienna: Löcker, 1989

Podbrecky, Inge; Franz, Rainald (eds.): *Leben mit Loos*, Vienna: Böhlau, 2008

Pogacnik, Marco: *Adolf Loos und Wien*, Salzburg and Vienna: Müry Salzmann, 2011

Porsch, Johannes (ed.): *The Austrian Phenomenon. Architekturavantgarde Österreich 1956–1973*, Architekturzentrum Wien, Basel: Birkhäuser, 2009

Posch, Wilfried: "Josef Frank, eine bedeutende Persönlichkeit des österreichischen Kulturliberalismus," in: *UM BAU* 10, 1986, 21–38

Posch, Wilfried: *Clemens Holzmeister. Architekt zwischen Kunst und Politik*, Salzburg and Vienna: Müry Salzmann, 2010

Prechter, Günther: *Architektur als soziale Praxis. Akteure zeitgenössischer Baukulturen: Das Beispiel Vorarlberg*, Vienna: Böhlau, 2013

Radebold, Hartmut (ed.): *Kindheiten im II. Weltkrieg und ihre Folgen*, Giessen: Psychosozial Verlag, 2004

Radebold, Hartmut; Bohleber, Werner; Zinnecker, Jürgen (eds.): *Transgenerationale Weitergabe kriegsbelasteter Kindheiten. Interdisziplinäre Studien zur Nachhaltigkeit historischer Erfahrungen über vier Generationen*, Weinheim and Munich: Juventa, 2008

Rainer, Roland: *Planungskonzept Wien*, hg. v. Stadtbauamt der Stadt Wien und dem Institut für Städtebau an der Akademie der bildenden Künste, Vienna: Jugend & Volk, 1962

Rainer, Roland: *An den Rand geschrieben. Wohnkultur-Stadtkultur*, Vienna: Böhlau, 2000

Rainer, Roland: *Das Werk des Architekten 1927-2003. Vom Sessel zum Stadtplan: geplant, errichtet, verändert, vernichtet*, Vienna and New York: Springer, 2003

Rathkolb, Oliver: *Die paradoxe Republik. Österreich 1945 bis 2005*, Vienna: Zsolnay, 2005

Ringel, Erwin: *Die österreichische Seele*, Vienna: Böhlau, 1984

Risselada, Max; van den Heuvel, Dirk (eds.): *Team 10, 1953-81. In Search of a Utopia of the Present*, Rotterdam: NAI Publishers, 2005

Ritter, Arno (ed.): *Konstantmodern. Fünf Positionen zur Architektur; Atelier 5, Gerhard Garstenauer, Johann Georg Gsteu, Rudolf Wäger, Werner Wirsing*, (Architektur und Tirol), Vienna and New York: Springer, 2009

Roe, Ian F.; Warren, John (eds.): *The Biedermeier and Beyond*. Selected Papers from the Symposium held at St. Peter's College, Oxford, 19-21.9.1997, British and Irish Studies in German Language and Literature, Vol. 17, Berne: Peter Lang, 1999

Rowe, Colin: *The Mathematics of the Ideal Villa and Other Essays*, Cambridge, MA: The MIT Press, 1976

Rowe, Colin; Slutzky, Robert: *Transparenz*, Basel, Boston and Berlin: Birkhäuser, 1997

Rühm, Gerhard (ed.): *Die Wiener Gruppe. Achleitner, Artmann, Bayer, Rühm, Wiener. Texte, Gemeinschaftsarbeiten, Aktionen*, Reinbek bei Hamburg: Rowohlt, 1967

Rühm, Gerhard: "das phänomen der 'wiener gruppe' im wien der fünfziger und sechziger jahre," in: Peter Weibel (ed.): *die wiener gruppe*, 1997, 17-29; Engl. "the phenomenon of the 'wiener gruppe' in the vienna of the fifties and sixties," trans. Tom Eppleton, in: ibid., 16-28

Rukschcio, Burkhardt; Schachel, Roland: *Adolf Loos. Leben und Werk*, Salzburg and Vienna: Residenz, 1982

Rukschcio, Burkhardt (ed.): *Adolf Loos* (exhibition catalog), Vienna: Löcker, 1989

Russell, Bertrand: "Mysticism and Logic," *Hibbert Journal* 12, No. 48, July 1914, 780-803

Safran, Yehuda (ed.): *Adolf Loos. Our Contemporary | Unser Zeitgenosse | Nosso Contemporâneo* (Ger./Engl./Port.), New York and Vienna: GSAPP/MAK, 2012

Sarnitz, August: "Realism versus *Verniedlichung*. The Design of the Great City," in: Harry Francis Mallgrave (ed.): *Otto Wagner*, 1993, 85-112

Sarnitz, August: *Otto Wagner 1841-1918. Wegbereiter der modernen Architektur*, Cologne: Taschen, 2005

Sarnitz, August: *Adolf Loos 1870-1933*, Cologne: Taschen, 2006

Sarnitz, August: *Josef Hoffmann 1870-1956*, Cologne: Taschen, 2007

Sarnitz, August: *Architektur in Wien. 700 Bauten*, Vienna: Springer, 2008

Schorske, Carl E.: *Fin de Siècle Vienna: Politics and Culture*, New York: Vintage Books, 1981; Ger.: *Wien. Geist und Gesellschaft im Fin de Siècle* (1982), Munich: Piper, 1997

Scully, Vincent: *Modern Architecture. The Architecture of Democracy* (1961), New York: George Braziller, 1974

Sedlmayr, Hans: *Der Verlust der Mitte. Die bildende Kunst des neunzehnten und zwanzigsten Jahrhunderts als Symptom und Symbol der Zeit*, Salzburg and Vienna: Otto Müller, 1948

Shapira, Elana: *Assimilating with Style: Jewish Assimilation and Modern Architecture and Design in Vienna – The Case of "The Outfitters" Leopold Goldman and Adolf Loos and the Making of the Goldman & Salatsch Building (1909-1911)*, Dissertation, Universität für angewandte Kunst, Vienna, 2004

Shapira, Elana: "Tailored Authorship. Adolf Loos and the Ethos of Men's Fashion," in: Podbrecky; Franz (eds.): *Leben mit Loos*, 2008, 53-72

Shapira, Elana: "Jüdisches Mäzenatentum zwischen Assimilation und Identitätsstiftung in Wien 1800-1930," in: Claudia Theune; Tina Walzer (eds.): *Jüdische Friedhöfe. Kultstätte, Erinnerungsort, Denkmal*, Vienna: Böhlau, 2011

Silverman, Lisa: *Becoming Austrians. Jews and Culture between the World Wars*, Oxford and New York: Oxford University Press, 2012

Smithson, Alison (ed.): "Team Ten Primer," in: *Architectural Design*, December 1962, London: Studio Vista, 1968

Smithson, Alison and Peter: "'Wie gefunden' und 'gefunden,'" in: Lichtenstein; Schregenberger (eds.): *As Found*, 2001, 40–41

Somavilla, Ilse (ed.): *Wittgenstein – Engelmann. Briefe, Begegnungen, Erinnerungen*, Innsbruck and Vienna: Haymon, 2006

Somol, Robert; Whiting, Sarah: "Notes around the Doppler Effect and Other Moods of Modernism," in: *Perspecta 33. The Yale Architectural Journal*, Cambridge, MA: The MIT Press, 2002, 72–77; Ger.: in: ARCH+ 178, 2006, 83–87

Spalt, Johannes: "Josef Frank und die räumliche Konzeption seiner Hausentwürfe," in: *UM BAU* 10, 1986, 59–74

Spalt, Johannes: *Johannes Spalt*, Vienna: Böhlau, 1993

Spiel, Hilde: *Rückkehr nach Wien. Ein Tagebuch*, Frankfurt: Ullstein, 1989; Engl.: *Return to Vienna: A Journal*, trans. Christine Shuttleworth, Riverside, CA: Ariadne Press, 2011

Stadler, Friedrich; Haller, Rudolf (eds.): *Wien – Berlin – Prag. Der Aufstieg der wissenschaftlichen Philosophie. Zentenarien Rudolf Carnap, Hans Reichenbach, Edgar Zilsel*, Vienna: Verlag Hölder-Pichler-Tempsky, 1993

Steger, Bernhard: *Vom Bauen. Zu Leben und Werk von Ottokar Uhl*, Vienna: Löcker, 2007

Stölzner, Michael; Übel, Thomas (eds.): *Wiener Kreis. Texte zur wissenschaftlichen Weltauffassung von Rudolf Carnap, Otto Neurath, Moritz Schlick, Philipp Frank, Hans Hahn, Karl Menger, Edgar Zilsel und Gustav Bergmann*, Hamburg: Meiner, 2009

Strauven, Francis: *Aldo van Eyck. The Shape of Relativity*, Amsterdam: Architectura & Natura, 1998

Tafuri, Manfredo: *Vienna Rossa: La politica residenziale nella Vienna socialista, 1919–1933*, Milan: Electa, 1970

The Presence of the Past. First International Exhibition of Architecture, La Biennale di Venezia 1980, New York: Rizzoli, 1980

Thurm-Nemeth, Volker (ed.): *Konstruktion zwischen Werkbund und Bauhaus. Wissenschaft – Architektur – Wiener Kreis*, Vienna: Verlag Hölder-Pichler-Tempsky, 1998

Thurner, Erika: *Nationale Identität und Geschlecht in Österreich nach 1945*, Innsbruck: Studienverlag, 2000

trigon 69 (exhibition catalog), published by the Neue Galerie Graz (Wilfried Skreiner), Graz: Neue Galerie am Landesmuseum Joanneum, 1969

Tugendhat, Ernst: "Antike und moderne Ethik" in: idem.: *Probleme der Ethik*, Stuttgart: Reclam, 1984, 33–56, Engl.: "Ancient and Modern Ethics," trans. Martin Livingston in: Darrel E. Christensen (ed.): *Contemporary German Philosophy* Volume 4, University Park, PA: Pennsylvania State University Press, 1984

Turnovský, Jan: *Die Poetik eines Mauervorsprungs*, Bauwelt Fundamente 77, Braunschwieg and Wiesbaden: Friedrich Vieweg & Sohn, 1999

Uhl, Ottokar: *Moderne Architektur in Wien von Otto Wagner bis heute*, Vienna and Munich: Anton Schroll, 1966

UM BAU 10. Dokumentation und Nachlese zum Josef-Frank-Symposium vom Dezember 1985, Vienna: ÖGfA, 1986

Veigl, Hans: *Wiener Kaffeehausführer*, Vienna: Kremayr & Scheriau, 1989

Venturi, Robert: *Complexity and Contradiction in Architecture*, New York: The Museum of Modern Art, 1966; Ger.: *Komplexität und Widerspruch in der Architektur*, Bauwelt Fundamente 50, Braunschwieg and Wiesbaden: Friedrich Vieweg & Sohn, 1978

Venturi, Robert; Scott Brown, Denise; Izenour, Steven: *Learning from Las Vegas*, Cambridge, MA: The MIT Press, 1972; Ger.: *Lernen von Las Vegas. Zur Ikonographie und Architektursymbolik der Geschäftsstadt*, Bauwelt Fundamente 53, Braunschwieg and Wiesbaden: Friedrich Vieweg & Sohn, 1979

von Moos, Stanislaus: *Venturi and Rauch. Architektur im Alltag Amerikas*, Niederteufen: Niggli, 1979

von Moos, Stanislaus: *Venturi, Rauch & Scott Brown*, Munich: Schirmer-Mosel, 1987

von Moos, Stanislaus; Gimmi, Karin (eds.): *SvM. Die Festschrift für Stanislaus von Moos*, Zurich: gta, 2005

Vossoughian, Nader: "Die Architektur der wissenschaftlichen Weltauffassung," in: Meder (ed.): *Josef Frank 1885–1967*, 2008, 59–65

Vossoughian, Nader: *Otto Neurath. The Language of the Global Polis*, Rotterdam: NAI Publishers, 2011

Wachsmann, Konrad: *Wendepunkt im Bauen*, Cologne: Otto Krausskopf, 1959; Engl.: *The Turning Point of Building: Structure and Design*, trans. Thomas E. Burton, New York: Reinhold Publishing Corporation, 1961

Waditschatka, Ute: "Im Vordergrund das Bauen" (Teil1), in: Pisarik; Waditschatka (eds.): *arbeitsgruppe 4*, 2010, 20–77

Waechter-Böhm, Liesbeth (ed.): *Wien 1945 davor/danach* (exhibition catalog), Museum des 20. Jahrhunderts, Wiener Festwochen, Vienna: Verlag Christian Brandstätter, 1985

Wagner-Rieger, Renate: *Wiens Architektur im 19. Jahrhundert*, Vienna: ÖBV, 1970

Wagner, Otto: *Einige Scizzen, Proiecte u. ausgeführte Bauwerke* (1889), (complete reprint of the four original volumes of 1889, 1897, 1906 and 1922, with an introduction by Peter Haiko), Tubingen: Wasmuth, 1987; Engl.: *Sketches, Projects, and Executed Buildings*, trans. Edward Vance Humphrey, New York: Rizzoli, 1987

Wagner, Otto: *Die Großstadt. Eine Studie über diese von Otto Wagner*, 1911; Engl.: "The Development of a Great City," *The Architectural Record* 31 (May 1912): 485–500 <http://urbanplanning.library.cornell.edu/DOCS/wagner.htm>

Wagner, Otto: *Die Baukunst unserer Zeit: dem Baukunstjünger ein Führer auf diesem Kunstgebiete* (1895), 4. Auflage 1914, reprint, Vienna: Löcker, 1978; Engl.: *Modern Architecture: A Guidebook for His Students to This Field of Art*, trans. Harry Francis Mallgrave, Los Angeles: Getty Center Publications, 1988

Weibel, Peter; Steinle, Christa (eds.): *Identität: Differenz: Tribüne. Trigon 1949–1990. Eine Topografie der Moderne*, Vienna: Böhlau, 1992

Weibel, Peter; Stadler, Friedrich: *The Cultural Exodus from Austria (Vertreibung der Vernunft)*, Vienna: Löcker, 1993; expanded edition, Vienna: Springer, 1995

Weibel, Peter (ed.): *die wiener gruppe. a moment of modernity 1954–1960. visual works and actions*, (catalog of eponymous exhibition in the scope of the Biennale 1997 in the Austrian Pavilion), Vienna and New York: Springer, 1997

Welzig, Maria: *Josef Frank 1885–1967. Das architektonische Werk*, Vienna: Böhlau, 1998

Welzig, Maria; Steixner, Gerhard: *Die Architektur und ich. Eine Bilanz der österreichischen Architektur seit 1945 vermittelt durch ihre Protagonisten, geboren in der Ersten Republik – Roland Rainer, Ernst Hiesmayr, Viktor Hufnagl, Harry Seidler, Harry Glück, Gustav Peichl, Friedrich Achleitner, Ottokar Uhl, Günther Domenig*, Vienna: Böhlau, 2003

Werkner, Patrick (ed.): *Kunst in Österreich 1945–1995*, ein Symposion der Hochschule für angewandte Kunst in Wien im April 1995, Vienna: WUV, 1996

Wien 1938 (exhibition catalog), Historisches Museum der Stadt Wien, Dokumentationsarchiv des österreichischen Widerstandes, Vienna: ÖBV and Jugend & Volk, 1988

Wiener Gruppe (exhibition catalog), Kunsthalle Wien, 1998

Wiener, Oswald: *Die Verbesserung von Mitteleuropa. Roman*, Reinbek bei Hamburg: Rowohlt, 1969

Wiener, Oswald: "einiges über konrad bayer," in: Weibel (ed.): *die wiener gruppe*, 1997, 43–49; Engl. "some remarks on konrad bayer," trans. Tom Eppleton, in: ibid., 42–48

Wiener, Oswald: "das 'literarische cabaret' der wiener gruppe," in: Weibel (ed.): *die wiener gruppe*, 1997, 308–321; Engl.: "the 'literary cabaret' of the vienna group," trans. Tom Eppleton, in: ibid., 308–321

Wilhelm, Karin: "Zurück in die Zukunft," in: Pisarik; Waditschatka (eds.): *arbeitsgruppe 4*, 2010, 160–175

Wittgenstein, Ludwig: *Tractatus logico-philosophicus. Logisch-philosophische Abhandlung*, Frankfurt: Suhrkamp, 1976; Engl.: *Tractatus logico-philosophicus*, trans. C. K. Ogden, New York and London: Kegan Paul and Harcourt Brace and Company, 1922

Wodak, Ruth: "Herrschaft durch Sprache? Sprachwandel als Symbol und Ausdruck des gesellschaftlichen Wandels," in: Waechter-Böhm (ed.): *Wien 1945 davor/danach*, Vienna: Verlag Christian Brandstätter, 1985, 75–89

Zweig, Stefan: *Die Welt von Gestern. Erinnerungen eines Europäers*, Frankfurt: Fischer TB, 1970; Engl.: *The World of Yesterday*, trans. Benjamin W. Huebsch and Helmut Ripperger, London, Toronto, Melbourne and Sydney: Cassell and Company, Ltd., 1947

Register

Aalto, Alvar 125

Abraham, Raimund 9 165

Achleitner, Friedrich 18 59f 62 65 68f 74ff 79 83 113 120f 127 132f 162 165 239f 280

Adorno, Theodor W. 13 89f 143 148 152 157

Adrian, Marc 65

Alberti, Leon Battista 176f 202 412

Alexander, Christopher 19 103f 194 243 252 264f 354 391 410 413

Altenberg, Peter 29

Alvera, Alessandro 85f

Anderson, Stanford 42 152

Andraschek, Iris 10

Angonese, Walter 420 424

Appelt, Werner (s. IGIRIEN)

arbeitsgruppe 4 57 61 65 67 69f 79 84f 91–94 107 112 116 118f 122 124 127 168 273f 348f 413

Archigram 113

ARTEC Architekten (Bettina Götz, Richard Manahl) 11 420 424

Artmann, H. C. 65 74ff 79 83

Ashby, Charlotte 185ff 336f

Atatürk, Kemal Pascha 60

Atelier 5 112

Attersee, Christian Ludwig 259

Auböck, Maria 10

Bachmann, Ingeborg 53 62

Badura-Triska, Eva 9

Bakema, Jacob 90

Ball, Hugo 57 66

Bandur, Markus 77

Banićević-Pöschl, Monika 200 244 246 248f

Banićević, Tale 248

Bartenbach (Firma) 164

Basil, Otto 49

Bau 82 115f 119 125f

Baufrösche 362

Bauhaus 16 32–35 37 39ff 75 124 309 397

Baum, Peter 238

Baumeister, Willi 63

Bayer, Konrad 47 64ff 74f 76 79 83 165

Bedoire, Frederic 23f 28 32

Beethoven, Ludwig van 51

Behrens, Peter 41 85 123

Beller, Steven 21

Benedikt, Heinrich 51

Beniston, Judith 36

Benn, Gottfried 50

Berg, Alban 78 331

Bergquist, Mikael 352 415

Biennale 15 62 74 85 146 349 376

Birkholz, Franke, Gassauer 362

Blau, Eve 36 40 42 286 288

Blau, Luigi 127

Bobek, Hans 202

Bodoni, Giambattista 20

Boeckl, Herbert 63

Boeckl, Matthias 23 59 61

Bohleber, Werner 45f

Böhme, Gernot 157 374

Bollerey, Franziska 143 343

Bolterauer, Klaus 136

Boltzmann, Ludwig 25 46 (-Institut)

Bolzano, Bernhard 25

Bonaparte, Marie 189

Borodajkewycz, Taras 47

Brandstaller, Trautl 81f

Brecht, Bertolt 56 66

Brenner, Anton 299

Brentano, Franz 25

Bretterbauer, Gilbert 367

Breyvogel, Wilfried 46

Brus, Günter 117f

Buckley, Craig 84 116

Burckhardt, Lucius 90

Bürkle, Johann Christoph 380

Burlingham, Dorothy Tiffany 427

Busse, Carl Ferdinand 26

Canetti, Elias 59

Carnap, Rudolf 26 34

Carroll, Lewis 244

463

Cendes, Peter 202

Cerha, Friedrich 77

Chamberlain, Sigrid 46

Chramosta, Walter 352

CIAM 38f 61

Clair, Jean 298

Colomina, Beatriz 32 84 116

Cook, Peter 9 81 113

Coop Himmelblau 9 113 115

Czech, Anna Jane (Mother) 43ff 48 55

Czech, Josef (Father) 43ff 47 48 55 70 137 168 175

Demner und Merlicek 296

Detzlhofer, Anna 380

Diderot, Denis 56

Die Fackel 29 56ff 122 124

Die Furche 81f 89 94 96 104 106 111ff 118f 121 124 132f 331 399 403

die reihe 65 77

Diener & Diener 86 380

Dimitriou, Sokratis 115f

Drasche, Heinrich von 24

Duchamp, Marcel 319

Dudler, Max 380

Eames, Charles and Ray 368

Egli, Ernst 60

Eichholzer, Herbert 60

Eimert, Herbert 77

Einstein, Albert 71 74

Eisenman, Peter 15 17 152

Enengl, Claudia 67f 127

Engelman, Edmund 425 427

Engelmann, Paul 30 33

Englert, Uwe 45

Ertl, Roland 136

Eto, Shinichi 19

Eugen von Savoyen, Prince 170

EXPORT, VALIE 117

Faber, Monika 392

Faber, Richard 82

Falke, Jakob von 31

Faschingeder, Kristian 17 190 299 381 397 400f 403

Fecht, Tom 133

Feiersinger, Martin 11

Fellerer, Max 39 59ff

Ferstel, Heinrich 23 338 343 404

Ferstel, Max 219

Feuerstein, Günther 9 81f 84 115f 119 124

Feyerabend, Paul 155

Figl, Leopold 54

Filmakademie 55f 62 78 163

Fischer von Erlach, Bernhard Johann 18 121 127 133 170 172 240 256

Fischer von Erlach, Josef Emanuel 256

Flasch, Kurt 147

Fleck, Robert 54 62f 65 83 117 134

Flick, Uwe 18

Flierl, Bruno 358

Fontana, Lucio 50

Förg, Günter 367

Förster, Ludwig von 23f 26 216 218 220 327

Förster, Wolfgang 36

Frampton, Kenneth 17 263 280

Frank, Anna 41

Frank, Heinz 126 266 280

Frank, Josef 14 16–19 28 33–42 57 60f 67f 74 84ff 118–121 125ff 133 136f 144 154f 162 170 172 175 176 194 201 203ff 219 229f 232 239–242 244 251f 263 265 273f 285ff 289ff 299 302ff 306f 334f 344 348 367 394 404 406–412

Frank, Philipp 34 36 74 154

Franz Joseph I. 30

Franz, Rainald 16 18 32 285

Frei, Hans 13

Freud, Anna 425 427

Freud, Martha 420

Freud, Sigmund 35 189 205 354 420ff

Friedell, Egon 24

Friedler, Georg 85

Fuller, Richard Buckminster 113

Funder, Friedrich 82

Functionalism 15f 61 83 89f 120 127 136f 143 176 304

Furuya, Seiichi 386

Gábor, László 302

Gabriel, Leo 34 66f 147

Gadamer, Hans-Georg 150

Galerie (nächst) St. Stephan 54f 62–65 67 75 81–84 95 112f 119

Galerie Olivetti 92

Galerie Würthle 63 68 70 124

Galison, Peter 35

Gaudí, Antoni 149

Geretsegger, Heinz 26 94 279f 385

Gerl, Eva 200

Gerngross, Heidulf 9

Giedion, Sigfried 38

Glück, Harry 112 126

Göderitz, Johannes 61 102

Goldman, Leopold 321

Gorge, Hugo 38

Gorsen, Peter 117

Götz, Bettina (s. ARTEC)

Götz, Sabine 45 370 372

Graf, Otto Antonia 26

Grafe, Christoph 143 337

Graff, Rainer 352

Grandjean, Étienne 185

Gredinger, Paul 77

Grill, Dagmar 118 409

Grillparzer, Franz 51

Gropius, Walter 38 123

Gross, Alan, G.

Gruen, Victor 90

Grüning Michael 71 74

Grüning, Christa 71

Gschnitzer, Rudolf 164

Gsöllpointner, Helmuth 238 243

Gsteu, Johann Georg 67ff 124 127 132 342f
Guévrékian, Gabriel 302
Haarer, Johanna 46
Hackenschmidt, Sebastian 406 412
Hackhofer, Josef 281
Hadid, Zaha 370
Haerdtl, Oswald 39 59ff
Hagmüller, Roland 118
Hahlweg, Sabine 77
Hahn, Hans 34
Halbrainer, Heimo 60
Haller, Rudolf 25f 34f 51 66
Hämer, Hardt-Walther 352
Hanisch, Ruth 34
Hansen, Theophil 24 175 216 218 220 321
Hareiter, Angela 238
Häring, Hugo 229 302 407
Hasenauer, Carl 91
Hauptmann, Gerhart 59
Haus und Garten 39 118 120 302
HausRucker-Co 9 116 243
Haydn, Joseph 51
Heer, Friedrich 66 82
Hegel, G.F.W. 66f 148f 151f
Heidegger, Martin 66
Heine, Heinrich 122 290
Heintel, Erich 66f 147f 152
Heller, André 201
Henderson, Nigel 165
Herbart, Johann Friedrich 25

Herzog & de Meuron 407
Hildebrandt, Lukas von 256
Historicism 23f 26 28f 218 220 330 333
Hitler, Adolf 41 45 46 54 295f
Hlaweniczka, Kurt 112
Hoffmann-Axthelm, Dieter 352 354 356
Hoffmann, Hubert 61 102
Hoffmann, Josef 28 39 41 56 59f 67 80 85 116 118–121 125 162f 165f 171f 175 302 333 406
Hofmannsthal, Hugo von 25 33 58 321
Hollegha, Wolfgang 65
Hollein, Hans 9 15f 18 57 81–84 91 106 112f 115f 119 125 134 263 270f 273 370 372
Hollein, Lilli 266
Holzbauer, Wilhelm 65 67 273 279
Holzmeister, Clemens 41 59f 67f 83 84
Hoppe, Schönthal, Kammerer 327
Horkheimer, Max 148 157
Hrachovec, Herbert 160
Hufnagl, Viktor 112 121
Hummel, Julius 226
Hundertwasser, Friedensreich 10
Ibsen, Henrik 45
IGIRIEN 127 280 304
International Style 14 41 120 123 302

Ishikawa, Sara 104
Izenour, Steven 14
Jabornegg, Christian 10f
Janik, Allan 29 57f
Jeanée, Michael 117
Jeanneret, Pierre 387
Jencks, Charles 14f
Johnston, William M. 53
Jonas, Franz 90
Jonas, Walter 112
Joseph II. 21
Judd, Donald 280
Jugendstil (Art Nouveau) 28f 32 123 126 133f 330 333
Jutz, Gabriele 78
Kabus, Ludewig 356
Kaesser, Monika 313
Kaiser, Gabriele 69 93 116 119 273
Kalb, Kurt 117
Kaltenbäck, Franz 117
Kamper, Dietmar 133
Kampits, Peter 25
Kant, Immanuel 89 153
Kapfinger, Otto 23 132 306 335 362 364
Kárász, János 10
Kaserer, Otto 43
Keel, Daniel 59
Kiesler, Friedrich (Frederick) 116
Kirchweger, Ernst 47
Klenze, Leo von 384
Klimt, Gustav 32
Klocker, Hubert 9

Klubseminar 81f 84 112 124
Kneissl, Franz Eberhard (s. IGIRIEN)
Kniefacz, Katharina 66
Knoll, Harald 46
Koch, Ernst 36
Kohoutek, Rudolf 116 188
Kokoschka, Oskar 73 331
Kollhoff, Hans 374
König, Karl 406
König, Kasper 268
Koolhaas, Rem 304 406ff 410
Kornhäusel, Joseph 127
Kos, Wolfgang 53 65
Koschel, Christine 53
Kraft, Viktor 62 66
Kraus, Karl 20 25 29 31ff 56 57ff 62 66 80 122 124 149 166 331
Kren, Kurt 65
Krischanitz, Adolf 127 132 167 306 360f 368f 370 374f 390
Kubelka, Peter 65 78f 165 188
Kühn, Christian 33 60f 68 102
Kulka, Heinrich 123–127 194 206
Künstler, Gustav 36 112 124
Kurdiovsky, Richard 330 338
Kurrent, Friedrich 60f 65 67ff 74 83ff 91f 104 118ff 124 126f 132 165 205 263 273 318 406

Kuss, Eva 9 11 160
Lampe, Jörg 62
Langer, Bernhard 30 188
Lao Tse 86
Laub, Jakob 62f 136
Le Corbusier 17 66 84f 112 125 172 229 303 362 387
Lechner, Ödön 24
Lefaivre, Liane 15 45 146 204 290
Lehár, Franz 58
Leitner, Otto 67
Leo, Annette 352
Lewis, Jerry 205
Lewis, Wyndham 50
Libeskind, Daniel 356
Lichtenberger, Elisabeth 202
Lichtenstein, Claude 166
Lichtenstein, Roy 116
Lihotzky, Margarete (s. Schütte-)
Lobnig, Hubert 10
Löcker, Erhard 194 196 316
Long, Christopher 30 35 38ff 60f 121 287 334f
Loos, Adolf 14 16–19 24 29–33 36ff 40 42 45 56ff 61 67ff 84ff 107 112 116 118ff 122–127 128 133 136 143f 148f 166 168 170 174f 176 183 188 193 194 196 203 206 209f 220f 238f 249 251 263 285–289 302 306 318–321 323 330–334 338 348 384 393ff 397 406f 410

Lueger-Schuster, Brigitte 45
Lurçat, André 303
Lurje, Viktor 38
Lynn, Greg 370
Lyotard, Jean-François 14
Mach, Ernst 25f 35
Mallgrave, Harry Francis 27 42
Manahl, Richard (s. ARTEC)
Mann, Golo 89f
Marinetti, Filippo Tommaso 50
Märkli, Peter 374
Matejka, Viktor 51
Mattl, Siegfried 51
Mau, Bruce 304
Mauer, Otto 62ff 134
Maulbertsch, Franz Anton 300
Mauthner, Fritz 25 62
Mayer, Horst Friedrich 81
Mayne, Thom 370
Mayr Fingerle, Christoph 179
Mayrhofer, Bernadette 321
Meder, Iris 36 306 408
Meili, Marcel 360ff 364 368
Meister Eckhart 86
Merlicek, Franz 296
Mesmer, Franz Anton 300
Michelangelo 78 193
Michélsen, Olof 409

Mielke, Fred 47
Mies van der Rohe, Ludwig 37 123 302
Mikl, Josef 65
Missing Link 9 280
Mistelbauer, Wolfgang 20 69f 73 80 122–127 136 162 164ff 170 176 194 201 205 288
Mitscherlich, Alexander 47
Mittnik, Heinrich 278
Moldovan, Kurt 165
Mölter, Veit 53
Moravánszky, Ákos 23f 26 30 188 397
Morgenstern, Soma 335
Mosayebi, Elli 188
Mozart, Wolfgang Amadeus 51
Mühl, Otto 17 117f
Münz, Ludwig 32 36 112 124
Münz, Maria 68
Musil, Robert 17 53 331
Nachkriegszeit (Postwar Period) 9 43 48 54 59 61 68f 83 91 124 145
Nash, John 107
National Socialism 34 43f 46 47 50 54 56 60 64 66 68 107 147 246 291 321 352
Nelböck, Hans 34
Nestroy, Johann 59
Neubacher, Hermann 39
Neufert, Ernst 284
Neuffer, Hans 176 190

Neumann Büttner Braun 356
Neurath, Otto 34–38 39 144 155 274 290f 394
Neutra, Richard 90 302
Neuwirth, Werner 390
Nierhaus, Andreas 302
Nitsch, Hermann 117
Nohàl, Reinald 70 80 122 162 164ff
Nouvel, Jean 370
Novy, Klaus 36
Oberhuber, Oswald 116
Oertel, Rudolf 91
ÖGfA 106 112f 118f 121
Ohmann, Friedrich 280f
Olbrich, Joseph Maria 28 32 119 175
Olgiati, Valerio 343
Opll, Ferdinand 202
Orosz, Eva-Maria 302
Ortner, Laurids 113 238
Ottillinger, Eva B. 31 34 338
Otto, Frei 71 97 184 262 342
Pacholkiv, Svjatoslav 21
Pálffy, András 10f
Palladio, Andrea 106 177
Paxton, Joseph 243
Peichl, Gustav 115
Peintner, Max 26 94 279f 385
Pelinka, Anton 53
Pereira, Adolph 23f
Pereira, Ludwig 216 218

Perriand, Charlotte 387

Pessler, Monika 420 423 425

Peter, Markus 360ff 364 368

Pevsner, Nikolaus 32

Pflaum, Hannes 216

Pflaum, Stefanie 398

Pichler, Cathrin 298

Pichler, Walter 9 16f 81ff 94 106 113 115f

Pircher, Wolfgang 298

Plato 151

Plaum, Moritz 219

Plečnik, Josef (Jože) 67 119

Plischke, Ernst Anton 33f 40 55 60 68 82 84–87 93f 107 120f 129 136 171 176 190 200 204 328 407

Podbrecky, Inge 16 18 32 285

Podgorschek, Wolfgang 268f 276

Podrecca, Boris 15

Poe, Edgar Allan 189

Ponti, Gio 407

Porsch, Johannes 81

Posch, Wilfried 28 36 39f 60 394

Pöschl, Hanno 176 187

Pöschl, Monika (s. Banićević-)

Postmodernism 14f 17 136 146 205 243 265

Potyka, Hugo 104

Pound, Ezra 50

Prachensky, Markus 65

Prantl, Karl 189

Price, Cedric 129

Prix, Wolf (s. Coop Himmelblau)

Prochazka, Elsa (s. IGIRIEN)

Puchhammer, Hans 112 127 318

Qualtinger, Helmut 10

Radax, Ferry 65

Radebold, Hartmut 45f

Rainer, Arnulf 65 78f 116

Rainer, Roland 61 82 84 92–96 102 104 328

Rathkolb, Oliver 9 51 321

Reder, Wolfgang 346

Reich, Wilhelm 300

Reinagl, Herbert 136

Reinhardt, Max 33

Requat & Reinthaller & Partner 112

Reulecke, Jürgen 45

Richter, Wilfried 136

Rietveld, Gerrit 302

Ritter, Arno 57

Roe, Ian F. 25

Rogers, Ernest N. 124

Rosdy, Ladislaus 81

Rossellini, Roberto 50

Rossi, Aldo 124

Rowe, Colin 211

Rudofsky, Bernard 407

Rühm, Gerhard 64f 74f 76f 79

Rukschcio, Burkhardt 36 112 318

Russell, Bertrand 35

Safran, Yehuda 32 148

Salz der Erde 9

Salzburg Summer Academy 68 70 73 154 162 342

Sarnitz, August 26ff

Sartre, Jean-Paul 66 148 152 157

Sauvage, Henri 107 112

Schachel, Roland 36 112 318

Schilbach, Rudolf 294

Schindler, Rudolph 116

Schlick, Moritz 25 34

Schmeller, Alfred 63

Schmid, Peter 136

Schnitzler, Arthur 21

Schönberg, Arnold 17 35 78

Schorske, Carl E. 22 31 57

Schregenberger, Thomas 166

Schrom, Georg 103

Schubert, Franz 51

Schüller, Philipp 398

Schuppan, Ingrid 117

Schuster, Franz 59 61

Schütte-Lihotzky, Margarete 36 60 394

Schütte, Wilhelm 60

Schwanzer, Karl 61 81

Schwarzenberg, Karl Johannes 256

Schwarzkogler, Rudolf 117

Schwertsik, Kurt 77

Scorsese, Martin 205

Scott Brown, Denise 14

Scully, Vincent 107 123

Seccession(ists) 24f 28f 32 37 56 333

Seehof, Stephan 316

Sedlmayr, Hans 50 52 68

Semper, Gottfried 41 91 175 204

Senarclens de Grancy, Antje 60

Shakespeare, William 59

Shapira, Elana 21 32 219 321

Sicard von Sicardsburg, August 26 316 344

Silverman, Lisa 33f

Silverstein, Murray 104

Simon, Axel 412

Singer, Adalbert 304 306

Sitte, Camillo 27 119

Skalnik, Kurt 81

Slutzky, Robert 211

Smithson, Alison 165ff 407

Smithson, Peter 165ff 407

Soane, John 107 238f 241 260

Sobotka, Walter 39

Somavilla, Ilse 30 33

Somol, Robert 231

Spalt, Johannes 61 65 67ff 83 91 104 118–121 126 132 165 194 229 239 273 286 318 332 344 349 406

Speer, Albert 107 250 252

Spiel, Hilde 49f

Spiluttini, Margherita 386
Spühler, Martin 86
Stadler, Friedrich 26 66
Stanislawski, Konstantin 56
Stauffer, Marie Theres 188
Steger, Bernhard 74
Steidle, Otto 352 374
Steiger, Dominik 117
Steiner-Herz, Denise 248
Steiner, Dietmar 408
Steinle, Christa 50 53
Steinmann, Otto 104
Steixner, Gerhard 68 73
Stockhausen, Karlheinz 77
Stonborough-Wittgenstein, Margarete 30 116
Strasberg, Lee 230
Strnad, Oskar 38f 85 112 119 306
Superstudio 115
Svenskt Tenn 120
Subotinic, Nada 425
Swoboda, Hannes 327
Tafuri, Manfredo 57
Tamms, Friedrich 91
Team X (Ten) 87 143 407
Tesar, Heinz 15 280 374
Tessenow, Heinrich 191
Theune, Claudia 21 219
Thonet 330
Thun-Hohenstein, Christoph 406

Thurm-Nemeth, Volker 216
Thurner, Erika 50 52
Thurner, Herbert 60
Todesco, Eduard und Moritz 24 321
Todesco, Sophie von 321
Tonon, Benedict 352
Toulmin, Stephen 29 57f
Truffaut, François 164
Trümpi, Fritz 321
Tschapeller, Wolfgang 423 428
Tscherkassky, Peter 78
Tugendhat, Ernst 150 152f 155f
Tzonis, Alexander 15 146 204 290
Uhl, Ottokar 57 74 127 132 165
Van Berkel, Ben 370
Van der Nüll, Eduard 26 175 316 344
Venturi, Robert 14 121 125 205 263 407
Vilain, Robert 36
Viollet-le-Duc, Eugène 204
Vocelka, Karl 202
Von Moos, Stanislaus 205 364 391
Vossoughian, Nader 36f 144 274 290
Wachsmann, Konrad 19 55 57 67f 70f 73f 80 97 127 136 162 205 342 344
Waditschatka, Ute 92

Wagner-Rieger, Renate 23f 28 218
Wagner, Otto 14 16 18f 24 26ff 40 42 57 67 81 85 93ff 119 123 127 145 175 194 241 250f 259 276 278–281 289 304 307 324 327 329 333 385 388 406 410f
Walzer, Tina 21 219
Wärndorfer, Fritz 28
Warren, John 25
Wawrik, Gunther 112 127
Webern, Anton von 78
Wehdorn, Manfred 278
Weibel, Peter 9 50 53 62 64 66 74f 117 166
Weidenbaum, Inge 53
Weigel, Hans 59
Weiler, Max 54
Welz, Friedrich 73
Welzenbacher, Lois 59ff
Welzig, Maria 35 38 61 68 73 286
Werkbund, Deutscher 28f 39 39 334
Werkbund, Neuer 41 60
Werkbund, Österreichischer 41 334
Werkbundsiedlung, Stuttgarter 120 302
Werkbundsiedlung, Wiener 39f 84 119 172 289 302f 307
Werkgruppe Graz 112
Werkner, Patrick 61 117
Wessely, Rolf 304 306
West, Franz 278

Whiting, Sarah 231
Wiener Aktionisten (Viennese Actionists) 9f 83 117 134
wiener gruppe 9f 62 64f 66 74ff 77 79f 83 166
Wiener Kreis (Vienna Circle) 25 29 33–37 62 66 74 147f 154f 290f
Wiener Moderne (Viennese Modernism) 18f 32 41 51 62 67 84f 132f 172 224 252 321 348
Wiener Werkstätte 28f 32 39 121f 333
Wiener, Oswald 62 64ff 75ff 83 117
Wilhelm, Karin 92
Windbrechtinger, Traude und Wolfgang 112
Wittgenstein, Karl 28
Wittgenstein, Ludwig 29f 33 58 62 66 75 116
Wlach, Oskar 38f 119f 286
Wodak, Ruth 54 58
Wögenstein, Walter 194
Wolff, Kurt 59
Wörle, Eugen 59f
Wright, Frank Lloyd 66 85
Zeemann, Dora 75
Zinnecker, Jürgen 45f
Zünd Up 9
Zweig, Stefan 186 426

About the Author

Born in Graz in 1970. Studied architecture at the Graz University of Technology, postgraduate studies in architecture at the ETH Zurich (Hans Kollhoff), doctorate at the University of Applied Arts in Vienna (Institute of the Theory and History of Architecture – Liane Lefaivre).
2001–2007 university assistant at the Graz University of Technology (Institute of Architecture Technology – Roger Riewe). 2011–2014 research assistant in the Austrian Science Fund (FWF) research project "Hermann Czech – Architecture and Critique of Language in Postwar Vienna" at the University of Applied Arts in Vienna under the direction of Liane Lefaivre. Teaching assignments at the Graz University of Technology. Since 2021 board member of Docomomo Austria.
Since 2009 architecture office coabitare in Graz.

Thanks

This book would not have come about without the support of numerous people, to whom I owe my heartfelt thanks: Liane Lefaivre's encouragement made me tackle the project in the first place, and without her critical perspective from outside much of the work would have gone unnoticed. Hermann Czech took the time for countless conversations and opened his archive to me.
His clients Catherine Schmidt, Hannes Pflaum, Philipp Schüller, Erhard Löcker, Manfred Holy, Irmgard Kuhner and Susanne Geissler welcomed me willingly and told me about the collaboration with Hermann Czech.
I had stimulating conversations about my work with Christopher Long, Claudia Mazanek and Elana Shapira in particular. In the implementation phase, Markus Bogensberger from the Haus der Architektur in Graz and Thomas Kramer from the publishing house Park Books became important supporters, as did Eva Guttmann, who, together with Claudia Mazanek, brought her expertise as an editor to the structuring and finalization of the book. With her topical photographs, Gabriele Kaiser shows how timeless Czech's work is. Michael Neubacher has given the book a coherent graphic appearance in which the heterogeneous image material follows the flow of the text as a matter of course. The Support Art and Research Department at the University of Applied Arts aided me throughout the entire work, first in the person of Eva Blimlinger, and then of Alexander Damianisch.
I always found a place to stay with my dear friend Lilu Steinbach and her daughter Emma in Vienna, and my husband Klaus Kuss tirelessly had my back and repeatedly encouraged me in recurring moments of doubt to keep working.

Image Credits

The Creative Commons Attribution-Non-Commercial 4.0 International (CC BY-NC 4.0) licence does not apply to all third party imagery listed below.

All images not specifically listed are from the Czech Archive/Architekturzentrum Wien Collection. Page numbers in italics refer to reference images.

Alexander, Christopher: *264* [from: Alexander: *Das Linz Café*, Vienna: Löcker, 1981]

Anonymous: *196 bottom left* [from: *Loos. Läden und Lokale*, Vienna: Album Verlag für Photographie, 2001, 23], *249 bottom* [from: Kulka: *Adolf Loos*, rpt., Vienna: Löcker, 1979, Ill. 7], *286 top* [from: Spalt; Czech: *Josef Frank 1885–1967*, Vienna: Hochschule für Angewandte Kunst, 1981, 150]

Arbeitsgruppe 4 94, 95 / Archiv F. Kurrent 92, 273 / Architekturzentrum Wien Collection [from: *Wien der Zukunft*, Vienna 1963]; *350 center*

Bassewitz, Gert von: 259 top

Bernsteiner, Katrin: 402

Duchamp, Marcel: *318 bottom* [from: Moure: *Marcel Duchamp*, New York: Rizzoli 1988, 25] © Association Marcel Duchamp / 2023, ProLitteris, Zurich für Werke von DUCHAMP MARCEL

Faust, Marina: 212 center, right, 215, 243 right

Flora, Gerhard: 198 right, 278 top, 347, 350 top right, 405, 416, 417 left, 419

Frank, Josef: *290* [from: Vossoughian: *Otto Neurath*, Rotterdam: NAI Publishers, 2011], *415 bottom right* [from: Welzig: *Josef Frank*, Vienna: Böhlau, 1998, 121]

Frank, Josef / Wien Museum Sammlung: *308 top*

Frank, Josef and Wlach, Oskar: *286* [from: Spalt; Czech: *Josef Frank*, Vienna: Hochschule für Angewandte Kunst, 1981, 40]

Gallis, Johann: 85

geoconten / google: 359

GeoEye, i-Cubed/Yahoo! INC.: 365

Gerlach, Martin: *183 bottom right, 210, 390 center* [from: Münz; Künstler: *Der Architekt Adolf Loos*, Vienna/Munich: Anton Schroll, 1964, Ill. 17, 151, 243/Adolf Loos Archive of the Albertina, Vienna]

Guttmann, Eva: 253 left, 254

Hauenfels, Uwe: 304

Heller, Gerhard: 296

Hejduk, Pez: 381

Hueber, Eduard: 196 top

Hurnaus, Hertha: 420, 421, 423–429

Innendekoration 41 (1930): *340 bottom*

Kaiser, Gabriele: 183 top left, top right, 187, 191 right, 193 left, right, 195 top, 212 left, 213, 214, 224, 225, 226, 228, 239 left, right, 240 left, right, 241, 243 left, 245 left, right, 246 right, 247 top, bottom, 248, 255 left, 257, 262, 284, 288, 289 right, 311, 315, 316, 317, 318 left, right, 320, 321, 323, 324 left, 355, 357 top, 384 right, center, 388 top left, right, 395, 398, 406, 407, 408, 409, 414, 415

Kreidl, Philipp / *H.O.M.E*: 384 left, 385

Kubelka, Peter: 78

Kuss, Eva: 63 right, 113, 172 right, 350 top left, 388

Le Corbusier: *309* [from: Boesiger (ed.): *Le Corbusier und Pierre Jeanneret – Ihr gesamtes Werk von 1929–1934*, Zürich, 2nd ed., Zurich: Verlag Dr. H. Girsberger, 1941, 28] © F.L.C. / 2023, ProLitteris, Zurich für Werke von LE CORBUSIER

Lindner, Gerhard: 220 top, center, 221, 222, 223

Loos, Adolf/Adolf Loos Archive of the Albertina, Vienna: *216* [from: Gravagnuolo: *Adolf Loos*, Milan: Idea Books, 1982, 165], *329, 399* [from: Münz; Künstler: *Der Architekt Adolf Loos*, Vienna/Munich: Anton Schroll, 1964, Ill. 113, 212–216], *390* [from: Czech; Mistelbauer: *Das Looshaus*, Vienna: Löcker, 1984, 104]

Mazanek, Claudia: 172 left, 281 top, *310*, 334 bottom left, 417 right

McGrath, Norman: 273 bottom [from: Hollein: *Design – MAN transFORMS – Konzepte einer Ausstellung*, Vienna: Löcker, 1989, 42]

Meyer, Karl: *337 bottom* [from: Kulka: *Adolf Loos*, rpt. Vienna: Löcker 1979, Ill. 57/Adolf Loos Archive of the Albertina, Vienna]

Mistelbauer, Wolfgang: 70

Rainer, Roland: 93 [from: *Rainer. Das Werk des Architekten*, Vienna/New York: Springer, 2003, 250]

Reiffenstein, Bruno: *220 bottom left* [from: Münz; Künstler: *Der Architekt Adolf Loos*, Vienna/Munich: Anton Schroll, 1964, Ill. 160/Adolf Loos Archive of the Albertina, Vienna]

Roth, Thomas: 278 bottom left

Scherb, Julius: 308 bottom

Schönfellinger, Harald: 249 top, 253 right, 260, 267, 270, 279, 285, 293, 295 top, 300–303, 335, 337, 338, 340 top, 345

Sekita, Mikio: 266

Spalt, Johannes / Fotowerkstätte der HS f. angew. Kunst, Vienna: *229 center right* [from: *Johannes Spalt*, Vienna: Böhlau, 1993, 237]

Speer, Albert: *250 left*

Spiluttini, Margherita / Architekturzentrum Wien Collection: 67, 238, 242, 353, 357 1.+2.from the bottom, 366, 369, 371, 373 bottom, 374, 390–393

Surwillo, Jerzy: 201, 204 left, 233

TerraItaly: 329 top

Wagner, Otto / Wien Museum Collection: 96, *241 bottom right*, 276 bottom, 390 bottom

Zschokke, Walter / Architekturzentrum Wien Collection: 289

In some cases, the copyright and reprint rights could not be determined despite extensive research. Legitimate claims will be settled within the framework of the usual fee agreements if appropriate proof is provided.

This publication is based on research results from the FWF stand-alone project "Hermann Czech – Architecture and Critique of Language in Postwar Vienna," conducted at the University of Applied Arts Vienna, Institute of the Theory and History of Architecture (Austrian Science Fund [FWF]: P23734-G15).

This publication was subject to an anonymous, international peer review process.

This publication is licenced, unless otherwise indicated, under the terms of the Creative Commons Attribution-Non-Commercial 4.0 International (CC BY-NC 4.0) licence (https://creativecommons.org/licenses/by-nc/4.0/), which permits use, sharing, adaptation, distribution, and reproduction in any medium or format, provided you give appropriate credit to the original author(s) and source, provide a link to the Creative Commons licence, and indicate any modifications. Use for commercial purposes is not permitted. The images or other third-party material in this publication are covered by the publication's Creative Commons licence, unless otherwise indicated in a reference to the material. If the material is not covered by the publication's Creative Commons licence and the intended use is not permitted by law or exceeds the permitted use, permission for use must be obtained directly from the copyright holder. Despite careful editing, all information in this publication is provided without guarantee; any liability on the part of the author, the editor, or the publisher is excluded.

Published with the support of the Austrian Science Fund (FWF): [PUB 702-G]

Funding Authorities and Sponsors

Bundesministerium
Kunst, Kultur,
öffentlicher Dienst und Sport

ART'ıst

dɪːˈʌngewʌndtə

coabitare

Imprint

Copy editing
Hermann Czech, Eva Kuss

Translation and proofreading
Brian Dorsey

Translation of the texts "No Need for Panic" and "For a Change" by Elise Feiersinger

Cover design and book concept
Peter Duniecki

Layout
Atelier Neubacher, Graz

Printing and binding
DZA – Druckerei zu Altenburg GmbH

Paper
Luxo Art Samt

Typeface
Adobe Garamond, Berthold Bodoni, Real Text Pro

© 2023, Eva Kuss, Graz, and Park Books, Zurich

Park Books AG
Niederdorfstrasse 54
8001 Zurich, Switzerland
www.park-books.com

Park Books is being supported by the Federal Office of Culture with a general subsidy for the years 2021–2024.

All rights reserved; no part of this publication may be reproduced, stored in a retrieval system or transmitted in any form or by any means, electronic, mechanical, photocopying, recording, or otherwise, without the prior written consent of the publisher.

ISBN 978-3-03860-346-7